Pranksters

Pranksters

Making Mischief in the Modern World

KEMBREW McLEOD

NEW YORK UNIVERSITY PRESS

New York and London

NEW YORK UNIVERSITY PRESS
New York and London
www.nyupress.org

References to Internet websites (URLs) were accurate at the time of writing.
Neither the author nor New York University Press is responsible for URLs that
may have expired or changed since the manuscript was prepared.

Library of Congress Cataloging-in-Publication Data

McLeod, Kembrew, 1970-
Pranksters : making mischief in the modern world / Kembrew McLeod.
p. cm.
Includes bibliographical references and index.
ISBN 978-0-8147-9629-0 (cl : alk. paper)
1. Practical jokes--History. 2. Hoaxes--History. 3. Impostors and imposture--History. 4.
Subculture--History. I. Title.
PN6231.P67M35 2014
001.9'5--dc23
2013029825

New York University Press books are printed on acid-free paper,
and their binding materials are chosen for strength and durability.
We strive to use environmentally responsible suppliers and materials
to the greatest extent possible in publishing our books.

Manufactured in the United States of America

10 9 8 7 6 5 4 3 2 1

Also available as an ebook

For Alasdair Nugent-McLeod,
my number-one mischief maker;
long may you rock.

CONTENTS

ACKNOWLEDGMENTS

I am indebted to NYU Press's Eric Zinner, Ciara McLaughlin, and Alicia Nadkarni, who put up with several blown deadlines while I tried to finish this book. Thanks to Andrew Katz, who is the best copyeditor I've ever worked with; his feedback substantially improved this book. And as always, thanks to the world's most rockin' literary agent, Sarah Lazin. For feedback on early drafts and parts of this book, I want to acknowledge Lynne Nugent, John Durham Peters, Benjamin Peters, Ted Striphas, Jonathan Sterne, Bruce Gronbeck, NYU Press's peer reviewers, and those who provided helpful commentary at my POROI Rhetoric Seminar and Communication Studies Department Seminar presentations at the University of Iowa. Some of the elements that made their way into this book were tested out in my column for *Little Village,* and I thank my wonderful editors, Matthew Steele, Melody Dworak, and Andrew Sherburne, for indulging me. Mad props to my several research assistants, most notably Jonathan Hansen, who pointed me toward some key information that shaped this book. And thanks to my other RAs: Jin Kim, Jane Munskgaard, Zane Umsted, Collin Syfert, Christine Moorehead, and Emily Torricelli. For other informal conversational contributions, thanks to Billy Hunt, Paul Collins, Harry Stecopoulos, Kathy Lavezzo, Laura Rigal, Naomi Greyser, Chris Nelson, Chris Offutt, Orion Meyer, Benjamin Burroughs, and Chuck D. Once again, I appreciate Prairie Lights Bookstore and the Times Club for offering me an inspiring place to write with others. Lastly, I am appreciative to the University of Iowa's Office of the Provost, whose Faculty Scholar program gave me the research time needed to work on this book, and thanks to the Office for the Vice President of Research's Book Subvention Program. This book is dedicated to the memory of Stuart Downs.

*I*ntroduction

American wit and wisdom began with some mass-mediated mischief. In the December 19, 1732 edition of the *Pennsylvania Gazette*, Benjamin Franklin penned the following advertisement: "Just published for 1733: *Poor Richard: An Almanack* containing the lunations, eclipses, planets motions and aspects, weather, . . . [and the] prediction of the death of his friend Mr. Titan Leeds." Writing under the name Richard Saunders, he not only narrowed down Leeds's time of death to the date and time—October 17, 1733 at 3:29 p.m.—but also the exact moment when two worldly bodies aligned: "at the very instant of the conjunction of the Sun and Mercury." Franklin was a rationalist product of the Enlightenment. He was a cynic who valued science over superstition, and heaped scorn on astrologers such as Titan Leeds. More crucially, Leeds was a business rival, and the printer's way up the ladder of wealth was often achieved by stepping on his competitors. Franklin claimed that the two friends frequently debated when the cosmos had scheduled Leeds's appointment with the grim reaper: "But at length he is inclinable to agree with my judgment. Which of us is most exact, a little time will now determine."[1]

When Titan Leeds did not die on that date, phase two of Operation: Ridicule Astrologer kicked into gear. In the next *Poor Richard's Almanack*, Franklin/Saunders bemoaned the fact that he couldn't attend to his best friend during his final moments on earth. Oh, how he wished to give Leeds a farewell embrace, close his eyes, and say good-bye one last time! This infuriated the astrologer, who ranted in his not-quite-posthumous 1734 almanac about this "false Predictor," "conceited Scribbler," "Fool," and—last but not least—"Lyar." Poor Richard was shocked by these rude utterances. With a wearied tone, he wrote, "Having received much Abuse from the Ghost of Titan Leeds, who pretends to still be living, and to write Almanacks in spight of me and my Predictions, I cannot help saying, that tho' I take it patiently, I take it very unkindly." He added that there was absolutely no doubt Leeds had died, for it was "plain to everyone that reads his last two almanacks, no man living would or could write such stuff." Franklin wasn't the first to mock astrology, which by the early eighteenth century had become a time-honored tradition. Two centuries before, François Rabelais published at least two such lampoons: *Almanac for 1532* and *Pantagrueline Prognostification* (signed "Maistre Alcofribas Nasier," an anagram of his name). The satirist wrote vague forecasts such as "This year the blind will see very little, and the deaf will hear poorly" and "In winter wise men will not sell their fur coats to buy firewood."[2]

Rabelais's lighthearted jabs, however, were nothing compared to what Leeds endured. Benjamin Franklin owned and operated the printing house that churned out his competitor's almanac, giving him a crucial advantage in this war of words. This inside knowledge allowed Franklin to read his attacks and respond to them in *Poor Richards' Almanack* before Leeds's publication even went to press. "Mr. Leeds was too well bred to use any Man so indecently and scurrilously," Franklin wrote, further egging him on, "and moreover his Esteem and Affection for me was extraordinary." The astrologer's protests continued to pour fuel on the fire, which by now had captivated much of the colonies' reading public. Franklin kept this up for several years, even after the astrologer really did die in 1738. The 1740 edition of *Poor Richard's Almanack* described a late-night visit from the Ghost of Titan Leeds, who entered Richard Saunders's brain via his left nostril and penned the following message: "I did actually die at that moment," he confessed, "precisely at the hour you mentioned, with a variation of 5 minutes, 53 sec." After this belated apology, the spirit issued one more prediction: John Jerman, another almanac maker who used Franklin as a printer, would convert to Catholicism. This was an outrageous claim to make during those antipapist times, and the author was not amused. Because of Franklin's "witty performance," Jerman huffed, he would be taking his business elsewhere.[3]

Learning from Pranks

Benjamin Franklin's ruse is one of the first modern examples of what I call a prank. In the groundbreaking book *Pranks!*, Andrea Juno and V. Vale suggest that the "*best* pranks invoke the imagination, poetic imagery, the unexpected and a deep level of irony or social criticism." By staging these semiserious, semihumorous spectacles, pranksters try to spark important debates and, in some instances, provoke social change. Unfortunately, the word *prank* is more often used to describe stunts that make people look foolish and little more. I'm not interested in celebrating cruelty—especially the sorts of mean-spirited practical jokes, hazing rituals, and reality-television deceits that are all too common in today's popular culture. Although "good" pranks sometimes do ridicule their targets, they serve a higher purpose by sowing skepticism and speaking truth to power (or at least cracking jokes that expose fissures in power's facade). A prank a day keeps The Man away, I always say. Nevertheless, I should stress at the outset that this book is not solely about pranking. Many of the characters who populate these pages aren't driven by noble impulses, and even those who are more pure of heart can muddy the ethical waters with dubious tactics.[4]

With this in mind, *Pranksters* examines everything from political pranks, silly hoaxes, and con games to the sort of self-deception that fuels outlandish belief systems. Though these may seem like very different examples, they are linked by fact that all varieties of deceit engender confusion, uncertainty, and ambiguity. Spectators (whether they have been scammed by a swindler or have witnessed a satirical street-theater spectacle) can experience a single event in radically different ways. One person's prank can become the fodder for another's con or, as we will soon see, conspiracy theory. Pranks, hoaxes, cons, and conspiracy theories share another key similarity: people buy into them when they resonate with their own deeply entrenched worldviews. Conversely, they can also push us to think more critically about how and why we come to embrace false beliefs—while at the same time reminding us not to repeat past mistakes. As the old proverb goes, "Fool me once, shame on you; fool me twice, shame on me." By viewing modern history through the lens of trickery, this book offers an offbeat and overlooked account of political, religious, and social life in the West. Yes, Reason and other Enlightenment principles shaped modernity, but so did chicanery and irrationality.

Mischief makers also left their mark on media. Most textbook histories offer a parade of Big Broadcasters, Great Men, New Technologies, and Noble Ideas. Lost in the cracks are the more peripheral figures who worked outside convention but still impacted the norms and uses of media. Subversive pranksters, opportunistic hoaxers, greedy con artists, and clever hackers all have played formative roles in the evolution of media. In 1903, for instance, a lone troublemaker helped kill off a sector of the wireless telegraphy industry before it got off the ground. Italian inventor Guglielmo Marconi was attempting to promote his patented radio system as a way to send confidential messages (even though total secrecy is impossible with broadcast media). During the device's unveiling, moments before it was to receive a transmission from Marconi himself, the wireless telegraph mysteriously came to life, tapping away. It had been hacked! "Rats. Rats. Rats," the message announced, followed by a series of obnoxious rhymes that began, "There was a young fellow of Italy, who diddled the public quite prettily." It was a PR disaster for Marconi, and it doomed his company's new product. The perpetrator was a stage magician named Nevil Maskelyne, who gleefully explained to reporters that he was trying to expose the invention's fatal flaw. Maskelyne's wireless-telegraph hack is a reminder that rule-breaking has long been a part of media's DNA.[5]

My history of trickery—or trickstory, if you will—starts at the dawning of the Age of Enlightenment and spans four centuries. Among other things, *Pranksters* chronicles the exploits of Jonathan Swift, Benjamin Franklin, and Mark Twain. It also explores P. T. Barnum's humbugs and the nineteenth-century culture of cons, the youthful hacking adventures of Apple cofounders Steve Jobs and Steve Wozniak, and a number of politicized pranks orchestrated by WITCH (Women's International Terrorist Conspiracy from Hell), ACT UP (AIDS Coalition To Unleash Power), and a dynamic duo named the Yes Men. In doing so, this book vividly illustrates how pranksters can stimulate constructive public conversations and, on some unfortunate occasions, unintended consequences—or what I call *prank blowback*. This occurs when a satire is taken seriously by its intended target and provokes a reactionary response. For example, the 1960s feminists who founded WITCH designed their outrageous protests to appeal to reporters and appall conservatives. Little did they know that their stunts (along with similar pranks pulled by others) would help jolt the Moral Majority into existence, reshaping American politics in the process. On a much grander scale, one can draw a twisted-but-unbroken line from today's New World Order conspiracy theories to the mind-control paranoia of the Cold War era, the post–French Revolution Illuminati scare, and all the way back to a satirical prank pulled in the early 1600s, which kicks off chapter 1.[6]

If reduced to a mathematical formula, the art of pranking can be expressed as *Performance Art + Satire × Media = Prank*. Put simply, pranks are playful critiques performed within the public sphere and amplified by media. They allow ordinary people to reach large audiences despite constraints (such as a lack of wealth or connections) that would normally mute their voices. Storytelling is an important tool that makes this possible, especially when a prank produces memorable morals or lessons that cry out to be retold. I had this in mind when I successfully trademarked "freedom of expression." My quiet little joke went public after I hired a lawyer who threatened to sue AT&T for using this iconic phrase in an ad *without permission!* In 2003, the *New York Times* broke the story with a wry article that began, "Freedom of expression, it turns out, may not be for everyone." When wire services picked it up, more reporters came calling. This gave me a platform to say ridiculous, provocative things such as "I didn't go through the time, effort, and expense of trademarking freedom of expression˙ just to have people use it whenever they want." I dangled many more tasty hooks, but if journalists savored the humor of this serious joke, they also had to swallow the critique that came with it. The absurd nature of my fake lawsuit certainly got people talking, but all good things must come to an end—including my beloved trademark. I forgot to file a "Section 8" form a few years into its lifetime, an oversight that terminated my ownership of the phrase. But there is an amusing silver lining. A U.S. government website now declares that freedom of expression is "dead" (in all caps, no less). *Dead* is just a legal designation for a lapsed trademark, but I prefer to think of it as an unintentionally hilarious example of bureaucratic performance art.[7]

Pranking is a form of edutainment—an instructive amusement that can make perpetrators, victims, and witnesses wiser. And as I said earlier, even hoaxes and cons can sharpen our critical-thinking skills. After Hurricane Sandy hit New York City in 2012, an obviously Photoshopped image of a scuba diver swimming in a fully submerged subway station circulated on social media. Rather than taking a few seconds to realize that every element of this picture was implausible, I quickly and credulously reposted it. I should have known better, especially because this happened while I was writing this book! Notorious publicist and self-proclaimed media manipulator Ryan Holiday discusses a tried and true technique that he calls "trading up the chain." Holiday writes, "I can turn nothing into something by placing a story with a small blog that has very low standards, which then becomes the source for a story by a larger blog, and that, in turn, for a story by larger media outlets. I create, to use the words of one media scholar, a 'self-reinforcing news wave.'" A 2010 survey of working journalists, for example, found that 89 percent admitted to turning to blogs and social media for story research. The speed at which news now travels makes antiquated concepts such as "fact-checking" and "verification" that much more difficult. If you trace the path of a news story back to its origins, more often than not a publicist is at the beginning of the chain (after all, "PR" is the first two letters of the word *prank*).[8]

Pranks encourage audiences to pause and reflect, even if it is only for a few seconds. Sometimes pranksters craft clear and direct messages that persuade, and sometimes they deliberately befuddle. The latter act is also useful—especially when an unexpected guerrilla performance jolts people out of their daily routines. When the world is temporarily turned askew, it can be seen from a new perspective. "Imagination is the chief instrument of the good," philosopher John Dewey argued, emphasizing the transformative power of art. Drawing on Dewey, sociologist

James Jasper used the term *artful protest* to describe the same tactics I attribute to pranksters. "Much like artists," he writes, "they are at the cutting edge of society's understandings of itself as it changes." Jasper believes that artful protestors offer us "new ways of seeing and judging the world." One of the reasons why pranking can be so compelling for everyone involved is because it's fun, theatrical, *and* participatory. By dispensing with stage lights and other barriers that separate audiences from performers, it lies somewhere between acting, gaming, and free play. A prank is like a humorous role-playing adventure in which people, ideas, and language all have leading parts. "Jokes are active, social things," media scholar Stephen Duncombe argues. Humor requires engagement from spectators, especially when irony is employed (one has to figure out what the joke teller *doesn't* believe to get it). With enough repetition, these cognitive acts can bleed over into the social world, moving people to action.[9]

SILLY SOCIAL ENGINEERING

Pranks also provide a real-life learning lab for conducting social experiments. Anyone with enough pluck, luck, and imagination can open the hood of the culture industry's engine and watch the gears turn. One useful example is the Banana Hoax. In early 1967, a rumor circulated that one could get high by smoking banana peels—though, in reality, the only way to trip on a banana is to step on one. The instigators were most likely "Country" Joe McDonald and Gary "Chicken" Hirsh, from the acid-damaged jug band Country Joe and the Fish. In late 1966, they started spreading the word among friends that banana peels contained psychedelic ingredients. "Even if it didn't work," Hirsh said of their druggy effects, "it was great fun." Not only would this fruit be absurdly difficult to outlaw, but the thought of puffing on bananas contained more than a whiff of slapstick silliness. The story initially traveled via word of mouth, and the first printed account appeared in a March 1967 issue of the *Berkeley Barb*. Conveniently, Ed Denson served as Country Joe's band manager and also contributed a regular music column to that underground paper. "I was fully involved in perpetrating the hoax when I wrote that article," Denson later admitted, though he denied penning a letter to the editor about a cop in a local food co-op who was "lurking in the fresh produce section." The writer predicted that possessing large amounts of bananas would soon become a criminal offense.[10]

The smokable-banana myth is a bit frivolous, sure, but we can still learn a lot from how it took root. Historian John McMillian notes that this prank reveals much about the social and media landscapes of the time. Underground papers created a virtual community connecting weirdos, radicals, and dropouts living in cities, suburbs, and rural areas. This alternative communication network ensured that few things remained local. Mainstream outlets also propagated the put-on, starting with a *San Francisco Chronicle* article titled "Kicks for Hippies: The Banana Turn-On." Within a month, *Time* and *Newsweek* piled on with a wink, and soon it was part of popular folklore. "From bananas, it is a short but shocking step to other fruits," said Congressman Frank Thompson, who cheekily proposed the Banana Labeling Act of 1967. In a speech on the floor of the House of Representatives, he declared, "Today the cry is 'Burn, Banana, Burn.' Tomorrow we may face strawberry smoking, dried apricot inhaling or prune puffing." Thompson claimed a "high official in the FDA" urged him to introduce the bill, but the Food and Drug Administration actually didn't find the banana-smoking rumor very funny. The FDA posted a press release that soberly stated that it failed to find "detectable quantities of known hallucinogenics" in bananas. Pop music also helped to spread this mischievous meme. Donovan's recent hit "Mellow Yellow" was widely rumored to be about you-know-what—"Electrical banana is gonna be the latest craze," he sang—but the song was actually written before the prank was hatched. It was just a kooky cosmic coincidence. The constant repetition of "Mellow Yellow" on radios amplified the Banana Hoax as it spread through subterranean tributaries, corporate channels, and word of mouth.[11]

A famous rumor about the Beatles' Paul McCartney, known as the "Paul Is Dead Hoax," followed a similar pattern. In 1969, news spread that he died in a car accident and was secretly replaced by a look- and sound-alike. The story originally appeared in an Iowa college newspaper and fanned out through underground papers, freeform FM radio, and other counterculture media outlets. *Time* and *Life* magazines also ran with it, and soon legions of stoned hippies were poring over the Fab Four's albums in search of clues about McCartney's demise. It was all in good fun, but not everyone appreciated this kind of tomfoolery.

In the case of the Banana Hoax, some radicals even called it counter-revolutionary. Students for a Democratic Society president Todd Gitlin insisted that it was a politically misguided stunt that ignored the United Fruit Company's unfair labor practices. "These circumstances come to mind," he grumbled, "whenever bananas are flaunted with humor or symbolic meaning, as a means of liberation." Although Gitlin did have a legitimate point, he was fighting an uphill battle. The ruptures produced by the gay and women's liberation struggles, combined with the black power and antiwar movements, created multiple openings for irreverent tricksters. Many of them simply could not resist stirring it up—including a pair of computer nerds who embraced the counterculture's worldview.[12]

Before Steve Jobs and Steve Wozniak built their first computer, they engineered pranks. Jobs started in elementary school, where he countered his boredom by making "Bring Your Pet to School Day" posters. "It was crazy," he recalled, "with dogs chasing cats all over, and the teachers were beside themselves." By the late 1960s, Jobs's pranks were mostly technological in design, such as wiring his childhood home with hidden speakers and microphones to mess with his parents (they were not pleased). Jobs "likes to do pranks like you do," a mutual friend told Wozniak, by way of introduction, "and he's also into building electronics." After becoming fast friends, Jobs and Wozniak targeted a graduation ceremony at Jobs's Silicon Valley high school. Using ropes and pulleys, they planned to drop a bed sheet tie-dyed in the school's colors—complete with a painting of a middle-finger salute and the words "Best Wishes." (Alas, another student told on them.) Jobs said that it was "the banner prank that sealed our friendship." Their pranking adventures continued after Woz created a device that could remotely screw up television reception. While in public spaces, like a dorm lobby, they would fill the screen with static—only to restore the picture once a frustrated viewer touched the television or made an awkward move. In doing so, the two Steves got their unwitting lab rats to contort themselves into human pretzels. Jobs said, laughing, "Just as they had the foot off the ground he would turn it back on, and as they put their foot back on the ground he'd screw it up again." Wozniak recalls that a bunch of students watched "the second half hour of *Mission: Impossible* with the guy's hand over the middle of the TV!"[13]

Jobs and Wozniak transitioned into the world of hacking, a practice that is not unlike pranking. Hacking is often depicted as electronic breaking and entering, or cyber-terrorism, but this technique has very a different meaning in computing circles. It involves modifying software or hardware in a way that shows style, simplicity, creativity, and technical virtuosity. More generally, hacking can be defined as making a technology do things it wasn't originally designed to do. The term originated in the early 1960s at the Massachusetts Institute of Technology, where students messed around with computers and telephones (the latter pursuit is known as phone phreaking). Hacking has another important connotation. *The Journal of the Institute for Hacks, TomFoolery & Pranks at MIT* defines a hack as "a clever, benign, and 'ethical' prank or practical joke, which is both challenging for the perpetrators and amusing to the MIT community." This might include covering the school's giant dome with reflecting foil to make it look like R2D2 or placing a police car on top of it. "Hacks provide an opportunity to demonstrate creativity and know-how in mastering the physical world," explains MIT alum André DeHon, now a University of Pennsylvania engineering professor. "An important component of many hacks is to help people see something in a different way, to give it a humorous, satirical, or poignant twist." Another alum adds, "In their ideal form, hacks are a melding of art, inspiration, and engineering."[14]

Like pranking, hacking requires ingenuity and creative thinking—as well as a playful and rebellious attitude, which was certainly the case for Jobs and Wozniak. In the fall of 1971, Woz read an *Esquire* article about blue boxes, illicit devices that could hack the AT&T telephone network by using specific sounds. This mainstream magazine, with a readership of half a million readers, was the first to shine a light on the clandestine world of phone phreaking. Four decades later, Wozniak remains awestruck. "Who would ever believe you could put tones into a phone and make calls free anywhere in the world? I mean, who would *believe* it?" The duo's very first business venture involved making and selling blue boxes (which Woz once used to make a prank call to the Vatican, almost getting the pope on the line). The pair marveled at how their homemade device could manipulate AT&T's multibillion-dollar phone network. "I wanted to find out what the limits of the telephone system were," Woz says. "What were the limits of *any* system? I've found that for almost anybody who thinks well in digital electronics or computer programming, if you go back and look at their lives they'll have these areas of misbehavior." His comment highlights how mischief can remake media and, occasionally, transform an entire industry. "If it hadn't been for the Blue Boxes, there wouldn't have been an Apple," Jobs said. "I'm 100% sure of that. Woz and I learned how to work together, and we gained the confidence that we could solve technical problems and actually put something into production."[15]

Though AT&T and the phone phreaks seemed worlds apart, they developed a mutually constitutive bond. This massive corporation provided a laboratory for hackers, whose illicit experiments pushed it to transition to a digital switching system that couldn't be triggered by tones. AT&T rolled out this new technology in 1970, when phone phreaking was reaching a critical mass. Although the company claimed it would increase efficiency, hamstringing phone phreaks was a major motivation. This digital infrastructure eventually made it possible for computer modems to talk to each other over the telephone network, paving the way for a thing called the Internet. (Again, people don't just make mischief with media; their mischief can also *remake* media in the process.) The spread of phone phreaking hinged on another dynamic: the convoluted interconnections that bind mainstream and alternative media and culture. That *Esquire* article drew many curious people into the phone-phreaking fold, and it also subtly influenced members of that subculture. They initially referred to themselves as freaks—with an *f*—but from then on these hackers proudly adopted *Esquire's* spelling of *phreaks*. It was a feedback loop, sort of like how underground papers and establishment news media propelled the Banana Hoax into the pop-culture stratosphere. Cultural studies scholar Sarah Thornton argues that dichotomies such as subculture/mainstream do not do a good job of accurately describing the world, because social life is more complicated than simple binaries. Similarly, the distinctions between amateur and professional media makers tend to be overly exaggerated. Like mythological trickster figures, mischief makers in the material world constantly blur the borders between insider and outsider, center and margin.[16]

The Trickster Tradition

Russian literary critic Mikhail Bakhtin believed laughter has played an underrecognized role in steering history. When hilarity erupts, it can also interrupt the status quo. He claimed that the old feudal order wasn't just brought down with cannonballs and Enlightenment thought but also by waves of uninhibited laughter. Medieval carnivals gave peasants the license to turn existing power relations upside down, if only for a day, by ridiculing kings and princes. Bakhtin noted that these festivities were marked by "a continual shifting from top to bottom, from front to rear, of numerous parodies and travesties, humiliations, profanations, comic crownings and uncrownings." They stood in stark contrast to the serious tone set by the ruling powers of Europe. "Besides carnivals proper, with their long, and complex pageants and processions," Bakhtin writes, "there was the 'feast of fools' (festa stultorum) and the 'feast of the ass.'" These raucous rituals occurred in all countries throughout Europe, creating an alternative space that thrived outside the official political and religious spheres.[17]

Even Christmas had an early unruly incarnation. Although some Christians did piously observe this holiday and shunned the wild celebrations associated with it, those folks were few and far between. Late-December festivities took place for centuries, and they coincided with a moment of leisure and abundance that came with the end of the harvest. During this time of year, the social hierarchy was symbolically turned upside down. The lowly became "Masters of Misrule," men dressed as women and vice versa, and children gained the status of their elders—who were ruthlessly mocked. At Christmastime, bands of boys and young men demanded food, drink, and goods from the rich, a tradition called Wassailing that continued into the modern era. In seventeenth-century New England, the holiday troubled religious leaders so much that they banned it entirely. Attention Fox News: the Puritans waged the first War on Christmas! Historian Stephen Nissenbaum notes, "when the Church, more than a millennium earlier, had placed Christmas Day in late December, the decision was part of what amounted to a compromise, and a compromise for which the Church paid a high price." Folding a rowdy secular festival into this holy Christian holiday created serious headaches for religious authorities.[18]

Despite the liberatory promise of medieval carnivals, they sometimes unleashed violent frustrations against Jews and other minority groups. These officially sanctioned subversions also functioned as instruments of social control (by letting people blow off a little steam before tensions exploded). Nevertheless, they did plant seeds that occasionally overturned the ruling order. As Lewis Hyde puts it, "Every so often Fat Tuesday *does* leak over into Lean Wednesday, and into the rest of the year as well." In Germany, the ceremonial debasement of the pope helped lay the groundwork for the Reformation: "The ritual container broke, the pollution leaked out, and the Church itself was fundamentally altered." It was the guffaw heard around the world, a reminder of media theorist Dick Hebdige's claim that the "modern age was laughed into being." Invoking Bakhtin, he writes, "The dust and the cobwebs, the angels and the devils, the necromancers and the priests, the barbaric inquisitions, the inflexible hierarchies, the sober, deadly serious *ignorance* of the medieval powers were blown away not by guns or great debates but by great gusts of belly laughter."[19]

Carnivalesque trickster figures—who appear in myths throughout the world, from Native American to Australian Aboriginal cultures—attack the things that society reveres most. The more sacred the belief, the more likely it will be profaned. Most trickster tales position a weak animal, such as a rabbit or monkey, against a physically powerful opponent. The prey becomes the hunter, and with mental jujitsu the king of the jungle can be knocked from his throne. Given the slave's lowly position in American society, it's no surprise that trickster tales such as those about Br'er Rabbit thrived in African American culture. These escapist fantasies made daily life slightly more bearable, and they offered practical models for resistance and survival (stealing food and other necessities were common themes). The escaped slave Henry "Box" Brown surely learned some valuable lessons from those stories. Brown secretly mailed himself from a Virginia plantation to Philadelphia's freedom, then became a theatrical star in the North. He reenacted his escape in an elaborate one-man stage show, *Mirror of Slavery*, which functioned as both thrilling entertainment and artful propaganda for the abolitionist cause. Fleeing slavery in a shipping crate was an act of desperation, and not a prank, to be sure. Nevertheless, Brown's unique form of edutainment aligned him with a long lineage of political pranksters and trickster figures discussed throughout this book.[20]

During the 1960s, the counterculture perfected pranking as a form of progressive political action. In one infamous incident, Abbie Hoffman and Jerry Rubin tossed hundreds of dollar bills from the gallery overlooking the New York Stock Exchange. The white-collar workers became unwitting actors in this staged drama when they started diving for dollars (it stopped the stock ticker for a few minutes, costing millions in lost trading). During this Wall Street–Theater performance, the buttoned-down mob revealed the avarice that bubbled just beneath the Stock Exchange's veneer of respectability. "Some stockies booed," compatriot Ed Sanders recalled, "but others groveled on the floor like eels of greed to gather the cash." Taking cues from the PR industry, the Yippies merrily used mass media to advertise alternative lifestyles, the peace movement, and other causes they held dear. The same was true of the radical feminist pranksters who founded WITCH. These women unnerved Mr. Jones and other squares by casting satirical hexes, wearing wicked costumes, and crashing bridal fairs.[21]

Two decades later, these tactics were adopted by ACT UP. This activist organization was founded in 1987 as a reaction to the pharmaceutical industry's, government's, and corporate media's nonresponse to the AIDS crisis. Its members dispensed with conventional protest models by using novel, attention-getting tactics. ACT UP got a ton of press coverage after placing a gigantic yellow condom over the home of Senator Jesse Helms, who opposed public funding for safe-sex initiatives. At a different protest, police officers enacted their homophobia and hysteria over "catching AIDS" by wearing bright yellow rubber gloves during arrests. The activists spontaneously chanted, "Your gloves don't match your shoes! You'll see it on the news!"—a catchy hook that ensured it *would* be seen on the news. This sassy humor was also on display in ACT UP's tradition of naming its subgroups. Echoing the feminists who founded WITCH, one splinter cell called itself CHER: Commie Homos Engaged in Revolution. Because the organization focused on issues of media representation, the *New York Times* was an early target. During one guerrilla sticker campaign, ACT UP members plastered the newspaper's vending machines with the following message: "*The New York Times* AIDS REPORTING IS OUT OF

ORDER." The last three words were prominent enough to discourage potential customers.[22]

In the twenty-first century, a decentralized collective named Anonymous has blurred the lines between hacking, pranking, and political protest. It uses inventive tactics to battle Internet censorship and other offenses perpetrated by corporations and governments. In 2011, Anonymous hacked the Syrian Defense Ministry website and replaced it with a flag associated with the country's prodemocracy movement. These hacktivists also took down the CIA's website for the better part of a day in 2012, which prompted a phone call between the FBI and Scotland Yard about how to take action. It turned out that Anonymous operatives were listening in, and they thumbed their noses at these agencies by releasing a recording of the conversation online. Their sophisticated programming skills allow them to trick computer networks into masking their activities so to remain, well, anonymous. That technique is aptly named "spoofing," and it has been used by many tech-savvy activists living under authoritarian regimes. Spoofing is one of many ways hackers have rewired the architecture of the Internet, or at least found cracks in the system that its designers were blind to.[23]

Pranks have their downsides, the most obvious of which are the dangers involved in baiting an unsympathetic audience. They require courage to pull off, especially in the face of hostile taunts and threats of physical violence—which shows how these provocations can tear at the social fabric. Another risk is losing control of how one's message is interpreted by the public, but there are ways of mitigating uncertainty after the prank's "big reveal." It is not enough to make people laugh or outrage them (though, admittedly, that can also be fun!). After the initial shock wears off, the next step is to explain the prank's purpose for as wide or—alternatively, specific—a public as possible. There needs to be an educational component, and this book is an extension of that oddball pedagogy. I hope to give you, dear reader, some conceptual gizmos to add to your critical-thinking toolkit. "I like to think people will learn something from my hijinks," pioneering prankster Alan Abel wrote in his 1970 book *Confessions of a Hoaxer*. "Because the next time around, their hoaxer might truly be diabolical and rob them of things far more important and meaningful." Abel is warning about everyone from underworld con artists to trusted authority figures of all stripes.[24]

Despite the productive potential of prankish tactics, they have been condemned on several fronts. In the book *Reclaiming Fair Use*, media and legal scholars Patricia Aufderheide and Peter Jaszi criticize copyleft activists, culture jammers, and others who gravitate toward monkey-wrenching and monkeyshines. More specifically, they describe and then dismiss the previously mentioned "freedom of expression'" prank as being counterproductive. After conceding that my "antics did indeed provide a broad-brush critique," Aufderheide and Jaszi claim that the prank also undermined possibilities for pragmatic reform. I would totally agree with them had I merely basked in the publicity surrounding the fake lawsuit, but that was just the beginning. In the wake of the coverage, I explained myself to a general audience whose eyes would normally glaze over during discussions of the free-speech implications of intellectual property law. It's a trick I picked up as a teacher: finding creative ways to engage people with ideas that might at first seem "boring." When working for change, a range of approaches is useful. That is more interesting than adhering to a programmatic One True Way ethic. For instance, the Old Left's stoic denial of pleasure was inherited to a certain extent by the sixties New Left, which was sometimes at odds with the Yippies, Merry Pranksters, and other Groucho Marxists.[25]

THE FULL SPECTRUM OF TRICKERY

By upsetting the apple cart, pranksters aspire to change the world—or at least to inspire visions of a better one. But even though I have a keen interest in critique and social change, *Pranksters* digs deep into the darker sides of deception. The origins of *The Protocols of the Elders of Zion*, for instance, highlight the disturbing ways trickery has shaped modern history. The causes of the Jewish Holocaust are complex, but *The Protocols* helped provide its social, ethical, and (a)historical justifications. And to be clear, this forged document does not count as a *prank*—which, as I have defined it, is a staged provocation meant to enlighten and stir up debate. A *hoax* is a kissing cousin of a prank, but its primary purpose is to fool people and attract attention. Lastly, I use *con* as an all-purpose term for a wide range of scams meant to defraud or gain an advantage. They all use similar methods to mislead, but the main difference lies in the perpetrator's intentions and the audience's interpretations. Further complicating matters, mischief makers often have multiple motives, which was certainly true of Benjamin Franklin's attack on Titan Leeds. Yes, he tried to educate the public by lampooning irrational astrological beliefs, but it was mostly a publicity stunt used to drum up almanac sales. To flesh out these differences, I'll preview some of the key stories and themes that run through this book.

Pranks

Chapter 1 begins with a provocation that had unintended, earthshaking consequences. In the early seventeenth century, a small group of radical Protestants invented an "Invisible College" of mystical adepts known as the Rosicrucians. Their prank was meant to spur a public debate about scientific and theological ideas that the Catholic Church vehemently opposed. But in doing so, their fabricated fictions ended up fueling four centuries of paranoia—including the mother of all conspiracy theories, the Illuminati myth (which I'll return to shortly). Keeping with the book's chronological organization, I follow that account with a profile of the first prominent practitioner of the modern prank: Jonathan Swift. The early eighteenth century witnessed a revival of the classical tradition of satire and the rise of print culture, which multiplied the scope and size of audiences that could be duped and/or entertained. The boundary-breaking transgressions of pranksters and hoaxers shaped the popular culture of that period, which is why Benjamin Franklin holds a prominent place in this trickstory. He was an independent media pioneer whose do-it-yourself (DIY) style and shape-shifting persona created a template used by generations of pranksters, hoaxers, and confidence men.

Léo Taxil was one of the most notorious pranksters of the nineteenth century, though he is largely forgotten today. Starting in 1885, he posed as a whistleblower who uncovered satanic Masonic secrets for an audience of credulous French Catholics. Taxil invented his stories out of thin air, but they were still believed by conservatives who hated Freemasons—an organization of freethinkers that had a history of annoying the Vatican. After staying in character for a dozen years, he came clean at an 1897 Paris press conference. After "the sweet pleasure of pranking took over," Taxil told the assembled clergymen and reporters, he decided to stage "an altogether amusing and instructive mystification." Like Benjamin Franklin, Taxil had multiple motives. Despite the "instructive" aspect of his prank, he also made a ton of money selling anti-Freemasonry books and pamphlets that were filled with hallucinogenic lies. Taxil's right-wing audience lapped up his tales about teleportation, magical bracelets used to summon Lucifer, and a worldwide telephone system operated by devils. This imaginary communication network was allegedly used to carry out a global plot to destroy all established religions and create a one-world government. Despite being revealed as fabrications over a century ago, many of Taxil's writings (or at least recycled versions of them) continue to be cited by contemporary conspiracy theorists.[26]

Hoaxes

Hoaxes resemble pranks, but the key difference is the perpetrator's intentions. For pranksters, trickery is a means to an end: prompting discussion, upending the naturalized rituals of everyday life, enraging and educating, and so on. Hoaxers have no such pretentions. For them, the goal is to make others look foolish or to seek fame. The latter was likely true for George Psalmanazar, who took London by storm upon his arrival in 1703. This blond, blue-eyed man said he was a native of an Asian country named Formosa, and he explained away his pale features by claiming to be part of the upper class. The island's elites lived in elaborate underground apartments, Psalmanazar said, while the dark-skinned working class slaved away aboveground, baking in the heat. Ridiculous? Sure. But rather than dismissing those who fall for pranks and hoaxes as dumb dupes, it's more useful to understand *why* certain tricks work. A successful deception tells us much about the culture or people who embraced it. In Psalmanazar's case, prevailing assumptions about race and skin pigmentation allowed this Aryan to pass as an Asian. It also didn't hurt that his backstory had an antipapist spin, which involved being kidnapped by treacherous Jesuit missionaries. (The Catholic world, particularly France, was in the midst of a raging battle with Protestantism and, by default, England.)

Throughout the eighteenth and nineteenth centuries, newspaper hoaxes thrived. Most famous was 1835's *New York Sun* Moon Hoax

("POWERFUL TELESCOPE DISCOVERS LUNAR BAT-MEN!") and the *New York Herald*'s Central Park Zoo Hoax of 1874 ("BEASTS BLUD-GEON BYSTANDERS ON BROADWAY!"). Less well known is the devious etymological origin of the term *miscegenation*. In late 1863, two racist New York journalists invented the word to undermine Abraham Lincoln's election campaign. It first appeared in an irony-filled pamphlet titled *Miscegenation: The Theory of the Blending of the Races, Applied to the American White Man and Negro*. This supposed proabolition publication was explicitly engineered to outrage white supremacists (think Stephen Colbert, if he were a raging bigot who sarcastically "praised" race mixing). Newspapers regularly printed straight news alongside hoaxes and tall tales until the early twentieth century, when this brand of mischief making largely came to an end. Satirists such as Mark Twain, who hatched several surreal hoaxes as a newspaper writer, forced the industry to more clearly define the limits of journalism. New standards of professionalism moved these playful styles of writing to the proverbial margins of the paper or eliminated them altogether.

Cons

In the second half of the nineteenth century, P. T. Barnum built a hugely successful business that blurred the line between good-natured publicity stunts and devious confidence games. His traveling shows and Manhattan-based American Museum captivated crowds with a variety of far-fetched curiosities, including an alleged mermaid. The master humbugger's mid-nineteenth-century popularity coincided with the emergence of confidence men who preyed on newly relocated big-city suckers. During this time, a criminal character named William Thompson roamed the streets of New York asking strangers if they had enough trust in him to loan their watch for a day. He then walked off, goods in hand, laughing. Thompson was playing a game of confidence, and the gullible were the losers. This naiveté had much to do with the fact that an increasing number of Americans were moving away from rural areas, where reputations were built and maintained within a tight-knit community. In urban settings, surface appearances were often used to judge a stranger's character. As cultural historian Karen Halttunen has shown, the American middle class wanted to believe that respectable exterior displays were projections of wholesome interiors. In this context, sharply dressed and well-mannered con men could easily relieve trusting victims of their possessions.[27]

P. T. Barnum's humbugs were popular because they helped spectators navigate an unruly capitalist marketplace: misleading advertising claims, real-estate frauds, and all. Barnum biographer Neil Harris notes that many of those who bought tickets to his exhibits fully expected to be hoodwinked. Much of the entertainment value was derived from analyzing and deconstructing the deception. "The public appears disposed to be amused," the showman observed, "even when they are conscious of being deceived." His entertainments functioned like an elaborate discursive game that encouraged people to spiritedly hash out arguments about social, technological, and economic transformations that were taking place in America. Audiences learned to make up their own minds about the veracity of Barnum's displays, a skill that became useful in everyday life. But even though he claimed to be sharpening his customers' wits, which is a key goal of pranks, that was merely a happy byproduct of his profitable amusements. In that regard, Barnum falls somewhere between a prankster, a hoaxer, and a con man—one whose spirit still haunts today's media and entertainment landscapes.[28]

And Don't Forget Self-Deception

As I suggested earlier, in order for audiences to be fooled by a prank, hoax, or con, it should resonate with one's deep-seated assumptions about how the world works. This is also true of conspiracy theories, which are similarly rooted in fantasy, ideology, and myth (concepts that are not necessarily interchangeable but that still overlap). These paranoid fictions spring to life when a tooth-chipping kernel of truth is elaborated on by religious fanatics, political partisans, devious fakers, attention seekers, the mentally ill, or all of the above. Conspiracy theories are often organized around an impossibly perfect model of communication. Plots are flawlessly executed over the centuries and across the globe, letters always arrive, transmissions are clearly understood, and there is no chance of plans going awry. This is not how life works, but imagination is a powerful thing. The West's most resilient conspiracy theory can be traced back to 1614, the year of the previously mentioned

Rosicrucian prank. This "Invisible Brotherhood" created the blueprint for a paranoid worldview that is centered around an ancient satanic plot to create a New World Order. This grand narrative was cemented after the French Revolution, which destabilized that country's traditional religious and political powers. Many conservatives believed that a subversive secret society named the Bavarian Illuminati was pulling the strings.

The religious right was also freaked out by Spiritualism, a quasi-religion that resonated with millions of people starting in the mid-nineteenth century. Cynics dismissed it as a hoax, but Spiritualism was deeply felt by believers—making it more of a fantasy than a straight-up hoax or con job. Women occupied leadership positions within this progressive movement because they were said to be sensitive to signals from the dead. The dream of spirit communication, which was inspired in part by the newly invented telegraph, helped promote feminism on both sides of the Atlantic. It also left an imprint on a twentieth-century mystic named Edgar Cayce. "The Miracle Man of Virginia Beach," as he was dubbed, turned *clairvoyance, channeling, past lives,* and *meditation* into household words. He was a pivotal figure who deeply influenced the 1960s counterculture, and its adversaries. "The Edgar Cayce Foundation was making a big play for the minds of people," fretted televangelist Pat Robertson, who also lived in Virginia Beach. "People were calling in from all over Tidewater pleading with us to pray because their loved ones were being caught up in séances and occult groups. The whole area was rife with Satan's power." Robertson is merely one in a long line of preachers who railed against devilish secret societies. In the late 1700s, a New England minister named Jedediah Morse caused a moral panic by claiming that the Bavarian Illuminati had infiltrated America. Samuel F. B. Morse followed in his father's footsteps by writing two books of conspiracy theory before inventing the telegraph (which, ironically, indirectly ignited the Spiritualist movement).[29]

In the 1960s, irreverent figures such as Church of Satan founder Anton LaVey pulled pranks and publicity stunts that fanned the flames of Illuminatiphobia. "The High Priest of the Church of Satan" was a former carny who freaked out his ideological opponents by staging events such as the "Satanic Baptism" of his young daughter. This Barnumesque showman had a knack for the spectacular, and he was well aware that sex sells. For instance, his "Satan Wants You" promotional posters featured LaVey in a horned, black, pajama-like costume while pointing at the viewer, à la Uncle Sam (albeit with a buxom naked woman draped on an altar behind him). The existence of a radical feminist organization cheekily named WITCH also confirmed in the minds of religious conservatives that occult villains were the driving force behind that decade's social upheavals. A ragtag group named the Discordians stirred up even more trouble. They worshiped the goddess of chaos, made fun of organized religion, and satirized what historian Richard Hofstadter calls the "paranoid style in American politics." Among other things, these Discordian prophets mailed comical letters on Bavarian Illuminati letterhead to evangelical churches and organizations such as the Christian Anti-Communism Crusade.[30]

These sorts of impish acts triggered some serious prank blowback after their satires were misinterpreted by concerned conservatives. (One person's humor can be another's horror.) As a result, the religious right soon began pushing back against many of the sixties' progressive advances. Mainstream media also stirred this movement into existence after esoteric ideas reached millions of people through popular culture. The Beatles placed Aleister Crowley on the cover of *Sgt. Pepper*, the Rolling Stones had a huge hit with "Sympathy for the Devil," and sensational news reports regularly linked hippies with Satanism. Television pumped out lighthearted occult sitcoms such as *Bewitched*, *I Dream of Jeanie*, *The Munsters*, and *The Addams Family*, as well as the bleaker *Outer Limits*, *Twilight Zone*, and *Dark Shadows*. *Rosemary's Baby* and other Hollywood films also popularized symbols that later resurfaced in the "recovered" memories of alleged ritual-abuse survivors. The devilish connotations of 666, for instance, were not widely recognized until its prominent use as a plot device in the 1970s *Omen* movies and their advertising campaigns.[31]

Conservative independent media, anchored by the John Birch Society's vast publishing arm, distilled those pop-culture fantasies into chilling narratives. Churches also served as communication hubs by spreading these stories through Sunday sermons and word-of-mouth gossip. Others, such as Pat Robertson, fought Spiritualist mediums with electrified media. For over half a century, he used his Christian Broadcasting Network to call out the Illuminati, Satanists, One Worlders, and other conspirators. Fundamentalists have often been caricatured as antimodern, despite being early adopters of most every new medium that has come along (from tent revivals, radio, and television to mimeograph machines, roadside billboards, and online bulletin boards). Alternative media regularly gets framed as a liberal project, leading many people to ignore the influence of right-wing indie media. This is a huge oversight. Its existence helps explain why such a cohesive set of beliefs—centered around mystical, evil elites who steer world events—have remained so consistent throughout the modern era. Former vice president Dan Quayle expressed this conspiracy-steeped anxiety when discussing the Russian mystic Grigori Rasputin: "People that are really very weird can get into sensitive positions and have a tremendous impact on history."[32]

These fears climaxed in the 1980s during the Satanic Panics, when heavy metal, Dungeons & Dragons, and other nefarious pop-culture staples became sources of hysteria. Worries about Satanism largely subsided by the 1990s, only to be replaced by Illuminatiphobia. Pat Robertson and *Left Behind* coauthor Tim LaHaye implicated a web of secret societies, liberal elites, and United Nations technocrats in a plot to establish a godless global government. New World Order conspiracy theories bred like bionic bunnies on the newly emerging Internet, multiplying further in the Age of Obama. Tea Party foot soldiers railed against manipulative social scientists, shouted from the rooftops about the UN and the Federal Reserve, and obsessed over Rockefeller elites and Rothschild bankers. After Barack Hussein Obama became president, "Say No to the Social Engineers!" became an unlikely but winning Tea Party election slogan. Although Congressman Ron Paul put a less unhinged spin on these notions, he still earned legions of conspiracy-theory fanboys by warning of a coming global currency and plans for a multilane "NAFTA Superhighway." This worldview seemed to erupt from nowhere, but it had been incubating for years—even though it was built on a house of cards, drawn from a deck full of jokers.

1

This Is the Dawning of the Age of Enlightenment ... and Pranks

Pulling a prank is like throwing a rock in the pop-culture pond. Observing the ripple effect can help us better understand how the modern world was formed—though that raises the question of why modernity has been so tangled up in trickery. The short answer is that media technologies made it easier to misrepresent reality. Through tape editing, 1940s radio producers could add applause, cut out risqué jokes, and place laughs over ones that bombed. This shifted recordings away from being a fairly straightforward "record" of a performance, opening the doors to all kinds of studio trickery. "Magnetism itself may be a universal truth," Greg Milner observes in *Perfecting Sound Forever*, "but magnetic recording taught music to lie." The invention of photography created other blind spots, largely stemming from the privileged role that vision plays in our society (seeing is believing, after all). "Photography allows us to uncritically think," documentarian Errol Morris argues. "We *imagine* that photographs provide a magic path to the truth." What we can't see is the process that led to their creation, from unconscious decisions about image composition to calculated, staged hoaxes. Moving back further in time, the printing press created radically new ways of consuming information. By the 1600s, an increasingly literate public was interpreting texts without the intervention of a priestly authority. This new media environment muddled the epistemological question— "How do we know what we know?"—by pushing many people to sputter, "Are we *really* sure we *truly* know what we *think* we know?"[1]

Jean Hardouin, for example, was fairly certain that everything everyone else knew was a lie. This Jesuit scholar, who lived from 1646 to 1729, wrote a head-spinning magnum opus titled *Ad Censuram Scriptorum Veterum Prolegomena*. It asserted that the vast majority of classical Greek and Roman art, coins, and written histories were outright fabrications. In the late thirteenth and fourteenth centuries, a shadowy network of atheistic pagans planted forged archival documents in monastic libraries. Hardouin claimed that this cabal was led by Severus Archontius, a dastardly fellow who pulled the strings from behind the scenes. In order to undermine the faith of believers, his followers subtly altered early Christian writings and mixed them with blasphemous counterfeit documents that were attributed to Church fathers. Hardouin insisted that only the works of Herodotus, Pliny the Elder, Cicero, and some—but not all—of Homer's and Virgil's writings were authentically ancient. The writings of Plato and Aristotle? Augustine's *Confessions*? The Hebrew text of the Old Testament? All fakes! While these ideas might seem a bit deranged, Hardouin did have a sharp mind and was revered for his erudite writings on the classical world. He was no crackpot fringe figure.

The Jesuit scholar's revisionist history was a desperate attempt to tame the contradictory range of ideas that erupted from print culture. Hardouin reacted to this information overload by forging order out of chaos, an impulse that continues to this day. His ideas are nearly identical to contemporary conspiracy theories—which can be understood as explanatory narratives that arise in response to a complex, unstable world. English professor Harold Love whimsically suggests that this pioneering conspiracy theorist can also be remembered as an early modern media theorist—one whose writings foreshadowed the work of a more significant Jesuit scholar named Walter J. Ong. "Hardouin regarded the period when religious knowledge had been transmitted largely through the oral medium as in every way preferable to the age of print," Love writes, "and would have liked to see it return." He wasn't the only one. Christian theology had been shared for thirteen centuries in an unbroken line from pope to pope, believer to believer, through the living imitation of Christ. This spoken-word tradition ensured ideological stability because communication could be directly surveilled and managed by Church authorities. Then came those satanic forgers and the diabolical printing press—a menace to faith and the first weapon of mass deception. Three decades before Hardouin was born, the printing press played a key role in spreading a satire that caused a massive amount of prank blowback after a small group of rabble-rousing Protestants invented a fictitious secret society. It cast a long shadow over the Jesuit's imagination and, for that matter, modernity itself.[2]

THOSE RASCALLY ROSICRUCIANS

The modern era was ushered in by a prank. In 1614, a mysterious tract appeared in Kassel, Germany, announcing the existence of an Invisible College of mystical adepts. *Fama Fraternitatis Rosae Crucis*, or "The Fame of the Brotherhood of the Rose Cross," told the tale of a man named Christian Rosencreutz. Among other things, he acquired ancient insights from Muslim scholars (Islamic knowledge began seeping into Christian Europe beginning in the twelfth century, bringing alchemy and astrology with it). Rosencreutz founded the Brotherhood in 1408, and it met yearly in the mysterious "House of the Holy Spirit." The trope of a young Christian who traveled east and gained new wisdom was not uncommon within the popular culture of the time, though the story of a hero's journey and homecoming has much older roots in myth. Within that context, *Fama* clearly reads like an allegory, though that didn't stop many people from taking it literally. This first tract—combined with an anonymous 1615 pamphlet titled *Confessio Fraternitatis* and 1616's *The Chymical Wedding of Christian Rosenkreutz*—formed the core of what became known as the "Rosicrucian Manifestos." These documents claimed that the Brothers of the Rose Cross were engineering a coming Golden Age that would transform all existing political and religious institutions. Not only could these men bring about global utopian harmony; they could make themselves *disappear!* Readers who wanted to meet a Brother were told that if they concentrated really, really hard, one would probably drop by for a visit.[3]

The *Fama* manuscript initially circulated in rarified circles, stimulating thoughtful debate and contemplation. The published version, which took the prank public, was reframed as a full-blown politico-religious diatribe that downplayed the original's subtlety. It blew up like a mass-mediated bomb. This had the comical effect of sending people scrambling in search of an invisible fraternity, even though *Fama* clearly made the hippy-dippy claim that one could only realize the true nature of the Brotherhood by looking deep within oneself. The authors of the Rosicrucian Manifestos were primarily drawn to esoteric learning, science, and technology. They also shared an irreverent or outright hostile attitude toward Catholicism—a belligerence that was on display in the first published edition of the manifesto. It was paired with a popular satirical essay called *The General Reformation of the Whole World* (whose title echoed a line from *Fama*, which promised "a general reformation, both of divine and human things"). It further stoked partisan passions by including a report about a man, Adam Haselmeyer, who was incarcerated by Jesuits for commenting on the original *Fama* manuscript. The second manifesto, 1615's *Confessio Fraternitatis*, made it even clearer that the Brotherhood stood against the papacy. This had the catalytic effect of splitting public opinion down religious lines: Catholics blasted these heretics, while others sought to join, claimed they were already members, or knew someone who was.[4]

What started out as a playful experiment in publicity transformed into a powerful, history-making myth. The Rosicrucian Manifestos rocked Europe by triggering a highly charged set of cultural, religious, and political associations. In the sixteenth and seventeenth centuries, many German thinkers were in the thrall of millenarian and messianic thought. Protestants had long been waiting for a redeemer figure who would complete the work of the Reformation and banish the papacy's "evil empire." The start of the Thirty Years' War in 1618 exacerbated Catholic anxieties about the Rosicrucians, who were thought to be Protestant supermen intent on conquering Europe. Germanic states were consumed by a power struggle between the political powers connected to the Catholic Church and the popularly elected Frederick V of the Palatinate, who was associated with Protestant England. Some Protestants found their savior in Frederick V, whose heraldic animal was the lion—an important signifier that circulated within the popular culture of that time. (*Confessio Fraternitatis*, for instance, had previously declared that the pope "shall be scratched to pieces with nails, and end be made of his ass's cry, by a new voice of a roaring lion.") In 1623, a conjunction of Saturn and Jupiter formed the sign of Leo, which was seen as an omen at a time when astrology was enjoying greater cultural currency. With Leo the Lion roaring high in the sky, a second wave of panic about the Rosicrucians swept the land.[5]

Reports from the period spoke of a "hurricane" of excitement, both pro and con, whipped up by this imaginary secret society. The Catholic Church insisted that the Rosicrucians were devil worshipers (whose promise of enlightenment was clear evidence of a diabolical agenda). The Brotherhood's self-proclaimed shape-shifting abilities let them infiltrate political and religious institutions, and their interest in "natural philosophy"—a precursor to modern science—was assumed to be wicked bait used to twist the minds of Christians. The lines between occultism, esoteric knowledge, and natural philosophy were quite blurry in this era. Even Sir Isaac Newton spent more time on alchemy than on gravitational science, and he was also a proponent of "natural magic." This term referred to a rational understanding of nature's laws that could help reveal the workings of God's universe (*Fama* claimed that "in Theology, Physics, and the Mathematics, the Truth doth manifest itself"). René Descartes was rumored to be a Rosicrucian, something he famously had to deny. Nevertheless, the mathematician was excited enough to write in his notes about "the distinguished brothers of the Rose Croix in Germany." Descartes sought after them in 1619, but it was a fruitless quest. As the manifestos instructed, one could only find a Brother by entering a world of imagination or a new consciousness. As the Beatles sang, "Turn off your mind, relax, and float downstream." (Appropriately enough, *The Alchemical Wedding* was the title of an infamous 1968 performance art "happening" by Yoko Ono and John Lennon, who spent the entire show hidden inside a large bag.)[6]

The Rosicrucian Brotherhood wasn't the only fantasy flowering at the time. Interest in Atlantis was being rekindled by Europe's encounters with the New World, prompting people to float all sorts of wild theories about the lost continent. Most imaginative was a professor named Olof Rudbeck, who insisted that its ruins could be found in . . . *Sweden!* His three-thousand-page tome *Atlantica* grew more bizarre with each turn of each page, and it provoked ridicule from his Uppsala University colleagues. One snapped, "In theology as well as jurisprudence, as well as medicine, chemistry, philosophy, Herr Rudbeck knows nothing." The nutty professor responded to this accusation in the fall 1679 lecture catalog by announcing a brand new class. "Olof Rudbeck is going to treat his listeners to a very useful, very intricate, and very subtle subject that is never praised enough: Nothing." University administrators (who aren't known for their senses of humor, then and now) were not amused by Rudbeck's "tasteless gesture." However, he was revered by England's Royal Society for the Improvement of Natural Knowledge, whose journal published a glowing review of *Atlantica*. He was invited to join this esteemed group, but Rudbeck was far too busy with his important work to bother responding. The Royal Society's interest in his research was partly rooted in the fact that its guiding spirit, Francis Bacon, wrote a classic utopian essay titled *The New Atlantis*—which was steeped in Rosicrucian thought. Fantastical ideas about Atlantis were later embraced by nineteenth-century occult revivalists such as the Theosophists, who were also influenced by the Rosicrucian Manifestos.[7]

Some incredulous observers believed that the entire Rosicrucian affair was nothing more than a hoax. "The invisibility of the Brothers, their apparent refusal to give any sign of their existence to their disciples," Frances Yeats writes in *The Rosicrucian Enlightenment*, "naturally encourages this view." Despite the manifestos' shadowy origins, some consensus has formed about who authored them. A radical German theologian named Johann Valentin Andreae later confessed to writing *The Chymical Wedding*, and he was also the probable author of *Fama Fraternitatis Rosae Crucis*. (Andreae was twenty-three when the latter was published, though he wrote it a few years earlier when he was in college.) The fact that *Fama* began as a handwritten manuscript, rather than a printed document, indicates that he did not initially intend it for general consumption. It circulated privately among a handful of university classmates and professors, but by 1610 it spread outside their orbit. Differences in handwriting and changes in the text suggest that *Fama* passed through many hands before it came to the attention of the Jesuits. Authorities soon began arresting "adherents of the same sect . . . to prevent the spread of their heresies." In response, a provocateur printed a mass-produced version, and that's when all hell broke loose. The relatively new technology of the printing press was key to the prank's success, especially because *Fama* invited "all of the scholars and rulers of Europe" to "declare their minds in print." In a stroke of marketing genius, no return address was given. European intellectuals tried their best to attract the Brotherhood's attention, and within a dozen years imitators (and detractors) produced several hundred pamphlets, books, and broadsides—an astounding amount for the period.[8]

Andreae characterized what he did as a youthful *"ludubrium,"* or a joke with a serious objective. In his autobiography, he expressed shock that people took his parody seriously, claiming that the *Chymical Wedding* was intended to trap the credulous. Andreae explicitly used theatrical and gaming metaphors to talk about his prank—describing how he wrote the script, set the scene, and watched the drama unfold. "When . . . some on the literary stage were arranging a play scene of certain ingenious parties, I stood aside as one who looks on," he recalled. "As a spectator, it was not without a certain quality of zest that I beheld the battle of the books and marked subsequently an entire change of actors." By wrapping *Fama's* cry for spiritual revolt in a dramatic tale about a quest and discovery, it pulled a curious public even further into this web of intrigue. Andreae hoped this theatrical game would encourage people to be more accepting of new ideas about science, philosophy, and spirituality. But by 1619, he grew exasperated. "Listen ye mortals," Andreae advised, "in vain do you wait for the coming of the Brotherhood, the Comedy is at an end." He also called it the "parent of all follies." Despite those fair warnings, many people continued to believe that this Invisible College was quite real. Five years after *Fama's* publication, Andreae noted that the Brotherhood was now a "fantasy" that had become "the heart and scandal of occultism" in his time. The pranksters lost control of the narrative, and the resulting furor ended up obscuring their intended message. It was the first in a long line of pranks that took on a life of their own, going viral in ways the original authors/actors/directors never intended.[9]

Tensions rose in Paris after a series of mysterious placards appeared in 1623. "We, being deputies of the principal College of the Brothers of the Rose Cross," one sign declared, with tongue planted firmly in cheek, "are making a visible and invisible stay in this city through the Grace of the Most High." The posters mocked the occult backlash that was sweeping Europe, especially in the French capital, and it inspired several sensational publications. *Horrible Pacts Made between the Devil and the Pretended Invisible Ones* claimed there were thirty-six Invisible Ones who ruled the planet (*six* international groups each contained *six* deputies, *six* of whom came to Paris to spread their devilish doctrine). Adepts were promised purses forever filled with money if they rejected Christ. They were also given the ability to eloquently speak all languages, as well as charismatic qualities that ensured respect and admiration. Shocked Catholic authorities responded with tribunals, but some more levelheaded people remained skeptical. "The Rose Cross is an imaginative invention by a group of persons who use it as their symbol and mark," the anonymous author of *Researches of the Rose Cross* dismissively wrote. "Besides this it means nothing."[10]

The poster prank was most likely pulled by a doctor named Étienne Chaume, who was described as being driven by "youthful jocularity and a juvenile spirit." In recounting this episode, the late-seventeenth-century scholar Nicolas Chorier described the common people of France as gullible by nature. "There are no other people on earth who allow themselves to be fooled more easily," he sneered. "Fear, distress, indignation invaded nearly every house." Swindlers came out of the woodwork and defrauded those who wanted to meet the Brotherhood or who begged for protection against them. One prominent Jesuit called for all Rosicrucians, Lutherans, empiricists, and witches to be thrown on the pyre's flame. Later in that century, between 1677 and 1682, Catholics were once again aghast when members of the French aristocracy were poisoned. After a series of forced confessions, some of Louis XIV's inner circle were charged with fraud, abortion, infanticide, and kidnapping. Most infamous was the case of Catherine Deshayes Monvoisin, a midwife and self-proclaimed clairvoyant. Before she was burned to death, inquisitors kept her in an intoxicated state that stimulated her psychedelic tales of aphrodisiacs, gardens of human remains, and black masses. Many of the key tropes that signify Satanism were developed during the Affair of Poisons, including naked women on altars, infant ritual sacrifice, the Lord's Prayer spoken backward, and other parodies of the Catholic mass. Few of these stories were substantiated, but they proved to be long lasting.[11]

Many assumed that the Rosicrucians were behind the Affair of Poisons, and fear once again rippled throughout the nation. These events provided the backdrop for the 1681 play *The Philosophers' Stone*, written by Thomas Corneille and Donneau de Visé. The comedy's plot centered around the 1623 poster incident, which indicates how deeply this elaborate ruse impacted French society. Johann Valentin Andreae's circle of friends—and the mischief makers they inspired—openly advertised their subversive inclinations. This dialed up the paranoia among religious conservatives, who adopted a siege mentality. The resulting prank blowback exploded into a social force that impacted four centuries of Western culture. Regardless of whether this Invisible College was a genuine secret society or just a provocative prank, the Rosicrucian Manifestos left a deep footprint on the material world. After trying to get the attention of the Brotherhood in print, to no avail, many interested parties started their own orders. The meme continued to self-replicate, and it went on to influence the religious pluralism of Freemasonry and others who challenged tradition. The myth of the Rosicrucian Brotherhood also created the template for virtually every occultic conspiracy theory that followed: an elite body of initiates—a satanic secret society *within* a secret society, sometimes known as the Illuminati—that wants to overthrow all established religious-political authority and create a New World Order.[12]

FORTUNE TELLING AND BABY EATING

Church authorities insisted that astrologers were satanic heretics, while Enlightenment enthusiasts just thought they were idiots. Writing under the name Isaac Bickerstaff, Jonathan Swift claimed that the popular English astrologer and almanac maker John Partridge would exhale his last breath at 11 p.m. on March 29, 1708. As you may recall, Benjamin Franklin did the exact same thing to Titan Leeds three decades later. Franklin was well aware of the Bickerstaff Affair, but much of the American public was not; so he recycled the prank to help advertise *Poor Richard's Almanack*. However, Swift was making a more serious point. He once described himself as a "rational surgeon" who dissected mass delusions such as astrology, which Swift and his peers believed was dangerous quackery. (And as dean of St. Patrick's Cathedral in Dublin, he also had a few doctrinal reasons for disapproving.) Astrologers, Swift said, did little more than offer "a yearly stock of nonsense, lyes, folly, and impertinence, which they offer to the world as genuine from the planets, tho' they descend from no greater a height than their own brains." John Partridge, he added, was one of those "fools and knaves" with whom he had "always been at open war." For those reasons, and more, he engineered an intricate prank that exploded in Partridge's face on April 1, 1708.[13]

April Fools' Day was Swift's favorite holiday, for it allowed him to inflict (on friends and foes alike) the sorts of puns and practical jokes that were second nature to him. His prank began with a pamphlet titled *Predictions for the Year 1708*. "My first Prediction is but a Trifle," Swift/ Bickerstaff wrote. "It relates to *Partridge* the Almanack-Maker; I have consulted the Star of his Nativity by my own Rules; and find he will infallibly die upon the 29th of March next, about eleven at Night." For fun, Swift used Partridge's own almanac as fodder for the prank. He zeroed in on a passage in which the astrologer solemnly predicted that April 1708 would bring "a Spring Distemper . . . with a Disorder in the Bowels." Riffing on this, Swift prophesized that Partridge would die at the hands of "a raging Fever." Within a week, *Predictions* sold thousands of copies, and pirate publishers distributed many more half-price editions. Partridge, who was very slow to catch on throughout the affair, did Swift an unintended favor by writing and publishing an *Answer to Bickerstaff*. Not only was it a labored attempt to dismiss *Predictions*; it also had the effect of keeping the joke alive through the entire month of March.[14]

"Now can any man of common sense think it . . . beneath the dignity of a philosopher," Partridge cluelessly responded, "to stand bawling before his own door? — Alive! Alive ho! The famous Dr. Partridge! No counterfeit, but all alive!" The self-proclaimed "*student in physick and astrology*" ended his *Answer* with the boastful couplet, "His whole Design was nothing but Deceit, The End of March will plainly show the Cheat." With that setup, Swift/Bickerstaff published the second phase of his April Fools' joke, *An Elegy on the Supposed Death of Partridge, the Almanack-Maker*. It practically begged the astrologer to say more stupid stuff.[15]

> Strange, an Astrologer shou'd die,
> Without one Wonder in the Sky!

Not one of all his Crony Stars
To pay their Duty at his Herse?
No Meteor, no Eclipse appear'd?
No Comet with a flaming Beard?
The Sun has rose, and gone to Bed,
Just as if partridge were not dead[16]

Elegy suggested an apt epitaph for Partridge: "Here, five Foot deep, lies on his Back, A Cobbler, Starmonger, and Quack." Then came the third and final deathblow: *The Accomplishment of the First of Mr. Bickerstaff's Predictions; Being an Account of the Death of Mr. Partridge, the Almanack-Maker.* The pamphlet claimed that a former government official who knew Partridge rushed to his side upon hearing about his imminent demise. Published immediately after *Elegy*—on the day before April 1, 1708—it included a deathbed confession in which Partridge acknowledged that astrology was nothing more than a money-making "Deceit." *Accomplishment* propelled Swift's prank into the stratosphere, and Partridge woke up as the laughingstock of London that April Fools' Day. As I suggested in this book's introduction, pranks are compelling because they encourage the participation of audiences. In the wake of the Bickerstaff Affair, an undertaker visited Partridge's home, a sexton inquired about a grave, church bells tolled for him, and the Reader of his parish sent messages insisting that he should be buried properly. Random pedestrians accused the hapless mystic of not paying his funeral bills, and others kept him awake at night with wails of mock mourning. The Stationers' Company, which published Partridge's almanac, took the news seriously and removed his name from its rolls. It took six years for him to recover from lost almanac sales, and the incident cast a pall over astrology—which began declining in reputation.[17]

Enthusiastic collaborators such as Richard Steele and Nicholas Rowe, along with countless other imitators, helped Swift keep the prank going long after its April 1, 1708 expiration date. But not everyone was in on the joke. The Catholic Church's Holy Inquisition in Portugal was under the mistaken assumption that Partridge really did die, so it burned copies of *Predictions*. Bickerstaff's forecast was so terrifyingly accurate that it could have only been the work of the devil! Partridge also missed Swift's humor, telling everyone who would listen that HE WAS STILL

ALIVE AND HAD NOT DIED over the course of the year. This inspired Swift/Bickerstaff to follow up on April 1, 1709 with *A Vindication of Isaac Bickerstaff Esq.* It "clearly proved, by *invincible demonstration*, that [Partridge] died, at farthest, within half an hour of the time" Bickerstaff foretold. Using language Benjamin Franklin borrowed a quarter century later, he complained, "[The ghost of] Mr. Partridge hath been lately pleased to treat me after a very rough manner." Swift's proof of death? The thousands of people who bought Partridge's almanac were "sure no man alive ever writ such damn'd stuff as this." Franklin swiped that line as well.[18]

Language was important to Jonathan Swift. He regularly used his poison pen to do battle, once punning that he hoped his writing would "Give your head some gentle raps / Only [to] make it smart a while." Swift used his rapier wit to make "sin and folly bleed," inviting—no, begging—people to think critically. He suggested that "*instead of lashing*," the most useful discourse is the kind that "*laughs men out of their follies, and vices*." Rather than straightforward condemnation, Swift regularly hid behind multiple literary guises and expressed the opposite of his true opinions. In the 1710 edition of his early satire *A Tale of a Tub*, Swift discussed this approach in the book's *Apology*: "some of those Passages in this Discourse, which appear most liable to Objection are what they call Parodies, where the Author personates the Style and Manner of other Writers, whom he has a mind to expose." Today, this comedic form of argumentation has become so familiar that audiences don't need that sort of hand holding.[19]

Ridicule was a common feature of eighteenth-century Anglo-American culture, but Swift and his colleagues Joseph Addison and Richard Steele believed it should be used sparingly. They advised against actions that do not yield personal "improvement," especially those that were mean-spirited. "The talent of turning men into ridicule," Addison and Steele wrote, "is the qualification of little, ungenerous tempers." Nevertheless, they acknowledged there were times when shaming was necessary in order to persuade people or to move them to action. Not only did Steele conspire with Swift during the John Partridge prank; he went so far as to list Isaac Bickerstaff as the editor of his first publication, the *Tatler*. (Throughout its run, Steele used this pseudonym as his journalistic persona and pen name.) Joseph Addison—who sought to "enliven

Morality with Wit, and to temper Wit with Morality"—joined Steele in 1711 to cofound the *Spectator*. The paper's goal was "to bring philosophy out of the closets and libraries, schools and colleges, to dwell in clubs and assemblies, at tea tables and in coffee houses."[20]

Swift's masterpiece was *A Modest Proposal*. Posing as an anonymous "Irish Patriot," he suggested that the starving people of Ireland could turn their malnourished frowns upside down by literally eating their young. Peter O'Toole once claimed that this 1729 essay has "a little something to offend everybody." Sure enough, the Irish actor's over-the-top recitation of *A Modest Proposal* provoked a mass walkout of dignitaries during the 1984 reopening of Dublin's Gaiety Theatre. "A child will make two dishes at an entertainment for friends," Swift dryly stated, "and when the family dines alone, the fore or hind quarter will make a reasonable dish." His grotesque instructions, if you'll pardon the pun, went far beyond the limits of good taste. "Those who are more thrifty (as I must confess the times require) may flay the carcass," he wrote, "the skin of which . . . will make admirable gloves for ladies, and summer boots for fine gentlemen." Swift crunched the numbers: of the 120,000 children society couldn't support, 20,000 could be set aside for breeding, and the rest would be served at the table. "I have been assured by a very knowing American of my acquaintance in London that a young healthy child well nursed is at a year old a most delicious, nourishing, and wholesome food, whether stewed, roasted, baked, or boiled." *A Modest Proposal* may be a bit long in the tooth, but it still has a bite.[21]

Although Swift certainly was attacking the English—particularly policymakers and absentee landlords—they weren't his main targets. Instead, he fixed his sights on his fellow Irish, whose lethargy in the face of disaster infuriated him. *A Modest Proposal* begged the question of how society could possibly engage in rational deliberation when total lunacy reigned. Because the people of Ireland had rejected all other reasonable options that might improve their condition, Swift wanted to deliver the most extreme and devastating assessment of their fate. He acknowledged that the practice of killing and eating babies *could* be perceived as abhorrent ("some scrupulous people might be apt to censure such a practice"), but at least it is better than doing nothing. The greatest irony of Swift's *Proposal* is that one of the English language's greatest writers essentially admitted that words have little impact. They can't fill stomachs or alter government policy, so in the absence of material change he at least wanted to give the public a cold rhetorical shower. Using shock and irony, two tactics still used by contemporary pranksters, Swift tried to prod his fellow citizens into action.[22]

Aryan Asian Kidnapped by Jesuits!

A Modest Proposal makes a passing reference to "the famous Psalmanazar, a native of the island Formosa." This blond, blue-eyed "savage" claimed people ate children in his homeland. "When any young person happened to be put to death," Swift recounted, "the executioner sold the carcass to persons of quality as a prime dainty." George Psalmanazar claimed to be a kidnapping victim who was snatched from Formosa (now known as Taiwan) by a Jesuit named Father de Rode of Avignon. This sinister missionary brought him to Europe and pressured the fair young lad to convert from paganism to Catholicism. He was thrown into prison after resisting their overtures but soon escaped their clutches. Soldiers belonging to the Elector of Cologne captured Psalmanazar and shipped him off to another batch of scheming Catholics, but he got away again. Then Dutch soldiers detained him and pushed Calvinism on him, to no avail (he just couldn't buy into the doctrine of predestination). While in the Netherlands, Psalmanazar crossed paths with an Anglican priest named Alexander Innes, who dazzled him with the Church of England's teachings. "At my arrival at London," he later recalled, "Mr. Innes, and some worthy clergymen of his acquaintance, introduced me to the bishop of London, and got soon after a good number of friends among the clergy and laiety."[23]

Psalmanazar gained the same level of fame or infamy as a modern-day reality-television-star train wreck. Nobles and rich merchants invited him to their dinner tables, where he spoke gibberish while inhaling mouthfuls of bloody food. (According to imaginary custom, Formosans ate their meat raw.) He impressed many, but Psalmanazar also had "a much greater number of opposers to combat with." At a meeting of the Royal Society—which on that day included discussions of ovarian cysts, possum penises, and this blond, blue-eyed specimen from Formosa—he was questioned by the group's resident astronomer.

Edmund Halley asked detailed questions about how long twilight lasted on the island, the amount of time the sun shone down chimneys, and other quantifiable queries. Psalmanazar calmly told Halley that Formosan chimneys were bent and, therefore, the sun couldn't shine down them. He remained fast on his feet and had an explanation for everything that was thrown his way, turning each objection against his story into evidence that it was for real.[24]

After fending off attacks from astronomers, botanists, and possumpenis enthusiasts, Psalmanazar was confronted by Father Fontenay. "You are a fraud," he declared, noting that Formosa was a province of China, not Japan. "You are wrong," replied Psalmanazar, who then asked if there were any other ways people referred to Formosa. "Tyowan"—that is, Taiwan—Fontenay said. *Ahhhh,* he told the Jesuit, that was a *different* island colonized by the Dutch! Psalmanazar said people from China referred to Formosa as Pak-Ando and natives such as himself called it Gad-Avia. Fontenay protested that "Pak" wasn't even a Chinese word. Other Royal Society members questioned why Psalmanazar had such light skin. "My complexion, indeed, which was very fair," Psalmanazar recalled, "appeared an unanswerable objection against me." (The Royal Society report on him noted that "he looked like a young Dutchman.") In the face of this skepticism, Psalmanazar told an elaborate story about how the upper classes of Formosa lived in "in cool shades, or apartments under ground," which kept their skin chilly and white. This explanation made sense within then-current assumptions about pigmentation. Although some ethnic distinctions existed during this period—such as the difference between light-skinned northern Europeans and sub-Saharan blacks—modern categories of race didn't yet exist. There was simply no conceptual framework in place to ask the question, "Aren't you Caucasian?"[25]

Psalmanazar's performance of a phony tongue was the most convincing feature of his masquerade. The "Formosan" alphabet had twenty letters that were written from right to left, as Psalmanazar probably imagined was true of all Asian languages. It was a mulligan's stew of "Hebrew (e.g., Mem, Nen, Kaphi), Greek (Lamdo, Epsi), and nonsense (Hamno, Pedlo, Dam, Raw)." By mixing pronunciations from "the many languages [he] had learned, and nations [he] had been conversant with," Psalmanazar made it impossible to pin down his dialect. The little evidence that remains suggests that he was from France, but when Father Fontenay was asked to guess Psalmanazar's origins, the Frenchman replied that he had never heard an accent like that in his life. Language also played a big role in Psalmanazar's posthumously published memoirs. "The *Memoirs*, in short, presents us with a long series of fluid and flexible identities," biographer Michael Keevak writes, "all of them constituted (or at least supported) by the acquisition of another tongue, living, dead, real or imaginary." Because no one that Psalmanazar crossed paths with had ever been to Formosa, it was up to him to define how a Formosan spoke, dressed, and acted. Also, he may have been a savage, but at least he was unthreatening, was light skinned, spoke fluent English, attended Anglican Church services, and hated Catholics.[26]

Genuine cross-cultural encounters during this era were much uglier. For example, a Jesuit priest named Jean-Francois Foucquet hired a Chinese man named John Hu to be his copyist in 1721. On the rocky nine-month trip across the Pacific and Atlantic, curving around South America and arriving in France, Hu grew increasingly disturbed. He brooded, had wild mood swings, and got into verbal altercations with other passengers. Foucquet's only conclusion was that he suffered from something he called "Chinese madness." This impression was bolstered when Hu had a meltdown in a French church after seeing males and females commingling during the services—something that was forbidden in China. When Foucquet mocked him for this, Hu crafted a drum and a foot-long banner with Chinese characters that read, "Men and women should be kept in their separate spheres." He then pounded the drum and waved his banner through the streets of Paris, gathering a curious crowd at the doors of St. Paul's Cathedral. Fearing Hu would be arrested for this strange behavior, Father Foucquet locked him away for two and a half years in an insane asylum. Eventually, Hu was summoned by a hospital cleric who was investigating his case. When asked if he had any questions, Hu only had one: "Why have I been locked up?" Life in Europe as an actual Asian man held only indignities.[27]

George Psalmanazar, on the other hand, had access to valuable cultural resources that offered him a relatively good life. After he wowed London with his colorful stories, customs, and far-out accent, the public clamored for more about his homeland. It took Psalmanazar only two months to knock out a 288-page volume titled *Description of*

Formosa, which sold out immediately. The book contained illustrations of native clothing and architecture and a lovely image of a grill used to roast the hearts of little boys. *Description* also featured foldout plates of the Formosan language and numerical system, along with information on botany, zoology, and gastronomy. British antiquarian Isaac D'Israeli dashed off a sarcastic exclamation-slathered summary of Psalmanazar's book: "wretched inventions! of their dress! religious ceremonies! their tabernacle and altars to the sun, the moon, and the ten stars! their architecture! the viceroy's castle! a temple! a city house! a countryman's house! and the Formosan alphabet!" And then there was the book's long, unwieldy title and subtitle.[28]

AN HISTORICAL AND GEOGRAPHICAL DESCRIPTION OF FORMOSA
AN Island subject to the Emperor of JAPAN

GIVING An Account of the Religion, Customs, Manners, &c. of the Inhabitants. Together with a Relation of what happen'd to the Author in his Travels; particularly his Conferences with the *Jesuits*, and others, in several Parts of *Europe* . . .

By GEORGE PSALMANAZAR, a Native of the said Island, now in London

Description covered every imaginable (or, to be more precise, *imagined*) topic. Chapter 3 outlined the island's "Form of Government, and of the new laws made by the Emperor Meriaandanoo," while chapter 8 discussed "the Worship of the Sun, of the Moon, and of the Ten Stars." Psalmanazar explained that the Formosan year was divided into ten months: Dig, Damen, Analmen, Anioul, Dattibes, Dabes, Anaber, Nechem, Koriam, Turbam. The primitive people of this island originally worshiped the sun, moon, and ten stars, but this changed in the early days of Formosan society. Throughout the book, Psalmanazar sounded like an anthropology major tripping on peyote. The Aryan Asian claimed that two philosophers, Zeroaboabel and Chorche Matchin, rose to prominence and insisted Formosans devote themselves to a single, powerful god. They built a gigantic temple for a High Priest named—yes, wait for it—Gnotoy Bonzo, who commanded them to annually sacrifice "the hearts of 18000 young Boys, under the Age of

9 Years, on the first day of the Year." This was obviously a major logistical flaw for such a sparsely populated nation. Psalmanazar smoothed it over by claiming that men were permitted to have multiple wives, so that "they may beget many Children every Year; of whom some of the Sons are Sacrific'd, but the Daughters are all preserv'd for Matrimony."[29]

Psalmanazar's book also offered a political history of Formosa, complete with conquests and daggered intrigue. It included a reproduction of a letter addressed to the Formosan king, written by the king of Japan (though no one asked how this wretched refugee acquired this rare document). To be sure, *Description* was outlandish, but Psalmanazar's account wasn't much different from that of an actual traveler such as George Candidius, the first missionary in Taiwan. Psalmanazar's con worked because he tailored it for an Anglican audience predisposed to hating the Catholic Church. (If you are going to spin a crazy yarn for antipapist Englishmen, it helps to say that French Jesuits kidnapped you.) Psalmanazar's critics grew louder, which prompted a group of his supporters—or perhaps George himself?—to publish 1710's *An Enquiry into the Objections against George Psalmanazar of Formosa*. The pamphlet cleared him of all charges, of course, but his novelty was wearing off. Within half a dozen years, he became a national joke, as is evidenced by an April Fools'–themed goof published in Addison and Steele's *Spectator*. The March 16, 1711 issue announced, "*On the first of April will be performed at the Play-house in the* Hay-market *an Opera call'd* The Cruelty of Atreus. N.B. *The scene wherein Thyestes eats his own children, is to be performed by the famous Mr.* Psalmanazar, *lately arrived from* Formosa: *the whole Supper being set to kettle-drums*."[30]

Psalmanazar drifted from odd job to odder job, such as marketing chinaware with the curious tagline "a White sort of Japan." A few years later, he took up fan painting, and when that failed to bring in a steady income, he tutored Latin and later reentered military service as a clerk. Psalmanazar lived the rest of his life as a hack—one of the many Grub Street writers that churned out encyclopedia entries, histories, and prefaces for the most minimum of wages. He wrote twelve hours each day and sustained himself with ten to twelve drops of opium mixed with a pint of punch. In 1732, Psalmanazar published another book, *A General History of Printing*, and in the 1740s, he wrote a chapter for a proposed sequel to Samuel Richardson's novel *Pamela*. The Pretended

Asian also contributed to 1747's *Complete System of Geography*—including, bizarrely, an entry on Formosa in which he referred to himself in the third person. In it, he finally admitted that Psalmanazar was a liar and assured readers that a full confession would be published after his death. Sure enough, he left behind an autobiographical manuscript in a desk drawer. If published today, it might be hailed as a postmodern masterpiece simply for the proto-pomo textual erasure in the book's title: *Memoirs of ****: Commonly Known by the Name of George Psalmanazar: A Reputed Native of Formosa.*[31]

Memoirs of **** was alternately low key and histrionic. It began with the line, "THE LAST WILL AND TESTAMENT OF ME: A POOR SINFUL AND WORTHLESS CREATURE COMMONLY KNOWN BY THE ASSUMED NAME OF GEORGE PSALMANAZAR." He described his hope for the book: "to undo, as much as was in my power, all the mischief I had done." But there were many major holes in Psalmanazar's story, especially because he provided no account of the dozen or so years after his arrival in England. Those indiscretions would only disgust the Christian reader, Psalmanazar said. He did not reveal his birth name or leave any trace that could identify him, his family, or even his country of origin. The man known as Psalmanazar is almost totally lost to history. In an unlikely postscript to this improbable tale, the disgraced hoaxer gained a famous admirer near the end of his life: Samuel Johnson. "I never sought much after any body," the writer remarked. "But I sought after George Psalmanazar the most. I used to go and sit with him at an alehouse in the city." Johnson regularly mentioned the faux-Formosan's name with enthusiasm, claiming he was so highly esteemed in the neighborhood that "scarce any person, even children, passed him without shewing him the usual signs of respect." Hester Thrale, a close confidante of Johnson's, recorded one such memory: "When I asked Dr. Johnson, who was the *best* man he had ever known? 'Psalmanazar,' was the unexpected reply."[32]

Benjamin Franklin, Merry Prankster

Around the same time Psalmanazar came to London, Benjamin Franklin was born into a family with rebellious roots. His grandfather Peter Folger was a firebrand county clerk once jailed for siding with Nantucket's growing class of artisans and shopkeepers. Folger also wrote a "near-seditious pamphlet" that sympathized with the Native Americans during King Philip's War in 1676. Franklin's grandfather wasn't the only gadfly in the family ointment. Benjamin's older brother James Franklin apprenticed under a "noisy dissenter" named Benjamin Harris, who published America's first newspaper, *Publick Occurrences*. Historian Louis Solomon describes Harris as "the first in a long list of ornery, nonconforming, trouble-making newspapermen who have insisted on being free despite the consequences." The first edition of Harris's four-page paper turned out to be the last. He wasn't the type to go through proper channels, and *Publick Occurrences* was suppressed after he enraged the Puritan-dominated colonial government. Counting Harris's paper, James Franklin's *New England Courant* was just the fourth in all the colonies. It often displaced sober news reports with items intended to be "entertaining and opinion-forming, rather than dully matter-of-fact." The *Courant* also took potshots at the church and government, ensuring that it definitely was *not* "Published By Authority."[33]

At the age of twelve, Benjamin Franklin was indentured by his parents to James's print shop. Lewis Hyde observes that "it is no exaggeration to say that there he literally helped to hand-set the emerging public sphere in Boston." At the shop, he acquired several skills that served him well in life. After Franklin's father criticized his prose, the young man set out to improve himself by studying Addison and Steele's *Spectator*. Using it as a model, Franklin developed a conversational writing style that was funny and direct, with few poetic flourishes. During this time, he also developed a love of pseudonyms. Franklin penned at least one hundred items under fake names throughout his life: Ephraim Censorius, Patience, the Casuist, the Anti-Casuist, Anthony Afterwit, Margaret Aftercast, and Silence Dogood, to name but a few. Pseudonyms were not uncommon for many eighteenth-century writers, in part because they reduced one's chances of being prosecuted for sedition and because the writing could be evaluated on its own merits, instead of being subjected to personal attacks. Joseph Addison observed, "Scarce one part in ten of the valuable books which are published are with the author's name."[34]

For Franklin's first prank, the sixteen-year-old conjured up Silence Dogood—a straitlaced widow who lived outside Boston. He knew his brother would never knowingly publish him, so Benjamin surreptitiously slipped Silence's letter under the *Courant*'s front door at night. Dogood was an immediate hit, and readers clamored for more. Using an affable, folksy voice, s/he launched understated assaults on religion and hypocrisy that would have gotten an identifiable author thrown in jail. Irony and subtlety can help keep one out of prison, a lesson that never got through to James Franklin—who once wrote, "Of all knaves, the religious knave is the worst." After he was jailed for three weeks for upsetting the clergy and magistrates, the *Courant* was briefly turned over to Benjamin. "I made bold to give our rulers some rubs in it, which my brother took very kindly," he recalled, "while others began to consider me in an unfavorable light as a young genius that had a turn for libeling and satire."[35]

This was merely the revisionist exaggeration of an old man writing his autobiography, puffing up his revolutionary street cred. The three issues produced on Benjamin Franklin's watch did not really challenge civil authorities, and the only thing that came close was a Silence Dogood letter that quoted a radical essay about free expression. He continued using this pseudonym until James discovered his imposture. "I began to be considered a little more by my Brother's Acquaintance," Benjamin wrote in his autobiography, "and in a manner that did not quite please him, as he thought, probably with reason, that it tended to make me too vain." It was a bad scene—especially because he was required to work at the print shop until the age of twenty-one—but Benjamin was still able to slip away. When James Franklin was arrested once again for mocking religion, the General Court barred him from publishing the *New England Courant*. To keep the paper running while he was in jail, James nullified his brother's apprenticeship, and the *Courant*'s masthead now read, "Printed and sold by Benjamin Franklin." James forced Benjamin to sign a new apprentice agreement, but Benjamin bolted anyway, knowing that this secret contract couldn't be enforced.[36]

Soon after starting a print shop in Philadelphia, Benjamin Franklin made plans to launch his own paper—the third such operation in a town that could barely support two. He foolishly discussed those plans with the apprentice to a rival printer, Samuel Keimer, who beat Benjamin to market by throwing together a slapdash paper titled *The Universal Instructor in All Arts and Sciences, and Pennsylvania Gazette*.

The publisher sheepishly admitted that the first issue had little content, so he compensated by pirating material from *Chambers's Cyclopaedia of English Literature*. With no money, Franklin turned to another resource to crush his competitor: wit. He penned pseudonymous pieces in a competing paper that seized on the fact that Keimer reprinted an innocuous *Cyclopaedia* entry on "abortion." Writing as Martha Careful and Celia Shortface, he wrote faux-indignant attacks on his rival's questionable morality and, in the process, manufactured America's first abortion debate. An irritated Keimer branded him a "Free-Thinker of the Peripatetic Sect" who was "Not one but every Ape's epitome." His humorless inability to ignore Franklin's barbs, combined with financial incompetence, led to the paper's demise. Its circulation dropped below one hundred, and Keimer ended up in debtor prison. Franklin snatched up the paper at a bargain and shortened its unwieldy name to the *Pennsylvania Gazette*. He could now print all the fabricated items he desired.[37]

This freedom allowed Franklin to experiment by adopting multiple personas that could argue every side of an issue. In his autobiography, the character "Benjamin Franklin" moves through a series of morphing identities that emphasize themes of personal reinvention and image management. "In order to secure my Credit and Character as a Tradesman," he wrote, "I took care not only to be in *Reality* Industrious and frugal, but to avoid all *Appearances* of the Contrary." Franklin famously advertised himself by pushing a barrow of paper and printing supplies through the streets of Philadelphia at the crack of dawn. He may actually have been working, but it was his *performance* of doing so that was most important. Early modern political thought often connected liberty with the accumulation of wealth, and Franklin's street-theater act dramatized how social mobility could be achieved in America. In the early eighteenth century, printers such as Franklin were liminal figures. Their feet were planted in a wide range of social networks but had no solid standing in society. "Printers were, without a doubt, artisans, but they could create special links to patronage networks," writes Franklin scholar David Waldstreicher, "and they played increasingly creative roles in religious and political battles."[38]

This creativity shines through in satires such as "Witch Trial at Mount Holly," which was couched as a scientific study. "*Burlington, Oct.*

12. Saturday last at *Mount-Holly*, about 8 miles from this place, near 300 people were gathered together to see an experiment or two tried on some persons accused of witchcraft," the *Pennsylvania Gazette* reported. "It seems the accused had been charged with making their neighbors' sheep dance in an uncommon manner, and with causing hogs to speak, and sing psalms." The defendants were weighed on scales opposite a Bible, with the assumption that the wizards and witches would be lighter. "But to the great Surprize of the Spectators, Flesh and Bones came down plump, and outweighed the great good Book by abundance." In another attempt to sort the good from the bad, the accusers and defendants were bound and dunked. Evildoers would float, they believed, while the innocents would sink; however, "every one of them swam very light upon the Water." One distraught accuser protested that she must have been bewitched, but the crowd concluded that it was the women's undergarments that made them buoyant. This set up the final punch line: "it is said they are to be tried again the next warm weather, naked."[39]

POLLY BAKER GOES VIRAL

One of Benjamin Franklin's greatest (literary) inventions was Polly Baker, who reportedly stood trial in New England for having five illegitimate children. "May it please the honorable bench to indulge me in a few words: I am a poor unhappy woman, who have no money to fee lawyers to plead for me," Polly told the court. "I think this law, by which I am punished, is both unreasonable in itself and particularly severe with regard to me." She then appealed to reason, compassion, and puns: "I cannot conceive (may it please your honors) what the nature of my offence is." Polly maintained that she had been no burden to her community, though she wryly added that she could have supported her children better if not for the heavy court-ordered fines that burdened her. The unwed mother then addressed the elephant in the room. Why did she have to endure public disgrace when the law didn't punish the men who got her pregnant? Rather than receiving a whipping, Polly insisted she ought to "have a statue erected in my memory."[40]

The Polly Baker speech went viral, eighteenth-century style. It was first published in the April 15, 1747 issue of the *General Advertiser*, a leading London daily newspaper. Within the week, other London dailies and weeklies reprinted it, and word soon migrated throughout the British Empire. Polly resonated with readers because her plight tapped into dominant trends in English culture and literature. A prank is like a virus that needs a host body to flourish, and Franklin's story fed on contemporary anxieties about tarnished womanhood. During this period, Samuel Richardson was in the process of drafting *Clarissa*, the follow-up to his novel *Pamela* (both of which were about women forced to defend themselves against amoral "rakes"). Henry Fielding was also in the midst of writing *Tom Jones*, and Daniel Defoe already had two hit books—*Moll Flanders* and *Roxana*—that spoke to these issues. In this context, Ms. Baker felt more real than real. The story got an extra boost from *Gentleman's Magazine*, a prestigious British publication that Samuel Johnson described as "one of the most successful and lucrative pamphlets which literary history has upon record." (It is quite possible that Johnson, who was employed by the magazine at the time, had a hand in printing Polly's speech.)[41]

Gentleman's Magazine publisher Edward Cave was known for his dreadful manners, two or three chins, an epic case of gout, and a close friendship with Benjamin Franklin. His magazine added an important wrinkle to the saga when it published a letter signed by William Smith, who claimed he met the "comely" sixty-year-old Polly Baker. This may be a clue that Franklin authored it, as he had a thing for older women. (He once penned an inappropriate list of reasons why "in all your Amours you should *prefer old Women to young ones*." Some excerpts: "3. Because there is no hazard of Children, which irregularly produced may be attended with much Inconvenience. . . . 6. Because the Sin is less. The debauching a Virgin may be her Ruin, and make her for Life unhappy. . . . 8th and Lastly. They are *so grateful!*") Mr. Smith claimed that Polly married Paul Dudley, a seventy-two-year-old judge whose stepfather and grandfather had been Massachusetts governors. Because Judge Dudley "struck with Awe the most daring Offenders," it was highly unlikely that he would run off and marry a serial bastard-baby maker. Revenge was the writer's most obvious motive. Back when Benjamin apprenticed at James's *New England Courant*, the paper regularly attacked Dudley—who was a member of the Puritan governing body that made life very difficult for the Franklin brothers.[42]

Ms. Baker's cause was taken up by several prominent figures, including an eccentric English deist named Peter Annet. In 1749, Annet published the speech in a book titled *Social Bliss Considered*. Although he was careful to state that it was *"said to be delivered by her"*—not *actually* delivered—Annet defensively wrote, "This story is attested for truth, but whether true or no, the reasons that follow are true." His twenty-five footnotes (oddly organized from A to Y) are the most significant elements of the deist's reprint. They allowed him to support Polly's assertions, interject comments, and transform her plea for understanding into a sidewalk-blistering diatribe against organized religion. Missing the humor in Polly's declaration that a statue should be built in her honor, Annet reverently wrote in footnote Y, "This speech is beyond all statues that can be erected to eternize her memory, which demonstrate her to have been a woman of excellent sense, virtue and honour." It was effective propaganda for the deist cause, but it also landed Annet in hot water. He was tried for attempting "to infuse and propagate irreligious and diabolical opinions in the minds of his majesty's subjects."[43]

Within a few years, Polly Baker morphed from a satire into a widely believed myth. In 1768, the Swedish periodical *Posten* soberly reported on Ms. Baker's trial, citing *London Magazine* as its source. The *Essex Gazette* (Salem, Massachusetts) printed the story in 1773, and that same year the *Virginia Gazette* (Williamsburg) also published the speech—coincidentally, or not, on April Fools' Day. But it was French historian Guillaume-Thomas Raynal Threadneedle who made Polly Baker a staple of that era's popular culture. Widely known as Abbé Raynal, he ran in fashionable intellectual circles and was described as being "intolerably loud, peremptory, and insolent." Raynal was a real know-it-all, but he could also be, as they say, without clue. His most significant work was *L'histoire philosophique et politique des établissements et du commerce des Européens dans les deux Indes*, which retold the Polly Baker story with brand-new details. In the concluding sentences, Polly no longer sarcastically suggested they build a statue of her. She now righteously declared, "I still ask for the punishment that awaits me rather than to hide the fruits of the fertility which heaven gave to man and woman as his first benediction."[44]

The ever-evolving Polly Baker story got a new lease on life after sections of Raynal's book were translated into English as *The History of North America*. "After some years during which [the public] grew tired of speaking about [Polly Baker]," one eighteenth-century commentator jibed, "along comes the Abbé Raynal, who recounts this tale in his book. Since then, it is firmly believed. Thirty years were sufficient to change fiction into history." At long last, Franklin had the chance to correct the record while living in Paris as the American minister to France. One day he struck up a conversation with Silas Deane of Connecticut about the mistakes contained in *The History of North America*, and at that exact moment Raynal walked into the room. "The Doctor and myself, Abbé, were just speaking of the errors of fact into which you have been led in your history," Deane said to him. "Oh no, Sir," Raynal replied, "that is impossible." Deane pointed out that Massachusetts never had a law on the books punishing women for having bastard children and insisted it was a hoax. "Be assured," the Abbé said, "you are mistaken, and that that is a true story." Forcing back laughter, Franklin finally spilled the beans. "Oh, very well, Doctor," Raynal conceded, "I had rather relate your stories than other men's truths."[45]

Throughout the nineteenth century, several other books represented Polly Baker as an actual historical figure. Franklin's story even made its way into a mid-twentieth-century sociology textbook that was widely taught in North America, furthering the cycle of misinformation. When people credulously embrace pranks, hoaxes, and cons, it is usually because they reinforce their own deep-seated worldviews. This was certainly true of the Polly Baker story. With its critique of eighteenth-century gender norms, a generous reader could interpret the tale as a protofeminist satire, but that would greatly exaggerate Benjamin Franklin's progressive record. He was full of contradictions that undermine any kind of rose-colored revisionism. Like his punch line for the Mount Holly witch trial—in which the women would be dunked naked when the weather warmed up, *har har*—much of Franklin's humor was of the good-ole-boy variety. His most pointed jokes, even those that made fun of himself, were usually made at the expense of women. Franklin could be liberal on some fronts and conservative on others, especially when it came to the question of slavery.[46]

The Wisdom of Enslaving Christians

Benjamin Franklin launched his most meaningful prank just a few weeks before he died. In a bold, irony-filled takedown of the proslavery position, he wrote a pseudonymous newspaper editorial arguing that Muslims should enslave Christians. It was smart and scathing, though it's important to remember that Franklin had a complicated relationship with the abolitionist movement. For starters, he was the author of the "three-fifths compromise" that made slaves only partly human in the eyes of the U.S. Constitution. Franklin owned slaves, used them in his print shop, and ran ads for human cargo in the *Pennsylvania Gazette* (print technologies facilitated slavery just as much as physical transportation did). Roughly one-quarter of the *Gazette*'s ample ad revenue relied on slave and indentured labor, which allowed Franklin to retire comfortably at the age of forty-two. On occasion, however, his paper and print shop did make room for antislavery dissenters. Most memorable was a rebellious Quaker merchant named Benjamin Lay, who embraced vegetarianism, occasionally lived in a cave, and refused to eat at the same table with slaveholders. He was the first abolitionist of the modern period, and he was quite a character.[47]

Over the course of the 1730s, Lay's tactics grew more confrontational. He once stood outside a Quaker meetinghouse shivering with one bare foot in the snow to shame parishioners about their underclothed slaves. He also detained a slaveholder's child, briefly, and then harangued the kid's parents about the aching sadness their own slave's family surely felt. Another colorful political prank took place in 1738 at an annual gathering of Quakers, where Lay loudly mocked his pacifist peers who looked the other way at human bondage. He insisted that they might as well put on armor and abandon their peaceful ways. Lay then ripped open his overcoat to reveal a military outfit and began wildly waving a sword while shouting, "Thus shall God shed the blood of those persons who enslave their fellow creatures." Lay punctuated his point by stabbing a hollowed-out Bible that contained a bladder filled with red pokeberry juice, which sprayed bystanders with fake blood. The two Benjamins were friends, though Franklin's only recorded reflections about Lay convey a pronounced sense of discomfort. After one visit,

Franklin wrote that the breath of this "Pythagorean-cynical-christian Philosopher" was "so acrid as to make his eyes tear and pain." It was a good metaphor for Franklin's relationship with the abolitionist movement: comfortable at a distance but nauseous up close.[48]

Franklin's full conversion to the antislavery cause culminated in 1787 when he became president of the Pennsylvania Society for Promoting the Abolition of Slavery. Then, in 1790, he presented a petition in favor of abolishing slavery to the newly formed United States Congress. It was met with hostility, especially from Georgia congressman James Jackson—who insisted that the Bible sanctioned slavery. Seizing on Jackson's logic, Franklin pulled off the last, and best, prank of his life. Writing under the name Historicus, he published a letter filled with faux citations and an elaborate backstory that ridiculed slave-owning Christians. In it, he quoted a speech supposedly given by a Muslim leader a century before. "Reading last night in your excellent paper the speech of Mr. Jackson in Congress, against meddling with the affair of slavery," he wrote, "it put me in mind of a similar one made about one hundred years since, by Sidi Mehemet Ibrahim, a member of the Divan of Algiers." This was followed by a translation of "the African's" speech, which read, in part, "If we cease our cruises against the Christians, how shall we be furnished with the commodities their countries produce, and which are so necessary for us? If we forbear to make slaves of their people, who, in this hot climate, are to cultivate our lands?"[49]

"Who are to perform the common labors of our city," Ibrahim added, "and in our families? Must we not then be our own slaves? And is there not more compassion and more favor due to us Mussulmen, than to these Christian dogs?" He piled on supporting arguments, including the fact that the labor pool enjoyed by Muslims would be annihilated if slavery ended. Property values would drop, as would tax revenues. And what on earth would be done with all those slaves if they were released from bondage? You can't trust those shifty Christians to stay out of trouble! Franklin/Historicus further needled the antiabolitionists by claiming that slavery uplifted Jesus-loving infidels: "they have an opportunity of making themselves acquainted with the true doctrine, and thereby saving their immortal souls." There was the added benefit that Muslim slave masters treated their slaves with more humanity than "free" laborers in Christian nations. Lastly, by remaining in bondage, the Christian slaves wouldn't be able to slit the throats of other warlike Christians—just as European savages had done for centuries. Franklin signed off in his usual deadpan style, "I am, Sir, your constant Reader and humble Servant, Historicus."[50]

*   *   *

Benjamin Franklin's final prank was successful because it skillfully used irony, satire, and media in an attempt to mold public opinion. He often borrowed from Jonathan Swift, whose Bickerstaff prank provided the template for Franklin's attack on the astrologer Titan Leeds. However, it was Swift's *A Modest Proposal* that remains that era's most important and instructive work. In Phillip Lopate's 1979 essay "Chekhov for Children," the writer recounts how he assigned the baby-munching manifesto to a class of eleven- and twelve-year-olds. The exercise was designed to help them understand the nature of irony, a concept not easily grasped by preadolescents. "I read from Swift's *A Modest Proposal*, got from the kids a list of things they hated, then asked them to select one and write an essay praising it." Lopate added, "I was attempting to teach them to lie and tell the truth at the same time." Pranksters often use falsehoods to reveal deeper truths—though this can backfire when a ruse takes on a life of its own and spirals out of control. That is but one of the many downsides of using this tricky tactic. Swift was well aware of satire's limitations, and he resigned himself to knowing that his *Proposal* would do little to eradicate hunger in Ireland. Biting satire sometimes does hold the potential to move people to action, but in the grand scheme of things, that rarely occurs. Speaking to this shortcoming, British comedian Peter Cook once sardonically praised the "great tradition of those satirical clubs of the 1930s that had done so much to prevent the rise of Adolf Hitler."[51]

2

Con Artists
and Consumer Culture

Near the end of Edgar Allan Poe's life, he published a lighthearted essay titled "Diddling Considered as One of the Exact Sciences." The word *diddling* referred to an elegant ruse that delighted audiences (though today, in some juvenile circles, it has taken on a more sordid subtext). The term was popularized by *Raising the Wind*, a popular 1803 play that featured a good-natured fellow named Jeremy Diddler. "Perhaps the first diddler was Adam," Poe wrote, though he was quick to add, "The moderns, however, have brought it to a perfection never dreamed of by our thick-headed progenitors." This assessment stemmed from the fact that swindles—artful and otherwise—were a pronounced feature of nineteenth-century life. Confidence men haunted city streets, fraudulent Spiritualist mediums made séance tables levitate, and newspaper hoaxes sat side by side with factual news stories. Herman Melville commented on this cultural condition in his 1857 novel *The Confidence-Man: His Masquerade*, as did his contemporaries. P. T. Barnum's fictionalized memoir, *Adventures of an Adventurer*, was laced with jokes, social commentary, and outrageous lies spun by a thinly veiled character named Barnaby Diddleum. "Now and then some one would cry out 'humbug' and 'charlatan,'" Barnum recalled later in his career, "but so much the better for me. It helped to advertise me, and I was willing to bear the reputation."[1]

With the public getting used to merchants making exaggerated claims, humbugs served as amusing warnings about the market economy's shadowy underbelly. Barnum blurred the lines between two of Manhattan's most prominent industries—larceny and entertainment—by mixing lawless confidence games with inventive advertising schemes. Presenting his exhibitions more as riddles than facts, Barnum reminded customers that deception was now an everyday fact of life. He didn't view himself as a confidence man, and the showman insisted that spectators left his exhibits with "a full equivalent for their money." Successful humbugs lured folks in with weird, wacky, and tacky displays, and audiences made repeat visits to figure out how they had been fooled. Humbugs and confidence games remind us that "if there is a false belief among us, we need to become conscious of how belief is created," Lewis Hyde writes in *Trickster Makes This World*. Even though conniving con artists and thought-provoking pranksters are driven by different impulses, their audiences can learn similar lessons from their deceptions. Swindlers sometimes do succeed in defrauding their victims, but (much like a prankster) at least they send people back into the world a little wiser.[2]

A Wooden Robot Crosses the Atlantic

Edgar Allan Poe had a lifelong obsession with deception. The writer often expressed, as one biographer put it, a "childish and almost unbalanced delight in a hoax of any kind." In addition to pulling pranks and hoaxes, he enjoyed exposing them. One of Poe's most famous targets was the Turk, a human-sized wooden figure that wore flowing pants and a turban—and also played chess. The automaton's name and clothing were inspired by a 1760s fad that had the Viennese indulging in all things Turkish. Its long and winding path across Europe and America began in 1769, when Hungarian engineer Baron Wolfgang von Kempelen debuted his creation at a command performance for Maria Theresa, the empress of Austria-Hungary. To prove no one was inside, at the beginning of each showing the operator opened several compartments to reveal the machine's inner workings. After it was wound up like a clock, the Turk bested most challengers. Word spread throughout Europe, and one excited witness buzzed, "It seems impossible to obtain a more perfect knowledge of mechanics than this gentleman has done."[3]

All this attention embarrassed Kempelen, so he started telling people the Turk was broken to avoid showing it off. By the time Maria Theresa died in 1780, it was largely forgotten. But then Kempelen was ordered by her successor to rebuild the Turk in time for a visit from Grand Duke Paul of Russia. He was far more interested in refining an invention that could manually synthesize the human voice—his "Speaking Machine"—but he had to comply with his patron's wishes. (Kempelen was eventually recognized as the founder of a discipline known as experimental phonetics.) During an extended European tour, in the spring of 1783, the Turk was presented to the French royal family in Versailles. While in France, it also crossed paths with Benjamin Franklin, a chess fanatic who sometimes played up to five hours a day. He reportedly lost, though no account of this incident was left by Franklin (who was known to be a sore loser). Years later, Napoleon Bonaparte challenged the Turk to a game. When he made a false move, the machine replaced the chess piece and motioned for him to play again. "Napoleon was delighted," the *Illustrated London News* reported. The general "once more played incorrectly, upon which the Automaton raised his arm, and, sweeping the pieces from the board, declined to continue the game."[4]

When Kempelen died in 1804, his son sold the disassembled automaton to Johann Nepomuk Maelzel—a Bavarian engineer whose real talent was showmanship. In his care, the Turk enjoyed a thrilling third act. It drew enormous crowds across Europe and provoked heated debates over the possibility of machine intelligence. Maelzel had expensive tastes, and his debts blossomed into lawsuits from angry creditors; so he fled Europe in 1826. After landing in New York City, he befriended newspaper editors and launched a publicity campaign that took the town by storm. The man and machine toured America for the better part a decade by tapping into a prominent form of nineteenth-century entertainment: the traveling road show. This touring circuit connected most eastern cities and reached as far into the frontier as was possible. It featured an eclectic talent pool, with respected lecturers such as Washington Irving and Benjamin Rush relying on the same networks used by itinerant showmen, fire-eaters, bearded ladies, puppeteers, and medicine men.[5]

In 1835, the Turk went on a minitour of the South. It ventured down to Charleston, South Carolina and back up to Richmond, Virginia, where Edgar Allan Poe worked as an editor for the *Southern Literary Messenger*. "Perhaps no exhibition of the kind has ever elicited so general attention as the chess-player of Maelzel," he breathlessly wrote. Poe's essay about the Turk was structured much like his own detective stories, in which mysteries were solved through logical deduction. After weighing the possibilities, he finally concluded, "the operations of the automaton are regulated by mind, and by nothing else." It was the only reasonable answer, given that calculating machines of the time couldn't possibly handle the number of moves the game of chess offered. Poe hypothesized that when the showman rolled the machine onto the stage, there was already a person inside. His exposé was a roaring success, and it gave the struggling author a much-needed ego boost. The *Charleston Courier* called it "highly ingenious," and Philadelphia's *United States Gazette* reported that it was "the most successful attempt we have seen to explain the *modus operandi* of that wonderful production."[6]

Despite conjecture that the Turk contained a dwarf, a child, or an amputee, its final owner revealed that a full-grown adult could fit inside. When the audience was shown its insides, the hidden chess player rearranged the machine's compartments to avoid detection. Cushions muffled his movements, and loud clocklike gears were used to mask other incriminating sounds. Like many of Benjamin Franklin's hijinks, Kempelen's invention blurred the lines between conning, hoaxing, and pranking. Some people viewed the automaton as an elaborate confidence game—because it was designed to trick audiences into coughing up admission fees—but it wasn't a malicious con. Likewise, the Turk fits the profile of a hoax because it was clearly designed to fool the public and attract attention. The machine's more enlightening qualities also aligned it with the pranking tradition. For example, cracking its code required Poe to use the same analytical methods he employed to solve puzzles and develop his detective-story plots. These critical-thinking skills would come in handy for denizens of the nineteenth century, who faced trickery around every shady corner.[7]

THE CULTURE OF THE HUMBUG

P. T. Barnum was named after his maternal grandfather, Phineas Taylor, an irreverent spirit who sported wild hair and permanently arched eyebrows. "My grandfather," he recalled, "would go farther, wait longer, work harder, and contrive deeper, to carry out a practical joke, than for anything else under heaven." In fact, heaven held little appeal for the man, a dissenter who had an irreverent attitude toward organized religion (when it came to Christianity, Universalism was about all he could stomach). Phineas often told a story about a ferry ride he took from Norwalk, Connecticut to New York City. He convinced all the male passengers, including a clergyman, to let him give them a shave—but only one half of their faces at a time. While in the middle of grooming, Phineas tried to sharpen his razor on the ship's stoop, and that's when the monkey business began. With the reverend standing first in line, the assembled men looked on in horror as he fumbled the blade. "Good heavens!" the mischief maker exclaimed, "The razor has fallen overboard!" Phineas doubled over with laughter as the half-bearded holy man disembarked into the city with his face covered by a handkerchief.[8]

Of all the pranks Phineas pulled, Ivy Island left the deepest impression on Barnum. For much of Barnum's boyhood, Phineas boasted that he had bequeathed his grandson the most valuable property in all of Connecticut. Barnum's parents and neighbors played along as well. "These constant allusions, for several years, to 'Ivy Island' excited at once my pride and my curiosity and stimulated me to implore my father's permission to visit my property." He got his wish during a long walk with his dad—a very long walk that saw the landscape grow progressively swampy. Barnum waded in waist-deep water for fifteen minutes while being attacked by bees, and once he arrived at his property, the truth flashed on him. "I had been the laughing-stock of the family and neighborhood for years," he recalled, "and while I stood deploring my sudden downfall, a huge black snake (one of my tenants) approached me with upraised head. I gave one shriek and rushed for the bridge." Upon returning home, Phineas loudly congratulated the red-faced boy as if he really did own the state's most expensive property. The prank served as a memorable lesson not to get fooled again, because next time the perpetrator would surely be more malevolent.[9]

Barnum grew up to be a struggling grocery-store owner, treading water in an unstable economy while looking for the next get-rich scheme. Early in 1835, he discovered a supposed 161-year-old slave woman named Joice Heth. The entrepreneur took a ten-day option on this "property," putting up $500 of his own money and securing the rest from financiers. When looking for a venue for Heth's New York City debut, Barnum was turned down by a respectable open-air saloon named Niblo's Garden. He was finally allowed to set up shop in a large apartment next door, where Barnum faced a formidable competitor from across the way: the Turk. It was on display in Niblo's main hall, but the robot turned out to be no match for the audience-drawing powers of George Washington's supposed nursemaid. A year earlier, the budding showman crossed paths with the Turk's handler, Johann Maelzel, who offered advice that clearly left an impression. "I see that you understand the value of the press, and that is the great thing," he said. "Nothing helps the showman like the types and the ink." Throughout Barnum's career, he cultivated close relationships with newspaper editors and publishers. "I am indebted to the press of the United States for almost every dollar which I possess," he wrote.[10]

Before Joice Heth's unveiling, Barnum invited the editors of the city's major papers for a private viewing; it also didn't hurt that he lavished them with paid advertisements. Between puffs on a pipe (she claimed to have been smoking for 120 years), Heth amused crowds with stories about the birth of "dear little George." She soon replaced the Turk as Niblo's primary attraction. "This old creature is said to be 161 years of age," the *New York Courier and Enquirer* reported, "and we see no reason to doubt it." The *New York Sun* added, "The arrival, at Niblo's Garden, of this renowned relic of the olden times has created quite a sensation among the lovers of the curious and the marvelous." There were surely doubters in New York City, but most accounts indicate Heth was widely believed to be quite old. Although some Americans did live into their nineties, the average lifespan was much lower—which made her age pretty preposterous. But as I have previously noted, hoaxes tell us much about the societies that embrace them. In this case, racism accounts for people's credulity, because most whites thought blacks had a fundamentally sturdier biological constitution (a notion that justified slavery).[11]

Heth's audiences eventually fell off, so Barnum and his fast-talking associate Levi Lyman began planting rumors in newspapers. One letter to the editor signed by "A Visitor" stated that that Heth was a robotic machine whose voice was supplied by a ventriloquist. Taking the bait, another newspaper published a scoop that Heth "is not a human being. What purports to be a remarkably old woman is simply a curiously constructed automaton, made up of whalebone, india-rubber, and numberless springs ingeniously put together." Audiences came rushing back to make up their own minds. "On one occasion," Barnum recalled, "an ex-member of Congress, his wife, two children, and his aged mother, attended the exhibition." With Lyman by his side, Barnum watched as the mother closely scrutinized "Aunt Joice."[12]

"There it is alive after all! . . ."

"Why do you think it is alive?" asked Lyman, quietly.

"Because its pulse beats as regularly as mine does," responded the old lady.

"Oh, that is the most simple portion of the machinery," said Lyman. "We make that operate on the principle of a pendulum to a clock."

"Is it possible?" said the old lady, who was now evidently satisfied that Joice was an automaton. Then turning to her son, she said: "George, this thing is not alive at all. It is all a machine."

"Why mother," said the son with evident embarrassment, "what are you talking about?"

A half-suppressed giggle ran through the room and the gentleman and his family soon withdrew.[13]

Cultural historian James W. Cook notes that all of Barnum's tricks are on display in this anecdote: "the deadpan denials from Lyman, which invited as much doubt as they dispelled; the suggestion that the deliberate act of promotional fraud was nothing more than good, clean Yankee fun; and the artful repositioning of the Boston audience from the role of observers to observed, looking and laughing here not only at Heth but at each other." Despite the clever gamesmanship, it's hard to view this as anything more than mean-spirited exploitation. It was a typical antebellum display, one that offered a racial caricature for the amusement of white northern urbanites. When Heth finally did die, Barnum staged an autopsy at the New York City Saloon for fifteen hundred paying customers. The examination, conducted by respected surgeon David L. Rogers, concluded she couldn't have been older than eighty. Barnum and Lyman whispered conflicting stories to the press suggesting all sorts of scenarios, setting off another storm of conjecture, claims, and counterclaims that raked in even more cash for Barnum. Sadly, after enduring a lifetime of slavery and showbiz scheming, Joice Heth became the butt of a practical joke that lasted years after her death. As one commentator wrote, "the funniest part came when the old wench died."[14]

BARNUM'S AMERICAN MUSEUM AND OTHER CURIOSITIES

P. T. Barnum realized that owning his own space could generate more revenue, so in 1842 he set his sights on a building near the Bowery. Competing with a wealthier group of investors, the showman resorted to his old tricks. Neglecting to mention that Ivy Island was a worthless swamp, he put his property up as collateral and spread rumors that caused the rival financiers' stock to decline. Soon after, Barnum's American Museum was open for business. It wouldn't be recognized as a "museum" today, but back then this term referred to establishments that mixed a wild variety of exhibitions. "Bowery museums were the true underworld of entertainment," Luc Sante writes, "and their compass could include anything too shoddy, too risqué, too vile, too sad, too marginal, too disgusting, too pointless to be displayed elsewhere." Bunnell's Museum on the Bowery, for instance, featured a tattooed man, his "double-brained" child, and several striking wax figures. Most memorable was Dante's Inferno, where despised public figures such as Boss Tweed writhed in flaming torment. Barnum's spectacle was the most garish of all. It exploded with banners, flags, color wheels, and the least modest touch of all: giant illuminated letters spelling out his name. "Powerful Drummond lights were placed at the top of the Museum, which, in the darkest night," Barnum boasted, "would enable one to read a newspaper in the street." It was a precursor to the Day-Glo consumption zone that is today's Times Square.[15]

In Barnum's commercial universe, the commodity and advertisement were inseparable—and the product was often Barnum himself.

He was that era's most well-known celebrity, and the showman practically invented the modern notion of fame. Barnum employed an army of salesmen to hawk his autobiography, and he regularly added and subtracted chapters to create demand for new editions. It reportedly became the second biggest-selling book in nineteenth-century America (after the Bible). Barnum's marketing campaigns also included attention-grabbing stunts such as "Free Music for the Million." Playing on people's desire for a free lunch, he lured New Yorkers to these outdoor concerts, but there was a prankish twist. "I took pains to select and maintain the poorest band I could find," Barnum said, "one whose discordant notes would drive the crowd into the Museum, out of earshot of my outside orchestra." Referring to his free music scheme, Barnum claimed that his humbugs offered moral instruction and sharpened people's critical faculties. "When people expect to get 'something for nothing' they are sure to be cheated, and generally deserve to be," he wrote. "Some of my out-door patrons were sorely disappointed; but when they came inside and paid to be amused and instructed, I took care to see that they not only received the full worth of their money, but were more than satisfied."[16]

With the ghastly Joice Heth exhibition now defunct, Barnum needed more curiosities. He searched the world for "educated dogs, industrious fleas, automatons, jugglers, ventriloquists, living statuary," and the like. The showman's next sensation was the Feejee Mermaid. This masterful taxidermy mash-up was little more than a monkey's head attached to the body of a large fish; Barnum described it as "an ugly, dried-up, black-looking, and diminutive specimen, about three feet long." He purchased it from Boston Museum proprietor Moses Kimball in 1842, but its roots date back at least to 1817. While in Calcutta, a ship's captain came across "a preserved specimen of a veritable mermaid, obtained, as he was assured, from Japanese sailors." He used $6,000 from the ship's funds to buy the furry, finned creature and then moved to London, where it initially packed in hundreds at a Piccadilly coffeehouse. The July 1822 issue of *Gentleman's Magazine* gave a detailed description of the fish-monkey-mermaid, which read, in part, "The head is turned back and the countenance has an expression of terror, which gives it the appearance of a caricature of the human face." The box office receipts didn't fully cover the borrowed money, so the sailor-entrepreneur went back to sea to repay his employer. He died penniless and left his only possession to an uninterested son, who promptly sold it to Kimball.[17]

Fearing ridicule, Kimball had second thoughts about displaying the Feejee Mermaid in his Boston Museum, so he invited Barnum to purchase it. He brought along a naturalist who, upon closer inspection, told the showman that he had absolutely no idea how the creature was made. "Why do you suppose it was manufactured?" Barnum asked. "Because I don't believe in mermaids," the scientist shot back. Knowing the public would be just as skeptical, Barnum fabricated a letter from Dr. Griffin—an "eminent Professor of Natural History" who was played by his sidekick, Levi Lyman. Barnum described his business associate as "a shrewd, sociable, and somewhat indolent Yankee" who "was admirably calculated to fill the position" for which Barnum engaged him. The dynamic duo quietly conspired to have reports on regional news from around the country sent to several New York newspapers, via postmarked letters. Barnum and Lyman made sure to include mentions of "Dr. Griffin, agent of the Lyceum of Natural History in London, recently from Pernambuco, who had in his possession a most remarkable curiosity." With this setup, the "doctor" showed off the specimen and entertained reporters at a fancy New York hotel in advance of the opening. "While Lyman was preparing public opinion on mermaids at the Pacific Hotel," Barnum recalled, "I was industriously at work (though of course privately) in getting up wood-cuts and transparencies, as well as a pamphlet, proving the authenticity of mermaids."[18]

FEEJEE MERMAID!
positively asserted by its owner to have been taken alive [in] the Feejee Islands, and implicitly believed by many scientific persons, while it is pronounced by other scientific persons to be an *artificial* production, and its natural existence claimed to be an utter impossibility. The manager can only say that it [h]as such *appearance of reality* as any fish lying [in] the stalls of our fish markets—but [who] is to decide when *doctors* disagree.... If it is artificial the senses [of] sight and touch are useless for *art* has rendered them totally ineffectual—if it is natural then all concur in declaring it

the greatest Curiosity in the World.[19]

In classic Barnum form, the advertisement cultivated uncertainty. The mermaid's authenticity is "implicitly believed by many scientific persons," on the one hand, but other experts dismissed it as a fabrication. He hired a rival promoter to denounce it as a hoax, which stirred up even more interest. Barnum's exhibits helped create a new kind of audience—one connected from great distances through print media and, later, the telegraph. While thousands saw the mermaid in person, many more read about it in the penny presses and talked about it among themselves. Rather than dismissing Barnum's customers as passive dupes, it makes more sense to ask *why* they enjoyed being tricked. "In other words," historian Neil Harris writes, "why the apparent naïveté about deception, and why the pleasure in experiencing deception after knowledge of it had been gained?" The reasons were both technological and social. Barnum's deceptions helped the public come to terms with a changing world where media and commercial exchange dominated daily life. Early capitalism produced many luxuries, but unpredictable fluctuations in the labor market shredded the social fabric. Many homesteaders arrived out West only to discover they had been swindled, and back East, confidence men regularly cheated big-city suckers. The economy itself felt like a gigantic con. Throughout the nineteenth century, practical jokes thrived because they helped tame this hostile environment by turning it into an entertaining game. The humbug was as enjoyable as sin, but without the messy consequences.[20]

Con Men and the Culture Industry

In 1849, a well-dressed gentleman named William Thompson pioneered a new type of criminal mischief. When striking up conversations with strangers on the streets of New York City, he asked if they would leave their watch with him until the following day. As the *New York Herald* reported that summer, "the stranger, at this novel request, supposing him to be some old acquaintance . . . allows him to take the watch, thus placing 'confidence' in the honesty of the stranger." Thompson then walked off, laughing, goods in hand. The press coined "confidence man" to describe Thompson, though news stories from this period indicate there were other grifters of this sort making the rounds. The term had a quick uptake, and it soon was used more generally to describe swindles in the world of commerce. A week after Thompson's arrest, the *Herald* characterized the stock market as "The Confidence Man on a Large Scale." Con artists operated openly on New York City streets between 1835 and the Civil War—when politicians, city officials, and police officers largely turned a blind eye to their scams. Card sharks, thimble-riggers, and other shadowy figures worked with stylish steerers, shills, and supernumeraries who redirected gullible marks to skinning houses. The respectable appearance projected by these "men of considerable address" made it easy to dupe strangers.[21]

During the first half of that century, in the midst of the transportation and industrial revolutions, people moved to cities in staggering numbers. Trustworthiness in agrarian villages was primarily cultivated through intimate interactions. For these new urban dwellers, a lack of communal ties made life tricky to navigate, so people looked to surface appearances to judge a stranger's character. An image-conscious middle class was taking shape in the United States, where one's social status was marked by the conspicuous consumption of clothing and other material goods. Cultural historian Karen Halttunen notes that close attention was paid to the smallest details of daily life, down to the proper positioning of hands on the lap. If aspiring social climbers didn't know how to fit in, they could consult dozens of advice manuals that often addressed the specter of the confidence man. The middle class was especially anxious about the proliferation of con games, which bankrupted many a family—as did gambling and irresponsible speculation. One such manual maintained that these behaviors undermined the "principle of *mutual confidence*" that was necessary to do business.[22]

The confidence man represented a worst-case scenario for many Americans. As shape-shifting identities became the norm, middle-class families fretted that their sons would slide into a life of criminal behavior. They also worried that their own performances of etiquette amounted to little more than a socially acceptable con game. Twentieth-century sociologist Erving Goffman argued in his classic work *The Presentation of Self in Everyday Life* that mutual conning is the very basis of social life. It is a game of appearances, concealment, and an interplay of poses—what he refers to as "identity management." An early example of this can be found in the life of Benjamin Franklin, who popularized the notion of the "do-it-yourself Self." In a famous essay titled

"Self-Reliance," Ralph Waldo Emerson held up Franklin as a model of self-invention. "We live amid surfaces," he observed in another essay, "and the true art of life is to skate well on them." This was a central theme of Herman Melville's novel *The Confidence-Man: His Masquerade*, published on April 1, 1857. Its plot revolves around a shifty character who sneaks onto a Mississippi River steamboat on April Fools' Day and proceeds to mess with the minds of its passengers.[23]

Melville uses the river's fluidity as a metaphor for the con man's morphing identities, which include a Missouri bachelor, a collector of funds for an orphanage, a "Black Guinea," and so on. *The Confidence-Man* also contains several references to the sorts of questionable handbills, print signs, business cards, tracts, and circulars that littered consumer culture at the time. Aside from the occasional big cons pulled on the public, most nineteenth-century frauds took place on a smaller scale (such as falsely advertised goods). As the most notable member of a new generation of entrepreneurs, P. T. Barnum taught the emerging middle class how to navigate the tricky, sticky world of commerce. His amusements created public spaces that facilitated problem solving, implying that behind all that good-natured obfuscation, Enlightenment ideals of rational deliberation still flourished. It was a skill that helped his audiences navigate the fraud-filled world of antebellum America— where no merchandise, commercial exchange, or social encounter was exempt from suspicion. But at the same time that Barnum's humbugs warned of the con man's dangerous schemes, they also made the world a more untrustworthy place.[24]

Tricksters, Scamps, and Thieves

A wide range of shady characters saturated nineteenth-century regional folklore: the wily western backwoodsman, the slippery northern Yankee, and the trickster. The latter term was coined in an 1868 study of Native American tales, and by the end of that century it was widely used within anthropology, folklore scholarship, and popular culture. Trickster figures appear in most societies, from the simplest aboriginal tribes to the most complex. The confidence man, on the other hand, emerged from a very specific moment in American history and should not be conflated with tricksters. Lewis Hyde highlights another important distinction in his book *Trickster Makes This World*. Run-of-the-mill liars and thieves don't count as tricksters because they do very little to trouble the established order. As cultural historian Lori Landay writes, tricksters "use impersonation, disguise, theft, and deceit to expose hypocrisy and inequality, to subvert existing social systems, and to widen their sphere of power." Tricksters tell lies, break rules, party hard, and rip the social fabric—only to nonchalantly stitch it back together in a new pattern. Their very practical, productive jokes yank the chair out from under society and remake it in the process.[25]

Trickster tales such as that of the Signifying Monkey are deeply rooted in African American culture. In this classic story, the Monkey manipulates the Lion into fighting the Elephant, who supposedly insulted the Lion's closest relatives (including his "mama" and even his "grandmamma, too!"). When the dethroned King of the Jungle limps back, bruised and battered, the Monkey laughs so hard he falls out of a tree and into his nemesis's hands. He convinces the Lion to start over and make it a fair fight, but once free, he jumps to safety and continues with his monkey business. The African American game of the dozens, or signifyin'—in which a physically weak opponent can beat a powerful one with clever wordplay—is rooted in this tale. The Signifying Monkey, Br'er Rabbit, and other such stories appealed to slaves because they implicitly addressed the brutal conditions black people experienced in America. "We had to lie to live," said Robert Falls, who endured plantation life in Tennessee. "They fed the animals better. . . . We would steal anything we could lay our hands on, when we was hungry." Trickster tales offered enslaved people subtle survival tactics that were passed on through storytelling, such as keeping their masters blind to their ingenuity by acting dumb or playing possum. This enabled slaves to take what they needed for survival, including stealing away to freedom.[26]

Henry "Box" Brown was a real-life trickster who staged a dramatic escape from a Richmond, Virginia plantation in 1849. The ex-slave wrote in his memoir, "The idea suddenly flashed across my mind of shutting myself *up in a box*, and getting myself conveyed as dry goods to a free state." With the help of abolitionist allies, Brown mailed himself in a small, three-by-two-by-two-foot box to Philadelphia, Pennsylvania. Calling it his "resurrection from the grave of slavery," he emerged seventy hours later as a free man. Soon after, Brown entered show business.

His elaborate multimedia stage show, *Mirror of Slavery*, was one half entertainment, one half abolitionist propaganda. The show debuted at Boston's Washingtonian Hall in April 1850, and it became an immediate hit due in part to Brown's use of moving panoramas and his "considerable theatrical flair." Racist images, imperialist narratives, and Manifest Destiny tropes were common in mid-nineteenth-century stage shows, but Brown flipped the ideological script by subverting these conventions. He presented blacks as active agents of their own fates, all while telling a gripping story about escape and survival that captured the public's imagination.[27]

The narrative of resurrection was a prominent aspect of Brown's performance, for he knew it would resonate within a religiously attuned society. The *Mirror of Slavery* stage show culminated in a reenactment of his journey, with him emerging from a tiny box singing a hymn. By disappearing and then reemerging, Brown dramatized Frederick Douglass's oft-quoted line, "You have seen how a man was made a slave, now you shall see how a slave was made a man." Brown also put his own unique spin on what became a staple of stage magic: substituting one thing for another. He anticipated the way cabinets, trunks, and other props would be used by Victorian magicians such as Harry Houdini (who performed a similar "escape act"). Brown later reinvented himself as a full-blown magic and mesmeric performer, pushing his shtick far beyond the limits of convention. After relocating to Great Britain, this worldly dandy could be seen marching "through the streets in front of a brass band, clad in a highly-colored and fantastic garb." Brown's eccentricities estranged him from the abolitionist movement, which valued polished orators trained in the rhetorical tradition. "Brown's brash and spectacular public acts," literary scholar Daphne Brooks writes, "may have indeed proved too excessive, too performative, too 'glam' to register as legible acts of social and political resistance to slavery."[28]

Frederick Douglass was another living, breathing trickster who blurred boundaries. The plantation system enforced certain rules to ensure its continued existence—including laws that forbade slaves from learning to read. A headstrong child, Douglass said that it was his master's "bitter opposition" that drove him to become literate. When Mrs. Auld began teaching the eight-year-old boy "the A. B. C.," her husband was furious. "A nigger should know nothing but to obey his master,"

Mr. Auld told her. "Learning would *spoil* the best nigger in the world. . . . He would at once become unmanageable, and of no value to his master." The slave master's words backfired. "From that moment," Douglass wrote, "I understood the pathway from slavery to freedom." Not only did he cross physical borders to gain independence, but his mixed racial background troubled the distinctions between white and black. On his road to literacy, Douglass initially acquired a "white" voice by absorbing knowledge from European classics by Plato, Milton, and Joseph Addison. Douglass recalled how he "entered upon this new life in the full gush of unsuspecting enthusiasm," though this optimism did not hold.[29]

Condescending white abolitionists reminded Douglass that the color line was still strong in America, even in the supposed utopia of the North. The angry white mob that broke his hands drove this lesson home, and as a result Douglass grew more self-consciously black. This transformation was reflected in the various editions of his autobiography. In the 1845 version, Douglass said he could barely remember his black mother, who, unlike his white father, was a stranger to him. By the final 1881 autobiography, the image of his mother was "ineffaceably stamped" on his memory, and he wrote, "Of my father I know nothing." Douglass's interracial heritage allowed him to deftly navigate between two societies. "Douglass dwelt on the boundaries of plantation culture," Lewis Hyde writes, "and in that setting he became a cunning go-between, a thief of reapportionment who quit the periphery and moved to the center." Yes, he made accommodations to some nasty American traditions, but he did so in a world he participated in remaking. "A truly domesticated Frederick Douglass would have remained a slave in Maryland," Hyde argues. "Truly domesticated, he would not have seen in his lifetime the abolition of slavery and the Constitution so regularly amended."[30]

Lions and Tigers and Merchandizing, Oh My!

The Great Oz was the fictional father of all humbugs. L. Frank Baum's iconic character functioned as a stand-in for P. T. Barnum, and his story dramatized this period's social upheavals. *The Wonderful Wizard of Oz*, published in 1900, begins with a bleak description of the west Kansas plains. "When Dorothy stood in the doorway and looked around, she could see nothing but the great gray prairie on every side," Baum wrote. "The sun baked the plowed land into a gray mass, with little cracks running through it. Even the grass was not green, for the sun had burned the tops of the long blades until they were the same gray color to be seen everywhere." The author wasn't so much writing about life in Kansas as he was describing the time he spent trying to eke out a living in South Dakota. Its treeless landscape was stricken by droughts, farm failures, and speculation-fueled real-estate crashes—not unlike Dorothy's native state. Homesteaders packed up, abandoned their property, and fled on wagons that read, "In God We Trusted / In Kansas We Busted."[31]

Baum eventually settled in Chicago, whose shop windows were a theater of marvels. "Through their plate glass, itself a product of technological revolution, Baum glimpsed a new kind of utopia," Zeese Papanikolas writes in *Trickster in the Land of Dreams*. Baum's trade magazine, *The Show Window*, introduced subscribers to a brave new world in which commerce was conjured through the magical art of merchandising. Baum filled it with eye-popping photos of the country's most marvelous department stores and other dazzling commercial zones. Baum's first novel, *The Wonderful Wizard of Oz*, was published the same year as his book on merchandising, *The Art of Decorating Dry Goods Windows and Interiors*. "You must arouse in your audience cupidity and a longing to possess the goods you sell," he instructed readers. Baum believed that the mise-en-scène of the "illusion window" could captivate the "passive throng" by using techniques borrowed from carnival sideshows, dime museums, and, of course, P. T. Barnum.[32]

The Wonderful Wizard of Oz was as much about Baum's adopted city as it was about Kansas and South Dakota. The spectacle of Chicago's 1893 Columbian Exposition surely was fresh in his mind when he dreamt up Oz's Emerald City. "White City"—which got its name from the glistening, classically inspired buildings erected for that year's World's Fair—was widely considered a wonder of modern industry. This consumerist spectacle had a dystopian dark side, one that Baum fictionalized in *The Wonderful Wizard of Oz*. Before Dorothy and her companions can enter Emerald City, they have to wear green sunglasses (a plot device that serves as the book's central metaphor). The Guardian of the Gates tells them, "If you did not wear spectacles the brightness and glory of the Emerald City would blind you." This is a lie, of course, much like how advertisements can shade the truth. The glasses imbue Kansas's sun-bleached landscape with alluring green qualities, though in reality it is little more than optical window dressing that disguises life's banal grayness.[33]

Baum likely borrowed the green-glasses trope from a story he wrote as a South Dakota newspaperman. His *Aberdeen Saturday Pioneer* reported on everything from financial and natural disasters to the women's rights movement and Spiritualism. (Frank and his wife, Maud Baum, both had an interest in the occult—which was enjoying a revival in Europe and America—and he sometimes upset the local church by challenging its teachings in print.) The *Saturday Pioneer* included a humorous weekly column, "Our Landlady," which Frank Baum pseud-onymously wrote under the name Mrs. Bilkins. One installment dis-cussed a fictitious innovation in animal husbandry: green goggles. This ocular confidence game allowed farmers to trick their animals into eating wood shavings that *looked* like grass, though with none of the nutrients. "I put the green goggles on my hosses an' feed 'em shav-ings an' they think it's grass," Mrs. Bilkins quipped, "but they ain't get-ting' fat on it."[34]

This scene is transformed in *The Wonderful Wizard of Oz* into a cap-italist fantasy. "Many shops stood in the street, and Dorothy saw that everything in them was green," Baum writes. "Green candy and green pop-corn were offered for sale, as well as green shoes, green hats and green clothes of all sorts." Naturally, the items are paid for with green pennies. Oz turns out to be an inverted version of Kansas, a place just as defective as what Dorothy left behind. Zeese Papanikolas asks, "Are Scarecrows and Tin Woodmen and Cowardly Lions—like the manikins behind the windows of the shops—more real than the deluded citi-zens who gaze upon them? It may have been a question that Baum, the actor and student of window dressing, might have asked about himself." The Great Oz, from behind his curtain, creates a spectacle (enhanced by those green spectacles) that substitutes substance with surface. He makes himself visible to the public only through a projected version of himself, but the wizard's ruse is revealed after Toto knocks over the screen. "How can I help being a humbug," he pleads, "when all these people make me do things that everybody knows can't be done?"[35]

❦ ❦ ❦

Pranksters and con artists are driven by very different impulses, but their actions produce comparable effects. Not only do they make mischief with media; their irreverent actions can also *remake* media institutions, norms, and practices (much like how mythical trickster figures turn the world upside down, shatter it to pieces, and glue it back together in their own warped image). Late-nineteenth- and early-twentieth-century media industries were shaped by the sorts of transgressive behavior spotlighted in this chapter. Because of the exaggerations and outright frauds found in advertisements, they were increasingly viewed with suspicion. The public likened them to confidence games, and illustrators working around the turn of the century often turned down advertising work because they didn't want their reputations tarnished by association. The ad industry responded with self-regulation and public-relations strategies in an attempt to instill trust. This is one important way that the culture of cons sparked the "Truth-in-Advertising" movement of the early 1900s and the related Pure Food and Drug Act of 1906, among other things. But I'm getting ahead of myself. Before exiting the nineteenth century, the next two chapters will navigate the murky waters of occultism and conspiracy theory. These esoteric and eccentric ideas—some of which were inspired by a combination of pranks, hoaxes, and cons—produced powerful ripple effects that reverberate to this day.[36]

3

Spirits in the Material World

Trickery ruled the school throughout the nineteenth century. In addition to confidence men and playful Barnumesque exhibitions that invited audience scrutiny, popular culture was haunted by the supernatural. Middle-class consumers embraced theatrical magic during this period, spawning a hugely profitable retail industry of instructional books, magazines, and goods used for parlor tricks. Magic slowly became a respectable entertainment after it began shedding its mystical pretentions in the late 1700s. An increasing number of conjurers distanced themselves from the insinuation or explicit suggestion that their manifestations were mystical in origin, and their clothing, props, and overall self-presentation were influenced by Enlightenment thought. Stage magicians now framed their tricks as a way of teaching logic and critical-thinking skills (for instance, they claimed their apparitions were nothing more than demonstrations of optical, acoustical, and electrical phenomena). The craft became secularized, and a new generation of celebrity magicians exposed the "supernatural humbugs" of shady charlatans. These changes reflected a cultural shift that occurred in the previous century, when science and reason increasingly held sway among the intelligentsia. Traditional magic was banished to the shadows of society—back-alley fortune-tellers, countryside cunning folk, and the like. But despite the best efforts of those Enlightenment cheerleaders, superstitious beliefs kept popping up like a Whac-A-Mole game in a creepy amusement park.[1]

Do You Believe In Magic?

Professional ventriloquists also worked hard to demystify irrational beliefs. "From the late seventeenth century onwards," Steven Connor writes in *Dumbstruck*, "ventriloquism moved from the jurisdiction of theologians and demonologists to that of anatomists and physiologists." Performers mastered multiple voices and threw them across rooms in an attempt to debunk the idea that God, or Satan, could speak through humans in the form of divine calls, demon voices, and the like. During these antipapist times, the most obvious targets of professional ventriloquists were Catholic priests, who were dismissed as miracle fakers who fooled their congregations into worshiping false idols. Even starry-eyed Spiritualists presented themselves as thoroughly modern in their thinking. Spiritualism, which emerged in the mid-nineteenth century, was considered a "religion of proof" that used scientific methods to observe, record, and examine communications from the Other Side. The mediums who led séances were known as "investigators," and they blurred the lines between mysticism and empiricism by analyzing "evidence" provided under certain "test conditions." Con artists soon got into the game by targeting those who desperately wanted to speak to their dearly departed loved ones. Some mediums were sincere, but it didn't really matter what their intentions were—it mattered how séance participants interpreted what they saw or heard. Self-deception is a powerful thing. People tend to embrace pranks, hoaxes, cons, conspiracy theories, and superstitious fantasies when they resonate with their deep-seated beliefs about how the world works.[2]

These were confusing, contested times. The fuzzy borders between science, religion, and entertainment opened up spaces for mischief makers to leave their mark on modernity. "Enlightenment fought constantly against the more notorious productions of this fictitious world," the nineteenth-century magician H. J. Burlingame wrote. "The magicians of the first half of our century . . . labored to make magic appear as entertainment only." One such magician was Étienne-Gaspard Robertson, a Belgian optician best known for popularizing a dazzling new amusement: phantasmagoria. His immersive spectacles used "magic lanterns" to project spectral images that were painted on glass slides. Robertson created the appearance of three-dimensional motion by mounting his primitive film projectors on small moving wagons and pointing them at swirling smoke. But even though this illusionist perfected the magic lantern, he didn't invent it. Back in 1671, a Jesuit named Athanasius Kircher designed the *lantern magica* as an awe-inspiring propaganda tool for the Catholic Church. "Through this art," he wrote, "godless people could easily be prevented from committing many vices if the devil's image is cast onto the mirror and projected into a dark place." The Church wanted to scare nonbelievers straight—with some magic-lantern-aided trickery.[3]

Robertson was among the first to position stage magic against the kind of mysticism that was falling out of favor in Enlightened circles. "I have now shown you all the phenomena of the phantasmagoria and have revealed to you all the secrets of the priests of Memphis and of the more modern Illuminati," Robertson said at the conclusion of his shows. "I will now show you the only really terrible spectacle, the only spectacle really to be feared by you all, whether you are strong or weak, rulers or subjects, believers or atheists, beautiful or ugly. Behold the destiny that is reserved for you all, and remember the phantasmagoria." With that dramatic flourish, he revealed a cute scythe-wielding grim reaper waving good-bye. However, not everyone took his lessons to heart. After Robertson conjured a ghostly image of a woman, an audience member raised his hand to his brow and uttered, "Heavens! I think that's my wife." A century of Enlightenment had not fully exiled superstition to the shadows, despite the best efforts of Robertson and another influential magician named Jean Eugène Robert-Houdin. "My interest in conjuring and magic and my enthusiasm for Robert-Houdin came into existence simultaneously," said Harry Houdini, whose stage name was a tribute to that illusionist. "I accepted his writings as my text-book and my gospel." Robert-Houdin's book *The Sharper Detected and Exposed* detailed how underworld swindlers often relied on stage-magic techniques. His other crusade, which Houdini also took up, targeted Spiritualism—something that both men viewed as a gigantic con.[4]

SPIRIT RAPPERS BUST A MOVE

Hydesville was Ground Zero for Spiritualism, whose quick uptake had much to do with where it took root. Word spread far and wide in part because this tiny town in upstate New York was a central node in America's expanding transportation systems: canals, highways, railroads, and the telegraph lines that ran alongside them. Spiritualism was set in motion by Kate and Maggie Fox, two adolescent sisters who moved with their family into an allegedly haunted Hydesville farmhouse. Mysterious noises caused the family much lost sleep, and on March 31, 1848, they grew louder late at night (and well into the early morning of April Fools' Day). The daughters stayed in their parents' bedroom amusing themselves by imitating the knocking. "Here, Mr. Split-foot," Kate said, using the nickname for a cloven-hoofed devil, "do as I do." She clapped three times, which was followed by three haunting knocks, or "raps." Mom asked the spirit more questions, and the family soon developed a Morse-like code in which one knock meant "yes," and two signified "no." The gates to the spirit world were soon blown wide open. Friends and curious visitors came to believe that chatty spirits followed them back to their homes, rapping away. Kate and Maggie's older sister Leah Fox soon had the idea to charge an admission fee, and P. T. Barnum eventually used the sisters as a sideshow attraction.[5]

"What would I have said six years ago," one skeptic wrote in 1855, "to anybody who predicted that before the enlightened nineteenth century was ended hundreds of thousands of people in this country would believe themselves able to communicate with the ghosts of their grandfathers?" Belief in the supernatural goes back to the beginnings of human civilization, but the idea that deceased spirits can commune with living beings through a medium is a modern development. With death a constant reality in the antebellum era, mourning became a default mode. People expressed their desire to connect with the dearly departed through poems, prose, and art—which helped lay the groundwork for Spiritualism's popularity. It found a welcoming audience in an era teaming with Christian revivalism, splinter sects, and millenarianism. There were certainly religious reasons for Spiritualism's uptake, but the same socioeconomic forces that gave rise to the nineteenth-century confidence man also played a role. Urban transplants were confronted with secular forces that emphasized surface appearances, leaving them yearning for something more meaningful. At the same time, the sorts of rituals and traditions that helped people make sense of life and death were in eclipse. People needed something to fill the void.[6]

Spiritualism was closely associated with feminism, another social movement that took shape during this era. In July 1848, when the Seneca Falls Convention kick-started the movement for women's equality, talk of ghostly communiqués rippled through the gathering. Elizabeth Cady Stanton and other activists became believers. Some led séances, and raps reportedly erupted from the table where the convention resolutions were drafted. In *History of Woman Suffrage*, Stanton and Susan B. Anthony noted, "The only religious sect in the world . . . that has recognized the equality of women is the Spiritualists." The attributes frequently ascribed to the "fairer sex"—passivity, purity, piety, and an excess of nervous energy—made women obvious candidates for receiving otherworldly messages. (Female mediums stood in stark contrast to confidence men, because ladies were thought to be constitutionally unable to hide their true feelings.) Spiritualism moved the site of religion from the public sphere of the church to the domestic sphere, placing women in leadership positions. "Victorian mediums were doing more than locating and carrying on conversations with the angel in the house," Marlene Tromp notes. "They were channeling her to reshape their lives."[7]

Under the cover of Spiritualism, these women felt free to act out unconventional behaviors that were frowned on by polite society. All of these mediums-gone-wild infuriated conservatives who wanted to preserve traditional gender roles. Rev. Hiram Mattison was one of many disgusted by the unfettered abandon of "spirit-dancers," whose theatrical displays drew from a hybrid jumble of nineteenth-century showbiz traditions and diasporic religious practices. In his anti-Spiritualist book *Spirit Rapping Unveiled!*, Mattison derided mediums that acted out "characters that had entered them" (including, he gasped, "a negro," a "Turk," and "an Indian chief"). As literary scholar Daphne Brooks observes, "A radical act of 'desegregating the dead,' the spirit-rapping sensation of midcentury North America further disrupted a country wrangling with borders between north and south, black and white, master and slave." By literally and metaphorically embodying the turbulence of 1850s American culture, mediums destabilized several other binaries: the personal and the political, religious and secular, and male and female. That was the most magical trick of all.[8]

Male Spiritualists also challenged social conventions. After John Shoebridge Williams made contact with his deceased daughter, he believed he was starting to grow mammary glands. The sixty-one-year-old wrote in his spirit journal, "Eliza said to me, 'You know, Dear Father, that of late years, your breasts have been partly developed like a females [*sic*]." His spirit-daughter continued, "This was from my influence. You were well prepared to receive me into your bosom, and already do our souls unite in substance so as to become one." Many sexagenarian males experience a loss of pectoral definition—you know, man-boobs—but Williams interpreted this in light of the cultural changes happening around him. It was a time when new conceptions of masculinity, femininity, and piety were taking form. Gaining prominence was the antebellum ideal of the rugged "self-made" man, which emphasized Benjamin Franklin–associated traits such as competitiveness, thrift, and hard work. But at the same time that the marketplace codified these masculine qualities, some religious leaders pushed in a different direction. Evangelicals, for example, admonished their followers to openly express their feelings and to apply "gentler virtues" in daily interactions. Male mediums felt the effects of this sexual confusion directly.[9]

Williams initially put himself in a submissive position by allowing his daughter's spirit to play a parental role. Claiming "there is no such thing as the I-myself-big-man-me in true mediumship," he entered a childish state of religiosity. Williams's mental gymnastics didn't end there. He later manned up by marrying his spirit-daughter, becoming the head of the house (in his head). Thereafter, Williams distanced himself from female mediums and adopted a stern religious theology, though he remained quite androgynous. Another prominent medium, Jesse Shepard, took his ambiguous sexuality even further. He was euphemistically described as a "beardless, boyish, *spirituelle* looking" creature who preferred the company of "vigorous young men." Shepard's ethereal voice was akin to a female soprano's—a divalike tone that could channel divine spirits. This was also true of Spiritualist superstar Wilberforce J. Corville, who spoke "in a girlish voice of very peculiar tone." These men were openly queer (in every sense of the term) at a time when science and medicine worked overtime to fix the lines between male and female and, later, homosexuality and heterosexuality. As a result, chest-thumping Transcendentalist Ralph Waldo Emerson complained that Spiritualism was "unmanly and effeminating."[10]

Despite all this gender bending and spiritual miscegenation, binaries remained central to the way séances were organized. Spiritualist Amanda Spence put it in terms of "the Masculine, or Positive organization" and "the Feminine, or Negative Organization." To prime the flow of spiritual energy, positive forces sat by the medium's left-hand side, and negative forces were to the right. Similarly, Andrew Jackson Davis's instructions for a "spirit battery" instructed that "males and females (the positive and negative principles) are placed alternately." Spiritualists drew this language from gendered theories of electricity that had been around since the early days of electrical research. These theories informed the natural sciences, and they later seeped into everyday understandings of gender, sexuality, psychology, and anthropology. Media scholar Jeffrey Sconce notes that female mediums were imagined as fully realized cybernetic beings: "electromagnetic devices bridging flesh and spirit, body and machine, material reality and electronic space."[11]

Spiritualism was initially influenced by mesmerism, or "animal magnetism," which came of age in the late eighteenth century during the heyday of electrical experimentation. Friedrich Anton Mesmer caused a stir in Paris when he claimed that an ethereal electromagnetic "fluid" existed in all living creatures. The Austrian doctor used the term *animal magnetism* (derived from *animus*, the Latin word for spirit) to differentiate it from mineral magnetism. In 1784, a commission of the French Academy of Sciences—which included Benjamin Franklin, among others—debunked his findings. Mesmer was run out of the country, though his theories later caught on in 1830s America, where signs proclaiming "MESMERIC EXAMINATIONS" and "DISEASES CURED BY MESMERISM HERE" were a common sight. The mesmeric circle, in which a small group of people held hands to increase the electrical charge, was later used as a template for Spiritualist séances.[12]

Even though Spiritualists used gendered jargon, it was with the strategic goal of imploding social binaries. Amanda Spence reminded her audiences "that a man of feminine organization should . . . assume the duties to which his nature calls him, and that a woman of executive temperament ought, without accusations of manliness and coarseness, to be permitted to take her due part in the executive branch of the business of the world." In short, mediums sought a balanced social, spiritual, and sexual life. "The experiment of masculine rule has been tried long enough," Spiritualist Thomas Hazard declared in 1868. "Six thousand years of war, bloodshed, hypocrisy and crime have pronounced it as a gross failure. It is high time that the feminine element was called to its aid." The fiction of spirit communion—which, to be fair, was deeply felt and quite real for many believers—allowed men to act in odd, "unmanly" ways and women to take control of their lives. This sort of prankish lie seems far less troubling than, say, the Catholic Church insisting that only men can be priests, because God said so.[13]

Spiritual Mediums and New Media

I suppose it's possible that one day in 1848 real spirits descended on Hydesville and opened a channel to the Other Side. But there are more plausible explanations. The rise of Spiritualism was fueled by the way new communication technologies shaped the public imagination. Because the associations between electricity, media, and mysticism had been widely recognized for years, the concept of spirit communication was embraced by many, though certainly not all. When Samuel F. B. Morse requested congressional funding for his telegraph research, a U.S. senator sarcastically suggested that half the funds should also subsidize mesmeric experiments. Within this context, it makes total sense that the telegraph provided a model for séances (cryptic messages were heard in raps: *tap, tap tap, tap, tap*—like Morse code). "The whole mystery is illustrated by the workings of the common magnetic telegraph," one Spiritualist scientist insisted. "The principles involved are identical." A Spiritualist friend of the Fox sisters, the Reverend Joseph Osgood Barrett, once dreamt that his church had been transformed into a massive broadcast station wired to the ghost world. He spoke of the "heavenly news along the attached wires, or chords of love-thought, uniting heaven and earth." Not coincidentally, Spiritualism's leading papers were named the *Spiritual Telegraph* and the *Celestial Telegraph*.[14]

These mystical and material communication technologies served two different purposes. The "spiritual telegraph" was used in the home and addressed issues important to women, whereas electrical telegraphy transmitted political and commercial information central to the patriarchal public sphere. Female mediums adopted scientific discourses and invoked respected figures that were associated with electrical research in order to legitimize themselves. In fact, the very first soul the Fox sisters conjured with their "spirit telegraph" was Mr. Electricity himself, Benjamin Franklin. On one spooky midcentury day, his sprit spoke through the rat-a-tat-tats of this newfangled device. "There will be great changes in the nineteenth century," Franklin predicted, vaguely, by way of transcription from Maggie Fox. "Mysteries are going to be revealed. The world will be enlightened." He also urged those who were present to establish "communications between two distant points by means of these rappings." In 1852, one of the country's more popular Spiritualist journals, the *Shekinah*, reported on a similar visitation from Franklin (who materialized many times in the decades that followed).[15]

Spirit communication shaped the ways people made sense of nineteenth-century electrical media, and vice versa. Media scholar John Durham Peters points out that the word *medium* was simultaneously used to describe the electrical transmissions of the telegraph and the people who facilitated communiqués from the Other Side. *Channel* is another term inherited from Spiritualism that is still in use today. The use of these terms highlights the socially constructed nature of media, and it also demonstrates how the architecture of media can restructure human consciousness. German communication theorist Friedrich Kittler argued that the dominant information technologies in any era can fundamentally transform our perceptions of the social world. The imagined workings of supernatural phenomena evolve with changes in media, such as when the telegraph compressed distances separating physical bodies. Before the mid-nineteenth century, it was inconceivable that people could send instant messages across the country or, for that matter, talk to the dead. Now that the telegraph broke down one barrier, why shouldn't other uncanny forms of communication be possible?[16]

This eeriness in the air seeped into popular culture. Two occult satires by Edgar Allan Poe, "Mesmeric Revelation" and "M. Valdemar," were so close to the mark that some readers confused them with reality. The latter story, written in the style of a medical report, was a gruesome tale about a man who was mesmerized just before passing away. He remained in tortured limbo for weeks, begging to die. After the trance was broken, he decomposed into "a nearly liquid mass of loathsome—of detestable putrescence." The story was so convincingly written that a publisher in England pirated it as a nonfiction work, and the *London Sunday Times* reprinted it without comment under the headline "Mesmerism in America: Astounding and Horrifying Narrative." In a Barnum-like move, Poe declined to comment on its fictional status. Morse's invention, which coded the alphabet as a series of dots and dashes, also inspired the author's interest in cryptography. "As the telegraph worked its way into the texture of daily life," literary scholar Shawn James Rosenheim writes, "it became far easier for Poe to conceive of a world structured around the concept of information, where knowledge itself was a form of decoding." From this point of view, the world was a deceptive puzzle that shouldn't be taken at face value (a key assumption of conspiracy theories, as we will see in the next chapter).[17]

Most of Poe's cryptographic writings were published from 1837 to 1844, between the time Morse began his experiments and the commercialization of the telegraph. During these years, he penned a rash of telegraphy-inspired essays, the *Dupin* trilogy, and "The Gold-Bug." These works further popularized the connections between cryptography, telegraphy, and the supernatural. When Poe died in 1849, a year after the Fox sisters first heard those rapped musings, his spirit became more popular than his corporeal counterpart ever was. One medium even lobbied to have her "Message from the Spirit of E. A. Poe" integrated into his cannon of published works. Several others dashed out messages from famous spirits, which developed into a bizarre literary subgenre. Isaac Post, the husband of the women's rights and abolitionist leader Amy Post, published a compilation of messages from Thomas Jefferson, George Washington, Benjamin Franklin, and William Penn (whom the state of Pennsylvania was named after). He used a process called automatic writing to compile a three-hundred-page book called *Voices from the Spirit World*, with a little help from "A. L. Fish (a rapping medium)."[18]

By the early twentieth century, the written legacies of William Shakespeare, Jack London, and Oscar Wilde expanded greatly. This publishing fad wasn't just limited to historical figures. The spirit of Patience Worth, who allegedly lived during the second half of the seventeenth century, was also "discovered." In 1916, Henry Holt and Company published *Patience Worth, a Psychic Mystery*, which collected this fictional woman's writings. In the 1920s, a large cottage industry produced a Patience Worth magazine, a Patience Worth publishing company, and an unending stream of transcribed poems and novels. With the assistance of some helpful (and inventive) mediums, she even produced a Victorian family melodrama. "Considering that neither Victorians nor novels had existed in Worth's day," historian Paul Collins notes, "this was an impressive achievement indeed." The most outrageous spirit memoir was Rev. Dr. Charles C. Hammond's *Light from the Spirit World: The Pilgrimage of Thomas Paine and Others to the Seventh Circle in the Spirit World*. He claimed to have written it under, ahem, an "invisible influence." Incredibly, the Library of Congress ascribed authorship to "Thomas Paine (Spirit)." Hammond took hilarious liberties with the religious beliefs of this contrarian, who now admitted that he had been wrong all along.[19]

> THOMAS: Indeed, this is none other than William Penn—the mind who
> never drew a sword to gain a victory, or repel an enemy.
> WILLIAM: I am William Penn; I have watched thy course, Thomas, and
> I have sympathized in thy efforts to rid minds of superstition and
> priestly rule; but thou seest now that thy labor was not successful,
> because the wants of nature must be supplied. . . .
> THOMAS: But my weapons were not malicious.
> WILLIAM: No; thou wast not malicious, but thou didst what thou wouldst
> not do again, as thou seest now. . . .
> THOMAS: I see my error.[20]

On *Light from the Spirit World*'s final page, the Spirit Formerly Known As Thomas Paine promised, "I will write another book." As it turned out, he didn't produce a sequel and was never heard from again. But if contemporary observers happened to be under the "invisible influence" of opiates, they might argue that "Thomas Paine (Spirit)" lived on to influence hip-hop music. The famous pamphleteer now signed his name "T. Paine"—which was surely a time-traveling homage to T-Pain, whose Auto-Tuned voice has haunted twenty-first-century radios. There was also a lot of talk about rap in the nineteenth century, a time when publishers pumped out books about "rapping mediums" and "spirit rappers." Reverend Hiram Mattison's *Spirit Rapping Unveiled!* was quite popular, as was the 1854 party-starting classic *The Rappers*, among many others. However, with a lack of historical evidence, we have no way of knowing whether there were any rivalries between East Coast and West Coast spirit rappers.[21]

HARRY HOUDINI TRIES TO MAKE SPIRITUALISM VANISH

By the late nineteenth century, Spiritualism had attracted its fair share of hucksters. The knocks, taps, and raps that marked the movement's early years didn't always make for exciting theater, so some mediums added pizzazz to their act. They graduated to telekinesis by making tables tilt and objects float, and a few magicians also made the cynical conversion to Spiritualism by giving their tricks a supernatural luster. The specter of fraud haunted true believers, for they knew those parlor charlatans could discredit the entire movement. Earlier in Harry Houdini's life, before becoming a vocal skeptic, he desperately wanted to speak with his deceased mother, but his experiences with mediums always ended in frustration. After he noticed something fishy during a séance, Houdini confronted a mystical con artist, who confessed, "Well, you've caught me; but you've got to admit that I do more good than harm by consoling sorrowing people who long for a message from their loved ones." Houdini asked if there was anyone he could recommend who wasn't a fake. "None that I know of," the medium replied. "They're tricksters—every one of them."[22]

Early in his career, Houdini found a copy of *The Revelations of a Spirit Medium*. This short book was written under the pseudonym "A. Medium," and it provided the budding magician with important tricks of the trade. It detailed the ways mediums could slip out of their bindings in a pitch-black room to manifest spirits, make otherworldly noises, shake tables, and return undetected. Using this book as a training manual, Houdini perfected skills that later came in handy as an escape artist. But before taking a more legitimate career path, Harry and his wife, Bess, made a living posing as fraudulent Spiritualists in an old-time medicine show. While in Gelena, Kansas, they amazed crowds with disclosures about the private lives of audience members. In reality, it was just another ploy Harry learned from *The Revelations of a Spirit Medium*. The Houdinis gathered information by visiting the local graveyard, memorizing names of the recently deceased, and getting tips from discreet local informants. The money was good, but they felt bad about preying on the vulnerable. "I was chagrined that I should ever have been guilty of such frivolity," he later said, "and for the first time realized that it bordered on crime." With no other job options, Harry and Bess joined a circus.[23]

Harry Houdini's crusade against Spiritualism culminated in a bizarre soap opera that costarred Sir Arthur Conan Doyle. It was a death-match clash of two pop-culture titans. The author was an ardent Spiritualist who believed in fairies (an odd contradiction for the creator of Sherlock Holmes, who was synonymous with rationality and empirical analysis). Doyle's conversion began in 1880 after attending a lecture on the topic, and his interest in the occult further intensified after marrying his second wife, Jean, in 1907. He became even more outspoken about his beliefs during World War One—when his son, brother, and several other family members died. Spiritualism's ranks swelled in the wake of the conflict's carnage, as did the number of skeptics. The soon-to-be antagonists met when the magician traveled to England to do research for the follow-up to his book *Miracle Mongers and Their Methods*. Houdini wanted access to Doyle's mediumistic contacts, so he invited the author to see his stage show—which totally blew the author away. It convinced him that Houdini was most *definitely* in touch with the spirits. During their first meeting, Sir Arthur insisted on showing off his most prized possession: photos of fairies taken by two young girls. "A fake! you will say," he said. "No, sir, I think not." As a member of Britain's upper class, he found it unfathomable that anyone "from the artisan class," as Doyle put it, would be clever enough to fool him.[24]

Doyle's earnest convictions were reinforced by nineteenth-century Anglo-American culture's blurring of rationalism, scientific inquiry, spirituality, and fantasy. Fairies, the widely accepted theory went, manifested their presence with the same "spirit matter" and "psychic force" that could be witnessed during séances. These mystical creatures exploded in popularity at the beginning of the nineteenth century, a trend that continued well into the twentieth century. Musical ballads, folktales, theater, and related fantasy literature appealed to British audiences hungry for portrayals of fairyland. Sir Arthur's uncle, Richard "Dicky" Doyle, was also the period's most celebrated fairy illustrator (a milieu that also planted the seeds for J. R. R. Tolkien's *The Hobbit* and his *Lord of the Rings* trilogy). Doyle first brought the Cottingley fairy photos to the public's attention in the Christmas edition of *Strand Magazine*, a British periodical that published his early Sherlock Holmes stories. The issue sold out in a matter of days, and he later published the photos in a book titled *The Coming of the Fairies*. An American magazine reviewed it with the headline "Poor Sherlock Holmes—Hopelessly Crazy?," and the British humor magazine *Punch* mocked him with an illustration of the detective scowling at Sir Arthur, whose dreamy head floated in the clouds. Years later, one of the girls who took the photos admitted to fabricating them. She simply cut out a fairy illustration from one of 1915's most popular children's books—which, embarrassingly, also included a story written by Sir Arthur.[25]

When the two met again in America, Houdini tried to give Doyle a good-natured lesson. He devised an illusion that caused whatever Doyle scrawled on a piece of paper to appear on a slate board (written out by a cork ball that left a trail of white ink). Things backfired when this was viewed as absolute, verifiable proof of the magician's supernatural powers. An exasperated Houdini begged Doyle not to jump to conclusions, but Sir Arthur thought he was just being cagey. Later, when Harry and Bess visited the Doyles in Atlantic City, they attended a séance conducted by Lady Doyle. She claimed to have conjured the spirit of Houdini's mother, but the showman knew she wasn't playing straight. For one thing, the spirit spoke perfect English, while his mom only spoke Hungarian. "In Heaven," Lady Doyle countered, "*everyone* speaks English." This inspired Houdini to mess with their minds by staging a "deliberate mystification." After being asked to try his hand at automatic writing, he grabbed a pencil and made a dramatic show of writing the name of one of Sir Arthur's recently deceased friends. The excitable author spread word of this in Spiritualist circles, intimating that Houdini would soon convert.[26]

"Dear Houdini," psychic researcher E. J. Dingwall inquired, "Is there any truth in the story of Doyle that you got an evidential message from your mother through Lady Doyle? Also that you have become an automatic writer?" To set the record straight, Houdini testified in a notarized deposition: "I can truthfully say that I have never seen a mystery, and I have never visited a séance, which I could not fully explain." He said much the same publicly, which Sir Arthur viewed as a direct attack on his wife's reputation. Doyle insisted to Houdini, "So long as you attack what I *know* from experience to be true, I have no alternative but to attack you in return." Houdini offered to send him a copy of his new book, *A Magician among the Spirits*, but he got no response. The book was criticized by Spiritualists for containing factual errors, something Houdini blamed on his publisher's decision to cut the manuscript by one hundred thousand words and rush it to market. In a letter to Upton Sinclair, he wrote, "I had a slight premonition that perhaps I would not live to see the book in print if I waited much longer, so I allowed them to rush it, against my judgment." Houdini's life was in fact coming to a close; two years later he was dead.[27]

THE SPIRITUALISTS STRIKE BACK

Houdini's anti-Spiritualist campaign provoked angry threats, particularly from a medium who went by the stage name Margery. Her career was thriving, and she worried that the crusading magician would expose her. If that happened, Margery told Houdini, "some of my friends will come up and give you a good beating." This wasn't a hollow threat, for her devotees could be brutal. "Something will happen to that man H," Doyle fumed in a letter to Margery's husband, Dr. Crandon. "You mark my words." The crazy train went off the rails after Sir Arthur got his very own spirit guide, Pheneas, who died "thousands of years ago in the East, near Arabia." Naturally, Pheneas spoke through Lady Doyle. "Your wife is invaluable to us," Pheneas said. "We use her a great deal." As the official channel of Doyle's spirit guide, Lady Doyle began playing a more prominent role in her husband's affairs. "Houdini is going rapidly to his Waterloo. He is exposed," Pheneas said during his first appearance. A few days later, the spirit guide grew more agitated: "Houdini is doomed, doomed!" Lady Doyle informed Margery the medium, "We were also told that Houdini is *doomed* & that he will soon go down to the black regions which his work against Spiritualism will bring him as his punishment."[28]

Soon after, Houdini self-published a pamphlet titled "Houdini Exposes Tricks Used by the Boston Medium 'Margery' to Win the $2500 Prize Offered by the *Scientific American*." He filled it with photographs and illustrations that revealed her deceits. Meanwhile, Margery and her spirit guide, "Walter," spread the word among Spiritualists that the magician was marked for death. Houdini was too well known among mediums to covertly visit séances, so he put together a network of undercover spies who posed as grieving widows. The magician also employed his niece Julia Sawyer to ensnare a particularly devious slate writer named Pierre Keeler. After Keeler dutifully channeled the spirits of Julia's nonexistent sister—along with two relatives who happened to still be alive—Julia casually mentioned that her rich uncle was waiting at the train station. Keeler happily accompanied Julia, who introduced him to her wealthy wheelchair-bound relative. Then, like in a scene straight out of a Sherlock Holmes story, or *Scooby-Doo*, "Uncle Bill" yanked off a long white beard and revealed himself. "I got you Keeler," Houdini exclaimed. His nurse, a reporter in disguise, stood by and took notes.[29]

It was now open war between the Spiritualists and Houdini, who hit the lecture circuit decrying the dangers of fraudulent mediums. A 1924 newspaper headline announced, "Houdini Hits Conan Doyle—Magician Says Englishman's Occult Teachings Are Menace to Sanity and Health." Mediums fought back with libel suits and much worse. Papers across the country trumpeted, "Houdini Gets Death Threat—'Evil Spirits' Put Curse on Him." Even though the magic man quipped, "[They] can't even give me a pimple by sticking hat pins through my photograph," he was being disingenuous. Houdini knew what lengths some Spiritualists went to in dealing with critics. "Those mediums are bad actors and would think nothing of putting you in the hospital or worse," he told his friend Joe Rinn, who helped debunk several fraudulent mediums (and endured multiple attempts on his life as a result). Around this time, Houdini placed a call to Fulton Oursler, the editor of *Liberty* magazine. "Listen, I'm leaving on tour in a little while," he said. "Probably I'm talking to you for the last time." The editor asked what was going on. "They're going to kill me." *Who?* "Fraudulent spirit mediums," Houdini told Oursler. "Don't laugh. Every night they are holding séances praying for my death." His enemies soon got their wish. After one fateful show, a McGill University student punched Houdini in the stomach before he could prepare for the blow. This ruptured his appendix, eventually killing him.[30]

"His death was most certainly decreed from the other side," said Sir Arthur, who believed the spirit world was furious at the magician for attacking mediums while also using supernatural abilities to advance his career. (Houdini: the self-loathing Spiritualist.) No autopsy was ordered because doctors were certain it was a case of a ruptured appendix, though some skeptics have floated other theories. Biographers William Kalush and Larry Sloman suggested that Spiritualists poisoned Houdini, but they offered no proof beyond vague circumstantial evidence. In lieu of hard facts, the authors executed a bit of prank, with a capital "PR." They staged a press conference in 2007 announcing the exhumation of Houdini's body. A famous forensic-science professor would lead the examination, and "the only known living descendant of the family" received permission from the cemetery. None of this turned out to be true (to begin with, Houdini has several living relatives). It was just a publicity stunt on the part of Kalush and Sloman, designed to revive the flagging sales of their book. Even though Spiritualists likely played no part in ending Houdini's life, they still used his death as a cautionary tale. When one of Doyle's favorite mediums was revealed to be a fraud, the author angrily told the debunker he would meet a similar fate. "If I die," Houdini said from his hospital bed soon before passing, "don't be surprised if phony spiritualists declare a national holiday." Appropriately enough, he passed away on Halloween.[31]

ENTER THE SLEEPING PROPHET

Spiritualism's steep decline in popularity occurred around the turn of the century. After the Fox sisters' initial burst of fame, they descended into alcoholism, unhappiness, and other ills. Near the end of Maggie Fox's life, in 1888, she publicly turned her back on Spiritualism when a *New York Herald* reporter visited her. Drinking heavily and despondent about the recent death of her husband, she gave a dramatic interview that blamed her older sister, Leah, for their deceptions. "A Celebrated

Medium Says the Spirits Never Return," the next day's headline trumpeted. Maggie deeply missed her husband but had no luck after several attempts trying to contact him (an irony that made her even more miserable). "Nothing came of it—nothing, nothing," she cried. The *New York World* followed up with a front-page story declaring, "Spiritualism Exposed: The Fox Sisters Sound the Death-Knell of the Mediums." A month later, Maggie appeared at New York City's Academy of Music to reveal how she and her sister produced those raps—by loudly popping their toe joints, apparently. Soon after, she recanted her repudiation. Though Maggie Fox denied being bribed by wealthy Spiritualists, the broke, broken woman hoped this return to the fold would earn her cash on the lecture circuit.[32]

By the late nineteenth century, Spiritualism became estranged from its utopian roots, especially after respectable suffrage leaders began distancing feminism from its unruly past. New technologies also accelerated Spiritualism's retreat from public life. Thomas Edison founded the Edison Electric Illuminating Company of New York in 1880, and within a couple of decades electricity was powering streetcars, factory machinery, and lighting for homes. Like many others who lived through these times, Edison was intrigued by the possibility of spirit communication. He once told Theosophist Henry Steel Olcott about an invention of his that connected one's forehead to a pendulum, so to test the kinetic powers of the mind. Edison also explained to a reporter that he wished to see "if it is possible for personalities which have left this earth to communicate with us." And in the final chapter of his memoir, titled "The Realms Beyond," the inventor discussed a valve he was building that could help one converse with the Other Side.[33]

The electric light bulb put the final nail in Spiritualism's coffin. It literally and metaphorically banished shadows from the darkened séance room, washing away the mystery. Electricity and telegraphy—which had both been profoundly associated with supernatural phenomena—eventually lost their magical luster. Spiritualist ideas lived on in the New Thought movement, which in turn influenced New Age ideas during the twentieth century. Many believers migrated to California and set up utopian communes, though the most influential Spiritualist descendant set up shop in a more unlikely locale. Edgar Cayce—"The Miracle Man of Virginia Beach"—bridged the old, weird world of the nineteenth century and more contemporary obsessions with reincarnation, astrology, ancient astronauts, and other trippy ideas that gained traction in the 1960s and 1970s. Slipping into a trancelike dream state, Cayce gave "readings" that discussed everything from prophetic predictions to homeopathic cures. (The *Journal of the American Medical Association* noted, "The roots of present-day holism probably go back 100 years to the birth of Edgar Cayce.")[34]

Cayce's fame had multiple acts. He initially gained notice in 1910 when the *New York Times* published a lengthy article titled "Illiterate Man Becomes a Doctor When Hypnotized." The psychic found himself in the limelight again soon before his death in 1945, and in the 1960s he became more popular than ever. His alleged powers manifested themselves as a boy, when he was able to see people's auras and hold conversations with dead relatives. Cayce's parents dismissed this as the overactive imagination of a child—a reasonable conclusion, given that he liked to play in the vegetable garden with "little folk" no one else could see. As an adult, he continued to see these tiny, invisible creatures, along with angels and other spirit guides. Rather than channeling a specific entity, the mystic claimed he was tapping into the origin of all knowledge. He called this The Source or, sometimes, The Information. Even though he remained resolutely Christian throughout his life, Cayce drew some of his ideas from Hindu teachings espoused by late-nineteenth-century Theosophist Madame Blavatsky. (The theosophists also revived interest in astrology and reincarnation, concepts Cayce helped popularize in the next century.)[35]

The Sleeping Prophet gave well over twenty thousand "readings" in his lifetime, some of which were a bit crackpot—with an emphasis on the *crack* and the *pot* smoking. For starters, Cayce said he was well into his eighth incarnation on this earth. He was previously an Egyptian high priest named Ra Ta and a sculptor/chemist/artisan named Xenon, one of the defenders of Troy. The faithful downplay his more absurd predictions, such as the discovery of an Atlantean "death ray" in 1958 or that Atlantis would surface near the Bahamas a decade later (an idea that intrigued stoned hippies at the dawning of the Age of Aquarius). According to Cayce, an explosive "Terrible Crystal" sunk Atlantis, which would soon rise again: "Expect it in '68 and '69," he declared. "Not so far away!" Cayce likely absorbed the Atlantis myth from

Madame Blavatsky, though he was also influenced by the popular culture of his youth (such as Edgar Rice Burroughs's *The Lost Continent*). Much like his Spiritualist predecessors, he was fascinated with electrified communication technologies. Like-minded people flocked to him, including Thomas Edison, Nikola Tesla, NBC founder David Sarnoff, and FM radio pioneer Mitchell Hastings. Edison reportedly told Cayce, "When we see the entire world seeking, seeking, seeking, there must be something [to it]."[36]

Cayce's stories may have been wild, but he wasn't a confidence man. He was widely regarded as a decent person who often gave readings for free, even when his family was nearly destitute. And unlike the more over-the-top mediums of the time, Cayce just spoke softly while appearing to be asleep. This is probably the reason why Harry Houdini remained curiously silent about him after observing a session in 1921. By the end of the 1920s, the Cayce Hospital for Research and Enlightenment was finally up and running, as was Atlantic University. "Men and women admitted on equal terms," an advertisement stated. The women's soccer team was called the Mermaids, and the school's band was named, yes, The Atlanteans. For a bunch of New Agers, the men's football team had a surprisingly winning debut season, even defeating American University 31–0. The Great Depression forced the university's doors shut in 1932 (which perturbed the financial backers, who wished the psychic had warned them about the impending downturn). Atlantic University also failed because of some fiscally irresponsible decisions. While in a trancelike state a few months before the stock-market crash of 1929, Cayce was asked if the university should continue with a plan to "appropriate ten million dollars, to be obtained from the [perpetual-motion] machine for the university." The Source—via Cayce—replied, "Absolutely correct!" Regrettably, success hinged on a pretty far-fetched business plan.[37]

❦ ❦ ❦

Inspired by that era's new media, Spiritualists conjured an alternative spirit realm that left very visible traces on the material world. This fantasy helped reorganize social relations by giving women leadership roles for one of the first times in Western history. Though some shady opportunists did infiltrate the Spiritualist ranks, true believers shouldn't be lumped in with con artists, pranksters, or hoaxers. Nevertheless, one thing they all had in common was a desire to play with media. Boundary-blurring tricksters, who typically exist on the margins of society, often make communication technologies do things their inventors never intended. In the early stages of the development of media, before their uses are routinized and naturalized, the possibilities are wide open. There is nothing inherent in the wiring of the telephone, for instance, that ensured it would only be used for point-to-point communication. During the late nineteenth century, telephone lines were used to broadcast music to the masses—much like today's radio stations. Inversely, early radio was often used to communicate from person to person, as opposed to a single station broadcasting to multiple listeners. The uses of media are shaped by the habits of mind shared by those who operate them—habits that can be transformed with imagination, creativity, and conviction. It therefore makes sense that Spiritualists repurposed the concept of electrical media to "break on through to the Other Side" (as a twentieth-century pop-culture shaman once sang).

4

Meet
the Illuminati

The intentions of political pranksters, attention-seeking hoaxers, and criminal con artists vary greatly, but they fool people for the same reasons. In each instance, their deceptions are engineered to exploit a victim's belief system. The same is true of conspiracy theorists, whose self-deceptive tendencies prime them to buy into fictions that validate their worldviews. As this chapter colorfully illustrates, conspiracy theories are often based on source material drawn from a combination of genuine historical events, satirical pranks, and the sorts of self-serving hoaxes and cons that prey on the credulous. In the case of the Rosicrucian prank, the blowback from this satire exploded into a conspiracy theory of epic proportions. Back in the early seventeenth century, a few radical Protestants invented the Rosicrucian Brotherhood to provoke a public debate about scientific and theological concepts that the Catholic Church wanted to suppress. Even if this secret society was a fiction, its doctrines were embraced by religious liberals and freethinkers who desperately *wanted* to believe. These fantasies rippled through the modern age, causing the religious right to react with horror and disgust.

"In 1959 the Tidewater area of Virginia was literally a spiritual wasteland. For years it had been in the grip of demon power," said Pat

Robertson, who settled in the region that year. "Virginia Beach was advertised as the psychic capital of the world. It was the headquarters of Edgar Cayce and the Association for Research and Enlightenment." Cayce's spectral presence profoundly warped Robertson's conspiratorial outlook. "Stories abounded of people who discovered their psychic sensitivity while visiting in the area," the televangelist claimed. "Spiritualist centers dotted the Norfolk, Virginia Beach area." For Robertson, New Agers weren't harmless flakes—they were satanic demons in hippy disguise. In his best-selling 1991 book *The New World Order*, he insisted, "The New Age religions, the beliefs of the Illuminati, and Illuminated Freemasonry all seem to move along parallel tracks with world communism and world finance." If you're wondering what Spiritualists, Masons, bankers, and communists have to do with each other, they are all key players in a centuries-old political drama. Though we may think of the late twentieth century as a high-water mark for conspiracy mania, it swept through the West much earlier. The French Revolution cemented a paranoid style that attributed every world-historical event to the machinations of the Bavarian Illuminati. Late-eighteenth-century conspiracy theorists based this all-powerful secret society on the legend of the Rosicrucian Brotherhood. Fiction or not, the rash of writings about the Rosicrucians actually did inspire the formation of real-life secret societies like the Freemasons (who were also accused of sparking the French Revolution). Later in the nineteenth century, the Illuminati myth grew more ubiquitous with the help of a gadfly named Léo Taxil. His elaborate satire targeted the religious conservatives of his time—who fell for his outlandish stories hook, line, and sinker.[1]

Sinister Secret Societies

Despite the mythical status of the Bavarian Illuminati, it really did exist. It was founded on May 1, 1776 by a canon-law professor named Adam Weishaupt, who wanted to unshackle the world "from all established religious and political authority." Just imagine Enlightenment philosophy on LSD-laced energy drinks. By 1782, three hundred members had joined the Illuminati after Weishaupt and his followers infiltrated European Masonic lodges. Freemasons had long been associated with subversion because its members had a fondness for the Rosicrucians, whose "invisible" members are the archetypal freethinkers of the modern era. Masons certainly didn't go out of their way to discourage this radical-chic image. This outlaw status was bolstered by members who fabricated or exaggerated Freemasonry's roots to make it appear more ancient, arcane, and impressive than it actually was. Some claimed a connection to the medieval Knights Templar, warrior monks that rebelled against the papacy in the fourteenth century. (Aligning themselves with the Templars and Rosicrucians was a strategic way to annoy the Vatican and other French conservatives.) Some even claimed that Freemasonry stretches all the way back to the builders of King Solomon's Temple. However, it probably just developed during medieval times—when stonecutter guild members used covert signs to identify one another to guard their knowledge against outsiders and protect their jobs.[2]

It wasn't until 1717 that the first Masonic Grand Lodge was formed, in London. Its members were middle-class liberals whose meetings were largely nonpolitical, save for endorsing secular Enlightenment principles, free speech, and open elections. This inevitably led to charges of "radical egalitarianism" by the Catholic Church, and in 1738 the pope banned Catholics from joining. Clement XII declared that Masons were "depraved and perverted, . . . most suspect of heresy." It was therefore a no-brainer for conspiracy theorists of the time to blame the French Revolution on the Freemasons and the more elusive Bavarian Illuminati (which became more powerful in myth than it ever was in reality). By 1784, the Illuminati's ranks swelled to three thousand, but the leader's big mouth and reckless behavior led to the group's downfall. The Bavarian government soon outlawed all secret societies in its territory, and in the process it seized and made public several incriminating documents. Weishaupt faded into obscurity while exiled in Gotha and died in 1830—which is more or less the end of the story, though some folks let their imaginations run wild.[3]

In 1797, the Scottish physicist and inventor John Robison published *Proofs of a Conspiracy against All the Religions and Governments of Europe, Carried On in the Secret Meetings of Freemasons, Illuminati and Reading Societies*. Robison was the senior scientific contributor to the *Encyclopedia Britannica*'s third edition and a respected professor at Edinburgh University. After *Proofs of a Conspiracy* became a massive hit—selling out within days in Britain and, later, America—he became famous for other reasons. Robison claimed that French aristocrats such as Mirabeau and Orleans joined underground groups that plotted the French Revolution, and he placed Adam Weishaupt at the center of this plot. The conspirators brewed tea that caused abortions, made a poison that instantly killed when squirted in the face, and—yikes!—developed a "method for filling a bedchamber with pestilential vapours." You could joke that he was on drugs, but that wouldn't be far off the mark. Starting in 1785, Robison suffered from painful groin spasms that put him on a steady diet of opium and bed rest. Isolated, paranoid, and tripping, he worried that the unfolding mayhem in France would reach his shores.[4]

Abbé Augustin Barruel, a Frenchman who wrote the massive five-volume *Mémoires pour servir à l'histoire du Jacobinisme*, confirmed Robison's belief that the Revolution was caused by a "triple conspiracy" of anti-Christians, Freemasons, and the Bavarian Illuminati. Also published in 1797, Barruel's book was swiftly translated into English as *Memoirs Illustrating the History of Jacobinism*. It traced the roots of this conspiracy back to the Knights Templar, those fourteenth-century warrior monks who turned against the pope. The Abbé believed that the rise of liberalism—which championed equal rights and individual liberty—was evidence of their continued influence. Over the centuries, the Knights Templar supposedly founded the Rosicrucian Brotherhood, infiltrated the Freemasons, established the Bavarian Illuminati, and spread their devilish agenda throughout Europe. Back in the real world, Barruel didn't notice any of this when the French Revolution was raging, nor did anyone else. The only exception was Marquis de Luchet's anonymously published *Essay on the Sect of the Illuminists*, which warned of an occult order that sought to "govern the world." However, this reference to an "Illuminist" was just a generic allusion to a mystical Freemason and not the Bavarian Illuminati itself.[5]

In the late eighteenth century, many people were still scratching their heads about the causes of the French Revolution. *It had nothing to do*, the conspiracy theorists insisted, *with the Bourbon dynasty's political and financial misrule*. Instead, they blamed a secret cabal that quietly pulled strings. "We shall demonstrate," Barruel wrote, "even to the most horrid deeds perpetrated during the French Revolution, everything was foreseen and resolved on, was combined and premeditated." Barruel's and Robison's books continued to be discussed well into the twentieth century, especially after Pat Robertson heavily drew on them in 1991's *The New World Order*. "The satanic carnage that the Illuminati brought to France," he writes, "was the clear predecessor of the bloodbaths and successive party purges visited on the Soviet Union by the communists under both Lenin and Stalin." The televangelist also echoed the positions of the John Birch Society, a far-right American organization founded in the 1950s. "The first and greatest enemy of Eighteenth Century *Illuminati* was Catholicism," founding Bircher Robert Welch insisted. "This is why, at the height of the Revolution in Paris, all worship of God was formally abolished, and a statue was erected to the 'goddess of reason,' to be venerated instead."[6]

Illuminatiphobia Sweeps America

Much like how anticommunism offered a simple rendering of complex global politics during the Cold War, Robison's and Barruel's narratives filled a similar void. Their books fanned the flames of Illuminatiphobia throughout Europe, and alarm bells soon sounded in America. The French Revolution, combined with the rise of Jeffersonian democracy, struck fear in the hearts of reactionary religious leaders. A pastor named Jedediah Morse took to the pulpit and used tactics straight out of the Joseph McCarthy playbook. "I have, my brethren," Morse declared, "an official, authenticated list of the names, ages, places of nativity, professions etc of the officers and the members of a Society of Illuminati . . . consisting of one hundred members." Foreign enemies, he said, wanted "to subvert and overturn our holy religion and our free and excellent government." Newspapers took up the debate over "Illuminated Masonry," and a war of words erupted between the Hamiltonian Federalists and the Jeffersonian Democrats in 1798 and 1799. One Federalist claimed Thomas Jefferson was "the real *Jacobin*, the very child of *modern illumination*," while a Jefferson supporter alleged that Illuminati-affiliated Federalists had infiltrated the New England clergy.[7]

The president of Yale University took Morse's unhinged rhetoric to the next level. "Shall our sons become the disciples of Voltaire, and the dragoons of Marat," Timothy Dwight warned, "or our daughters the concubines of the Illuminati?" George Washington received a copy of Robison's book, and while he was skeptical, he didn't reject it entirely. "It is not my intention to doubt that the doctrine of the Illuminati and the principles of Jacobinism had not spread in the United States," Washington wrote. "On the contrary, no one is more satisfied of this fact than I am." But he insisted that American Masonic lodges were not affiliated with the Illuminati. Washington's defensiveness likely stemmed from the fact that Benjamin Franklin, Thomas Jefferson, and the president himself were all Freemasons. While it is true that Franklin was beloved by Italian Illuminati philosophers and scientists who took a shine to his electrical experiments, there is no evidence that he or any other founders were Illuminati agents. At least, that's what they want you to think! (Jefferson had a less diplomatic take on Barruel's book, dismissing it as "the ravings of a Bedlamite.") When Morse was challenged to be more specific in his proof, he could only vaguely point to a group of forty Massachusetts freethinkers as "evidence that the devil is at this time gone forth, having great influence." Like many conspiracy theorists, it turned out that Morse—an ardent Federalist—had a partisan ax to grind.[8]

Freemasonry regained its respectability in the United States after Washington's death, but the pendulum swung back a couple of decades later. Anti-Masonism spread through New York State and New England after the September 11, 1826 kidnapping and murder of William Morgan, who enraged Masons by revealing their mysterious rites. The killers were brought to justice but got off with light sentences—something that was attributed to the secret society's behind-the-scenes machinations. It was widely believed that Masonic editors had muzzled the press, a charge that reverberates today in conservative attacks on elitist mainstream media. Fifty-two anti-Mason newspapers popped up around the country, and several Anti-Masonic Party candidates were elected in the decade following Morgan's murder. (It remains an enduring footnote in political history because it was the first party to hold a national convention, on September 11, 1830.) The moral panics that erupted over Freemasonry and the Illuminati were fueled by a belief that a privileged few were closing off opportunities for common people. Anti-Masonic Party members regularly cited Robison's and Barruel's books, and concerns about shadowy puppet masters continue to course through contemporary conservative movements.[9]

In the 1830s, the crosshairs were retrained on Catholics after they began immigrating from Ireland in record numbers. By midcentury, anti-Catholic conspiracy theories reached a fever pitch. "We have the best reasons for believing that corruption has found its way into our Executive Chamber," a Texas newspaper declared in 1855, "and that our Executive head is tainted with the infectious venom of Catholicism." In addition to bloody violence and mile-high piles of propaganda, the papal haters executed several hoaxes. One deceit involved Maria Monk, who suffered a severe brain injury at an early age after a pencil punctured her ear. She grew up to be a wild child, so her parents sent her to live with nuns—who forced Monk to leave the convent after she became pregnant. She was taken in by nativist crusader William K. Hoyte, who helped Monk pen an outrageous book, *Awful Disclosures*. It made a huge splash after being hyped in the popular newspaper *American Protestant Vindicator*. Aside from Harriet Beecher Stowe's *Uncle Tom's Cabin*, it was the most widely read book of that era, selling over three hundred thousand copies by 1860. (Harriet's father, Lyman Beecher, also happened to be a raging anti-Catholic; "Whatever we do," he wrote of this threat, "it must be done quickly.")[10]

Monk's lurid exposé included an account of her first experience in the confession booth, where the priest shocked her with his "licentious expressions." She was also forced to service the horny men in the monastery next door. The nuns told Monk that if she became pregnant, her child would be "baptized and immediately strangled." *Awful Disclosures* also revealed mass graves filled with babies, underground torture chambers, and lots of sex! As historian Richard Hofstadter put it, "Anti-Catholicism has always been the pornography of the Puritan." A prominent Protestant nativist debunked Monk's story after visiting the convent in question. He saw no evidence of such shenanigans, but that has not prevented the book from remaining a steady seller well into the twenty-first century. The 2010 catalog of the right-wing mail-order company CPA Book Publishers includes a listing for *Awful Disclosures*—along with John Robison's *Proofs of a Conspiracy*, Charles Lindbergh's populist (and Jew-baiting) book *Banking, Currency, and the Money Trust*, and several books published by the John Birch Society.[11]

Jedediah Morse's son Samuel F. B. Morse also saw conspiracies everywhere. In 1835, he penned two nutty books, titled *Foreign Conspiracy against the Liberties of the United States* and *Imminent Dangers to the Free Institutions of the United States.* "A conspiracy exists," he said of the Catholic menace, and "its plans are already in operation." Ironically, at the very moment that the European Catholic Church was accusing Freemasons and the Illuminati of plotting to destroy civilization, American Catholics were being accused of doing the exact same thing, in precisely the same manner. Morse was soundly defeated when he ran for office on a nativist platform, but he more than made up for that failure by developing the telegraph. But he still remained in the grip of paranoia, something that influenced the inventor's initial idea to bury his telegraph lines. That decision proved to be disastrous, because the soil corroded the uninsulated wires. Stringing them overhead would be cheaper and easier, but he was afraid of saboteurs: "mischievously disposed persons," Morse fretted, could "injure the circuit." The inventor was just walking in his father's footsteps. "Like Jedediah, Samuel was haunted by the specter that insidious conspirators were subverting the republic," media historian Richard R. John writes. "Telegraph saboteurs were but one more peril that Samuel felt impelled to combat."[12]

A Grand Unified Conspiracy Theory Is Born

One of the nineteenth century's oddest ideological twists was the fabricated association between Judaism, Freemasonry, and Satanism. In medieval Europe, Jews were sometimes viewed as quasi-oriental sorcerers or disguised demons that worshiped the ancient text of the "satanic" Kabbalah. A common depiction of the Devil resembled a clichéd image of the Jew: "goat-hoofed, bearded, curly-haired, redheaded, and horned." The occasional massacres of Jewish communities during the eleventh and twelfth centuries were but one expression of that era's anti-Semitism. Also rampant were charges that Jews were secretly committing atrocities against Christians, especially little boys—which became known as the "blood libel." Infants were supposedly being kidnapped and slaughtered by Jews, who drank their blood during Passover. (I had no idea babies were kosher.) In 1255, a rumor panic exploded in England after a boy's body was found in a cesspool near the house of a Jewish man. The man confessed after being tortured, and about a hundred Jews were arrested, tried, or murdered outright.[13]

After the French Revolution, the archaic connection between Judaism and Satanism was revived in the form of a grand unified conspiracy theory. This was one of the central premises of *Le Juif, le Judaïsme et la Judaïsation des peuples Chrétiens* (translated as *The Jew, Judaism and the Judaization of the Christian Peoples*). This 1869 book was the bible of French anti-Semitism, and it was written at the height of a conflict between the Catholic Church and Freemasonry. Even though the Masons did not singlehandedly spark the French Revolution, as many Catholics suspected, the secret society was more than happy to take credit for the headaches it caused the Church. From there, it was just a short (illogical) leap to believe Freemasonry was in cahoots with Satan-worshiping Jews. Among other claims, the *Le Juif* authors insisted that the Masons developed an "intimate alliance with the militant members of Judaism, princes and imitators of the high cabal." To better understand how this Judeo-Masonic conspiracy theory congealed, we need to turn our attention back to early-nineteenth-century France.[14]

At first, none of the French Revolution conspiracy theories mentioned Jews. This changed in 1806 when Abbé Barruel got a letter from a man named J. B. Simonini (likely a pseudonym used by the French political police). Simonini congratulated Barruel on having "unmasked the hellish sects which are preparing the way for Antichrist" but then pointed out something he missed: "the Judaic sect." Barruel came to believe that a "supreme council" made up of twenty-one people, of which at least nine were Jews, had an iron grip on European Masonic lodges. Within that covert council was *yet another secret inner council of three*, who elected a Grand Master that controlled all international Masonic lodges. As I have already noted, the modern notion of a satanic secret society *within* a secret society was first popularized in the early 1600s by the pranksters who invented the Rosicrucian Brotherhood. This Judeo-Masonic conspiracy theory was merely an updated version of that meme. Barruel dreamt up an elaborate communication network—complete with relay runners—which allowed orders to be speedily carried out in a pre-telegraphy era. This idea may have been inspired by the Rothschilds, a prominent Jewish banking family that grew rich using courier pigeons to get finance-related news in advance of competitors.[15] Drawing on Simonini's letter, Barruel wrote,

From neighbour to neighbour and from hand to hand the orders are transmitted with incomparable speed, for these pedestrians are delayed neither by bad weather, nor by the mishaps that normally befall horsemen or carriages. . . . They stop neither to eat nor to sleep, for each one covers only two leagues. The mail-coach takes ten hours from Paris to Orleans, stopping for an hour; the distance is thirty leagues. Fifteen or twenty pedestrians, replacing one another, can reach Orleans from Paris in nine hours, using short-cuts and above all never stopping.[16]

According to Simonini, not only did Jewish conspirators establish Freemasonry and the Bavarian Illuminati; they also infiltrated the Church hierarchy. Over eight hundred Italian ecclesiastics, including bishops and cardinals, were actually crypto-Jews (who planned to install one of their own as pope). These claims were nothing new. During the Spanish Inquisition in the late fifteenth century, many Catholics suspected that Jewish *conversos* to Christianity remained clandestine Jews—or were atheists and perhaps even Satanists. Also implicated were the "Illuminists," or *alumbrados*, who were associated with Erasmian humanism, a proto-Enlightenment tradition reviled by the Church. Even though the French Revolution solidified the imagined links between Judaism and illuminated thought, the facts say otherwise. Freemasons largely resisted allowing Jews in their lodges, Weishaupt's Bavarian Illuminati was also unwelcoming, and Orthodox Jews viewed Freemasonry as an abomination. After Napoleon grudgingly granted Jews universal rights, all the pieces of the Judeo-Masonic conspiracy theory fell into place. In 1806, the year Barruel received the Simonini letter, Napoleon gathered an advisory committee of prominent French Jewish scholars and rabbis to help bolster his political power. But he made the mistake of calling it the "Great Sanhedrin," which reinforced the belief that a secret Jewish tribunal was steering world events.[17]

To avoid "the effect which might be produced by the 'Sanhedrin,'" Barruel shared the Simonini letter with Church officials and French security forces. He wrote a massive manuscript about this conspiracy but destroyed it two days before his death in 1820 (Barruel feared it would lead to a massacre of the Jews). Nevertheless, the book's key claims became public knowledge, and a new wave of anti-Semitism rolled through the land. Because Jews had previously been denied entry into traditional professions, they were disproportionately associated with banking, journalism, and other symbols of modernity. Mystery veiled their religious rituals, which were sometimes misunderstood as witchcraft by outsiders. This perception, compounded with resentment toward Jewish bankers such as the Rothschilds, fomented hatred on all sides of the political spectrum. The landed aristocracy viewed Jews as a political threat; Protestants and Catholics saw them as uncanny, occult beings; and socialists despised them for keeping the proletariat down. As the nineteenth century wore on, Illuminatiphobia, anti-Masonry, and anti-Semitism merged to form a hugely influential worldview. By 1893, a Catholic archbishop confidently insisted that "everything in Freemasonry is fundamentally Jewish, exclusively Jewish, passionately Jewish, from the beginning to the end."[18]

An Evil Hoax

In *Warrant for Genocide*, the definitive book on the origins of *The Protocols of the Elders of Zion*, Norman Cohn traces the roots of this infamous forgery back to the early nineteenth century. *The Protocols* presents itself as a transcript of the first Zionist Congress held in Basel, Switzerland— where Dr. Theodor Herzl outlined plans to install a supreme Jewish ruler. If this sounds a lot like the Bavarian Illuminati's plot to control the world, that's because *The Protocols* heavily plagiarized from Barruel's *Memoirs Illustrating the History of Jacobinism*. Additionally, at least 15 to 20 percent of *The Protocols* was copied from Maurice Joly's 1864 political satire about Emperor Napoleon, *Dialogue in Hell between Montesquieu and Machiavelli*. The latter took the form of an imagined conversation between the infamous political philosopher Machiavelli and Montesquieu, a champion of Enlightenment principles. "Like the god Vishnu," Machiavelli said, "my press will have a hundred arms, and these arms will give their hands to all the different shades of opinion throughout the country." Compare this with the almost-identical *Protocols* passage, allegedly uttered by a sinister Jew: "These newspapers, like the Indian god Vishnu, will be possessed of hundreds of hands, each of which will be feeling the pulse of varying public opinion." Joly's line "Evil instincts among men are much stronger than the good" was adapted within *The*

Protocols as "I maintain that men of evil instinct are more numerous than those of good character." And so on—and on and on.[19]

The Protocols also borrowed from a book by Hermann Goedsche, written under the pseudonym "Sir John Retcliffe." This writer's day job was split between laboring at a post office and working as an openly anti-Semitic journalist—all while acting as an agent provocateur for the Prussian secret police. In this capacity, Goedsche forged letters and documents that discredited left-wing politicians, radical rabble-rousers, and Jews. For an unrepentant hate-monger, he had a soft side: by night, Goedsche was a romantic novelist. His melodramatic novel *Biarritz* contained a chapter titled "In the Jewish Cemetery, Prague," which starred a satanic rabbi intent on annihilating Christianity. (Coincidentally, this chapter also plagiarizes from Joly's *Dialogue,* among other sources.) Goedsche's story, which took place during the Feast of the Tabernacles, described a gathering of powerful Jews, named—what else?—the Sanhedrin. At midnight, in a graveyard, a blue flame illuminated the conspirators as a hollow voice intoned, "I greet you, heads of the twelve tribes of Israel." Zombielike, they replied, "We greet you, son of the accursed."[20]

The year Goedsche published *Biarritz,* 1868, was significant. Years of Napoleonic rule over Germanic states resulted in the partial liberation of the Jews, which provoked some violent anti-Semitic reactions in that region. "It is therefore not surprising," Cohn writes, "that the first comprehensive formulation of the modern myth of the Jewish conspiracy should have appeared in Germany at the very moment when Jews were about to be granted full emancipation." Fears of the Jewish menace, also prevalent in Russia, helped turn Goedsche's fictional story into fact. Someone in St. Petersburg published the *Biarritz* chapter in 1872 as a stand-alone pamphlet, along with a note that stated it was based on a true story. This was followed in 1876 by the publication of a similar pamphlet titled *In the Jewish Cemetery in Czech Prague (the Jews Sovereigns of the World).* By 1881, it appeared in France—this time presented as a historical document, *Annals of the Political and Historical Events of the Last Ten Years.* This version consolidated all the speeches from Goedsche's original novel into one long monologue that was delivered by the chief rabbi. That text was eventually interpolated into *The*

Protocols, whose authors added a hodgepodge of Joly's *Dialogue* and Barruel's *Memoirs*.[21]

This head-spinning game of telephone is a disturbing example of how hoaxes, fantasies, and satire can take on a life of their own. To summarize: *The Protocols'* mutant family tree includes an Illuminati-phobic history of the French Revolution, a political satire targeting Napoleon III, and an anti-Semitic romantic novel that was later transformed into a nonfiction essay. *The Protocols* was first published in a 1903 edition of the *Banner*, a Russian newspaper in St. Petersburg. Two years later, a minor tsarist official named Sergei Nilus reprinted it in his book *The Great within the Small: The Coming of the Anti Christ and the Rule of Satan on Earth*. Nilus warned that the Antichrist would appear as a Jewish messiah who conspired with secret societies to establish a godless world empire—an explanatory narrative that has enjoyed tremendous staying power. It is, for instance, more or less the plot of Tim LaHaye and Jerry Jenkins's *Left Behind* novel. In this best-selling book, the satanic Jew is substituted for a charismatic United Nations secretary-general who espouses ideas loathed by conservatives. "We must disarm," the U.N. leader insists, "we must move to one currency, and we must become a global village."[22]

Nilus's *The Great within the Small* kept *The Protocols* on the radar in eastern Europe, but it might have been relegated to the historical dustbin if not for the efforts of two anti-Semitic peas in a pod: capitalist car manufacturer Henry Ford and mass-murdering warmonger Adolf Hitler. Ford reprinted parts of the forgery in his newspaper, the *Dearborn Independent*, which was widely distributed through Ford car dealerships. *The Protocols* also appeared in his best-selling book *The International Jew*. As the most famous and respected industrialist of the era, he played a central role in stoking American anti-Semitism. Ford was forced to repudiate *The Protocols* after being sued for libel, but the damage had already been done. In Germany, this document helped explain the country's economic woes after it was soundly defeated in World War One. "According to *The Protocols of Zion*," Hitler wrote, "the peoples are to be reduced to submission by hunger. The second revolution under the Star of David is the aim of the Jews in our time." Translations appeared in multiple languages, and it continued to spread around the world, despite a Swiss court ruling that deemed it a fraudulent patchwork. "I hope that one day there will come a time," the presiding judge stated, "when no one will any longer comprehend how in the year 1935 almost a dozen fully sensible and reasonable men could for fourteen days torment their brains before a court of Berne over the authenticity of these so-called Protocols." His assessment turned out to be overly optimistic.[23]

Friedrich Wichtl's 1919 book *World Freemasonry, World Revolution, World Republic: An Investigation into the Origin and the End Goal of the World War* recycled the Judeo-Masonic conspiracy theory for the post-war era. Published in Germany, this influential screed blamed World War One on Freemasons, Jews, and the Bavarian Illuminati. A young Heinrich Himmler, who became a leading member of the Nazi party, wrote in his diary that Wichtl's book "tells us against whom we must fight." Satanic Semites were going to destroy the world! Winston Churchill echoed these sentiments when he published an article in a 1920 issue of the *Illustrated Sunday Herald*. He blamed the war on a "sinister confederacy" of international Jewry that quietly conspired with European secret societies. The future prime minister cited a British fascist named Nesta Webster, who claimed that the Jewish-led Illuminati was part of a "world-wide conspiracy for the overthrow of civilisation." Churchill noted that, as "Mrs. Webster has so ably shown," this secret cabal played "a definitely recognisable part in the tragedy of the French Revolution."[24]

Predictably, Nesta Webster insisted that *The Protocols*' authenticity was "an entirely open question." Years later, in 1991, Pat Robertson introduced a new generation to Webster's wacked-out ideas by citing her writings in *The New World Order*. He avoided quoting her more anti-Semitic opinions, but they are in plain view throughout her writings. "Beneath all these occult sects one common source of inspiration is to be found," she argued in *Secret Societies and Subversive Movements*, "the perverted and magical Cabala of the Jews." Robertson insists that he doesn't have a prejudiced bone in his body, but one passage from his 1972 autobiography is particularly telling. Describing his first experience with other evangelicals who spoke in tongues, he writes, "In those days we had a deep-seated fear of what church people would think of our experience with the Holy Spirit, and our prayer meetings were often held late at night, like a gathering of conspirators." He adds, "As was true of the disciples after the crucifixion, we made a practice of locking the doors to our prayer meetings, 'for fear of the Jews'" (a quote from John 7:13 but also a nod to the accusation that the Jews killed Jesus).[25]

Nesta Webster traced her history of secret societies all the way back to the Rosicrucians, who she said were inspired by "the perverted Jewish Cabala of the Rabbis." In fact, she believed that Jews have *always* been the source of all things mystical and evil. "Throughout the Middle Ages it is as sorcerers and usurers that they incur the reproaches of the Christian world," Webster wrote. The presence of Jews, she added, could be detected "behind the scenes of revolution from the seventeenth century onward" (referring in part to the influence of the Rosicrucian Brotherhood). In addition to being obsessed with Jews, Webster's books regularly returned to a time-worn theme: secret societies inside secret societies. Discussing the Order of the Golden Dawn, a late-nineteenth-century occult organization, she said, "the real directors of the Order were in Germany and known as the 'Hidden and Secret Chiefs of the Third Order.'" The Secret Chiefs, it was said, were supremely intelligent god-men who controlled the fate of humankind. Webster didn't realize, however, that it was a hoax invented by one or more of the Golden Dawn's founders (in order to bestow mystery and legitimacy on their brand-new organization). This was a common impulse at the time. Many European adepts contrived supposedly ancient cults, designed ceremonies around dimly understood rituals, and claimed connections to ancient civilizations.[26]

Oddly enough, Nesta Webster was a bit of a mystic herself. Around 1910, she became convinced that she was the reincarnation of a French Revolution–era countess, which prompted a lifelong obsession with the Bavarian Illuminati. Webster's worldview was rooted in "magical thinking," a reasoning process that imagines a causal relationship between real-world events and rituals, utterances, and thoughts. For instance, the Judeo-Masonic conspiracy theory she promoted requires one to believe that witches, Jews, and Satanists have steered history through the ages. After all, it is much easier to blame the French Revolution on the devil than to wrap one's head around the complicated social and economic forces that gave rise to it. Webster also argued that the Illuminati recruited "militant suffragettes" into their ranks and that "terrible bands of harpies" cast spells and ran wild in the streets of Paris. Pat Robertson lapped all this up. Citing Webster, he blamed the Russian

Revolution on the Illuminati, Freemasons, "German-Jewish intellectuals," and—wink, nudge—international financiers. Embarrassingly, it turns out that Webster's and Robertson's books credulously cited several satirical hoaxes masterminded by Léo Taxil, a pen name used by journalist-provocateur Gabriel Jogand-Pagès.[27]

LÉO TAXIL, PRANKSTER

Between 1885 and 1897, the self-proclaimed "greatest joker of all times" transfixed the public with lurid revelations about Freemason black masses, orgies, and good ole Satan worship. Born in 1854 to a devoutly religious French family, the rebellious Jogand-Pagès developed a reputation as a prankster throughout his troubled Catholic education. In 1880, he broke off ties with his family, changed his name to Léo Taxil, and gleefully entered into a career of "poison-pen, yellow journalism." He edited such journals as the *Mudslinger* and authored a popular sacrilegious text, *The Amusing Bible for Grown-Ups and Children*. Taxil also published outrageous political tracts such as *Down with the Cloth!* and wrote several pornographic novels (*The Pope's Mistress* and *The Debauches of a Confessor*, to name a couple). He faced many duels, mostly over defamation, and by 1876 he had been put on trial thirteen times. But business was good. *Down with the Cloth!*—which labeled Pope Pius IX a "debaucher, forger, adulterer, and assassin"—sold 130,000 copies. The profits were more than enough to make up for the court-ordered damages.[28]

So it came as a shock when, in April 1885, Taxil walked into a Catholic church and claimed the Holy Spirit moved him to convert. He renounced his old writings, and in June 1887 he received a personal audience with Pope Leo XIII. When asked what he truly desired, the prankster fell to his knees and gushed, "Holy Father, to die at your feet, right now!" Over the next decade, he churned out several books such as *Confessions of an Ex-Free-Thinker*, *The Anti-Christ and the Origin of Masonry*, and *The Masonic Assassins*—all of which sold in the hundreds of thousands. It was the most celebrated conversion of the time, and one detractor dismissed Taxil as "the spoiled darling of the conservative Catholics." The only explanation for the Church's naiveté was that he exceeded its most far-fetched conspiracy theories about Freemasonry.

It made no difference how unbelievable Taxil's claims were, even when he revealed that the fraternal organization welcomed female members. *The Existence of the Lodges of Women* is also notable because it included "Secret Instructions" supposedly written by Albert Pike, the American head of Scottish Rite Freemasonry: "The Masonic Religion should be, by all of us initiates of the higher degrees, maintained in the purity of the Luciferian doctrine." French Catholics immediately held up "Pike's Secret Instructions" as proof of Masonic devil worship, even though Taxil was the true author.[29]

Taxil had help from his childhood friend Charles Hacks. Under the name Dr. Bataille, Hacks wrote a two-thousand-page exposé that revealed a worldwide conspiracy of Freemasons, Buddhists, Hindus, Spiritualists, Masons, and Englishmen. *The Devil in the Nineteenth Century* was published by the most respected Catholic publishing house in 1892, and it became a best-seller. The book alleged that Albert Pike had a telephone system that allowed him to instantly communicate with other Freemasons in seven of the world's capitals. Devils, of course, were employed as operators. Pike also wore a magical bracelet used to summon Lucifer, and Satan once took him on an excursion to Sirius. While in Calcutta, Bataille witnessed a "Baptism of the Serpents" in a Masonic temple, attended a blasphemous "Marriage of the Apes," watched Indian girls dematerialize, and was present for a human sacrifice. In Singapore, Bataille saw a Presbyterian Church turn into a Masonic lodge with the touch of a button. He was also shocked—*shocked!*—to discover that the Rock of Gibraltar contained hidden factories that churned out weapons for a coming global war against all Catholic nations. Authors outside of Taxil's circle eagerly embellished these stories. Leon Meurin, the bishop of Port-Louis, imaginatively merged anti-Anglo animosity with anti-Semitism in the book *The English, Are They Jews?*[30]

Taxil's prank came to a thunderous close after he invented Diana Vaughan, a mysterious woman who was born on February 29, 1874 (a date that didn't actually exist, but no one seemed to notice). This devil in a red dress—the bride of "Hell's Four Hundred"—was the high priestess of Lucifer, an honor supposedly bestowed on her by Albert Pike. Taxil first exposed the nefarious doings of Miss Vaughan in his four-volume book *Are There Women in Freemasonry?*, which revealed the existence of a previously unknown "Palladian Order." The book's introduction reprinted seventeen letters of goodwill from gullible bishops, archbishops, and cardinals. Catholic journals began printing letters from Vaughan that described a variety of implausible scenarios—including, as an 1897 issue of *Literary Digest* deadpanned, "remarkable stories about piano-playing alligators." More Taxil-penned letters, articles, and books laid out a convoluted series of factional splits among Freemasons: some sided with Satan, others with Lucifer.[31]

By now, Taxil's stories had completely dispensed with any pretenses of believability. Miss Vaughan went on "excursions to Mars" with the aid of devils, traveled to the Garden of Eden, and defeated its guardian angels. She also mounted a gigantic white eagle that took her to the planet Oolis and returned to Earth via volcano (arriving, naturally, at Pike's Scottish Rite temple in Charleston, South Carolina). Just another day in the life of a Luciferian high priestess of Freemasonry. Taking a page from P. T. Barnum, Taxil acted as Diana Vaughan's business agent, and he used every promotional gimmick under the sun. Photographs of Miss Vaughan clad in Masonic vestments appeared alongside articles about how she had relocated to Paris in search of new souls to devour. Horrified Catholics prayed for her to convert, and then—lo and behold—she did so in 1897. Vaughan immediately stopped publishing the journal of the New and Reformed Palladium and began serializing her next project, *Memoirs of an Ex-Palladist*.[32]

After Charles Hacks / Dr. Bataille confessed that his book was a lie, doubts about Vaughan's existence intensified. (Hacks made it clear why he wrote *The Devil in the Nineteenth Century*: there was money to be made on the "known credulity and unknown idiocy of the Catholics.") Taxil finally called a press conference at the Geographical Society in Paris, where he promised that Vaughan would at last make her public debut. After twelve eventful years, the prankster came clean. "My Reverend Fathers, Ladies, Gentlemen," Taxil told the assembled priests and journalists. "First of all, it is appropriate to convey some thanks to those of my colleagues of the Catholic Press. . . . Do not get angry, my Reverend Fathers, but do laugh heartily when you are told now that what did happen is the very opposite of what you expected." Taxil chose to begin and end his "funny as well as instructive hoax" in "April, the month of gaiety, the month of pranks." He explained that the satanic woman pictured in the Catholic press was actually his typist, a Protestant who happily played along with the charade. Taxil then ridiculed Catholics as ignorant imbeciles all too willing to wallow in their own stupidity.[33]

> My first books on Freemasonry were a mish-mash of rituals with inter-pretations; each time that a passage was obscure, I explained it in a sense agreeable to Catholics who would see Lucifer as the Grand Master of the Freemasons. There were several books by authors who ran in the train of my marvelous revelations. The most extraordinary of these works was that by a Jesuit bishop, Monsignor Meurin, bishop of Port Louis, who came to see me in Paris and consult me. He got well informed![34]

Taxil was referring to Leon Meurin, the author of *The English, Are They Jews?* and *Freemasonry: The Synagogue of Satan.* The latter was a work of fiction in more ways than one (his account of "an authentic apparition of Satan" was plagiarized from a short story in *Blackwood's Magazine*). "Palladism," Taxil trumpeted, "my most beautiful creation, never existed except on paper and in thousands of minds!" He then apologized to Free-masons for his nonsensical attacks: "they could not foresee the outcome," he boasted, "which will be a universal roar of laughter." Taxil left through the back door under police protection when a near riot broke out, but at least he had the foresight to have all umbrellas and canes checked at the door. Plenty of pro-Catholic publications denounced him, though some accepted it as an important lesson. "For all our deep disgust at Léo Taxil and his helpers we can not deny that they have, unintentionally of course, done some good," one paper noted. "An end should be put to all the numerous stories which fantastic souls, addleheads, fake converts, and conscienceless liars continually offer the public in the shape of rev-elations, secrets, and predictions." Taxil's confession was followed by his immediate retirement, which was funded in part by those who (literally and figuratively) bought his stories. He moved to a stately home outside Paris and lived a comfortable life until his death in 1907.[35]

💣 💣 💣

Taxil's mischief produced several unintended consequences. Most significantly, Albert Pike continues to live in infamy as a result of the satanic "Secret Instructions" that were attributed to him. Nesta Webster popularized this lie, as did Lady Queenborough in her 1933 book *Occult Theocrasy*. Queenborough came across Taxil's forgery in *Woman and Child in Universal Freemasonry*, an 1894 book by Abel Clarin de la Rive (who was just as guilty of incompetent research as those who cited his book). After the Christian Book Club of America reprinted Queenborough's tome, "Pike's" instructions became a staple of the conspiracy theories that were embraced by the John Birch Society, Pat Robertson, and others on the far right. This chain of citations helps explain why an obscure historical figure such as Pike continues to resurface in popular culture. Most recently, he was used as a key plot device in Dan Brown's novel *The Lost Symbol* and in the Nicolas Cage film *National Treasure: Book of Secrets*. Another resilient Taxil-penned hoax involved the prominent liberal Italian politician Adriano Lemmi, who succeeded Pike as the "Luciferian pope." Even though Taxil admitted at his press conference, "it was not in the Palazzo Borghese, but in my study that he was elected pope of the Freemasons," this story has been persisted for over a century.[36]

The Rosicrucian Brotherhood prank, the self-mythologizing tendencies of the Freemasons, the post–French Revolution emancipation of Jews, the rise of Spiritualism, and Taxil's dozen-year ruse all created a perfect storm. By the end of the nineteenth century, the Judeo-Masonic conspiracy theory evolved into an electrifying explanatory narrative. With the help of a thriving right-wing publishing industry, generations of religious and political conservatives have cited and recited a series of fabricated atrocity stories until they became gospel. Since the early 1600s, a wild array of fantasies, forgeries, hoaxes, pranks, cons, and conspiracy theories merged, mutated, and took on a life of their own. This reshaped the modern world's social, religious, and political landscape in ways that reverberate to this day. "It is self-evident that Masonic beliefs and rituals flow from the occult," Robertson wrote in *The New World Order*. "Beliefs from Egyptian mysticism, Chinese Buddhism, and the ancient mysteries of the Hebrew Kabalah [*sic*] have been resuscitated to infuse their doctrines. What a splendid training ground for a new world / New Age citizen!"[37]

5

The Golden Age
of Newspaper Hoaxes

In the 1830s, with literacy hovering around 90 percent for white New Yorkers, the city was primed to become America's newspaper capital. But it wasn't quite there yet. New York's eleven daily newspapers had a combined total circulation of only 26,500, a small number compared to the total population of Manhattan and its surrounding boroughs. The top-selling papers (such as the *Journal of Commerce* and the *Commercial Advertiser*) focused on political and economic news only of interest to the mercantile and upper classes. And at a whopping six cents per issue, they priced most residents out of the market. The emerging penny presses stepped into this vacuum by catering to the middling classes, mixing straight news stories with the most sinful, outrageous, and tragic reports of the day. Of particular note was Benjamin Day's *New York Sun*. This paper specialized in crime—if it bled, it led—and it featured other eye-popping articles geared toward the working masses. The *Sun* entertained its readers with huge headlines, slang-filled prose, sensational stories, and several bald-faced hoaxes.

Since the eighteenth century, newspapers regularly mixed factual reports with fictional stories, but this changed by the early 1900s. Advances in communication technologies and shifts in journalistic norms put the breaks on older, more frisky journalistic traditions. Nineteenth-century hoaxers and pranksters created a backlash that helped establish new standards of newsroom professionalism that frowned on overt deception. Nevertheless, these changes opened up possibilities for a new kind of hoaxer: the PR man. The types of trickery covered in this chapter certainly differ in terms of motive (such as a racist prank that was intended to undermine Abraham Lincoln's presidency, a newspaper hoax designed to increase sales, and various corporate public-relations campaigns and government propaganda efforts meant to mold the minds of the masses). However, there are important similarities. In each case, the perpetrators didn't just make mischief with media; they fundamentally *remade* media in the process.[1]

Moon and Balloon Hoaxes

During the summer of 1835, a Halley's comet year, the *Sun* reported on shocking new astronomical discoveries made from a South African observatory. The sightings were attributed to a famous astronomer named Sir John Herschel, who published his findings in the (nonexistent) *Supplement to the Edinburgh Journal of Science*. Knowing the world was waiting in anticipation for news from this remote outpost, reporter Richard Adams Locke unleashed his imagination within the pages of the *Sun*. The story began with Sir John scanning the moon and discovering a field of poppies: "Then appeared as fine a forest of firs, unequivocal firs, as I have ever seen cherished in the bosom of my native mountains." This was an earthshaking discovery, for it proved that the moon had a life-sustaining atmosphere. Herschel had once and for all "affirmatively settled the question whether this satellite be inhabited, and by what order of beings." And what an order of beings it was! After panning across the poppies and a red-hilled valley, Herschel could hardly believe his eyes: Moon. Animals. With. Horns.[2]

"The horned goats seemed to prefer the glades to the woods, racing fast over the gently sloped ground, pausing a while to nibble on the grass, then bounding and springing about as playfully as kittens." Locke, the joker—and probable midnight toker—named this area "The Valley of the Unicorn." By starting his tall tale in a lunar poppy field, he was surely alluding to the psychedelic states recently described in Thomas de Quincey's *Confessions of an English Opium Eater*. The surreal sight grew trippier when the scientific team observed a group of man-bats, or *Vespertiliohomo*, who enjoyed active sex lives. (Their "improper behavior," Locke intoned, would "ill comport with our terrestrial notions of decorum.") The *Sun* did report on the man-bats' more G-rated activities, such as how they spent "their happy hours in collecting various fruits in the woods, in eating, flying, bathing, and loitering about." Because the articles mentioned that Herschel's team made engravings of these creatures, readers flooded the *Sun* with requests for lithographs. Sensing a potential windfall, the paper commissioned a print titled *Lunar Animals and Other Objects*.[3]

The man-bats bit the Big Apple, hard. An illustrated pamphlet compiling the entire series sold sixty thousand copies in under a month, and the *Sun*'s circulation soon topped eighteen thousand. It was now the biggest paper in the world. The famous journalist Horace Greeley spoke of the story's "unquestionable plausibility and verisimilitude," claiming it had fooled "nine-tenths of us, at the least." It also made an impression on P. T. Barnum, who was launching a career in the deceptive arts the very same year. "The sensation created by this immense imposture, not only throughout the United States, but in every part of the civilized world," he noted, "will render it interesting so long as our language shall endure." Even such respectable outlets as the *New York Times* fell for it. The hoax-loving Edgar Allan Poe observed with an air of bemusement, noting that "the astonishment of that public grew out of all bounds." He recalled, "A grave professor of mathematics in a Virginian college . . . told me seriously that he had *no doubt* of the truth of the whole affair!" A group of excited Yale professors also took the bait. After they traveled to New York City in search of the elusive *Supplement*, *New York Sun* publisher Benjamin Day sent them on a wild goose chase across Manhattan. They took the ferry back home empty-handed.[4]

Doubts grew louder, and the buzz spread around town that Richard Adams Locke was—gasp—*a hoaxer*. He began drinking more heavily after his boss ordered him to keep quiet. One night at a bar, Locke confessed to an old friend who worked at the *Journal of Commerce*, which was planning to publish the moon series. "Don't print it right away," Locke blurted out. "I wrote it myself." News of the ruse quickly rippled across the country. Papers in Europe piled on, but it took months for this curious story to reach South Africa. Herschel first learned of it when a friend presented him with a pile of newspapers and a pamphlet titled *A Complete Account of the Late Discoveries in the Moon*. His good-humored mate took a dramatic bow and excused himself, leaving the astronomer to explore his own discoveries. "This is a most extraordinary affair!" he exclaimed. "Is this really a reprint of an Edinburgh publication, or an elaborate hoax by some person in New York?" The astronomer was flooded with mail, including a missive from a Baptist missionary seeking advice on how to spread the word of God to lunar inhabitants. In a letter to his aunt, an exasperated Herschel wrote, "I have been pestered from all quarters with that ridiculous hoax about the Moon—in English French Italian & German!!"[5]

Coincidentally, Edgar Allan Poe published a similar story three weeks before Richard Adams Locke's news broke. As was the case for the *Sun* journalist, Herschel's *A Treatise on Astronomy* provided the inspiration for Poe's piece. "The Unparalleled Adventures of One Hans Pfaall" appeared in the June 1835 issue of the *Southern Literary Messenger*. It was about a voyage to the moon in a hot air balloon "manufactured entirely of dirty newspapers." His story sunk without a trace, another bitter reminder that the world didn't appreciate his talents. Poe became convinced that Locke had ripped him off, and he also obsessed over the scientific flaws in his rival's story. He harrumphed, "bat-men could not fly on the moon because the moon had no air." Though Poe felt the *Sun*'s series was poorly written, he gave a backhanded compliment by describing it as "the greatest hit in the way of sensation—of merely popular sensation—ever made by any similar fiction either in America or Europe." Whereas Locke's story appeared in a newspaper and struck a serious tone, Poe's piece appeared in a literary journal and was marked as fiction. Given that the latter was "half plausible, half bantering," as Poe later lamented, it had no chance of succeeding as a prank.[6]

The dejected writer abandoned the second part of his Pfaall story after Locke's success, though he got a second chance at mass-mediated mischief a decade later. In 1844, he convinced the *Sun* to publish his hoax about a seventy-five-hour hot-air-balloon ride across the Atlantic. In preparing it, Poe studied Locke's story to avoid his earlier tactical errors. This time he used a well-known figure, Monck Mason, and paid careful attention to the details—right down to the type of equipment the balloonist used in real life. The *Sun*'s five-thousand-word extra edition featured an explosion of random fonts, punctuation, italics, and boldface type.[7]

ASTOUNDING NEWS

BY EXPRESS VIA NORFOLK!

THE ATLANTIC CROSSED IN THREE DAYS!

SIGNAL TRIUMPH OF MR. MONCK MASON'S FLYING MACHINE!!![8]

On the day the story was published, Poe wobbled to the top of the newspaper building's steps, drunk on wine, and revealed to an assembled crowd that the great *Edgar Allan Poe* was the genius author of the hoax! "The crowd scattered," one witness recalled, and "sales fell off." Poe had a history of alcohol-fueled self-sabotage. In the next issue, the *Sun* printed a simple retraction: "we are inclined to believe that the intelligence is erroneous." Philadelphia's *Saturday Courier* was the only paper that bothered reprinting parts of the *Sun*'s extra edition, but it skeptically advised, "The celebrated 'Moon Hoax,' issued from the office of the New York *Sun*, many years ago, was an ingenious essay; but that is more than can be said of the 'Balloon Story.'" Poe, who was clearly in total denial, gave a very different account of its success in a letter printed in the *Columbia Spy*. "I never witnessed more intense excitement to get possession of a newspaper," he wrote. "As soon as the few first copies made their way into the streets, they were bought up, at almost any price, from the news-boys, who made a profitable speculation beyond doubt."[9]

Miscegenation Shakes Up an Election

Sutured together from the Latin terms *miscere* (to mix) and *genus* (species), the word *miscegenation* was invented at the tail end of 1863. It first appeared in a pamphlet titled *Miscegenation: The Theory of the Blending of the Races, Applied to the American White Man and the Negro*. This anonymous seventy-two-page publication was part of an elaborate political hoax timed for the presidential election season. Its endorsement of race mixing and insistence that it was the Caucasian man's "noble prerogative to set the example of this rich blending of blood" caused an immediate sensation. Predictably, white supremacists went into apoplectic fits. David Goodman Croly, an editor at the *New York World*, wrote *Miscegenation* with one of his reporters, George Wakeman. The *World* was like the Fox News of the mid-nineteenth century, and its reports regularly stirred up white, working-class racial resentments. "And now, behold!" the authors sarcastically announced, "the great Republican party has merged into the little abolition party. The drop has colored the bucket-full." *Miscegenation* drew on scientific theories about race that were gaining traction at the time, as well as concepts ("grafting," "crossing") borrowed from horticulture and animal husbandry. "All that is needed to make us the finest race on earth," it stated, "is to engraft upon our stock the negro element."[10]

From a contemporary vantage point, *Miscegenation* reads like an ideologically confusing game of Mad Libs: "Look at those anti-white Republicans, with their awful progressive agenda! Who will they vote for next, a black president with a white mother?" The pamphlet was a big hit, and its passages were even read in the halls of the U.S. Congress. Representative Samuel Sullivan Cox, a Democrat from Ohio, quoted from it when he attempted to block the Freedman's Bureau bill. The congressman concluded his recitation by claiming that Republicans were "moving steadily forward to perfect social equality of black and white, and can only end in this detestable doctrine of—Miscegenation!" It was exactly the kind of pot-stirring reaction Croly and Wakeman hoped for, and they expertly managed the hoax like a public-relations campaign. First, they sent out advance copies to abolitionist tastemakers with a warm letter soliciting their opinions. Parker Pillsbury, the editor of the *National Anti-Slavery Standard*, wrote back to say that *Miscegenation* had "cheered and gladdened a winter morning." Pillsbury's paper ran a glowing review that hoped "there will be progressive intermingling and that the nation will be benefited by it."[11]

Croly and Wakeman quietly provided their political allies with ammunition. Congressman Cox crowed to his colleagues that Parker Pillsbury, Lucretia Mott, and many other Progressive leaders endorsed the doctrine. Some suspicious abolitionists did not take the bait, believing it would "retard" their efforts to end slavery. Mott acknowledged that her Massachusetts Anti-Slavery Society had lobbied to repeal the law against interracial marriage, but she was careful to note that it had never advocated "such unions." And even though Pillsbury liked the pamphlet, he still warned that it might do "more harm than good." Proslavery forces also singled out Spiritualists for ridicule. The *London Times* noted that "the advanced spirits" of the Republican Party believed blacks were "in many important respects the superior of the whites." Similarly, the prosouthern *London Morning Herald* mocked the reactions of these "hare-brained spiritual mediums of the land—and there are a score or more of these ethereal individuals in every northern village."[12]

When the hoax was still under way, *New Hampshire Patriot* concocted an article titled "Sixty-Four Miscegenation." It implausibly claimed that sixty-four proabolitionist teachers in New England's Port Royal school gave birth to mulatto babies. The *New York World* reported on a Democrat's speech that insisted interracial unions would lead to polygamy. Sounding like a warped Benetton ad, the politician said, "a man could have a yellow wife from China, a brown wife from India, a black wife from Africa, and a white wife from his own country, and so have a variegated family and put a sign over the door: 'United Matrimonial Paint Shop.'" These racists may have been horrible people with hate in their soul, but you can't say they were totally humorless. *Miscegenation* successfully turned interracial marriage into one of the central campaign issues of the 1864 elections at a time when the electoral tide was turning against Lincoln. His campaign was in shambles, and the president privately believed it was "exceedingly probable" he would lose the election. The proslavery press reiterated the false claim that Lincoln advocated race mixing, which he most certainly did not (the president could be as racist as the worst of them).[13]

The *London Morning Herald* was the first to reveal that the pamphlet was a politically motivated fake. "The 'Moon Hoax' in the Shade," another headline declared, referring to Richard Adams Locke's *Sun* series. A year later, Congressman Cox wrote in his memoirs, perhaps disingenuously, "No one in Congress thought of questioning the genuineness and seriousness of the document." Others were clued in that it was a hoax. The *National Anti-Slavery Standard* stated, "The little book upon 'miscegenation' has very generally been regarded here as a burlesque, or satire." *Miscegenation* succeeded in turning interracial mingling into an enduring political boogeyman, and only a few radical abolitionists continued to publicly endorse the concept. The hoax had very long legs, and it helped shape the course of American race relations well into the twentieth century. In 1864, the *New York World* noted that the word *miscegenation* had "passed into history" and accurately predicted that it "will live forever in the grateful midriff of a nation." Miscegenation went into heavy rotation, and it remained a powerful rhetorical tool used to police color lines. It took until 1967, in the *Loving v. Virginia* decision, for the U.S. Supreme Court to rule that laws banning interracial marriage were unconstitutional.[14]

THE GOLDEN AGE ENDS

On November 9, 1874, the *New York Herald* whipped the city into a frenzy after it published a story about a Central Park Zoo animal riot that killed forty-nine people and injured over two hundred. The headlines screamed:

AWFUL CALAMITY
The Wild Animals Broken Loose
from Central Park
TERRIBLE SCENES OF MUTILATION
A Shocking Sabbath Carnival
of Death
SAVAGE BRUTES AT LARGE
Awful Combats Between The Beasts
and the Citizens[15]

Dozens of vicious animals stalked city residents after a cruel zookeeper poked Pete the Rhinoceros with a stick, making him go berserk. When another zoo employee fired his gun, the bullets bounced off the rhino's hide as it charged the shooter. "The horrid horn impaled him against a corner cage and killed him instantly," the *Herald* breathlessly reported, adding that Pete was "tearing the cage to pieces and releasing the panther." Lincoln the Lion planted its paw on a human corpse, roaring as shots whizzed by his head. "Almost on the heels of the puma came the black and spotted leopard, followed by the jaguar, the African lioness, and tiger." People fled the blood-soaked avenues when a Bengal tiger killed over twenty bystanders on the corner of Thirty-Fourth Street and Madison Avenue. The city had never seen so much bloodshed; arms, legs, and heads littered the gutters. New York governor John A. Dix arrived with a gun in hand, and several other prominent New Yorkers took part in an animal hunt on Broadway. The *Herald* also quoted a proclamation by the city's mayor warning citizens not to go outside: "There is a sharp lookout for the black wolf."[16]

Because of the slow speed at which news traveled back then—there was no telephone or radio, for instance—many New York City residents lived in fear until the following morning. Readers locked themselves indoors, and even journalists fell for the story. The editor of the *New York Times* reportedly left his home "with a brace of pistols, prepared to shoot the first animals that would cross his path." Dr. George W. Hosmer, a celebrated war correspondent, appeared in the *Herald*'s offices with two large navy revolvers, shouting, "Well, here I am." And James Gordon Bennett, the owner of the paper that published the hoax, collapsed in his bed after reading the story and remained there all day. Like many of his paper's readers, Bennett did not make it to the final paragraph, which began, "Not one word of it is true." The *Herald* continued, "Not a single act or incident described has taken place. It is a huge hoax, a wild romance, or whatever epithet of utter untrustworthiness our readers may choose to apply to it." The article's stated goal was to "test the city's preparedness to meet a catastrophe," though selling tons of papers was surely the main objective.[17]

Before the turn of the century, pulling a successful hoax was considered as much a badge of honor as getting an exclusive is today. It was not uncommon for newspapers to print tall tales, which were sometimes marked with the preamble "important, if true." Many of the yarns published in the American West were obviously preposterous, such a story about a bird that hid from its enemies by swallowing itself. In the South, newspapers printed similar tales that were typically provided by readers. Another form used by unreliable narrators was the sketch, which reported on real events using the literary tropes of fiction writing. In the eighteenth century, Daniel Defoe, Benjamin Franklin, and contributors to Addison and Steele's *Spectator* routinely wrote sketches. This slippery journalistic style thrived well into the nineteenth century, when Mark Twain wrote for the *Virginia City Territorial Enterprise*. His most significant hoaxes had a southwestern regional spin, such as an 1862 tale about a hundred-year-old "petrified man" who was found embedded in a cliff (simultaneously winking and thumbing his nose at the world). "I was a brand-new local editor in Virginia City, and I felt called upon to destroy this growing evil," Twain said of a fad that was sweeping the area, where people obsessed over all things fossilized. "I chose to kill the petrifaction mania with a delicate, a very delicate satire."[18]

In another piece, "A Bloody Massacre Near Carson," Twain described the misadventures of a man who went nuts after losing money in a mining scheme. He murdered his family, rode into town clutching a chunk of his wife's head, and died on a saloon's steps "with his throat cut from ear to ear and bearing in his hand the reeking scalp from which the warm, smoking blood was dripping." Much of Twain's homegrown humor was an exaggerated version of the often-brutal everyday realities out West, where frauds, cons, and violence were regular occurrences. Years later, Twain recalled the "feats and calamities" that he "never hesitated about devising when the public needed matters of thrilling slaughter, mutilation and general destruction." Twain's massacre story was no exception. "Well, in all my life I never saw anything like the sensation that the little satire created," he boasted. "Most of the citizens dropped gently into it at breakfast, and they never finished their meal." Twain pointed out that his story had many telltale signs of a hoax, including such impossibilities as the existence of a "great pine forest" in the middle of the desert. Local readers picked up on other clues, such as the fact that the murderer, Philip Hopkins, was known in those parts as a bachelor. Also, folks around town were well aware that Twain's friend owned the saloon where the killer supposedly expired.[19]

The *Territorial Enterprise* was among the most influential papers in the West, and several other news outlets reprinted the story. Those who weren't in on the joke were outraged when Twain published a simple, unrepentant retraction the next day: "I take it all back." Readers howled in protest "from Siskiyou to San Diego." One newspaperman complained, "The ass who originated the story doubtless thinks he is 'old smarty'—we don't," and a San Francisco paper promised a boycott of the *Enterprise* until Twain was fired. The paper retorted in its defense,

"Truth is not an indispensable requisite in the local columns of a newspaper," adding, "the more outrageous the hoax, the greater the evidence of talent." Throughout the nineteenth century, newspaper articles were not judged solely on their "truthfulness." The quality of their wit and storytelling was key, but by the beginning of the twentieth century these kinds of hoaxes would become an endangered species. However, that doesn't mean deception would be completely erased from the pages of the newspaper.[20]

PR Is Merely the First Two Letters of the Word Prank

While working as a journalist and press agent in the 1910s, Edward Bernays helped invent the field of public relations. During World War One, he sharpened his media persuasion skills while serving as a member of the U.S. Committee on Public Information (CPI). It was, Bernays said, "the first organized use of propaganda by our Government, and its work was the forerunner of modern psychological warfare." CPI was charged with selling the war to the public, and the agency sought to "guide the mind of the masses" with a publicity apparatus that dwarfed everything that came before it. Bernays's colleague Walter Lippmann worked for years as a public intellectual and a shadow consultant to corporate power brokers and politicians—including President Woodrow Wilson, for whom he served as an adviser. The president ran for reelection in 1916 on the slogan "He kept us out of war" but then shocked the country by changing course early in his second term. Wilson installed the esteemed Progressive investigative journalist George Creel as the head of CPI to deflect criticism from his electoral base, which was skeptical of this "capitalists' war." Creel's impeccable anticorporate credentials helped sell the American public on the campaign to "Make the World Safe for Democracy."[21]

Creel used his social and professional connections to bring Progressive journalists, editors, and opinion leaders into line. CPI distributed its newspaper to opinion leaders, worked with college professors who published prowar pamphlets, printed millions of posters and buttons in a dozen languages, and weaved its messages into advertising, political cartoons, and state fair exhibitions. It also coordinated the activities of the "Four-Minute Man" (not to be confused with the very different

"Sixty-Minute Man," of popular music fame). The Division of Four-Minute Men was primarily composed of businessmen and other well-regarded professionals, who delivered weekly speeches to their communities. CPI distributed a newsletter with government-sanctioned talking points, and over seven million speeches were delivered in fifty-two hundred communities between 1917 and 1918. On any given week, hundreds of men addressed their friends and neighbors—all while sticking to a centrally coordinated script.[22]

After the war, Edward Bernays assisted corporate efforts to persuade consumers and citizens. "Newsworthy events, involving people, usually do not happen by accident," he said. "They are planned deliberately to accomplish a purpose, to influence our ideas and actions." Bernays believed social-science-informed propaganda efforts would make America's large-scale society operate more smoothly. (At the time, the p-word didn't carry the same negative baggage it does today; it was originally conceived as a tool that could help citizens cut through the noise of media.) An "intelligent few" would be charged with shaping the minds of the masses, a technique that Walter Lippmann famously called "the manufacture of consent." It could be achieved through a "an independent, expert organization for making the unseen facts intelligible to those who have to make the decision." Bernays's influential handbooks *Crystallizing Public Opinion* (1923) and *Propaganda* (1928) helped popularize Lippmann's ideas. Each of them believed that technocrats should frame stories for journalists, who would then deliver the prepackaged news for the public. Media critic Stuart Ewen characterizes Bernays's ideal model of communication as merely a hallucination of democracy: "A highly educated class of opinion-molding tacticians is continuously at work, analyzing the social terrain and adjusting the mental scenery from which the public mind, with its limited intellect, derives its opinions."[23]

Many conservatives draw a straight line from the nefarious Progressive agenda of President Woodrow Wilson—*a former university professor*—to "Professor in Chief" Barack Obama, another Ivy League elite. The far right has long despised Wilson for his association with such figures as Lippmann, Bernays, and a social-science-loving philosopher named John Dewey. Talk-show host Glenn Beck seethed that Wilson "is an evil SOB" and a "horror show, possibly the spookiest president we've ever had." Beck was following the lead of the John Birch Society and its founder, Robert Welch, who loathed Wilson and his propagandistic social engineers. "It was under Wilson that the first huge parts of the Marxian program, such as the progressive income tax, were incorporated into the American system," he writes. "And they undoubtedly rejoiced at the success of their satanic schemes." Welch also claimed that college professors pulled the strings of Adam Weishaupt's Bavarian Illuminati: "the diligence and skill with which they worked at promoting each other is illustrated by the fact that within a comparatively few years all of the chairs at Weishaupt's own University of Ingolstadt, with two exceptions, were occupied by *Illuminati.*" With ruthless precision, they marched in lockstep to carry out their socialist plot. (Back in the land of reality, anyone who has witnessed a university faculty meeting is aware of the impossibility of getting some professors to agree on the sky's color.)[24]

President Wilson's ally John Dewey, whose educational reforms helped establish kindergartens in America, is another pariah of the right. "Since Dewey began his notorious career at Columbia, twisting and shaping the values and behaviors of American scholars and teachers," Pat Robertson declared, "the secular establishment has been patiently and persistently dismantling America's value system and its ethical foundations." Progressivism's sinister associations were further solidified by fact that Wilson was associated with mystics such as Edgar Cayce, who reportedly advised him during the planning stages of the League of Nations (an internationalist project that was another bogeyman feared by the right). Although no official record of the visit exists, there is plenty of evidence connecting the two. Cayce's friendship with the president's brother and his two first cousins is well documented, and they all received "readings" from Virginia Beach's Sleeping Prophet. Also, just like Wilson, Cayce was a Freemason. *Cue sinister music.* Because Bernays was associated with Wilson, this public-relations man has made appearances in right-wing conspiracy theories involving mind control.[25]

To be fair to Bernays's more sane conservative critics, he did often sound like an elitist, technocratic puppet master. "We are dominated by a relatively small number of persons," he wrote, admiringly. "It is they who pull the wires which control the public mind, and who harness old social forces and contrive new ways to bind and guide the world." The consolidation of media ownership in the first decades of the twentieth century promised to make Bernays's dream-factory-of-persuasion a reality. During this time, newspaper chains gained a near stranglehold over publishing, and radio networks dominated the airwaves. Media messages were being steered by a decreasing number of news sources, which greased the wheels for centrally coordinated PR messages. This age of monopolistic media offered many opportunities for trickery, particularly in the world of propaganda and public relations. Today's more decentralized communication landscape has rendered some of Bernays's and Lippmann's methods less effective, though not entirely.[26]

Back in 1955, Bernays succinctly summed up the role of the public-relations man: "the engineer of consent *must create news.*" Lippmann outlined how this could be done. "He arranges a stunt," he wrote, "obstructs the traffic, teases the police, somehow manages to entangle his client or his cause with an event that is already news." A hoax, prank, or PR stunt is like a virus that needs a host body to carry it (such as a big story that is already in the news). Discussing how PR techniques were used to promote women's equality in the early twentieth century, Lippmann wrote, "If the publicity man wishes free publicity he has, speaking quite accurately, to start something. . . . The suffragists knew this, and kept suffrage in the news long after the arguments pro and con were straw in their mouths." Pranks, at their most productive, inspire critical inquiry and thoughtful reflection—goals that were not highly valued by Bernays. Nevertheless, he was happy to use social movements in the service of corporate marketing efforts, such as when he convinced women's liberation activists to march in the New York Easter Parade holding Lucky Strike cigarettes high in the air. Bernays dubbed them "Torches of Freedom," and he enlisted the help of feminist leader Ruth Hale (who, in turn, used the event as an opportunity to advance her own cause). "Our parade of ten young women lighting 'torches of freedom' on Fifth Avenue on Easter Sunday as a protest against woman's inequality caused a national stir," he trumpeted. "Front-page stories in newspapers reported the freedom march in words and pictures."[27]

☙ ☙ ☙

By the turn of the twentieth century, newspapers were being reimagined as instruments that could foster a healthy democracy. This ideal coincided with a mounting faith in empiricism and social-scientific inquiry. There were these objective things called "facts," and it was the role of journalists to transparently transmit them to citizens. Moreover, news was increasingly being compartmentalized into different sections of the newspaper: local news, entertainment, sports, political opinion, and so on. This altered the way reporters framed their stories and described the world. More imaginative forms of journalism—such as hoaxes and sketches—were relegated to sections that weren't explicitly marked as "news," or they were left out completely. Advances in transportation and communication technologies also disrupted older models of journalism. During Thomas Jefferson's presidency, he set out to bolster the country's roadways and canals—pathways that were later used to mount telegraph and telephone lines. At the same time, steam engines were dramatically increasing the speed of travel. By the century's end, those powerful engines made printing presses more efficient, inaugurating a publishing revolution that finally turned newspapers into a genuinely *mass* medium.[28]

As Edward Everett Hale wrote in 1903 about the not-so-distant past, "It seems impossible" to express "how far apart the States were from each other, and how little people knew each other." In 1861, the telegraph network beat the railroads in a race across the country, and London and New York were successfully connected via transatlantic cable in 1866. By the 1920s, the two major telegraph companies rolled out over a million miles of wires, something that quite literally rewired the United States' political and financial systems. In order to keep this economy ticking—including, famously, the Wall Street stock ticker—time had to be better managed. Previously, communities established the time of day on the basis of the position of the sun. "When it was noon in Chicago," media historian Ruth Schwartz Cowan writes, "it was 12:30 in Pittsburgh (which is to the east of Chicago) and 11:30 in Omaha (to the west)." Train schedules were in disarray, so railroad managers and captains of industry lobbied for a law that established four uniform time zones. The capitalists won the Time Wars, despite howls of protest over the imposition of "railway time" and, along with it, industrial norms of punctuality and efficiency.[29]

These technological, cultural, and economic factors changed the face of journalism. The newsroom grew more factory-like, and the massive volume of information flowing through the wires turned news into a valuable commodity. This necessitated a spare economy of language, which further standardized news writing. "If the same story were to be understood in the same way from Maine to California, language had to be flattened out," media scholar James Carey writes. "The telegraph, therefore, led to the disappearance of forms of speech and styles of journalism and story telling—the tall story, the hoax, much humor, irony, and satire." These changes were also prompted by such folks as Richard Adams Locke, Edgar Allan Poe, and Mark Twain. Their shenanigans pushed the news industry to tame its wild side and adopt new codes of professionalism, but these impish impulses couldn't be fully suppressed. As Orson Welles's *War of the Worlds* radio broadcast reminds us, the twentieth century enjoyed its fair share of media hoaxes and pranks—and no decade was marked by mischief more than the 1960s. During this time, the counterculture's alternative network of underground newspapers and freeform FM radio stations crackled with irreverence. A new round of prank blowback was just around the corner.[30]

6

*P*olitical
*P*ranksters

The San Francisco Bay Area house occupied by Ken Kesey served as a communal spot where creative types hung out, took drugs, and pondered the cosmos. From this launching pad, the Merry Pranksters drove their psychedelic vision right into the heart of Middle America. Their famous 1964 road trip was a rolling social experiment, or a "superprank," as Tom Wolfe called it in *The Electric Kool-Aid Acid Test*. Sparks flew after Kesey bought a used school bus that the Pranksters dosed with traffic-accident-inducing swirls of color. They placed a "Caution: Weird Load" sign on the back and "Further" on the destination manifest up front. Kesey's crew wired the bus for sound and cut a hole in the ceiling so they could rock out (or space out) with electric guitars, bass, and drums on the rooftop. They also "rigged up a system with which they could broadcast from inside the bus, with tapes or over microphones, and it would blast outside on powerful speakers on top of the bus." It was a multimedia installation on wheels—equipped to turn on America with feedback, magnetic tape, and LSD. During the magic bus's maiden voyage, pedestrians stopped and stared. Wolfe had an epiphany: "there was going to be holy terror in the land." The same could be said of the Merry Pranksters' Acid Tests, a series of mid-1960s parties they hosted up and down the West Coast. The psychedelic songs of the Grateful Dead, the Acid Tests' house band, complemented light designer Roy Seburn's pulsating projections. It was like a prank on reality, a way to yank people out of their daily routines and imagine a new world of weirdness.[1]

The sixties exploded with pranks and provocations that challenged social conventions. Media was a key ingredient that rabble-rousers used to cook up trouble, and they deftly manipulated underground newspapers and their aboveground, mainstream counterparts. Counterculture activists didn't just publicize their antiestablishment messages with press releases and other traditional techniques; they also staged street-theater actions for an audience of television and newspaper reporters. During the 1968 Democratic National Convention protests, the Youth International Party, or the Yippies, ran wild in Chicago's streets and lobbed quotable sound bites at journalists. A few weeks later, the women who founded the Women's International Terrorist Conspiracy from Hell (WITCH) launched a carnivalesque feminist protest against the Miss America beauty pageant. Several civil rights leaders—from the more moderate Martin Luther King Jr. to Black Panther Party cofounder Huey Newton—used similar methods. While their tactics varied wildly in tone, they all shared the same basic goal of stirring up debate and inciting social change.

The Realist Brings the Weird

In 1958, a decade before Paul Krassner went on to cofound the Youth International Party, he started the *Realist*—a magazine that inspired a generation of satirists and alternative-media moguls. (When *People* dubbed him the "father of the underground press," Krassner shot back, "I demand a blood test.") Several other influences helped build the left's raggedy indie media system—including the early 1960s "Mimeograph Revolution." During this time, a growing number of micropresses pumped out everything from radical political pamphlets to incendiary literary magazines such as Ed Sanders's *Fuck You: A Magazine of the Arts*. In 1964, the *Los Angeles Free Press* debuted and quickly became the first newspaper the youth movement could truly call its own. The underground papers that emerged in its wake connected dispersed local scenes by sharing news, stories, comics, and information. Additionally, the Liberation News Service (LNS) and the Underground Press Syndicate (UPS) functioned as alternative wire services for the counterculture. This communication system also increased the pace at which pranks, hoaxes, and rumors spread. When an inflammatory lie about an American Vietnam War atrocity was planted in an underground paper, LNS cofounder Raymond Mungo came to its defense—insisting that the story was *impressionistically* true, even if it wasn't factual. As far back as Benjamin Franklin's Polly Baker hoax, people have embraced falsehoods when they feel authentic and resonate with their belief systems.[2]

Although other independent publications such as *I. F. Stone's Weekly* and the *Village Voice* debuted before the *Realist*, Paul Krassner's magazine had the biggest impact on the 1960s literary landscape. It pioneered an envelope-pushing style that laid the groundwork for "New Journalists" such as Tom Wolfe; its contributors included Ken Kesey, Kurt Vonnegut, Norman Mailer, Lenny Bruce, and Joseph Heller. Because Krassner launched it with nothing more than a title and some loose change, he relied on friends and favors to keep the magazine afloat in the early days. He reached out to *Mad* magazine art director John Francis Putnam, who designed its logo and contributed a regular column named "Modest Proposals." The *Realist* emerged as an adult analogue to that subversive kid's magazine, and its popularity grew throughout the 1960s—reaching one hundred thousand subscribers at its peak. It had many taglines over the years, but the most apt was "The Truth Is Silly Putty."[3]

Krassner's first prank was inspired by a 1960 news story about a southerner who went ballistic after seeing a black man kissing a white woman on a television program. It turned out that both actors were white, and there was something wrong with the local station's equipment. Nevertheless, the show's sponsor flew in an account executive to give a private screening that proved the kiss was racially pure. If a company would go to such ridiculous lengths to appease a single viewer, Krassner thought, what if hundreds protested? And what if these complaints made zero sense? He targeted an innocuous television program—an NBC game show called *Masquerade Party*—and chose a future airdate when an incident would supposedly take place. Providing his readers with NBC's address, Krassner instructed them to "write a letter complaining about the offensive thing that was said on the program. Use your own wording. *But don't mention anything specific.*" The deluge of letters freaked NBC out, especially because no one could figure out what folks were so up in arms about. The network threatened legal action once it found out what Krassner did, though it never followed through with a lawsuit.[4]

The *Realist*'s infamous red, white, and blue "FUCK COMMUNISM!" poster was a kind of semiotic prank. "At the beginning of the 1960s, FUCK was believed to be so full of bad magic as to be unprintable," novelist and *Realist* contributor Kurt Vonnegut recalled. "COMMUNISM was to millions the name of the most loathsome evil imaginable." By having the two words battle it out in the same sentence, it showed how ridiculous it was for people to react to these words "with such cockamamie Pavlovian fear and alarm." One *Realist* subscriber bought twenty-five posters and had them sent to FBI director J. Edgar Hoover and the John Birch Society. Krassner joked, "If the post office interfered, I would have to accuse them of being soft on communism." Unsurprisingly, "FUCK COMMUNISM!" triggered some unintentionally funny responses. After a student at a midwestern college held it up in a yearbook photo, agitated administrators demanded that the naughty word be airbrushed out. This meant that he would be holding a "COMMUNISM!" poster, so that word was deleted as well. In the end, the student was pictured holding up a blank sign.[5]

The *Realist* was an underground publication, but it occasionally popped up on the mainstream media's radar when Krassner went to extremes. And in 1967, he certainly did with a scandalous piece about John F. Kennedy's death. After the 1963 assassination, the Kennedy clan tapped writer William Manchester to write *The Death of a President*. With JFK conspiracy theories reaching a boiling point, the situation was primed for a prank. "It only worked because it grew organically out of the situation," Krassner explains. "Jackie Kennedy tried to have certain parts of it suppressed and nobody knew *what.*" Speculation intensified after Random House editor in chief Bennett Cerf said the manuscript disclosed "unbelievable things that happened after the assassination." After a redacted version was published in 1967, Krassner was inspired to write and publish "The Parts Left Out of the Kennedy Book." It reprinted sections of the book that had supposedly been censored, such as the following: "During that tense flight from Dallas to Washington after the assassination," Jacqueline Kennedy "inadvertently walked in on Johnson as he was standing over the casket of his predecessor and chuckling."[6]

"That man was crouching over the corpse," Jackie was quoted as saying, "no longer chuckling but breathing hard and moving his body rhythmically. At first I thought he must be performing some mysterious symbolic rite he'd learned from Mexicans or Indians as a boy. And then I realized—there is only one way to say this—he was literally fucking my husband in the throat. In the bullet wound in the front of his throat." The *Realist* piece included handwritten marginal notes that played to growing doubts about the Warren Commission's lone-gunman theory: "Is this simply necrophilia, or was LBJ trying to change entry wound from grassy knoll into exit wound from Book Depository by enlarging it?" This was all too much for Krassner's longtime printer, who refused to touch the issue. After finding a printing house that would, word of mouth spread like wildfire—though the commentary from the mainstream media was confounding. For reporters to convey what made it so controversial, they needed to describe the lurid scenes. That was clearly out of the question, and so the ensuing coverage blended sensationalism and vagueness into a tasty absurdist stew.[7]

United Press International correspondent Merriman Smith issued a cryptic denial. "One of the filthiest printed attacks ever made on a President of the United States is now for sale on Washington newsstands. The target: President Johnson." Smith added, "The language referred to is not conventional hell or damn profanity—it is filth attributed to someone of national stature supposedly describing something Johnson allegedly did. The incident, of course, never took place." This impulse to refute the ridiculous reminded Krassner of another story involving LBJ. One of the president's favorite jokes involved the election of a popular Texas sheriff, whose staff member suggested that they spread a rumor that his opponent "fucks pigs." Another staffer objected, because the candidate actually did not have sex with swine. "I know," came the reply, "but let's make the son of a bitch *deny* it." Krassner gambled that no one would sue him because legal action would imply that LBJ's necrophilia was within the realm of plausibility. The bet paid off. Throughout the

Realist's publishing run, Krassner went out of his way never to label anything as satire because he didn't want to "deprive readers of the pleasure of discerning for themselves whether something was the truth or a satirical extension of the truth." This is yet another example of how pranks can cultivate critical-thinking skills.[8]

Yippies, Hippies, and Hipsters Dial Up the Chaos

"I started doing hoaxes to purposefully make a commentary about people," says Joey Skaggs, who is still at it today. "I thought humor was a great way of making people think, rather than hitting them over the head with something." Instead of pencil, paint, or sculpture, his expressive medium was mass media. For one of his first pranks—what he called a "Cultural Exchange Program"—Skaggs packed a bus full of hippies and took them on a sightseeing tour of suburban Queens. "They reacted like we weren't supposed to be there," he says, "yet it was okay for straights and suburbanites and out-of-towners to come to the East Village with Instamatics and point them at long-haired bearded, beaded people." After the Associated Press picked up the story, Skaggs's prank landed on the front page of most major newspapers. There was plenty more where that came from, such as his "Cathouse for Dogs" project, which began with a classified ad in the *Village Voice*. "CATHOUSE FOR DOGS: Featuring a savory selection of hot bitches," the notice read. "From pedigree (Fifi, the French Poodle) to mutts (Lady the Tramp). Handler and Vet on duty. Stud and photo service available. No weirdos, please." Owners could sit down, have a drink, and take a photo of the dog-on-dog action.[9]

"The response was *unbelievable*," Skaggs says. "I had people willing to pay fifty dollars to have their dog sexually gratified, as well as people who came 'out of the closet'—people who wanted to have sex with dogs, both male and female." On cue, the press came calling, so he hired twenty-five actors to play veterinarians, dog owners, customers, and so on. "The media were there—they were the only ones who weren't actors—and they just took it hook, line and sinker," Skaggs recalls. After the Cathouse debuted, ABC News asked to do a profile, but he couldn't go through the trouble and expense of reproducing the event. "Every hoax I do is like doing a film or a theater piece or a commercial," Skaggs says. "It's conceived, written, produced, directed, staged, acted; there are locations, props—it's very complicated. Rather than do that every time some other media source wanted to see the Cathouse, I provided them with a videotape of the dogs humping." ABC used it as b-roll for a short documentary that got an Emmy nomination for Best Newscast of the Year. City newspapers ran a campaign against the Cathouse for Dogs, as did the ASPCA, the Bureau of Animal Affairs, and the NYPD vice squad. When Skaggs was subpoenaed by the New York attorney general's office, he showed up with his entourage of actors and explained that it was a conceptual art piece. The AG staff was not pleased.[10]

Skaggs emphasizes that the most valuable work comes after the prank—by educating audiences about mass media's role in spreading misinformation. That can be hard, because most news organizations don't like to report on their own follies. For instance, ABC News never retracted its Emmy-nominated story, likely because it didn't want its credibility as a news outlet questioned. "My message is: You're already being pranked every day," he says. "If you think *I'm* the prankster, you are sadly mistaken. I'm just ringing the alarm." Skaggs also emphasizes that he doesn't take money from people who are fooled by his stunts. "Deceit—yes, fraud—no," he says, distinguishing his pointed pranks from criminal cons. The primary goal of Skaggs's spectacles is to encourage dialogue and contemplation, which is why he goes through the trouble of urging news outlets to correct the record once he reveals his ruse. "What worries me is when I'm not able to tell the truth," he says, "when for its own reasons the media doesn't want the truth to be told."[11]

Joey Skaggs wasn't the only counterculture joker of his kind, for the 1960s was bursting with trickster figures who manipulated media. "As a co-founder of the Yippies with Abbie Hoffman and Jerry Rubin," Paul Krassner recalls, "I observed how they were able to manipulate the media to further their antiwar mission. If you gave good quote, you got free publicity." Pranks allow people with few monetary resources to turn media outlets into their own personal megaphone. Hoffman added, "If you don't like the news, why not go out and make your own? . . . Guerrilla news events are always good news items and if done right, people will remember them forever." The Yippies' first great prank targeted the United States Stock Exchange in 1966. Krassner tells me that street-theater performer and gay-rights activist Jim Fouratt came up with the idea, but Hoffman ran with it. "We had $200 in dollar bills—enough to look like a lot of money—and we went and threw them down from the gallery of the Stock Exchange," Hoffman says. "Trading stopped for about six minutes; the tickertape stopped—it was great!" At first the police wouldn't let them in the building, so Hoffman and Rubin loudly accused the cops of being anti-Semitic in front of reporters. Pandemonium erupted after they were grudgingly allowed in. "Stockbrokers weren't used to seeing real money there," Krassner says, "and they immediately switched from screaming 'Pork Bellies!' to diving for dollars."[12]

The Yippies plotted ever-larger spectacles, including, as Krassner puts it, "an event in the nation's capital that would publicly cross-fertilize political protesters with hippie mystics." This 1967 protest/prank brought together the politicized antiwar wing of the counterculture and the spiritual descendants of Ken Kesey's Merry Pranksters. "There were 50,000 warlocks in costumes with noise-makers," Hoffman recalled. "We all drove across the freeways to Virginia and attacked." The *East Village Other* (known as *EVO*) colorfully described it as a "mystic revolution" led by "witches, warlocks, holymen, seers, prophets, mystics, saints, sorcerers, shamans, troubadours, minstrels, bards, roadmen, and madmen." To publicize this antiwar rally, the Yippies held a press conference that demonstrated a (fake) new drug. "So we invented a drug called *Lace*," Hoffman says, which makes "you take your clothes off and fuck! We had it in water guns. We held a Press Conference and demonstrated this with live hippies who fucked in front of all the press. It was a good put-on." *Time* magazine, the *New York Post*, and several other news outlets covered it.[13]

Krassner was to play the reporter who accidentally got sprayed—and laid—but to his dismay he was scheduled to speak at a literary conference at the University of Iowa. While in Iowa City, Krassner procured a bag of cornmeal the Yippies used to encircle the Pentagon for their magic ritual. "We applied for permits to raise the Pentagon 100 feet," Abbie Hoffman said, but the request was rejected. They appealed the ruling, and Krassner tells me that bemused officials finally agreed on a compromise: they could only levitate the Pentagon *three feet* in the air. When Hoffman was arrested while measuring the sides of the Pentagon, he explained to journalists that he was merely "finding out how many witches" they would need. Occult ideas circulated within the counterculture, much like how Spiritualism was associated with feminism, abolitionism, and other progressive causes of the nineteenth century. But with some notable exceptions, the hippies' interest was more aesthetic and intellectual than deeply felt. In the case of the levitation prank, the co-conspirators were inspired by a comment by Lewis Mumford suggesting that peace could only be achieved by expelling the evil embodied in the Pentagon.[14]

"Someone came up with the idea for exorcism and levitation modeled on the Catholic or Episcopalian exorcism," Ed Sanders recalled, "so we said, 'Let's do it.'" The poet-provocateur studied linguistics in college, so he consulted a Hittite book and wrote some "magical" incantations. The event's music was provided by Sanders's riotous band, the Fugs, which wrapped biting political messages in a cloak of satire. "Kill for Peace," performed at that 1967 rally, is positively Swiftian in spirit. The Fugs played on a flatbed truck, weaving chants into their musical performance. "Out, demons, out—back to darkness," Sanders screamed, flashing his Lucifer-tattooed chest. "Ye servants of Satan—out, demons, out!" More tongue-in-cheek incantations followed. "In the name of the Amulets of Touching, Seeing, Groping, Hearing and Loving we call upon the powers of the Cosmos to protect our ceremonies," Sanders howled. "For the first time in the history of the Pentagon, there will be a grope-in within a hundred feet of this place." These "superhumans," *EVO* reported, "cast mighty words of white light against the demon-controlled structure"—that is, until the riot police kicked their teeth in.[15]

The following year, this loose confederation of radicals formed a political party of sorts. "The Yippies themselves were kind of a massive hoax," Krassner says. "I came up with the name, although all I did was give a name to a phenomenon that already existed." He started with the exclamation *yippee!*—a reference to the newly coined word *hippy*—and reverse engineered an acronym. They were young, their movement was international, and it was a party, *man*. "Hippies are dead," Hoffman shouted during their brainstorm session. "Youth International Party—Y I P.—YIP—YIPPIE! We're all jumping around the room, Paul Krassner, Jerry Rubin, and I." The *Realist* and other underground newspapers spread the word about the Yippies' plans to disrupt the 1968 Democratic National Convention (DNC). Soon after, mainstream newspapers ran headlines such as "Yipes! The Yippies are Coming!" Instead of building a sustainable political party, the ragtag gang of Yippies was more interested in moving people to action. "We are faced with this task of getting huge numbers of people to come to Chicago," Hoffman recalled. "How do you do this starting from scratch, with no organization, no money, no nothing? Well, the answer is that you create a myth. Something that people can play a role in, relate to." The key ingredients for a powerful prank are imagination, fun, play, and—last but not least—audience participation.[16]

"Join us in Chicago in August for an international festival of youth music and theater," one announcement read. "Come all you rebels, youth spirits, rock minstrels, truth seekers, peacock freaks, poets, barricade jumpers, dancers, lovers and artists. . . . We will create our own reality, we are Free America." During the DNC, the Yippies ran an actual pig for president (named "Pigasus") and jokingly threatened to dose the entire city's water supply with LSD. Unfortunately for the Yippies, Chicago cops didn't share their sense of humor. The protopunk band MC5 provided the soundtrack for a summer day in Lincoln Park that grew increasingly sinister, culminating in bloody violence later that evening. "Contrary to common legend," writes music journalist Don McLeese, who was there that day, "the MC5 didn't spark a riot with their free concert on the eve of the 1968 convention. They simply lit the fuse, escalating the tension energizing the crowd to a fever pitch of musical militancy as the police encircled the park, with their riot gear and billy clubs, maintaining a stone-faced vigil." That night, the city exploded.[17]

In what became known as the Chicago 8 trial, eight protest leaders—including Abbie Hoffman, Jerry Rubin, and Black Panther leader Bobby Seale—were prosecuted for conspiring to incite riots. Paul Krassner testified as a character witness, but he made a disastrous decision to take the stand while on LSD (as you can imagine, it didn't go well). The presiding judge was the cantankerous Julius Hoffman, whom Abbie Hoffman annoyed by calling him "Uncle Julie," rather than "Your Honor." Defending his lack of formality, the Yippie quipped, "I believe in equality." The defendants wore a variety of costumes throughout the trial, such as Revolutionary War outfits. On another occasion, they came to

139

court dressed in judicial robes. When the judge ordered them removed, they complied, only to reveal Chicago police uniforms underneath. "We came to Chicago in August, 1968, to disrupt the ritual and sham which is ordinarily put over as the democratic process," said defendant Rennie Davis. "Now we are disrupting the ritual and sham which Judge Hoffman calls the judicial process."[18]

Much like how tricksters profane that which society holds most sacred, the Chicago 8 ceremonially defrocked Judge Hoffman and upset the court's stately decorum. During the trial, Abbie Hoffman tried to legally change his first name to Fuck, so that Judge Julius Hoffman would be forced to say the words "Fuck Hoffman." (The Yippie also listed his home address as "Woodstock Nation.") Because of these stunts, he was sentenced to eight months in jail for contempt of court. "When decorum is [political] repression," Hoffman seethed, "the only dignity that free men have is to speak out." And with that furious declaration, the trial came to an end. But before it did, Bobby Seale's outbursts angered the judge so much that he was bound and gagged in his courtroom chair. As the Black Panther Party chairman's co-defendants howled in protest, he was finally jailed for contempt. "This image of Seale," American studies scholar T. V. Reed writes, "the sole black defendant, receiving not blind but shackled and gagged justice in the white man's courtroom played powerfully in the court of black public opinion, confirming the Panthers' longstanding claim that they faced only kangaroo courts, not courts of justice."[19]

MUTUAL ESCALATION

A year before the Chicago 8 conspiracy trial, in the fall of 1967, the Black Panther Party made a dramatic nationally televised debut. Dressed in black berets and leather jackets—and carrying loaded rifles, handguns, and twelve-gauge shotguns—thirty African American men and women entered the California state capitol. Then-governor Ronald Reagan made a quick exit as a Panther shouted, "Look at Reagan run!" The group then returned to the building's steps, where newspaper reporters and network news crews were assembled. Chairman Huey Newton read a statement that began, "The Black Panther Party for Self-Defense calls upon the American people in general and the black people in particular to take careful note of the racist California Legislature which is now considering legislation aimed at keeping black people disarmed and powerless." The Panthers' provocative performance—complete with menacing costumes and props—ensured their access to the nation's airwaves. This scripted drama helped circulate a radical message that would typically never be broadcast through mainstream channels.[20]

At the height of the Black Panther Party's notoriety in the late 1960s and early 1970s, its members grew quite adept at media manipulation. But the black community also had to be won over in practical ways, such as with the Panthers' free-breakfast program, antiheroin crusade, and other public services. They pulled off a mixture of the pragmatic and the playful during a campaign to put a stoplight in an intersection where several children had been run over. Municipal authorities had taken no action, so the Panthers got creative. They informed city officials and the press that, until the stoplight was installed, armed Party members would be stationed on that corner (serving as a revolutionary crossing guard, of sorts). The ploy worked. Plenty of other civil rights leaders used street-theater tactics to make serious points, such as when Martin Luther King Jr. launched a massive protest campaign in Birmingham, Alabama. He knew it would provoke a vicious reaction from the racist commissioner of public safety, who unleashed police dogs and fire hoses. Eugene "Bull" Connor's tactics backfired when those televised images shocked the public and helped shift opinion on racial equality. The violent reality of American racism was often hidden from view, and King's performance shined a cathode-ray spotlight on it.[21]

In what social-movement scholar Doug McAdam described as "a genius for strategic dramaturgy," civil rights leaders harnessed the power of broadcast media. Even Rosa Parks's famous refusal to leave her bus seat was carefully staged by activists. She was not, as the oft-told story goes, a frustrated black woman who simply wanted to sit down after a hard day of work. Parks was the secretary of the local NAACP chapter and a community organizer trained at the progressive Highlander Institute. Nevertheless, this deliberately perpetuated fiction still resonates within the popular imagination. It's a modern-day fairy tale that has inspired people to embrace social justice much more than a fact-checked laundry list of civil rights trivia ever could. Media scholar Stephen Duncombe rhetorically asks, "What's more important, the history lesson or the myth?" Unfortunately, the Black Panthers' confrontational mythmaking resulted in a brutal U.S. government crackdown. Their posturing was one factor that prompted FBI director J. Edgar Hoover to call them the "most dangerous extremist group in America." The 1967 memo that kicked off COINTELPRO (the FBI's new counterintelligence program) stated, "The purpose of this new counterintelligence endeavor is to expose, disrupt, misdirect, discredit, or otherwise neutralize the activities of black nationalist, hate-type organizations and groupings." Undercover-agent provocateurs played a key role, and these "extras" helped turn the Panthers' violent iconography into a self-fulfilling prophecy.[22]

When COINTELPRO targeted an underground newspaper that collaborated with the Detroit Black Panther Party, it resorted to the most juvenile of ideas: a stink bomb. "The Bureau is requested to prepare and furnish to Detroit in liquid form a solution capable of duplicating a scent of the most foul smelling feces available," an internal memo stated. The plan was to force underground papers to "fold and cease publication" by using dirty tricks. The day President Nixon was elected in 1968, an emboldened Hoover directed field operatives to study "New Left-type publications" and to compile lists of advertisers, staffs, and printers. The FBI even created two fake newspapers—*Armageddon News*, in Indiana, and *Longhorn Tales*, in Texas—to promote more moderate views within the counterculture. COINTELPRO agents did use prankish tactics, but they were more like frat-hazing rituals than something that would kick open the doors of perception. This kind of mean-spirited mischief was a common feature of Greek life back when Abbie Hoffman attended college. "I've hated fraternities ever since," he says. "I could see there were good pranks and evil pranks." COINTELPRO definitely fell into the latter category.[23]

The ever-inventive FBI covertly distributed a variety of forgeries: pamphlets, posters, and even a bizarre *Miscegenation*-like hoax, *The Black Panther Coloring Book*. African American children were pictured doing the darndest things—such as wielding knives and guns or killing cops. "The pig is afraid of black children because they are brave warriors," one caption stated; another read, "The only good pig is a dead pig." The FBI designed it to look like an official publication of the Panthers to unnerve their white liberal supporters. In another evil prank, operatives distributed a "Wanted" poster sporting the likenesses of Yippies Paul Krassner and Jerry Rubin. It stated, "The only solution to Negro problems in America would be the *elimination* of the Jews. May we suggest the following order of elimination?" Under photos of Krassner and Rubin was a Nazi-atrocity-invoking caption: "lampshades! lampshades!" It was part of a broader government campaign to drive a wedge between African Americans and Jewish Americans, two groups that were close allies in the early years of the civil rights struggle.[24]

A few COINTELPRO memos struck absurdist tones that resembled Yippie tracts. One emphasized that a plot "must be approached with imagination and enthusiasm if it is to be successful." Another 1968 communiqué planted juicy ideas in the heads of FBI agents. "Some leaders of the New Left, its followers, the Hippies and the Yippies, wear beads and amulets." The memo proposed that "a few select top-echelon leaders of the New Left be subjected to harassment by a series of anonymous messages with a mystical connotation." Attached to the memo was a series of sketches, including a drawing of a beetle accompanied by text engineered to strike fear in the hearts of stoned hippies: "Beware! The Siberian Beetle," one caption warned, while another intoned, "The Siberian Beetle Can Talk." COINTELPRO operatives kept busy writing; after *Life* magazine profiled Krassner, one sent a pseudonymous letter to the editor. "Gentlemen, you must be aware that *The Realist* is nothing more than blatant obscenity. . . . To classify Krassner as some sort of 'social rebel' is far too cute. He's a nut, a raving, unconfined nut." Years later, the Yippie titled his memoir *Confessions of a Raving, Unconfined Nut*.[25]

Feminist Rage and Laughter

As in most counterculture groups of the 1960s, men dominated the Yippies. One minor exception was the Women's Caucus Within the Youth International Party, which formed a Yippie subgroup named SCREWEE!—or "Society for Condemning the Rape and Exploitation of Women, Etc., Etc." But for the most part, women were marginalized from leadership positions in New Left groups. Feminist trailblazer Robin Morgan noted at the time that they were relegated to typing speeches delivered by men and, as she put it, "making coffee but not policy." Ironically, the roles women played mirrored the straight society that chest-thumping radicals claimed they were making a break from. Many leftist men were dismissive and patronizing toward feminist activists or were openly hostile to the cause. One pamphlet published by a chapter of Students for a Democratic Society cluelessly stated, "The system is like a woman; you've got to fuck it to make it change."[26]

The 1968 demonstration against the Miss America Pageant was a turning point for the women's liberation movement. The sisters were doing it for themselves—coordinating with local governments, getting permits, and organizing press events. They designed their "zap action" to provoke a debate about beauty pageants and the patriarchal society that props them up. "There were about thirty-five of us," says Roz Payne, a member of the Newsreel Film Collective. "We got on the bus and traveled down from New York to Atlantic City to have a little fun." To dramatize women's enslavement to "beauty standards," some chained themselves to a gigantic Miss America puppet. They took a cue from the Yippies' pig-for-president campaign by using a sheep to "parody the way the contestants (all women) are appraised and judged like animals at a county fair," as one leaflet stated. "We crowned the sheep Miss America," Payne tells me. "Some men would give us thumbs down. I remember one guy saying, 'I like *the ladies.*'" The *New York Times* reported that the women performed their guerrilla-theater event on the boardwalk for "650 generally unsympathetic spectators."[27]

The action was collaboratively conceived, but Robin Morgan did much of the organizing work. She was a former child actress, and her extensive media contacts helped generate plenty of coverage. Her press release promised "Picket Lines; Guerrilla Theater; Leafleting; Lobbying Visits to the contestants urging our sisters to reject the Pageant Farce and join us; a huge Freedom Trash Can (into which we will throw bras, girdles, curlers . . .)." It slyly added, "In case of arrests, we plan to reject all male authority and demand to be busted by policewomen only. (In Atlantic City, women cops are not permitted to make arrests—dig that!)" A few did get arrested when an "inside squad" of twenty women disrupted the pageant's live broadcast. They screamed "Freedom for Women!" and unfurled a banner that trumpeted "women's liberation," which stopped the pageant for ten excruciating seconds. The television audience could tell something was wrong—Miss America trembled and stuttered after the shouting began—but it was unclear what exactly was going on. Another woman was arrested for spraying the mayor's seating area with Toni hair conditioner, a pageant sponsor. The police arrest report referred to it as a "noxious odor," which wasn't exactly the best product placement for the company.[28]

The women refused to speak with male reporters. Although this was spun by critics as knee-jerk man hating, it was a calculated gesture meant to highlight women's marginalized place in the newsroom. Morgan says, "We estimated correctly that it would raise consciousness about the position of women in the media—and help more women get jobs there (as well as helping those who were already there escape from the ghetto of 'the women's pages')." They had good reasons to distrust mainstream media, especially because the protest's most memorable event—bra burning—never took place. "I never saw a bra burn in my entire life," says Roz Payne, who filmed the Miss America protests. She adds, laughing, "It was probably a man who started that story." Actually, the bra-burning urban legend can be traced to a young female reporter at the *New York Post*. Lindsy Van Gelder wrote an article that drew parallels between the Miss America protest and another contemporary form of mass resistance: draft-card burning. Her satirical article, "Bra Burners and Miss America," backfired after its ironic tone was lost in translation. An annoyed Art Buchwald criticized the protestors in a syndicated column titled "Uptight Dissenters Go Too Far in Burning Their Brassieres."[29]

Bitch magazine cofounder Andi Zeisler reminds us that today's bras are nothing like the ones those women railed against. "Bras, girdles, and—*oof*—nylon hose were both restrictive and compulsory for women in professional settings, and dumping these underpinnings really was a tangible act of defiance." The mental image of bra burning quickly took root in public memory, even though there was no photographic evidence to verify it happened. People just filled in the blanks with their imagination. Robin Morgan noted at the time that the bras tossed in the Freedom Trash Can "was translated by the male-controlled media into the totally fabricated act of 'bra-burning,' a non-event upon which they have fixated constantly ever since." What she didn't say was that event organizers actually *did* plan to set fire to the trash can, but Atlantic City officials denied their permit on the grounds that it was a fire hazard (the boardwalk was made of wood). In feminist historian Alice Echols's history of the movement, she notes that at least one of the organizers, hoping to stir up media interest, leaked word of the planned bra burning to the press beforehand. "Those feminists who sanctimoniously disavowed the bra-burning as a media fabrication," Echols insists, "were either misinformed or disingenuous."[30]

Once the bra-burning meme was unleashed, the women's movement lost control of the narrative, and it was used as a bludgeon to caricature feminism. The organizers also admitted other tactical mistakes. Morgan laments that their flyers, press statements, and public protests didn't make it clear enough that they were not attacking the pageant contestants themselves. It also didn't help that protesters brought their own posters that read "Miss America Goes Down" and chanted victim-blaming slogans such as "ain't she sweet / making profit off her meat." This had the unfortunate effect of alienating some women who might have been brought into the feminist fold. Participant Carol Hanisch recalled, "Posters which read 'Up Against the Wall, Miss America,' 'Miss America Sells It,' and 'Miss America Is a Big Falsie' hardly raised any woman's consciousness and really harmed the cause of sisterhood."[31]

Despite those criticisms, there were plenty of radical feminists who were drawn to Yippie-style shock tactics. "Abbie, Jerry, and Paul called themselves 'The Crazies,'" Roz Payne tells me. "I was good friends with Abbie and Jerry. They were really wild and funny and were people I liked hanging out with." Payne was one of the founding members of WITCH, a.k.a. the Women's International Terrorist Conspiracy from Hell. Though the group originated in New York City, "Covens" soon popped up throughout America. One WITCH leaflet explained, "A certain common style—insouciance, theatricality, humor, and activism—unite the Covens, which are otherwise totally autonomous, and unhierarchical to the point of anarchy." Each cell was free to define WITCH however it wanted, including its acronym. One Coven changed its name to "Women Infuriated at Taking Care of Hoodlums" on Mother's Day. This (dis)organization was conceived when Krassner, Hoffman, and other movement men were called before the House Un-American Activities Committee (HUAC). Roz Payne, Robin Morgan, Peggy Dobbins, Judy Duffett, Cynthia Funk, and about half a dozen other women founded the group. Payne recalls that they dressed as witches and put a hex on the all-male members of the HUAC committee. They asked, "How come we, the real subversives, the real witches, aren't being indicted?"[32]

The most confrontational and carnivalesque WITCH action took place in 1969, at a bridal fair in Madison Square Garden. "There was a wedding event at a convention center near midtown," Payne recalls, "so we caused a little trouble." A WITCH promotional flyer read,

> *Come* witches, gypsies, feminists, students, our black and Puerto Rican sisters, professional women, housewives, welfare women—come all oppressed women of every age and marital status. Come to New York's first *and last* "Bridle Un-Fair." *We will create* our own rituals and festivals, perform our own anti-fashion shows, meet each other and the brides-to-be attending the fair in self-defense against the common enemy. We will distribute WITCH "shoplifting" bags, share free cocoa and experiences, cast spells, celebrate guerrilla theater, and demand an *end* to the patriarchal structure and the profit-oriented society.[33]

During the bridal fair, the witchy women performed an Un-Wedding Ceremony for an unwilling audience. "We promise to love, cherish, and groove on each other and on all living things," they said in unison. "We promise to smash the alienated family unit. We promise not to obey." The witnesses were not amused, especially when the protesters circulated a "Confront the Whoremakers" flyer (which was a play on the then-popular counterculture slogan "Confront the Warmakers"). "Incredibly," Alice Echols writes, "they had not considered the possibility that the women attending the fair might resent WITCH's characterization of them as prostitutes in the making." When the Coven released live mice into the crowd, the brides-to-be didn't jump onto chairs screaming, as the sexist stereotype would suggest. Instead, they scrambled to save the mice. As with the Miss America protests, some of the more pragmatic feminist activists criticized this action for turning off potential converts. Morgan later dismissed WITCH's tactics as "clownish protoanarchism," adding, "[We hadn't] raised our own consciousness very far out of our own combat boots." Morgan's former colleague Roz Payne, on the other hand, sees a place for this sort of activism. "It was a great way of making an impression, and I still do stuff like that. I don't want to just stand there with a sign and chant slogans."[34]

The wild confrontations planned by WITCH and others like them produced some severe blowback effects. First and foremost, the religious right interpreted their spoofs as proof that Satanism and witchcraft were poisoning society. "WITCH was featured in the *New York Times Magazine*," Payne recalls, "though it was for a story about actual witches and interest in the occult that was happening at the time." Andrew Greeley, a Roman Catholic priest affiliated with the University of Chicago's Sociology Department, wrote the article. "There's a New-Time Religion on Campus" opens with one of Greeley's departmental colleagues being hexed by members of a WITCH Coven. "Fie on thee, Morris Janowitz! A hex on thy strategy!" Although Greeley acknowledged that the women's actions contained a mix of the serious and the put on, he still worried, "WITCH is only one manifestation—though a spectacular one—of a resurgence of interest in the occult on the college campuses of the country."[35]

Greeley's piece made a big splash. For years, it and other similar stories were reprinted and disseminated by evangelical churches and conservative organizations. Another article that circulated widely in far-right religious communities was David Emerson Gumaer's "Satanism: A Practical Guide to Witch Hunting." The article was published by the John Birch Society magazine *American Opinion*, and it sarcastically observed that we shouldn't "be concerned when a revolutionary Communist group calling itself the Women's International Terrorist Conspiracy from Hell—the W.I.T.C.H.—makes front-page news for one of its radical forays in New York or Chicago or wherever." On the other side of the Atlantic, in England, Wicca tapped into the sexy Swinging Sixties zeitgeist. Flamboyant personalities such as Gerald Gardner, the self-styled high priest of the contemporary Wicca movement, actively courted the British press (whose bread and butter was sensationalism mixed with a dollop of disapproval). In the 1980s, during the height of the Satanic Panics, Christian radio host Bob Larson warned of a similar threat in his book *Satanism: The Seduction of America's Youth*. In a section titled "Witchcraft and Radical Feminism," he maintained that goddess worship "is one way teenagers, particularly young girls, are being influenced by witchcraft." From Wicca, it was a lubed slippery slope into hell.[36]

𐫱 𐫱 𐫱

We can learn a lot about media and the culture we inhabit by studying the ripple patterns produced by pranks. Tracing these mischievous memes as they weave their way back and forth through underground and aboveground channels shows how alternative and mainstream media are deeply intertwined. This sort of boundary blurring was also on display when the government borrowed tricky tactics from the counterculture, and vice versa—which contributed to a cycle of mutual escalation that pitted the FBI's COINTELPRO operation against the Black Panthers, Yippies, and other outrageous lefty groups. These were crazy, uneasy times. The 1968 assassinations of Martin Luther King Jr. and Robert F. Kennedy rocked America, and the movements for black, female, and gay equality also tore at the social fabric. Illuminatiphobia returned with a vengeance, especially after conservatives misinterpreted the ironic put-ons of those Pentagon-protesting warlocks and wedding-crashing WITCHes. The ensuing prank blowback reshaped America's political map by prompting the "silent majority" to scream bloody murder. Many leaders of the religious right (Pat Robertson, Tim LaHaye, and the John Birch Society's Robert Welch, in particular) genuinely believed that the counterculture was an Illuminati plot. These Christian warriors led a counter-counterculture that was enabled by the independent media systems they helped pioneer. Mass media picked up on these dissonant noises and amplified them, producing a feedback loop that lasted for decades.

*P*rank
*B*lowback

During the 1960s, pranking and paranoia exploded across the political spectrum—from the left, right, and those *Möbius-like* spaces where the two extremes joined up. Right-wing media, in particular, simmered with conspiracy mania. It occasionally bubbled to the surface and was picked up by mainstream media and lefty alternative newspapers before going back underground—only to resurface again, and again, and *again* in the decades that followed. This cycle has been repeating ever since those Rosicrucian pranksters first tweaked conservative church authorities four centuries ago. Each incarnation of the Illuminati myth was shaped by its historical moment, and during the mid-twentieth century, Cold War anxieties added new wrinkles to this grand narrative. Most influential was the brainwashing myth, a meme that entered popular culture in the 1950s through books and films such as *The Manchurian Candidate* and *Invasion of the Body Snatchers*. The John Birch Society adapted these fictions about mind control and synthesized them with paranoid fantasies involving social science, secret societies, witchcraft, and collectivism. The far right wove these threads into an overarching conspiracy theory whose evidence was drawn from a hodgepodge of factual historical events, literary forgeries, satirical pranks, and the products of other unreliable narrators. This condition of suspicion was duly satirized by a group of mind-bending pranksters known as the Discordians. Their irreverent actions, combined with those of other sixties troublemakers, helped fuel a conservative backlash that fundamentally altered America's social and political landscapes.

Just Because You're Paranoid Doesn't Mean Someone Isn't Brainwashing You

The Cold War, a period when communist plots seemingly lurked around every corner, was the backdrop to this madness. During the early 1950s, Americans learned that a majority of captured American POWs signed confessions or petitions calling for the end of the Korean War. There could only be one reasonable explanation for this behavior: *brainwashing*. A 1953 report noted that POWs leaving North Korea via the Soviet Union "apparently had a blank period or period of disorientation while passing through a special zone in Manchuria" (a rumor that later provided the premise for *The Manchurian Candidate*). The CIA-sponsored journalist Edward Hunter tackled this issue in newspaper articles, in books, and as the editor of the psychosocial-warfare journal *Tactics*. In his 1956 book *Brainwashing*, Hunter said that this technique could literally "change a mind radically so that its owner becomes a living puppet—a human robot—without the atrocity being visible from the outside."[1]

Cold warriors such as Senator Joseph McCarthy and FBI director J. Edgar Hoover sounded similar warnings. Hoover believed that a "communist thought-control machine" could wipe out any "undigested lump of independence." Pop culture dramatized this anxiety, especially in the 1956 film *Invasion of the Body Snatchers*. Alluding to the Leninist model of political subversion, one character says, "They're taking you over, cell by cell!" The fiction of mind control also sprung from a growing body of social-science literature that examined the propaganda efforts of Nazis and communists. From this fairly modest starting point, Edward Hunter turned it into a conspiracy of epic proportions. Within a few years, he was characterizing these techniques as a mix of oriental mysticism and hard socialist rationality. Brainwashing, Hunter insisted, was "like witchcraft, with its incantations, trances, poisons, and potions, with a strange flair of science about it all, like a devil cancer in a tuxedo carrying his magic brew in a test tube." This was little more than a Cold War spin on nineteenth-century conspiracy theories about the occult, and it had a quick uptake in conservative anticommunist circles. Several other scholars across the political spectrum—such as MIT's Edgar Schein—also lent this idea credibility.[2]

By the late 1950s, brainwashing had become a powerful cultural fantasy. When the CIA began testing LSD as a psychological weapon, it was a reflex reaction caused in part by Hunter's research. In other words, the CIA fell for its own propaganda! Director Allen Dulles was growing increasingly concerned about the Eastern Bloc's "parrotlike" population. Responding to this "brainwashing gap," he directed secret funds to MK-ULTRA, a project that conducted the LSD experiments. These government men concluded that America's only defense against the communist menace was *tripping* (in fact, it was army scientists who coined the term *trip*, not the counterculture). Starting in the mid-1950s, Technical Support Services quietly began dosing unsuspecting members of the TSS team and other interagency personnel. Surprise acid trips got so out of hand at the CIA that supervisors finally stepped in. The author of a security memo dated December 15, 1954 soberly advised that he did "not recommend testing in the Christmas punch bowls usually present at the Christmas office parties." There would be no government-sponsored electric Kool-Aid acid tests, at least not at holiday celebrations.[3]

A few years later, the CIA cooked up a plan to dose socialist and lefty leaders in other countries with P-1 (the agency's code name for LSD). That way, the logic went, Fidel Castro would speak gibberish to the public and provoke a regime-toppling chain reaction. In 1959, Major General William Creasy—the chief officer of the Army Chemical Corps—testified before Congress. It was a year after Richard Condon's best-selling book *The Manchurian Candidate* was published, and mind-control mania was sweeping the nation. In a session of the House Committee on Science and Astronautics, Representative James Fulton fretted, "What is the test to see whether we are already being subjected to them? Are we under it now?" He continued, "Are we the rabbits and the guinea pigs? . . . How do we know?" Creasy responded that if LSD were administered to members of Congress, "we could possibly have you dancing on the desks, or shouting Communist speeches." Taken aback, Rep. Fulton wanted to know if the CIA had ever tried this experiment on Congress. "I can assure you of one thing," came the army official's dry reply, "the Chemical Corps of the Army has not found it necessary to do it up until now."[4]

The Discordians versus the Conspiracy

The assassination of John F. Kennedy sunk the sanity of many people. One victim was Kerry Thornley, who had the unfortunate luck of being stationed briefly with Lee Harvey Oswald in 1959. Before joining the Marines, Thornley helped create a joke religion called Discordianism with his pal Greg Hill. The pair met in the mid-1950s at California High School, where they bonded by messing with other students (including an elaborate *War of the Worlds*–type hoax played over the school's intercom). Thornley and Hill also loved *Mad* magazine, which served as a touchstone for many countercultural pranksters. Their "religion" was invented in 1957, at a bowling alley. Thornley had been writing juvenile poems about how, through chaos, "order would at last unfold"—but his friend disagreed. Over the clattering of pins, Hill insisted that was impossible. "Order is something that the human mind projects on reality," he said, claiming that *everything* is chaos. The Greeks even had a deity for it: Eris, a troublemaking goddess. Soon after, the two wrote the first draft of the Discordian holy book, *Principia Discordia*. The number of coauthors expanded a decade later when the book evolved into a surrealist chain letter that invited recipients to add their own collaged text and images.[5]

Through the doctrine of Chaos, the Discordians half seriously believed, one could attain higher wisdom by upending the naturalized routines of everyday life. Because their motto was "We Discordians Must Stick Apart," it comes as no surprise that faux factionalism was central to their absurdist belief system. The first major splinter group was the Erisian Liberation Front (ELF), which espoused a more anarchist, antiauthoritarian worldview. Thornley, a.k.a. Ho Chi Zen, led this branch. Malaclypse the Younger, a Hill alias, led the Paratheo-Anametamystikhood of Eris Esoteric (POEE). Its mystical approach was imbued with a heavy amount of silliness.[6]

POEE (pronounced "POEE") is an acronym for the PARATHEO-ANAM-ETAMYSTIKHOOD OF ERIS ESOTERIC. The first part can be taken to mean "equivalent deity, reversing beyond-mystique." We are not really esoteric, it's just that nobody pays much attention to us. . . .

HOW TO BECOME A POEE CHAPLIN
  1. Write the ERISIAN AFFIRMATION in five copies.
  2. Sign and nose-print each copy.
  3. Send one to The President of the United States.
  4. Send one to
        The California State Bureau of Furniture and Bedding
        1021 "D" Street, Sacramento CA 94814
  5. Nail one to a telephone pole. Hide one. And burn the other.
  Then consult your pineal gland.[7]

"Many people consider Discordianism a complicated joke disguised as a religion," said Robert Anton Wilson, another co-conspirator. "I prefer to consider it a new religion disguised as a complicated joke." Wilson was a fledgling writer who, in 1959, began contributing to Paul Krassner's *Realist* after it published his article "The Semantics of God." He asked readers to draw a mental picture of the divine one's private parts. "The Believer had better face himself and ask squarely: Do I literally believe that 'God' has a penis?" Wilson wrote. "If the answer is no, then it seems only logical to drop the ridiculous practice of referring to 'God' as 'he.'" Wilson entered the Discordian universe in 1967 after striking up a correspondence with Kerry Thornley. He recalled how their political philosophies aligned perfectly: "We were both opposed to every form of violence or coercion against individuals, whether practiced by governments or by people who claimed to be revolutionaries." The libertarian-leaning Discordians responded to physical, psychological, and social repression with unbridled absurdity.[8]

It was all fun and games, until Thornley lost his mind. The trouble started on May 18, 1964, when he was called before the Warren Commission to discuss his association with Lee Harvey Oswald. "You might say I was [Oswald's] best buddy," he testified, "but I don't think he had any close friends. I was a close acquaintance." The commission reported that Oswald abruptly broke off ties with his fellow marine after Oswald overreacted to a lighthearted quip. "Well, come the revolution you will change all that," Thornley said when the soon-to-be assassin complained about having to march in a parade. Oswald looked at Thornley "like a betrayed Caesar" and then walked away for good. The commission's report also stated that Thornley "later wrote an unpublished novel in which he drew heavily on his impressions of Oswald." The commission seized *The Idle Warriors* manuscript, and after decades of collecting government archive dust, it was finally published in 1991. (It has the distinction of being the only fictional work written about Oswald *before* 1963.) All told, the star-crossed buddies spent no more than three months together before Thornley was shipped out to Japan. Even though they later lived near each other in the French Quarter neighborhood of New Orleans, the Discordian insisted they never crossed paths.[9]

At the time of Thornley's Warren Commission testimony, he believed Oswald was Kennedy's sole killer, but he later changed his mind. Thornley headed off to New Orleans for several discussions with district attorney Jim Garrison, who opened an investigation into JFK's assassination. Garrison was building a case around the testimony of a few unsavory characters who he claimed had ties to a shadow government. He believed Oswald was a closeted homosexual who conspired to kill Kennedy with the help of the CIA, the FBI, and a gay businessman named Clay Shaw. "Thornley and Garrison did not make a good team, to put it mildly," Wilson recalls. "In fact, at their last interview each told the other to go to hell. Discordianism and law do not mix." Garrison's office subpoenaed Thornley in early 1968. "I feel like I'm going to a mad hatter's tea party," Thornley told a Tampa newspaper after being deposed. A month later, the Discordian wrote much the same in an anxious letter to his old friend Greg Hill:[10]

At the moment I have every reason to believe I may get 20 years in a Louisiana prison for: 1) having gone to USC at the same time [alleged spy] Gordon Novel did; 2) having written a novel based on Oswald which re-inforced [*sic*] his apparent Marxist cover; 3) having been from that point out the victim of either the most fantastic chain of incriminating co-incidences or the most satanically evil plot in history.[11]

155

The New Orleans district attorney filed perjury charges against Thornley for lying under oath and sent out a press release that boldly asserted, "Kerry Thornley and Lee Oswald were both part of a federal operation operating in New Orleans." Because many lefty newspapers were in the thrall of Garrison's JFK conspiracy theories, they parroted these charges against Thornley. Wilson recalled, "In the underground press, Thornley and the other Garrison suspects were pictured as a weird gang of homosexual Satanic CIA Nazi fanatics. It was the McCarthyism of the '50s all over again, coming from the left this time." Thornley pled not guilty but then started introducing himself to strangers in ways that could not possibly have helped his case. "I'm Kerry Thornley," the Discordian would say. "I masterminded the assassination—how do you do?" Later, one of Garrison's aides concluded that the killing of JFK was the work of the Bavarian Illuminati. This was a strange turn of events, given that the Discordians had previously included that secret society in their comic cosmology. The crazy train totally went off the rails after Garrison theorized that the Discordian Society was in reality a clandestine CIA front.[12]

Ironically, Garrison unwittingly aided the production of a key Discordian tract. Back in the early 1960s, the DA employed a friend of Thornley's—who surreptitiously used the office Xerox machine to print an early version of *Principia Discordia*. Little did Garrison know that he too was a dupe of a Discordian/CIA/Illuminati conspiracy! "Synchronicity, by Goddess, was afoot," Wilson says, "and the weirdness was increasing." When Thornley was set to go on trial in 1970, he started to doubt himself. Garrison's investigation, Thornley recalled, "had laid out so many reasons on me for thinking that I was part of the conspiracy that I began very seriously questioning the validity of my own consciousness. I wondered if I was not some kind of Manchurian Candidate or if I had not been drugged or hypnotized to forget my role in the assassination. Fortunately for my sanity, very few 'coincidences' withstood the test of independent research."[13]

Around this time, Thornley created a Do-It-Yourself Conspiracy Kit that included Bavarian Illuminati letterhead stationery and other prankish paraphernalia. The Discordians also started a half-serious secret-society membership drive (the serious part helped raise money for the Kerry Thornley Defense Fund, whose slogan was "Don't let

Garrison wreck the Illuminati!"). "For only five bucks, folks—or a larger donation if you can afford it—you get a Bavarian Illuminati Membership Card, which is to Illuminate the Opposition," Thornley wrote in a letter to his friend Lady L. "You also get other junk and especially some ILLUMINATION STICKERS, which . . . feature the Illuminati Pyramid, and say on them either conspire or (depending on the sticker in question) ILLUMINATE." The Discordians' twisted version of the Illuminati myth was a satire of the far right's longstanding obsession with that mythical secret society. "There simply were no real Illuminati," Wilson observed; "it was all a right-wing fantasy—a sanitized version of the tired old Elders-of-Zion mythology."[14]

TALKIN' JOHN BIRCH PARANOID BLUES

By 1961, the John Birch Society boasted more than one hundred thousand members and had taken command of parts of the Republican Party in California, Arizona, and Texas. Mainstream Republicans such as William F. Buckley openly criticized the Birchers, and predictably, liberal entertainers ridiculed them. Jazz trumpeter Dizzy Gillespie, who was born John Birks Gillespie, made a satirical run for president in 1964 (he organized "John Birks Societies" in twenty-five states). In Bob Dylan's 1962 song "Talkin' John Birch Paranoid Blues," he sings, "Now Eisenhower, he's a Russian spy / Lincoln, Jefferson and that Roosevelt guy." Dylan exaggerated for comic effect when his narrator searched inside his toilet bowl and car glove compartment for "Reds." Nevertheless, the Birchers actually believed Eisenhower was a diabolical communist stooge, or worse. Founder Robert Welch, a former candy manufacturer, insisted the president "had been planted in that position, by Communists, for the purposes of *throwing the game*." Eisenhower, he claimed, was "a dedicated, conscious agent of the Communist conspiracy"—a sinister plot that stretched all the way back to Adam Weishaupt's Bavarian Illuminati.[15]

The original conspirators ("all of whom," Welch reminds us, "were professors") went underground before the French Revolution. Working behind the scenes, these nefarious academics sowed the seeds of socialism and Satanism throughout the nineteenth century. During this time, utopians such as Charles Fourier threatened the traditional order with their progressive vision of the future. Not only did these dreamers attempt to displace Christianity as the center of daily life; their ideas about social engineering were at odds with conservative notions of individual freedom. Fourier advocated communal living, radical social arrangements, and—as the celebrated Illuminatiphobe Nesta Webster fretted—"promiscuous intercourse." He also had an eccentric notion that the "three sexes" (women, men, and children) should eat in different dining rooms within the communes. "They will sometimes eat together in groups of various sizes at lunch or supper," Fourier wrote. "But ordinarily there will be no mixing at dinner, which is a meal during which each of the sexes will engage in its own gastrosophic cabals." This is exactly the sort of rhetoric that drives liberty-loving conservatives nuts, then and now.[16]

Robert Welch outlined the Bavarian Illuminati's monstrous plans, which went far beyond mere gastrosophic cabals. "The purpose of the Order was to rule the world," he said in a 1966 speech. "This incredibly ambitious undertaking was to be conducted as a conspiracy, and secrecy at every point and at all times was of utmost importance." The Illuminati assisted Karl Marx by teaming him with Freemasons and other secret societies that orchestrated European revolutions. "All of these objectives and methods," Welch insisted, "had either been specifically set forth by Weishaupt for his Order of Illuminati, or were the practical applications of his program." By the twentieth century, "there had evolved an inner core of conspiratorial power, able to direct and control subversive activities which were worldwide in their reach." At the center of Welch's alternate reality were the "Insiders," an all-purpose term for an omnipotent "ruling clique." It is essentially the ideological flipside to left-wing sociologist C. Wright Mills's "Power Elite" (though without the empirical evidence). Welch claimed that the Insiders first took control of popular culture by using the brainwashing powers of the novel. Charles Dickens, Upton Sinclair, and Sinclair Lewis were pinned as conspirators, and when radio and television came along, the Insiders seized these media as well. Welch assures us, "it has all been planned that way."[17]

In addition to the anti-Semitic fascist Nesta Webster, the Birchers regularly cited the Judeo-Masonic conspiracy theories of William Guy Carr. His 1958 book *Pawns in the Game* claimed that the Bavarian

Illuminati was the brainchild of a group of rabbis and high priests who followed the teachings of "Lucifer during the performance of their Cabalistic Rites." Citing Webster and her early-twentieth-century contemporary Lady Queenborough, Carr claims that Weishaupt conspired with Rothschild moneylenders. This prominent family of Jewish bankers followed "the age-old 'protocols' designed to give the Synagogue of Satan ultimate world domination." Carr's turn of phrase "Synagogue of Satan" was an artifact of Léo Taxil's extended prank on French Catholic right-wingers, and it wasn't the only time Carr cited one of his hoaxes. *Pawns in the Game* also credulously quoted the "Secret Instructions" allegedly authored by Freemason Albert Pike (but which were actually written by Taxil). The unhinged author wrote, "Can any thinking person deny that the conspiracy as revised by Weishaupt in the latter 1700's, and the plans drawn up by Pike in the latter 1800s, haven't matured exactly as intended?"[18]

The John Birch Society's massive publishing operations disseminated these ideas far and wide. Robert Welch's articles and speeches kept Carr's basic arguments intact but sanitized the anti-Semitism by deleting his references to "the Synagogue of Satan," "International Bankers," and "Jewish influence." Rather than blaming the creation of the Federal Reserve on the Jews, as Carr did, Welch attributed it to "highly placed Marxian influences in the Woodrow Wilson administration." The John Birch Society was sometimes characterized as a right-wing hate group, but it actually did go out of its way to recruit members of other races and religions. However, Welch didn't do himself any favors by asserting that Vladimir Lenin was the true author of *The Protocols of the Elders of Zion*. He claimed that Lenin and his allies planted the document among anticommunist sympathizers as part of an evil long-range plan to discredit conservatives. In a twisted kind of pretzel logic, Welch claimed some right-wingers hated Jews because they had been *tricked* into doing so. Leftists, he asserted, worked "both sides of this 'anti-Semitic' battleground in their efforts to weaken or destroy The John Birch Society."[19]

OPERATION MINDFUCK GETS OUT OF HAND

Accused conspirator Kerry Thornley amused himself while under indictment by kicking off a mind-bending Discordian Society propaganda campaign. Under the pseudonym Lord Omar Khayyam Ravenhurst, he sent missives on Bavarian Illuminati letterhead to organizations such as the Christian Anti-Communist Crusade. "We're amused you've discovered that we've taken over the Rock Music business. But you're still so naïve," he wrote. "We took over the business in the 1800s. Beethoven was our first convert." The Discordians stirred up trouble by, as Robert Anton Wilson put it, "issuing position papers offering non-violent anarchist techniques to mutate our robot-society." They planted stories in the underground press about how the Discordian Society had been waging a long-running, centuries-old war against the Ancient Illuminated Seers of Bavaria (AISB). Wilson recalls, "We accused everybody of being in the Illuminati—Nixon, Johnson, William Buckley Jr., ourselves, Martian invaders, all the conspiracy buffs, *everybody.*" It was an irreverent sociological research project, an attempt to figure out how conspiracy theories are born and spread. The Discordians experimented by dropping pebbles in the proverbial pond and then observed the ripple patterns that were created as the memes morphed and spread.[20]

They didn't view their behavior as conventional hoaxing. It was "guerrilla ontology," says Wilson, who gave it a more colloquial name: Operation Mindfuck. They hoped that "some less gullible souls, overwhelmed by this embarrassment of riches, might see through the whole paranoia game and decide to mutate to a wider, funnier, more hopeful reality-map." The turbulence of 1968 kicked their experiment into high gear. Wilson and Thornley wrote a pseudonymous letter that claimed the Illuminati was responsible for the assassinations of Martin Luther King Jr. and Robert F. Kennedy. They published the letter, along with an accompanying answer, in the "Forum" section of *Playboy* (which Wilson edited at the time). "I recently heard an old man of right-wing views—a friend of my grandparents—assert that the current wave of assassinations in America is the work of a secret society called the Illuminati," it stated. "At first all this seemed like a paranoid delusion to me. Then I read in *The New Yorker* that Allan Chapman, one of Jim Garrison's investigators in the New Orleans probe of the John Kennedy assassination, believes that the Illuminati really exist."[21]

New exposés began popping up in both lefty underground papers and conservative newsletters. A 1969 article in the *Los Angeles Free Press* reported on the "Black Mass," a supposed Afro-Discordian conspiracy that Wilson, Thornley, and the rest of the gang had nothing to do with. Then, in 1970, the John Birch Society's *American Opinion* magazine published an article that further stirred the pot. Sticking to the age-old script, author David Emerson Gumaer linked the Illuminati, Satanists, and Communists in a plot to overthrow capitalism and Christianity. But in a pattern that has become all too familiar by now, some of Gumaer's "evidence" was based on pranks and misunderstood satires. The impish acts of the Discordians, WITCHes, and other like-minded troublemakers deepened the siege mentality that coursed through the fringes of the political spectrum. It is interesting to note that the far right and far left mirrored not only each other's extreme rhetorical styles but also the media technologies they employed. For example, evangelical churches and antiwar radicals each used mimeograph machines and other cheap reproduction technologies to spread their messages.[22]

When Operation Mindfuck was going full steam, Robert Shea and Robert Anton Wilson began writing their cult classic, the *Illuminatus!* trilogy. It drank from the rich well of Illuminatiphobia. The first book of the series was dedicated to Discordian co-creators Thornley and Hill, and its epigraph was taken from Ishmael Reed's 1972 novel *Mumbo-Jumbo*: "The history of the world is the history of the warfare between secret societies." Shea explained in 1976, "*Illuminatus!* began with the idea of satirizing conspiracy mania." The book depicted several assassination teams racing to kill John F. Kennedy in Dealy Plaza and also floated the theory that Adam Weishaupt went to Virginia, murdered George Washington, and assumed his identity. Parodying the obsessive style of conspiracy researchers, Shea and Wilson supported this claim with several citations—including an innocuous NBC press release for a program called *Meet George Washington*, which mentioned that no one is sure what he truly looked like. "Contemporary portraits of the first President," it stated, "do not even seem to be the same man." Shea and Wilson also made much of the fact that Washington/Weishaupt wrote in his diaries about separating "the Male from the Female hemp" (implying that he and the other Founders were under the influence of the devil's weed).[23]

The *Illuminatus!* trilogy's barely comprehensible "plot"—about the Illuminati's plan to slaughter the audience at a rock festival held in

Ingolstadt, Bavaria—weaves together several conspiracy-theory staples. The book blurs fiction and nonfiction, reality and fantasy, in excerpts such as this:

ILLUMINATI PROJECT: MEMO #13

J.M.:

The survival of the Bavarian Illuminati throughout the nineteenth century and into the twentieth is the subject of *World Revolution* by Nesta Webster (Constable and Company, London, 1921). Mrs. Webster follows Robison fairly closely on the early days of the movement, up to the French Revolution, but then veers off and says that the Illuminati never intended to create their Utopian anarcho-communist society: that was just another of their masks. . . . I see no way of reconciling this with the Birchers' thesis that the Illuminati has become a front for the Rhodes Scholars to take over the world for *English* domination.[24]

Much of the Illuminati research popularized by Pat Robertson would feel at home in *Illuminatus!* The tone is equally ridiculous (though in the televangelist's case, the humor is unintentional). Exhibit number one: "[Weishaupt's] conspiracy was sufficiently successful from that point on to use French Freemasonry as a vehicle for placing members of the French Illuminati into key governmental positions." Exhibit number two: "This lodge, in turn, was made up of Rosicrucians—high Freemasons— and its preoccupation was mourning the death of the feudal system." You might have a hard time telling which passage is Robertson's and which is deadpan satire (for the record, the latter quote is from *Illuminatus!*). Shea and Wilson also heavily drew on *Principia Discordia*, and they incorporated many of the real-life pranks perpetrated by Thornley's motley crew. Greg Hill described *Illuminatus!* as "a rare example of extended and sustained Discordian art, and also makes an exemplary textbook of Discordian theory and practice." Timothy Leary loved this satire. The psychedelic guru told Wilson that his "experiences with the DEA, FBI, CIA, PLO, Weather Underground, Mansonoids, Aryan Brotherhood, Al Fattah, etc., were precisely like the most absurd parts of *Illuminatus!*"[25]

Thomas Pynchon's *Gravity's Rainbow*, Ishmael Reed's *Mumbo Jumbo*, and other 1970s novels also wrestled with conspiracy culture. The era's unease was also on display in popular motion pictures such as *The Parallax View* and *Three Days of the Condor* (whose main character sums up the zeitgeist: "Maybe there's another CIA *inside* the CIA.") These films departed from Hollywood conventions by making the U.S. government the bad guy. The Watergate scandal, the Pentagon Papers, and revelations about corporations covering up unsafe products created a fretful, uneasy feeling. Thomas Hine writes in *The Great Funk*, his cultural history of the 1970s, "Sometimes it seemed that rational thought had ventured into the Bermuda Triangle, that area in the Atlantic where, it was believed, boats and airplanes disappeared without a trace." Robert Shea later lamented, "Conspiracy mythology is a cop-out. . . . It's a way of evading our responsibility for history." To a certain extent, however, Shea and Wilson ended up reinforcing the very thing they were critiquing. Their mix of libertarianism, anarchism, mysticism, and sexual experimentation sometimes undercut their book's subversive pretentions. At its worst—in the way it embodied the regressive gender politics typical of the counterculture—the *Illuminatus!* trilogy was little more than a nerdy adolescent male's wet dream. But at its best, the book offered a blueprint for decades of mind-expanding pranks.[26]

Unfortunately for Thornley, this conspiracy-soaked alternate universe drove him insane. "We were all having a lot of fun with Discordianism," Wilson recalled. "None of us were aware, yet, that Operation Mindfuck could get out of hand." After Thornley had been targeted by the New Orleans district attorney for five years, the charges against him were finally dropped in 1973 when Jim Garrison lost an election to Harry Connick, Sr., the father of the jazz-pop singer (somewhere out there, there must be a JFK conspiracy theory involving Harry Connick Jr.—if not, someone needs to invent one, *ASAP!*). Thornley kept obsessing, and obsessing, believing that he had been set up like Lee Harvey Oswald. "At one point," Wilson recalled, "he went to a hypnotist to attempt to discover if Naval Intelligence could have brainwashed him, erased the memory of that, and controlled him for years." Thornley's letters to his friend became more unhinged, and by the late 1970s he insisted that "Robert Anton Wilson was murdered and replaced by a double on orders from Gerald Ford." He also became convinced, as was Garrison, that CIA agents really did infiltrate the Discordian Society and use it as a front for their assassination bureau.[27]

"The logic of this was brilliant in a surrealistic, Kafkaesque sort of way," Wilson says. "Try to picture a jury keeping a straight face when examining a conspiracy that worshipped the Goddess of Confusion, honored Emperor Norton as a saint, had a Holy Book called 'How I Found Goddess and What I Did to Her After I Found Her,' and featured personnel who called themselves Malaclypse the Younger, Ho Chi Zen, Mordecai the Foul, Lady L, F.A.B., Fang the Unwashed, Harold Lord Randomfactor, Onrak the Backwards, *et al.*" Wilson said he stopped speaking to Thornley because "it's hard to communicate with somebody when he thinks you're a diabolical mind-control agent and you're convinced that he's a little bit paranoid." Greg Hill told an interviewer that the two high school friends once discussed how their choice of deity—Eris, the goddess of discord—became a self-fulfilling prophecy. "You know," Thornley told him, "if I had realized that all of this was going to come *true*, I would have chosen Venus." His mental health deteriorated along with his physical well-being, and in 1998 Thornley died in an Atlanta hospital. At his memorial service, longtime friend Barbara Joye lovingly quipped, "Kerry had the best sense of humor of any paranoid schizophrenic I ever knew."[28]

A False Report from Iron Mountain

The Report from Iron Mountain: On the Possibility and Desirability of Peace emerged from the same milieu that pushed Kerry Thornley over the edge. This was, after all, the decade that produced the catchphrase "Just because you're paranoid doesn't mean they aren't out to get you." When *Iron Mountain* was published in 1967, this alleged government document was discussed everywhere from mainstream and underground media to serious sociology and political science journals. Five years later, the writer Leonard Lewin stepped forward to claim authorship of this lefty lampoon, and then it descended into obscurity. That should have been the end of the story, but by the early 1990s members of the far right were snapping up out-of-print editions. When those ran out, the Liberty Lobby and others began pirating it. In 1995, the *Wall Street Journal* ran a front-page story about how the patriot militia movement had embraced *Iron Mountain* as a "sort of bible." It was widely read in fringe circles alongside William Pierce's racist novel *The*

Turner Diaries and Pat Robertson's *The New World Order*. "The book is, of course, a satirical hoax," Lewin wrote in the 1996 reprint of *Iron Mountain*, "a fact not so obvious in 1967 when it first appeared and, disturbingly, still lost on some people today."[29]

"Its acceptance by super-patriots and conspiracy theorists of the far right," said Victor Navasky, who played a role in publishing the book, "is roughly akin to the Irish Republican Army considering Jonathan Swift's *A Modest Proposal* proof that eating babies is official British policy." Navasky (who went on to edit the *Nation*) was the editor and publisher of *Monocle*, a magazine of political satire that was active during the late 1950s and early 1960s. Its writers and editors had an irreverent streak. For instance, Navasky recalls that "when J.F.K. failed to integrate publicly assisted housing with 'a stroke of the presidential pen,' as he had promised he would, we started the Ink for Jack campaign, urging our subscribers to deluge the White House with bottles of ink." When *Monocle* folded, members of the editorial board paid back their creditors by writing quickie books for the thriving paperback market. They published *The Illustrated Gift Edition of The Communist Manifesto*, *The Beatles, Words without Music*—a transcribed collection of the Fab Four's press conferences—and *The Report from Iron Mountain*.[30]

Iron Mountain was originally inspired by a 1966 *New York Times* article about a "Peace Scare" that created a temporary downturn in the stock market. This unintentionally funny story, Navasky said, was "worthy of Jonathan Swift, H. L. Mencken, Mark Twain." The *Monocle* editorial board hatched the idea to fake a suppressed government report commissioned by the JFK administration. "To give the book credibility we needed an ultra-respectable mainstream publisher," Navasky wrote, "but one with a sense of humor and the pluck to pull off a hoax." Dial Press agreed to publish *Iron Mountain* sight unseen and placed it in the nonfiction section of its catalog. Satirizing the prose style of think tanks such as the RAND Corporation, the book's introduction dryly emphasized the importance of writing "about war and strategy without getting bogged down in questions of morality." *Iron Mountain*'s treatment of the conflict in Southeast Asia was similarly ironic: "The Vietnam war alone has led to spectacular improvements in amputation procedures, blood-handling techniques, and surgical logistics." The introduction concluded with the following summary of the benefits of war.[31]

1. *Economic.* War has provided both ancient and modern societies with a dependable system for stabilizing and controlling national economies. . . .

2. *Political.* The permanent possibility of war is the foundation for stable government; it supplies the basis for general acceptance of political authority. . . .

3. *Sociological.* War, through the medium of military institutions, has uniquely served societies, throughout the course of known history, as an indispensable controller of dangerous social dissidence and destructive antisocial tendencies. . . .

4. *Ecological.* War has been the principal evolutionary device for maintaining a satisfactory ecological balance between gross human population and supplies available for its survival. . . .

5. *Cultural and Scientific.* War-orientation has determined the basic standards of value in the creative arts, and has provided the fundamental motivational source of scientific and technological progress.[32]

A reporter for the *New York Times*, John Leo, spotted the listing in the Dial catalog and inquired if it was a hoax. The publisher told Leo that if he felt it was a fraud, he should look into the footnotes, which checked out, so he inquired with government agencies. An official from the State Department's Arms Control and Disarmament Agency issued a vague denial: "To our knowledge no such special study group ever existed." When Leo called the White House, he got a "no comment," which further fueled speculation. The *Times* ran a front-page news story on *Iron Mountain*, and later that year the paper published a book review that noted, "It is, of course, a hoax—but what a hoax!—a parody so elaborate and ingenious and, in fact, so substantively original, acute, interesting and horrifying, that it will receive serious attention regardless of its origin." Henry Kissinger took the joke personally and called *Iron Mountain* idiotic, while RAND Corporation president Henry S. Rowen dismissed it as a clunky satire that missed its mark.[33]

Leonard Lewin finally admitted that he wrote *Iron Mountain* in a 1972 *New York Times Book Review* essay. It came on the heels of a few recently leaked documents such as the Pentagon Papers, which exposed the government's lies about the Vietnam War. Lewin said he was inspired to confess because those genuine leaks seemed more like parodies of *Iron Mountain*, rather than the reverse. Some people continued to believe it was the real deal, including a national-security aide to the Kennedy administration named Colonel Fletcher Prouty. He later worked as an adviser for Oliver Stone's 1991 feature *JFK*, which used New Orleans district attorney Jim Garrison as its lead character. (The film's shadowy government whistleblower played by Donald Sutherland was modeled after the colonel.) Prouty's book *JFK: The CIA, Vietnam, and the Plot to Assassinate John F. Kennedy* is laced with many credulous references to the fictional Special Study Group. "All leaders of all nations know that, as stated in *Report from Iron Mountain*, 'The organization of a society for the possibility of war is its principal political stabilizer,'" he writes. The colonel convinced himself that Lewin had merely fictionalized real events, which explains his bizarre claim that *Iron Mountain* was actually a "novel."[34]

Prouty said the Special Study Group was an "organization whose existence was so highly classified that there is no record, to this day, of who the men in the group were or with what sectors of the government or private life they were connected." He of course was overlooking the most obvious answer: this group only existed in the mind of Leonard Lewin! Oliver Stone is similarly delusional when he writes, "The key question of our time, as posed in Colonel Prouty's book, comes from the fabled *Report from Iron Mountain on the Possibility and Desirability of Peace* by Leonard Lewin." Because Lewin revealed his prank decades before, his use of the word "fabled" is ironic, or merely moronic. Some of *Iron Mountain*'s prose was incorporated into *JFK*'s dialogue, which means Oliver Stone's film—which claims to uncover the truth—is based on a fictional satire posing as a footnote-slathered nonfiction title. No wonder Prouty, Stone, and patriot militia members all had their brains scrambled. *Iron Mountain* was so perfectly pitched that it had Birchers and neo-Nazis dancing in unison with JFK-obsessed lefties and Hollywood liberals.[35]

After Lewin discovered that far-right groups were bootlegging his book, he sued them for copyright infringement. In an ingenious move, the militias defended their actions by arguing that *Iron Mountain* really, *really* was a government document. (Works produced by federal agencies are public domain, which means there is no copyright to infringe.)

Lewin prevailed in court, but the legal struggles over *Iron Mountain*'s authorship nevertheless demonstrate how difficult it is to disprove a conspiracy theory. In the book *Conspiracy against God and Man*, Bircher Clarence Kelly mournfully writes that true believers "are the victims of a conspiracy of silence when they are not made the objects of witch hunts (as McCarthy in his time and The John Birch Society have been)." Similarly, Pat Robertson laments, "Authors who expose subversive secret organizations are usually ridiculed because, when asked for proof of the identity of participants in secret societies, they have to answer, 'That is impossible, since the names are secret.'" Conspiracy theories are inherently unfalsifiable, and any attempt to disprove a nefarious plot is considered suspect.[36]

Recall the discussion of the *Realist*'s "Parts Left Out of the Kennedy Book" prank in the previous chapter. Lots of folks bought Paul Krassner's big lie about LBJ having intercourse with JFK's bullet wound. "Lyndon Johnson's peculiar behavior on Air Force One was a metaphorical truth," he notes, "yet it was perceived as literal truth by literate people." An ACLU official, a Peabody Award–winning journalist, members of the intelligence community, and several others fell for it. Daniel Ellsberg, the man who leaked the Pentagon Papers, admitted to the *Realist* editor, "Maybe it was just because I *wanted* to believe it so badly." Krassner adds, "I also received a call from Ray Marcus, a critic of the Warren Commission Report, who had discovered a chronological flaw in my article. . . . Marcus deduced that *The Realist* must have been given the excerpts by a CIA operative in order to discredit *valid* dissent on the assassination." After Krassner revealed that it was a prank, many people assumed the CIA pressured him into retracting the story. Similarly, Lewin's confession that he authored *Iron Mountain* was seen as proof of a cover-up. As any good conspiracy theorist knows, it's the oldest trick in the book.[37]

BEHOLD A PALE HORSE

Aside from Pat Robertson's *The New World Order*, William Cooper's *Behold a Pale Horse* was the most influential conspiracy book of the 1990s. This doorstop of a paperback became a word-of-mouth hit after it was published in 1991, moving hundreds of thousands of units. It is a dizzying mix of fact and fantasy that draws from all the usual suspects: Robison's and Barruel's late-eighteenth-century urtexts, conspiracy classics by Nesta Webster and Lady Queenborough, and the John Birch Society's vast publishing output. *Behold a Pale Horse* also extensively quotes from a newer entry in the conspiracy canon—you guessed it—*The Report from Iron Mountain*. (Once again, a satirical prank was transformed into proof of a satanic scheme.) America's steady swing to the right primed a receptive audience to embrace Cooper's book. In 1994, during the rise of the patriot militia movement, the Oklahoma state legislature went so far as to pass a resolution calling on the U.S. Congress "to cease any support for the establishment of a 'new world order' or any form of global government." A year later, Timothy McVeigh blew up the Oklahoma City Federal Building in a first strike against this impending takeover.[38]

McVeigh was a fan of William Pierce's 1978 cult novel *The Turner Diaries*, which gained thousands of new followers in the 1990s. It told a story, set in 2099, about a white terrorist group called the Organization. Its members battled the System, a Jewish-run cabal propped up by armies of angry black men and the federal government (which banned all firearms under the Cohen Act). In a case of life imitating art, if you can call *The Turner Diaries* "art," the Organization's first major act was blowing up an FBI building. An extremist named Ray Lampley also embraced *The Turner Diaries*. He was a founder of the Universal Church of God and the Oklahoma Constitutional Militia, which networked with other militias and white-supremacist groups. In 1994, Lampley began sending out unhinged newsletters—with the confident tagline "Revealing Events Before They Occur"—that detailed dreadful events just over the horizon. Unlike some who hedge their bets with vague forecasts, the self-proclaimed "Prophet of the Most High God" was quite specific. "08/21/94 Activities: 30 Days until the blood-red moon. 16 days until the Jewish Feast of Trumpets and the False Messiah." In the first week of October, Lampley predicted, "PLAGUES OF DESTRUCTION CONTINUE TO FALL ON THE EARTH. YOU SHOULD CONTINUE TO REMAIN INDOORS."[39]

What followed came straight out of the Judeo-Masonic conspiracy-theory playbook, by way of the John Birch Society. Lampley warned of an all-out assault on the United States coordinated by a UN-backed coalition of Russian and Asiatic forces. "The American people are quickly waking up and the New Worlders know it," he wrote on August 12, 1994. "The planned invasion we spoke of will come to pass before September 23rd, this year." Lampley grew more urgent a couple of weeks later. "We are getting reports that the Communist/Edomite/Sodomite-loving federal government in Washington, DC, is preparing to begin its attacks upon American people." The assault would be coordinated by the U.S. government's Multi-Jurisdictional Task Force and carried out by sheriff's departments and Postal Service employees. Lampley said there were already 650,000 foreign troops moving on American highways and many more just over the border in Mexico. In making these claims, the millenarian militiaman recycled right-wing fears of a borderless North American government. Back in 1963, Republican Thomas R. Kuchel (then the minority whip of the Senate) said he received about six thousand letters *a month* warning of such plots. One claimed "35,000 Communist Chinese troops bearing arms and wearing deceptively dyed powder-blue uniforms, are poised on the Mexican border, about to invade San Diego."[40]

A few days after Lampley's predictions did not come to pass, he sent out one last mailing. "I made a mistake," he admitted. "The blame for this is not going to be placed on my co-workers here at the office. I am solely responsible for pushing the concept that we would see a blood-red moon before the Messiah returns. . . . I do not feel good about this at all." This wasn't the first false prediction of its kind. A New England farmer named William Miller claimed the Rapture would take place on March 21, 1844. After that date passed, his followers endured jeers from people on the street: "We thought you'd gone up!" or "Wife didn't go up and leave you behind to burn, did she?" Regardless, the Millerites remained confident that Judgment Day was coming. Sociologists have noted that strong ties to a like-minded community can maintain beliefs, though this faith can't survive forever. After Prophet Miller's revised prediction failed to transpire, Millerism crashed and burned on October 22, 1844. "Our fondest hopes and expectations," one adherent cried, "were blasted." As for Ray Lampley, the world would unfortunately hear from him one more time. As with the Millerites, his failed prophecy did not dampen the convictions of his followers, who adopted a bunker mentality. A year later, Lampley, his wife, and two others were arrested for plotting to bomb gay bars, abortion clinics, and civil rights groups such as the Southern Poverty Law Center. They were convicted on all counts.[41]

A sinister cast of characters populated the conspiracy theories that the 1990s patriot movement embraced. The Rothschilds, the Rockefellers, the Bilderberg Group, the Council on Foreign Relations, and Cecil Rhodes's English Round Tables all made frequent appearances. But for many people in the movement, the Rothschild family was the most satanic. Since the nineteenth century, that family has been singled out as the archetype of Jewish banking power. In *The New World Order*, Pat Robertson sticks to the script by linking together the occult, high finance, and Judaism. "It is reported that in Frankfurt," he writes, "Jews for the first time were admitted to the order of Freemasons." Robertson also claims that the Rothschilds took control of the Bavarian Illuminati and worked their wicked magic throughout Europe. But as I pointed out in chapter 4, many of his sources were drawn from a mixture of pranks, hoaxes, satires, and genuine historical documents. Not surprisingly, Robertson fell for Léo Taxil's most notorious fabrication. His book credulously discusses the "Secret Instructions" supposedly authored by Albert Pike (the evil Freemason who maintained an underground telephone network operated by devils).[42]

In addition to Robertson's *The New World Order*, Pike also shows up in William Cooper's *Behold a Pale Horse*. This confused, confusing book also reprints the entirety of the *Protocols of the Elders of Zion*, but with a twist. In the author's note, he says that the document actually dates back to the late 1700s and that everything contained in it has come to pass. Cooper tells readers that the word *Zion* should be replaced with *Sion* and that *Jews* should be substituted with the word *Illuminati*. In addition to standard-issue New World Order conspiracy theories, Cooper claimed aliens forged a secret pact with the U.S. government to use humans in mind-control experiments. These eerie ideas infected mainstream media like a virus. Discussing the popular 1990s television show *The X-Files*, journalist Jeff Chang writes, "Fox Mulder's Cooper-esque rantings about one-world government, master-race plotters, alien abductees, secret torture chambers and Tuskegee-style bioterror experiments felt realer than reality, a speculative history of the Cold War in which the actual struggle had always actually been between the leaders and the people, the Illuminati and the cattle, the one-worlders and the sheeple."[43]

The case of *The X-Files* serves as another example of how alternative and mainstream media are entangled in a dialogic relationship. This prime-time network television show fed on ideas that quietly circulated via small publishing houses, talk radio, and the Internet. In doing so, *The X-Files* led some audience members back to the obscure source material that originated in underground media. The online world, which at the time was much more of a marginal medium, played a huge role in accelerating the spread of New World Order and Illuminati conspiracy theories. It was used by radical groups on the left and right to communicate with other believers and to win new converts. William Cooper, for instance, hosted one of the Internet's first streaming talk shows, which was also broadcast through the much-older technology of shortwave radio. On his show—and in *Behold a Pale Horse*—Cooper declared that the Federal Emergency Management Agency was planning a coordinated assault on American democracy. (Considering FEMA's incompetent response to Hurricane Katrina in 2006, it's difficult to conceive how that agency could pull off such a feat.)[44]

This assumption about FEMA's omnipotence highlights how conspiracy theories rely on a perfect model of communication—one that doesn't allow for mistakes, misunderstandings, chance occurrences, and failure. In this dystopia, plans are flawlessly executed with the help of Masonic long-distance relay runners, devilish telephone systems, Cold War mind-control techniques, and, more recently, the hypnotizing rhetoric of President Barack Obama. The only way to uncover these secret plots is to carefully study signs and symbols hidden in plain view, whether they are pyramids on the dollar bill or statues outside Rockefeller Center. The following passage by William Cooper illustrates this habit of mind. "The numbers 3, 7, 9, 11, 13, 39 and any multiple of these numbers have special meaning to the Illuminati," he writes. "The Constitution has 7 Articles and was signed by 39 members of the Constitutional Convention. The United States was born on July 4, 1776. July is the 7th month of the year. Add 7 (for July) and 4 and you have 11; 1+7+7+6=21, which is a multiple of 3 and 7. Add 2+1 and you get 3. Look at the numbers in 1776 and you see two 7s and a 6, which is a multiple of 3." Then comes the kicker: "Coincidence, you say? I say, 'Baloney!' and I'd really like to say something a lot stronger."[45]

By the late 1990s, Cooper became more closely affiliated with the militia movement, and his delusions were inflamed by an ongoing conflict with the Internal Revenue Service. He believed he was being singled out by "The Illuminati Socialist President of the United States of America, William Jefferson Clinton" and the "bogus and unconstitutional Internal Revenue Service." By 2001, Cooper holed himself up in a trailer home in a desolate part of Arizona. He lived out the rest of his days with his dogs, a chicken, a rooster, and shortwave radio. When two Apache County sheriffs came to arrest him for an outstanding warrant, he was shot dead on November 5, 2001, after killing one of the officers. This incident forever secured William Cooper's martyr status among high-plains tax protestors. Illuminatiphobia enjoyed a revival during Bill Clinton's presidency, but it was the election of Barack Obama in 2008 that pushed these fantasies over the top.[46]

A Right-Wing Prankster

The history of political pranks is littered with lefty characters. Conservatives, on the other hand, do not gravitate toward irreverent hijinks. One exception is James O'Keefe, a right-wing prankster who uses hidden cameras to stage encounters with his ideological enemies. At the same time that progressive organizations such as MoveOn.org were hailed for their savvy uses of online media, O'Keefe, Andrew Breitbart, and other conservatives employed similar DIY methods. O'Keefe's provocations began in 2004 while attending Rutgers University. In a satire of political correctness, what he viewed as a pious sensitivity to ethnicity on college campuses, he launched a campaign to remove Lucky Charms from the dining hall. He secretly videotaped himself complaining to a food-service employee about the leprechaun on the cereal box. While the school official earnestly scribbled notes, O'Keefe deadpanned, "As you can see, we're not short and green—we have our differences of height—and we think this is stereotypical of all Irish Americans." While at Rutgers, he gained notoriety by organizing an "affirmative-action bake sale," in which whites paid exorbitant prices and African Americans got discounts.[47]

In developing his craft, O'Keefe read Saul Alinsky's *Rules for Radicals*, the bible of many liberal activists. Rule Four especially inspired him: "Make the enemy live up to its own book of rules." He applied this directive in 2007 when he punked Planned Parenthood in an attempt to expose white liberal hypocrisies about race, abortion, and eugenics. It is certainly true, for instance, that some early-twentieth-century Progressives could be racist. Planned Parenthood founder Margaret Sanger is a women's rights pioneer, but some of her projects ran hand in hand with a desire to reduce the size of "undesirable" populations. Particularly unsettling was Sanger's "Negro Project," which was arguably a thinly veiled eugenics scheme. This sordid history has enabled conservative commentators to take the moral high ground by claiming that white liberals are the real racists. To dramatize this claim, O'Keefe secretly taped a phone conversation with a Planned Parenthood staffer, who was asked if his donation could be used to abort black babies (so to prevent his future son from being discriminated against through affirmative action). He was told the organization would accept the money, for whatever reason. Even though Planned Parenthood dismissed the tapes as "heavily edited," the public-relations damage was done.[48]

An unsettling amount of racial resentment runs through O'Keefe's stunts, from his Rutgers University "affirmative-action bake sale" to one of the pranks he is most known for: the ACORN pimp tapes. In 2009, he targeted the Association of Community Organizations for Reform Now, or ACORN, which advocated for working-class citizens and minorities. Conservative talk-show hosts such as Rush Limbaugh and Glenn Beck turned it into a political punching bag during and after the 2008 election campaign, and O'Keefe piled on. Posing as a pimp—and accompanied by his associate Hannah Giles, who played the role of the prostitute—he videotaped low-level employees who appeared to endorse his proposed tax-fraud and child-prostitution schemes. The footage contained misleading cutaway shots of the skinny, white twenty-something in a pimp costume, making it look like he dressed this way in ACORN's offices. It was one of many manipulations in O'Keefe's viral videos (which, to be fair, are not unlike some edits found in films by liberal documentarian Michael Moore).[49]

The incendiary footage prompted multiple criminal investigations, though no charges were ultimately filed. A report on ACORN activities produced by the California attorney general found that the organization suffered from mismanagement, but the AG also concluded that the videos were "heavily edited to feature only the worst or most inappropriate statements of various ACORN employees." The report stated, "the impression of rampant illegal conduct . . . is not supported by the evidence related to the videos." Additionally, at least one employee who seemed to play along while on camera contacted the police after the "pimp's" visit. The District Attorney's Office in Brooklyn, where another hidden-camera sting occurred, also reported that "no criminality has been found." O'Keefe's tactics did not constitute investigative journalism, but as a prank—a staged provocation designed to persuade—they were very effective. The U.S. House of Representatives overwhelmingly voted to deny federal funding to ACORN, and by 2010 it was on the verge of bankruptcy. "That 20-minute video ruined 40 years of good work," a former Maryland chapter co-chairwoman lamented. In 2011, O'Keefe pulled a similar prank on National Public Radio, which prompted legislation to defund public broadcasting. This was change the right could believe in.[50]

TEA PARTIES AND MAD HATTERS

As a former community organizer with ties to ACORN, Barack Obama was the perfect foil that helped unify a conservative movement that was in disarray. His rise to power unleashed a torrent of repressed political energy: the formation of Tea Parties, the instant stardom of talk-show host Glenn Beck, the growing popularity of libertarian politicians Ron and Rand Paul, and the return of Illuminatiphobia. Demographic and economic shifts were transforming America, whose shrinking white majority was less prosperous than ever before. This created the impression that educated elites and racial minorities were closing down opportunities for Tea Partiers. Their ideas and slogans seemed to come from out of left field—or, more accurately, right field—but they had been lurking just below the surface for decades. In 1964, the John Birch Society lost its influence within top Republican Party circles after playing a key role in getting Barry Goldwater nominated as the party's presidential candidate. "Extremism in the defense of liberty is no vice," the candidate famously said, in a nod to the Birchers. "Moderation in the pursuit of justice is no virtue." His campaign slogan, "In your heart you know he's right," was easily lampooned by Democrats: "In your guts you know he's nuts." Goldwater was too out there for most voters and was trounced in the general election.[51]

After years in the political woods, the John Birch Society made a comeback in the Age of Obama. The month after his inauguration, it cosponsored that year's Conservative Political Action Conference (CPAC), which featured a wild keynote speech by Glenn Beck. On his radio and television programs, Beck helped reintroduce the organization to America. "When I was growing up, the John Birch Society, I thought they were a bunch of nuts," he told spokesman Sam Antonio during an on-air interview, but now "you guys are starting to make a lot more sense to me." Antonio earnestly confirmed, "Yes, we at the John Birch Society are not nuts." Echoing *The X-Files'* famous tagline, he added, "We are just exposing the truth that's been out there for many, many years." The society's website proudly ran *Glenn Beck* program clips that highlighted the similarities between the host's views and its own, and it lauded him for "presenting American history in the way that The John Birch Society has been doing it for over 50 years." That story goes: Woodrow Wilson socially engineered America's downfall; Dwight Eisenhower was a communist dupe, or worse; Richard Nixon was more treacherous; and his secretary of state was most certainly an Illuminati agent. In *Kissinger: The Secret Side of the Secretary of State*, a 1976 book published by the John Birch Society, Gary Allen concludes, "It is not too late to tell Henry Kissinger and his masters and mentors in the Shadow government that we want no part of their New World Order." You can only imagine what the Birchers think of (the foreign-born?) Barack Hussein Obama.[52]

Liberals smugly portray Glenn Beck as a crackpot who makes up crazy stuff off the top of his head, but a consistent logic and a large body of literature structure his worldview. When he devotes an entire program to exposing the evil forces behind the Federal Reserve or Rockefeller Plaza, he is mining the same paranoid load as the Birchers. Beck also draws heavily from a former Brigham Young University professor named W. Cleon Skousen, who never saw a progressive social cause, such as the civil rights movement, that didn't have a conspiracy stamped on it. When the Church of Jesus Christ of Latter-Day Saints was being pressured to allow African Americans to be ordained to the priesthood—it took until 1978 to do so—Skousen insisted that communist agitators were behind the movement. Finally, after accusing President Carter of being a puppet of an international conspiracy, the Mormon Church issued a national order to "avoid any implication that the Church endorses" his views.[53]

Skousen had been famous in far-right circles ever since he wrote 1972's *The Naked Capitalist: A Review and Commentary on Dr. Carroll Quigley's Book "Tragedy and Hope."* It presented itself as an exposé of a relatively obscure academic book by Quigley, a Georgetown University history professor who was Bill Clinton's college mentor (a bright red flag raised by many a conspiracy theorist). Since then, the 1,348-page *Tragedy and Hope* has been held up as a smoking gun. Skousen called it "a bold and boastful admission by Dr. Quigley that there actually exists a relatively small but powerful group which has succeeded in acquiring a choke-hold on the affairs of practically the entire human race." By the early 1970s, *The Naked Capitalist*'s print run topped fifty-five thousand copies—far more copies than Quigley's book ever sold—and in 1972 the Washington office of the Liberty Lobby reported that it was selling twenty-five copies a day. As a result of this attention, *Tragedy and Hope* was checked out of libraries and never returned. This made the out-of-print book even harder to find, provoking conjecture that lefty librarians were pulling it from the shelves to suppress its revelations.[54]

"Skousen's book is full of misrepresentations and factual errors," an exasperated Quigley insisted at the time. "He claims that I have written of a conspiracy of the super-rich who are pro-Communist and wish to take over the world and that I'm a member of this group. But I never called it a conspiracy and don't regard it as such." He was actually describing a web of corporate and nongovernmental bodies, such as the Council on Foreign Relations and J. P. Morgan, which sought to "coordinate the international activities" of commerce and governance. Unfortunately, the professor made the mistake of calling this network an "elaborate, semi-secret organization." Skousen believed that the Ivy League establishment—with its penchant for internationalism—was carrying out its wicked goals using the tentacles of the Rockefeller and Rothschild dynasties, the Federal Reserve, the Bilderberg Group, and the Council on Foreign Relations. *None Dare Call It a Conspiracy,* a book by Birchers Gary Allen and Larry Abraham, echoed Skousen's assertions. Four decades later, Glenn Beck was telling radio listeners, "I know it's not popular to quote Carroll Quigley but if you've ever read *Tragedy and Hope* from the 1960s, you see this being played out."[55]

In addition to reviving sales of *The Naked Capitalist*, the conservative talk-show host made Skousen's *The Five Thousand Year Leap* a best-seller. It was premised on the notion that the U.S. Constitution was based solely on biblical law, not Enlightenment principles. America was so remarkably different from any previous governmental system, Skousen argued, that it represented a five-thousand-year leap forward for civilization. Beck's foreword to the book begins, ironically enough, "This is a story you won't believe." Skousen's history was misleading, to say the least (the Mormon journal *Dialogue* condemned him for "inventing fantastic ideas and making inferences that go far beyond the bounds of honest commentary"). For instance, *The Five Thousand Year Leap* selectively quotes a letter written by Benjamin Franklin to make it appear that he was a champion of marriage and fidelity. Beck's intellectual hero neglects to quote the rest of the letter, in which the Founder says married men should seek out older mistresses ("the pleasure of corporal enjoyment with an old woman is at least equal, and frequently superior"). Hundreds of study groups throughout America now teach Skousen's unique "originalist" interpretation of the Constitution.[56]

Beck, Skousen, and the Birchers all believe that their beloved Constitution suffered a deathblow after the election of President Wilson. "As I study history," Beck told his audience, "I see that a lot of the problems—most of the problems, in fact—stem from Woodrow Wilson and the Progressive movement." John Birch Society founder Robert Welch similarly claimed, "By 1920 the *Insiders* attained such Communist goals for the United States as a graduated income tax, the Federal Reserve System, and"—the horror!—"the Seventeenth Amendment for the direct election of Senators." One of the most pronounced aspects of modern conservative thought is a deep-seated distrust of elites: international bankers, well-connected Ivy Leaguers, unelected technocrats, atheistic social scientists, and the like. In the book *Liberal Fascism*, Jonah Goldberg argues that early-twentieth-century Progressives were far greater warmongers, crueler jingoists, worse racists, and more fascist than the right ever was. The *National Review* contributing editor conveniently ignores a few elephants in the Conservative Hall of Shame, but he makes some valid points. Some Progressives were racist eugenicists, and a few even supported Hitler and Mussolini (though so did plenty of right-wing capitalists).[57]

New Republic founding editor Herbert Croly, an archetypical Woodrow Wilson Progressive, was an early backer of the Italian fascist. He was also a big booster of social science, another longtime conservative foil. In 1925, Croly asked, "Who will be the prophets and pilots of the Good Society?" He concluded that a "better future would derive from the beneficent activities of expert social engineers." The *New Republic* editor's father, David Goodman Croly, also promoted positivism (the application of the scientific method to explain and regulate human events). You may also remember him from chapter 5 as the racist newspaper editor who invented the word *miscegenation*. Five years after his hoax, the elder Croly founded an American branch of the Church of Humanity, which was dedicated to ideas espoused by sociologist Auguste Comte. Given that most antiabolitionists used biblical arguments to justify slavery, the fact that Croly embraced secularist rationalism is unusual. But history is littered with odd ideological bedfellows (sometimes quite literal bedfellows—his wife, Jane Croly, was one of the first syndicated feminist columnists in America).[58]

As for *New Republic* coeditor Walter Lippmann, there were times when he could sound downright conspiratorial when expressing his love of social engineering. Likewise, his colleague Edward Bernays enthusiastically noted, "It is now possible to control and regiment the masses according to our will without their knowing it." A century later, these Progressive dreams of a social-scientific utopia still strike fear in the hearts of conservatives. In 2010, Tea Party–backed candidates took control of North Carolina's Wake County school board, sweeping into power with the campaign slogan "Say No to the Social Engineers!" The majority Republican board promptly dismantled one of the America's most successful and celebrated integration efforts as a rebuke to pointy-headed bureaucrats. Two years after Obama was elected, Tea Party candidates in Republican primaries began unseating incumbents such as South Carolina congressman Bob Inglis. During the 2010 primaries, angry voters confronted the representative about how the existence of Social Security numbers was proof they had been sold into slavery by a secret bank. "And then, of course," Inglis adds, "it turned into something about the Federal Reserve and the Bilderbergers and all that stuff."[59]

Throughout the twentieth century, the political and religious right quietly disseminated these ideas through underground media channels. But by the new millennium, conservatives had Fox News, America's number-one cable news network. It helped popularize views that were previously relegated to small-print-run newsletters and AM talk radio. Fox News gave Glenn Beck a platform to broadcast numerous conspiracy theories, such as "FEMA camps" that were secretly being constructed in Montana. Just like *Iron Mountain*, it was a project so clandestine that no one could find evidence of its existence. When rumors about those detention centers first circulated in 2009, Beck interviewed Texas congressman Ron Paul, a longtime champion of the John Birch Society. In an awkward balancing act, they both implied that the FEMA camps might exist while also doing their best to sound sane. "So in some ways," the U.S. representative told Beck, "they can accomplish what you might be thinking about, about setting up camps, and they don't necessarily have to have legislation, you know, to do the things that we dread. But it is something that deserves a lot of attention."[60]

Paul has also sounded alarms about a "NAFTA Superhighway" that will supposedly bisect the United States. "Proponents envision a ten-lane colossus with the width of several football fields," Paul writes, "with freight and rail lines, fiber-optic cable lines, and oil and natural gas pipelines running alongside." Ron's son, Senator Rand Paul, said much the same thing while campaigning in Montana for his father's presidential bid in 2008. "So, it's a real thing," he said, "and when you talk about it, the thing you just have to be aware of is that, if you talk about it like it's a conspiracy, they'll paint you as a nut." Both father and son take care to present themselves as reasonable people, but they don't always succeed. The *Ron Paul Survival Report*, which the elder Paul published in the 1990s, contained the usual warnings about the Rockefellers, black helicopters, America's "disappearing white majority," and other far-right talking points. The senior Paul has also been a frequent guest on Alex Jones's bat-crap-crazy radio show, where the congressman railed against a "cataclysmic shift toward a new world order," made possible by "a new monetary order. . . . A world central bank, worldwide regulation and world control of the whole system, of all the commodities and all the natural resources, what else can you call it other than world government?"[61]

Paul's endorsement of G. Edward Griffin's *The Creature from Jekyll Island: A Second Look at the Federal Reserve*—along with several other positions he holds—has made him an icon for New World Order conspiracy theorists. Griffin's book is laced with standard-issue references to the Council on Foreign Relations, W. Cleon Skousen, Carroll Quigley, the Rothschild family, and the Bavarian Illuminati (a branch of which, the author suggests, played a role in assassinating Abraham Lincoln). Griffin was also a longtime affiliate of the John Birch Society, which published several of his nutty books. In Paul's blurb for *The Creature from Jekyll Island*, he calls it "a superb analysis deserving serious attention by all Americans. Be prepared for one heck of a journey through time and mind." It sure is. The congressman is a principled libertarian conservative whose positions on civil liberties, the wars in Iraq and Afghanistan, and the legalization of drugs overlap with those of many people on the left. He is a learned man and not a nut. However, when this congressman appears on Alex Jones's show, endorses Bircher books about a Federal Reserve conspiracy, and warns of nonexistent plans for a NAFTA Superhighway, it shows how the fringe ideas discussed throughout this book have infiltrated substantial parts of the political mainstream.[62]

💣 💣 💣

William Cooper's *Behold a Pale Horse*, Pat Robertson's *The New World Order*, and the John Birch Society's massive output of books and periodicals resonated widely because they used simple, gripping stories to explain complex socioeconomic changes. But their foundations were built on a sinkhole of deception. Few believers know, or care, that those books mixed citations of genuine historical documents with mean-spirited forgeries (*The Protocols of the Elders of Zion*), self-deluded historical scholarship (John Robison's *Proofs of a Conspiracy* and Abbé Barruel's *Memoirs Illustrating the History of Jacobinism*), government propaganda (CIA-sponsored brainwashing research and the FBI's COINTELPRO program), and several satirical pranks (the invention of the Rosicrucian Brotherhood, Léo Taxil's stories about Masonic devil worship, the Discordians' Operation Mindfuck, the playful protests staged by the Women's International Terrorist Conspiracy from Hell, and Leonard Lewin's *The Report from Iron Mountain*, to name but a few). Since the beginning of the modern era, an interconnected, self-referential web of evidence has been recycled and expanded on by new generations of credulous conspiracy theorists. By the late 1960s, the mounting paranoia had reached a tipping point. The prank blowback caused by the Discordians, WITCH, and other like-minded mischief makers helped reconfigure American politics and, as the next chapter reveals, religious life as well.

8

A Satanic Panic

Shadow secret societies and Satanism have been intertwined in the right-wing imagination throughout the modern era. This conspiratorial worldview helped American evangelicals make sense of the tumultuous 1960s, which witnessed several radical breaks from tradition. Many people in the youth movement came to believe that Western rationalism was dehumanizing, and they expressed their rebellion by retreating into Eastern religions, mysticism, and paganism. Social historian Theodore Roszak points out that there is nothing new about the existence of Theosophists, Spiritualists, Satanists, and other kinds occultists. "What *is* new," he wrote in the late 1960s, "is that a radical rejection of science and technological values should appear so close to the center of society, rather than the negligible margins." Hippies sent the far right into hysterics, and by the decade's end Charles Manson became a cautionary symbol of the movement's perceived immorality. The California press often portrayed him as the head of a satanic cult, and reported details about the Manson Family's killing spree provided the grist for many a far-fetched fantasy. Regional disruptions such as the Watts riots, Berkeley campus antiwar protests, and San Francisco's "Summer of Love" also put the fear of God—or Satan—in conservative Christians.[1]

Although tensions exploded in the 1960s, the fuse was lit decades earlier by the "New Thought" utopians and other like-minded souls who set up communes in California. The West Coast has been caricatured as a hotbed of leftist radicalism, but the religious right has also enjoyed a long and strong presence in the Golden State. Back in 1953, the California State Senate Committee on Education reported, "So-called modern communism is apparently the same hypocritical and deadly world conspiracy to destroy civilization that was founded by the secret order of the Illuminati in Bavaria on May 1, 1776." Additionally, the Los Angeles–area enclave of Orange County boasted more chapters and members of the John Birch Society than the rest of the country *combined*. Those households regularly received mailed warnings about the Illuminati from the Birchers, and they watched in horror as decadence and drug use crept closer to their own backyards. Orange County played a key role in sending Ronald Reagan to the governor's mansion in 1966 and, in 1980, the White House (the president half joked that the OC is where "all good Republicans go to die"). As the 1960s and 1970s wore on, it became clear that California wasn't big enough for both conservatives and the counterculture. They passionately competed for elbow room, and this close proximity led to more than a few ideological dustups.[2]

Shouting "Satan!" in a Crowded Theater

Anton LaVey's First Church of Satan, founded in San Francisco three years before the Manson murders, was an important backdrop for California's conservative backlash. Its high priest was a natural-born showman who previously worked as a calliope operator in carnivals and burlesque houses. He also played the pipe organ in churches, where he saw the same men who lusted after half-naked ladies the previous night dutifully sitting with their wives during Sunday service. This deepened LaVey's disdain for Christianity and the hypocrisies of its believers. He acquired a variety of occult books and looked around for satanic churches to join, but they were way too dull. "The true magus knows," LaVey wrote in *The Satanic Bible*, "that occult bookshelves abound with the brittle relics of frightened minds and sterile bodies, metaphysical journals of self-deceit, and constipated rule-books of Eastern mysticism." Very much the sixties swinger, LaVey began putting on burlesque shows with witch- and vampire-costumed strippers. In 1966, he founded his own place of worship, which he publicized with a colorful series of pranks. The high priest officiated a "Satanic wedding" that got worldwide press coverage, which was followed by the "Satanic baptism" of his six-year-old daughter, Zeena. "My mother was mortified," Zeena recalled, "because she just wanted to be like the Addams Family, but it all took off so quickly and spun very much out of his control."[3]

LaVey's lascivious shock tactics were akin to shouting "Satan!" in a crowded theater filled with members of the Moral Majority. The anxieties he created were heightened by a 1970 article that appeared in the John Birch Society's *American Opinion* magazine, which became one of the anti-Satanism movement's urtexts. Churches distributed photocopies of the article, and by the 1980s its outrageous assertions and anecdotes were appearing in Christian books, pamphlets, newsletters, and magazines. Author David Emerson Gumaer linked establishment media, Manson, Satanism, LaVey, and the Illuminati in a grand anti-Christian plot. "Satanism," he wrote, "next to Communism, has become the fastest growing criminal menace of our time." Gumaer then quotes a Los Angeles policeman who said it was dangerous to travel alone on his beat—in, um, *Beverly Hills*—because of the heavy "influx of Satanist dope fiends." When Gumaer interviewed Anton LaVey, the high priest was more than happy to give the Bircher what he wanted. He confirmed that Bavarian Illuminati founder Adam Weishaupt was "a practicing Satanist" and said Weishaupt's secret society was "quite a powerful force for evil."[4]

LaVey, however, wasn't the most reliable of mystical narrators. He had a habit of ripping off those who preceded him, particularly the nineteenth-century French magus Eliphas Lévi (who also took ideas that sprang from his imagination and presented them as ancient and arcane). It was Lévi who imbued the pentagram with its modern-day satanic connotations. When the "five-pointed star of occult masonry" was turned upside down, Lévi writes in his book *The Key of the Mysteries*, it became "a hieroglyphic sign of the goat of Black Magic." Léo Taxil prominently incorporated this "Baphomet" image into his anti-Catholic hoaxes in the 1890s, which cemented its devilish associations. Then, in 1969, LaVey reprinted it on the cover of his book *The*

Satanic Bible. LaVey also featured Baphomet in Roman Polanski's 1968 film *Rosemary's Baby*, for which he served as an adviser and played the role of Satan. It was all fantastic PR for his church. His rapid rise to pop-culture stardom was a symptom of widespread curiosity about the occult. J. R. R. Tolkien's *Lord of the Rings* trilogy was a massive hit in the 1960s, and it practically became required reading on college campuses. By 1968, about fifty million people had read Tolkien's books—which introduced readers to wizards, magic, and other fantasy-literature staples.[5]

Occultism seemed to lurk in every corner of mass media, even in the most innocuous places. Sammy Davis Jr. became affiliated with the Church of Satan after attending one of LaVey's nightclub parties (which Mr. Entertainment later described as "dungeons and dragons and debauchery"). In the early 1970s, Davis could be seen onstage wearing a Baphomet amulet, sporting a painted red fingernail, and flashing the devil horns. He also starred in a failed 1972 television-show pilot, *Poor Devil*, in which he played a bumbling demon who was instructed by Satan to procure a man's soul. Satan's office featured a giant upside-down pentagram, his minions wore Baphomet pendants, and the Dark One even gave a shout-out to LaVey's Church of Satan. As you can imagine, the show's silly and sympathetic take on Satanism provoked protests from religious groups. Eeriness was in the airwaves. During an episode of NBC's *Tonight Show* in 1968, Truman Capote told Johnny Carson that the recent King and Kennedy assassinations were part of an occult conspiracy. He claimed that the nineteenth-century mother of Theosophy, Madame Blavatsky, instructed followers to provoke revolutions through political assassinations. News media repeated this story about Blavatsky's "Manual for Revolution," even though Capote had made it all up. No such idea appeared in her writings, but that didn't stop the John Birch Society from purchasing full-page ads in California newspapers warning of the Russian mystic.[6]

Anton LaVey's irreverent publicity stunts and devilish product placements played a huge role in popularizing the tropes that currently signify Satanism. In addition to copying Eliphas Lévi, he also aped an infamous "black magician" named Aleister Crowley (another mystic who constructed an occult cosmology mostly from his opium addled brain). Born in 1875, at the height of the occult revival, Crowley became fascinated with séances, hypnotism, and other ideas that circulated in the era's popular culture. Crowley was a mystery writer, Freemason, British intelligence agent, drug addict, and all-around creep who promoted himself with the nickname "The Great Beast 666." ("The Great BSer" might be a more apt title.) After being run out of Europe, he settled in—where else?—California. Crowley still sends the religious right into apoplectic fits, despite being little more than a self-promoting P. T. Barnum–like character with a warped wit. He once stood before reporters at the Statue of Liberty, ripped up his British passport, declared war on England, and called for Irish independence. "How can you expect people to take your Magick seriously," his followers complained, "when you write so gleefully about it, with your tongue always in your cheek?" Crowley's sense of humor often ran dark, especially when it came to the topic of ritual sacrifice. His critics can be forgiven for their credulity because the only clear indication he wasn't serious about killing babies was buried in footnotes. "There is a traditional saying that whenever an Adept seems to have made a straightforward, comprehensible statement," Crowley writes, "then is it most certain that He means something entirely different."[7]

A snob, Crowley used shock tactics to separate the cool kids from the gullible, uptight squares. This was also true of LaVey, who was known as a flamboyant hipster who took his pet panther for strolls around San Francisco. Even though he rocked a medieval-magus style, he was clearly indebted to the tackiest pop-culture products he grew up with. With his shaved head and goatee, LaVey had more than a passing resemblance to Ming the Merciless from the *Flash Gordon* serials and comic strips. As a kid in Chicago, he devoured B-grade flicks and the horror pulp magazine *Weird Tales*, which published H. P. Lovecraft (LaVey said Lovecraft was a far greater occult teacher than Crowley was). The Bay Area was crawling with hippies, whom he despised for their groovy egalitarianism, cookie-cutter nonconformity, and dippy, half-baked Eastern mysticism. *I am the true individual*, the high priest sneered, literally cursing the tie-dyed masses. LaVey's "Rising Forth" ceremony, another prankish stunt, gathered a black-clad group of Satanists who urinated on marijuana, crushed an LSD-soaked sugar cube, and hung a picture of Timothy Leary upside down. "Beware, you psychedelic vermin! Your smug pomposity with its thin disguise of tolerance will serve you no longer!" These spectacles ensured that the showman would soon be spreading his message on such talk shows as *Donahue* and *The Tonight Show*.[8]

News outlets also reported that Susan Atkins, who was part of the Manson Family killing spree, once belonged to LaVey's Church of Satan. Another murderous Charles Manson associate, Bobby Beausoleil, provided music for Kenneth Anger's *Lucifer Rising*, an art film that featured Beausoleil in the role of Satan. These associations solidified the links in the public's mind between the counterculture and Satanism. One of Manson's victims was Sharon Tate, the wife of *Rosemary's Baby* director Roman Polanski—whose movie, it was said, generated such bad mojo that it killed her. (Tate actually had the horrible luck of moving into a house recently vacated by a record producer who Manson believed had sabotaged his music career. The closest the soon-to-be mass murderer ever got to a hit was when the Beach Boys covered one of his songs on the B-side of a 1968 single.) A month after Manson's arrest in 1969, the *Los Angeles Herald Examiner* carried the headline "hippie commune witchcraft blood rites told." Los Angeles–area police told reporters that certain "hippie types" were mixing animal blood with LSD to "heighten their trances." People read these stories and unleashed their sordid imaginations. One teen told police that he witnessed hippies "engaged in a weird dance around a parked auto that had five skinned animals, apparently dogs, on its hood."[9]

Anton LaVey, exasperated by this unsolicited infamy-by-association, told a *Los Angeles Times* reporter that he found the Manson murders "damned sickening." Claiming that his shtick was mainly "showmanship," he insisted that the Church of Satan was nothing more than "Ayn Rand's philosophy, with ceremony and ritual added." One ironic thing about the Birchers' antagonism toward LaVey is that they shared a fundamentally individualist and anticollectivist worldview. Rand's *The Fountainhead* and *Atlas Shrugged*—a favorite of the Church of Satan, the John Birch Society, and today's Tea Party movement—celebrated the "virtues of selfishness." The only difference is that one group worships God and the other "worships," *wink wink*, Satan. But they were all united in their loathing of hippies. *The Satanic Bible*'s "Nine Satanic Statements" highlights LaVey's mix of playful irreverence and rational self-interest.[10]

1. Satan represents indulgence, instead of abstinence! . . .
4. Satan represents kindness to those who deserve it, instead of love wasted on ingrates! . . .
6. Satan represents responsibility for the responsible, instead of concern for psychic vampires! . . .
9. Satan has been the best friend the church has ever had, as he as kept it in business all these years![11]

The rise of "Jesus Freaks" and other unconventional religious sects simultaneously stirred up trouble. The members of the Process Church, a Scientology splinter group, projected a sinister vibe by wearing black uniforms, red emblems, and capes. They were also notorious for walking attack-trained Alsatian dogs through San Francisco's Haight district. "Black is the color of the Bottomless Void to which the human race is doomed," the group declared, using language straight out of a teen's angst-filled notebook. "So Black we shall wear in mourning for the doom mankind has brought upon itself." They also had a loose connection to Manson, who contributed an article for the "Death issue" of the Process Church's magazine. Creepy associations aside, the Process Church was little more than a radical Christian sect that wanted to shock the bourgeoisie, sixties style. (Members got such a bad rap that they eventually traded in their black capes for gray leisure suits.) These sorts of flamboyant characters freaked out conservative Christians, who began trading all sorts of far-fetched stories. "There was a very active but behind-the-scenes satanic community here," disgraced megachurch pastor Ted Haggard said of Colorado's post-1960s landscape. He claimed it was littered with "covens, thousands of Satanists, sixties leftovers into really bloody Satanism." Those who were predisposed to believe that the devil walked among them feared the worst, and the religious right's emerging media system eagerly dialed up the paranoia.[12]

Fighting Mediums with Media

Preachers have populated the airwaves since the earliest days of radio, a time that coincided with the emergence of Christian fundamentalism. That religious movement pushed back against nineteenth-century Protestant leaders who adapted to more "modern" ways of thinking (such as interpreting biblical stories through the lens of science). Fundamentalists are often caricatured as backward and antimodern, but this perception masks the fact that they have regularly been early adopters of new media technologies. The first known Christian radio broadcast occurred in 1921, and during the 1930s Charles Fuller's *Old-Fashioned Revival Hour* was the most popular American radio program of any kind. (Fittingly, the preacher got his start in Orange County, California.) But in the second half of the twentieth century, mainstream media tended to shy away from religious programming. Evangelicals, fed up with the secularism creeping into their living rooms, began to build a vast alternative communication network during the 1960s. Using church sermons, religious tracts, books, magazines, radio, and television, they spread chilling tales about Satanism and the Illuminati to millions of Americans.[13]

Pockets of nuttiness peppered the Midwest, but California and Virginia formed a formidable axis of insanity. Hippies provoked a siege mentality in conservative West Coast strongholds, and on the other side of the country Edgar Cayce's flighty followers deeply troubled Pat Robertson, who fretted, "The Spiritualist Church was making a resurgence." Despite Robertson's animosity toward Spiritualists, the televangelist often invoked metaphors originally used by nineteenth-century mediums. Recounting his first experience speaking in tongues, he recalled, "It seemed as if a heavenly teletype machine had mysteriously been activated." Robertson and Cayce both ended up in Virginia Beach because their spiritual guides—God and The Source, respectively—instructed them to go. The evangelical was told to start a television station there, and the mystic was led to believe he could make better use of his powers near a large body of water. Upon arriving in this small beach town in the middle of winter, Cayce and his family found little more than a hardware store, a drugstore, a restaurant, and some boarded-up souvenir shops. They wondered aloud, "Why did the readings send us to Virginia Beach?"[14]

I asked similar questions while growing up in this seedy tourist trap. Even though my mom and dad were never hardcore cultish followers, they were each curious enough about the Sleeping Prophet to move across the country to Virginia Beach. There, Dottie's and Dallas's paths to illumination crossed, and they had a baby boy named Kembrew. (I was born on Halloween in 1970, the dawning of the Age of Aquarius, and grew up to be a university professor—which likely makes me the devil incarnate in Pat Robertson's eyes.) My parents' bookshelves were littered with standard-issue 1970s accouterments such as pyramid paperweights, along with several Edgar Cayce paperbacks. They were a treasure trove of wacky ideas: Astral projection! Atlantis rising! Death rays! Perpetual Motion Machines! Reincarnation! I also grew up watching Robertson's local UHF channel, which broadcast cartoons and sitcom favorites such as *The Dick Van Dyke Show*. It inundated me with Christian fundamentalist PSAs, such as an antidivorce spot that is still drilled in my head: "Love is not an *emotion*. Love is a *decision*." Those years of Cayce whispering in one ear and Robertson in the other helped me cultivate a fairly good BS detector.

"Virginia Beach was renowned as the prime receiving station of the Universal Transmitter (Satan)," the televangelist wrote. "Mediums, clairvoyants, and necromancers flocked to Virginia Beach saying the 'vibrations' in the air made their work easier." The fact that Cayce's Association for Research and Enlightenment was practically in Robertson's backyard further inflamed his obsession with Satan and Spiritualism. Overestimating the power of a handful of starry-eyed esoteric souls, he set out to fight mediums with mass media. In 1960, God instructed Robertson to buy a defunct television station for $37,000. This made for a strange negotiation with then-owner Tim Bright, especially after Pat pulled the old Jesus Mind Trick. "Yes, Tim, you've got to sign it. God wants you to," he said. "And $37,000 is your top figure?" Nodding, Robertson replied, "That's the top and bottom figure. . . . God said that was how much I was to pay you." He planned to call the station WTFC— Television for Christ—but when those call letters weren't available, it became WYAH (as in YAHweh). WYAH signed on the air on October 1, 1961 as the country's first television station to exclusively offer religious programming.[15]

Because alternative media is typically associated with the left, Pat Robertson rarely gets credit as an independent media pioneer. But he most certainly was, and WYAH was flying on a wing and a prayer during those early years. "Everything spoke of utter desolation," Robertson said of the station's poorly maintained state. A writer for the magazine of National Religious Broadcasters recalled, "When I visited WYAH-TV in 1962, about a year after it went on the air, I certainly didn't expect it to amount to much. . . . The studio looked like something put together with coat hangers." To produce a miracle, Robertson flooded sympathizers with prayer cards asking for "(1) wisdom to know how to start a TV station, (2) God's blessing in the negotiations to buy it, (3) favor with the Federal Communications Commission, (4) a nationwide ministry on radio and television tape." The $37,000 he paid turned out to be a mind-bogglingly profitable investment. The Christian Broadcasting Network (CBN) grew from its humble beginnings—decrepit studios, ancient equipment, and all—into a terrestrial network that boasted twenty-five affiliates by 1975. Two years later, it began distributing its programs via satellite, and now CBN has long been established as a formidable media behemoth. Robertson regularly uses it to rail against Satanists, New Agers, One Worlders, and the Illuminati.[16]

The CBN founder wasn't the first to broadcast these warnings. Radio preacher Gerald Winrod enjoyed massive popularity throughout the 1930s sermonizing about "the fundamentals." His Wichita, Kansas–based Defenders of the Christian Faith published a journal that spouted anti-Semitic views for a national readership in the tens of thousands. Winrod kept the Judeo-Masonic conspiracy-theory flame alive by drawing on *The Protocols of the Elders of Zion* and the Illuminatiphobic texts of Lady Queenborough and Nesta Webster. His 1935 tract *Adam Weishaupt, a Human Devil* concluded, "The real conspirators behind the Illuminati were Jews." In another pamphlet, *Communism Prophecy History America*, Winrod miraculously discovered and reprinted the Illuminati founder's private letters. (No one bothered to ask how this midwesterner found those documents, 150 years after the fact.) "My circumstances necessitate that I should remain hidden from most of the members as long as I live," Weishaupt allegedly wrote, explaining why he went underground to pull the strings from behind the scenes. "I am obliged to do everything through five or six persons. . . . In this way I can set a thousand men in motion and on fire in the simplest manner."[17]

Winrod's Catholic analogue was Father Coughlin, who eventually founded a political party with at least four million members. In 1931, the CBS network began broadcasting the radio priest's sermons nationwide, but his show was dropped after he accused international bankers wink, nudge, Jews—of causing the Great Depression. Coughlin started out as a supporter of President Roosevelt's New Deal, but by 1938 he was attacking FDR on the air and advocating for an authoritarian corporate state. He asserted that foreign conspirators were manipulating the working class (the president's electoral base) into carrying out their wicked plans. In testimony before the U.S. Congress, Coughlin blamed America's moral decay on the Illuminati and paraphrased Weishaupt as saying, "Destroy Christianity and civilization will be happy." *Social Justice*, the preacher's newspaper, regularly repeated Nazi propaganda about a global Jewish conspiracy. After Coughlin aligned himself with the profascist Christian Front, the government finally shut the paper down—securing his martyr status among Illuminatiphobes.[18]

The bloody aftermath of World War Two made anti-Semitism unfashionable, and for the most part, conspiracy politics were not a large part of the fundamentalist scene when Oral Roberts, Billy Graham, and Pat Robertson embraced the new medium of television. During these years, the religious right tended to stay out of politics, but progressive winds of change agitated a formidable social movement into action. Catholics, fundamentalists, and evangelicals fought back after a 1963 Supreme Court case banned prayer in public schools, the first of many perceived assaults on their faith. As President Ronald Reagan's "Morning in America" dawned, religious leaders turned their churches into powerful communication hubs. In addition to sermons, informal gossip, and leafleting, they used shortwave and AM radio, fax networks, videotapes, syndicated satellite transmissions, electronic bulletin boards, and every other media technology under the sun. Luddites, they were not.[19]

The cassette tape was another popular medium, and John Todd gained fame in the 1970s with his audiotape series. In 1973, evangelicals invited him to come to California—where he connected with Jack T. Chick, known for his comic-styled "Chick tracts." The religious publisher based a few of his tracts on Todd's stories, including tales of Masonic devil worship ripped directly from the pages of Léo Taxil's forgeries. Among other nutty pronouncements, the traveling minister said he was raised a witch and had been initiated into something called the "Grand Druid Council." (The military medical report that led to his discharge for psychiatric problems stated, "Todd finds it difficult to tell reality from fantasy.") He also said that the Illuminati installed one of their own—Jimmy Carter—who was preparing to declare martial law and ban firearms. Citing secret documents he claimed to be privy to, Todd piled up an ever-higher tower of babbling craziness: President Nixon had been removed from power and replaced by Carter; the president's sister Ruth Carter Stapleton was the "most powerful witch in the world"; and there would be a "world takeover" by the Illuminati in 1980s.[20]

The election of Ronald Reagan temporarily fended off this planned coup. Evangelical leader Tim LaHaye claimed the religious right foiled the Illuminati's plot by playing a crucial role in registering voters during the 1980 presidential election. Even though Reagan didn't solve all of America's moral problems, LaHaye maintains that his election "lit the way for other Christians who could turn the conspirators back another decade." The John Birch Society also claimed credit for this victory. "The Christmas holiday season," founder Robert Welch said, "would have been converted largely into a pagan festival, celebrating the brotherhood of man under the aegis of the United Nations." If not for Welch's efforts, these events surely would have come to pass. He may have been exaggerating, but the John Birch Society was quite effective in promoting its worldview. Through its publishing arm and other media holdings, the group helped lay the foundation for the religious right's alternative communication network. It began taking shape in the 1960s, and by 1983 one out of every seven radio stations in America was Christian owned (totaling thirteen hundred broadcasters with a listenership of 150 million). This massive communication network rivaled Léo Taxil's devil-operated telephone system, and its first order of business was to scare the hell out of believers.[21]

The Satanic Panics

The Satanic Panics swept America in the 1980s, when thousands of children were allegedly kidnapped, defiled, and murdered in devilish rituals. Even though police statistics made it clear there was no such epidemic, a nation of millions believed the hype. The most infamous case was sparked in 1983 by allegations that 360 children had been victimized by a "Devil worship" cult at the McMartin Preschool in Manhattan Beach, California. Judy Johnson (who had a history of making wild accusations and was later diagnosed with schizophrenia) claimed her son Matthew had been abused by preschool workers dressed as witches. She claimed that they put crayons in Matthew's rectum and made him "ride naked on a horse and then molested him while dressing as a cop, a fireman, a clown, and Santa Claus." There were also black candles, mutilated animals, oven-cooked infants, force-fed feces, liquid snacks of baby's blood, subterranean tunnels, and airplane rides to secret sites. It was the longest running and most expensive criminal trial in American history, and it ended in 1990 with all charges dropped (and many lives ruined). A similar case in Jordan, Minnesota reinforced the impression that satanic crimes were sweeping this country.[22]

Sociologists use the term "rumor panics" to describe how folk legends spread by word of mouth until they explode via mass media. As a teenager growing up in Virginia Beach, I vividly remember how these worries echoed through my school's hallways. One state over, students at Panther Valley High School in Lansford, Pennsylvania warned each other about a bloodbath that would take place at their 1987 prom. This rumor panic spread to a neighboring high school that was also holding a prom that weekend, and soon the entire community was freaking out. The high school's principal contacted the police department, which installed metal detectors and hired extra security to protect the students. Traveling "experts" on satanic ritual abuse popped up regularly in schools throughout the country, and several police departments offered public seminars. Virginia Beach detective Don Rimer warned parents of the evils of not only rock music but also *The Smurfs*: "Papa Smurf, a seemingly innocuous cartoon character, has appeared in several television episodes wearing a pentagram, symbolic of satanic worship." Former police officer Robert Hicks estimates that in Virginia, cops gave at least fifty of these seminars in 1988 alone—mostly in churches and schools.[23]

Research done by French anthropologist Sherrill Mulhern reveals that a powerful, interconnected social network was formed by religious leaders, police cult experts, and concerned parents' groups. Mulhern argues that this network "is sufficient to completely explain the creation, elaboration, and spread of the satanic-cult rumor." The hysteria was also stoked by civilian lecturers such as Jerry Johnston, who reportedly spoke at twenty-seven hundred schools in the 1980s. His book *The*

Edge of Evil: The Rise of Satanism in North America offers up a menu of the usual suspects, including the Illuminati and other "diabolically" evil secret societies. The always-reliable Geraldo Rivera insisted in *The Edge of Evil*'s introduction that Satanism "exists and it's flourishing," and the book's dust-jacket copy warned, "Satanism is a growing teenage subculture phenomenon, and not just among metalhead underachievers." Devil worshipers could even be found among—*gasp!*—"intelligent, upper-middle-class honor students." In another telling expression of the cultural anxieties at play, the most prevalent atrocity stories involved plots to defile blond, blue-eyed children—especially white, female virgins. Parents kept their kids home from school, and police departments were inundated with phone calls about satanic graffiti, mutilated animals, and human corpses.[24]

Even though rumors of Satanism seemed to explode from nowhere during the 1980s, these collective fantasies had already taken root for at least two decades. In the 1970s, stories circulated in the American Midwest and Southwest about thousands of dead cattle whose blood had been drained. Their eyes, lips, and genitals had been meticulously cut out, and no footprints could be found. The mutilation myth proved hard to quell, even after a three-hundred-page report by an FBI forensic expert identified animals, not humans, as the culprits. (The missing body parts were the same ones typically removed by scavengers.) Even multinational corporations such as Procter & Gamble did not escape scrutiny. Starting in 1980, it received a growing stack of letters complaining about devilish imagery in its logo—a crescent moon facing thirteen stars. The company insisted that the stars represented the original thirteen states of America, but more creative minds connected the dots and saw "666." From there, the rumors grew weirder. The owner of the company pledged all profits to the Church of Satan! He announced this on a nationally televised talk show!! Unbelievable!!![25]

The rumor certainly was far-fetched, but Proctor & Gamble's profits still suffered. Retailers stopped selling its products, vandals attacked company cars, and by 1982 it received five hundred letters a day about this issue. The company hired traditional public relations consultants, but it was no use because those stories were being spread through informal communication networks such as church sermons, gossip, parking-lot leafleting, and the like. Proctor & Gamble finally changed its logo in 1985, but by 1990 a new set of tales surfaced about its sup-posedly sinister activities. What in the hell was going on? Sociologist David Bromley suggests that these rumor panics arose in response to the upheavals of the 1960s, and they galvanized the right by provok-ing moral indignation among believers. These fantasies were powerful and convincing, and they followed a similar pattern. Bromley's research shows that one reoccurring theme in those atrocity stories was a loss of individual freedom in the face of collectivism (of the satanic-cult or socialist-state varieties). This concern resonates with conservative pre-occupations with personal and familial liberty that go back to the early days of modernity. It was the same old song, a record that refused to stop skipping.[26]

Mediated Madness

Mike Warnke's *The Satan-Seller*, published in 1973, provided the source material for many fantastical tales that proliferated in the 1980s. The surreal memoir details the exploits of a satanic salesman who climbed Lucifer's ladder of success. Warnke says he became a "Master Coun-selor" after impressing his supervisors with novel ideas such as sacrific-ing cats and luring victims with "hypnotic rock music." *The Satan-Seller*, which sold a reported two million copies, is a brain-scrambling occul-tic stew that pours adolescent fantasy on fantasy (with devilish babes thrown in for good measure). One night when Warnke was studying incantations and alchemistic formulas, "*flash!*—this chick materialized in the middle of my living room," he wrote. "I was not high; I was not hallucinating or flashing back. I fervently wished I was." He said one of the most disquieting things about the association of Satan-Sellers was how normal they all appeared. "We could have called ourselves Satan and Sons, Inc.," Warnke quipped. Then someone told him about a secret group *within* this group, the fourth step. "The fourth step?" he asked. "Yeah," came the reply. "Some people think it's the *Illuminati*, but you'd better not breathe that word to anyone!"[27]

In spinning this yarn, Warnke recycled fantasies that go back to the seventeenth-century Rosicrucian prank. "A worldwide, super-secret control group with perhaps as few as a dozen at the very top," he writes, "pulling the strings on every major international event." The Illuminati *must* be run by Satan, because "the most efficient human organization on earth could not possibly keep track of everything." Warnke claimed he met Anton LaVey at an Illuminati convention and crossed paths with Charles Manson twice. Manson was actually in jail the entire time Warnke said he was a Satanist—one of many details that didn't add up. *The Satan-Seller* also describes a 1967 visit to Scott Memorial Baptist Church in San Diego, where he informed pastor Tim LaHaye about the Illuminati's existence. "I brought up the term Illuminati first," LaHaye later retorted. "I tried testing him to see if he really knew anything about it. He didn't seem to have ever heard the word before." The pastor's version is more trustworthy because he has some serious anti-Illuminati street cred. For half a century, LaHaye has studied, as he puts it, "the satanically inspired, centuries-old conspiracy to use government, education, and media to destroy every vestige of Christianity within our society and establish a new world order."[28]

In addition to making a living as an author, occult crime expert, and anti-Antichrist motivational lecturer, Mike Warnke enjoyed an implausibly successful comedy career. He billed himself as "Former Satanist High Priest, Now America's Number 1 Christian Comedian." 1978's *Hey Doc!* was his breakout hit, and he recorded several other popular albums (*A Jester in the King's Court, Live . . . Totally Weird*, and the noncomedy 1979 spoken-word *A Christian's Perspective on Halloween*). They sold over one million copies, a rare achievement for this niche market. But as the Satanic Panics wound down, Warnke suffered an abrupt financial and reputational decline. An exposé by *Cornerstone* magazine, which earned an award for investigative journalism from the Evangelical Press Association, was largely responsible for his downfall. When Mike Hertenstein and Jon Trott contacted his former fiancée, she said, "I've been waiting twenty-five years for someone to ask me about Mike Warnke's story. He's a pathological liar." Warnke received millions of dollars in donations after reciting the sad story of "Jeffy," a nonexistent ritual-abuse survivor who was reduced to a vegetative state by devil worshipers. His ministry lost its tax-exempt status when the IRS discovered that, out of $800,000 brought in during 1991, only $900 went to charitable donations.[29]

"A generation of Christians learned its basic concepts of Satanism and the occult from Mike Warnke's testimony in *The Satan Seller*,"

Hertenstein and Trott wrote. "We believe *The Satan Seller* has been responsible, more than any other single volume in the Christian market, for promoting the current nationwide 'Satan-scare.'" Warnke's fame as a ritual-abuse expert skyrocketed after his appearance on a 1985 ABC news program. "Tonight, the startling, sobering results of a *20/20* investigation," the voice-over warned. "Satanism, devil worship is being practiced all over the country." It exploded like a mass-mediated bomb, and soon the airwaves, churches, and schools were buzzing. "Boy, after Mike appeared on *20/20* things really started happening," a former Warnke employee recalled. Geraldo Rivera's 1988 prime-time special on the subject, "Exposing Satan's Underground," became the highest rated two-hour documentary in the history of television. "The very young and impressionable should definitely not be watching this program tonight," Geraldo disingenuously pleaded. "I am begging you. . . . Please get them out of the room or change the station!" Warnke and other "survivors" made the rounds on *The Oprah Winfrey Show*, *Larry King Live*, *Nightwatch*, *Donahue*, and *Sally Jesse Raphael*.[30]

Proponents of the vast-satanic-conspiracy myth gravely pointed to the uniformity of survivor stories as proof of the existence of an evil underground. A more reasonable explanation is that they borrowed those tropes from *Rosemary's Baby*, *The Exorcist*, *The Omen*, and other well-known horror films. The most glaring offense of these modern-day witch hunters was their dismissal of popular culture as source material for "recovered memories." Another major sin was their uncritical acceptance of outlandish atrocity stories that investigators coaxed out of kids. As Bruno Bettelheim argues in *The Uses of Enchantment: The Meaning and Importance of Fairy Tales*, children have a rich fantasy life. The Freudian child psychologist writes, "far from being innocent, the mind of the young child is filled with anxious, angry, destructive imaginings." That is one reason why murder, torture, and cannibalism are staples of classic fairy tales such as "Snow White" and "Hansel and Gretel." Kids draw pleasure from those dystopian stories by facing down their fears (killing and cooking the fearsome witch who wants to eat them, for instance). Satanic Panic investigators created an explosive mix when they consciously or unconsciously introduced imagery from adult horror genres while questioning children. Fantasy bled into the real world, with frightening effects.[31]

Communication scholar Joshua Gunn reminds us that much of the imagery that is used as shorthand for Satanism is not very old. Dark-robed and hooded figures, inverted crosses, and pentagrams were popularized by Anton LaVey's publicity stunts. Most influential was his quasi-documentary, *Satanis: The Devil's Mass*. Its depiction of a garishly lit chamber, haunting hooded figures, and the obligatory naked sexy lady on an altar was far more silly than sinister. *Satanis* was meant to promote LaVey's Church of Satan, but this train wreck of a film bombed at the box office. No one bothered registering the copyright, so the film's public-domain status allowed newscasts to freely use it as b-roll in the 1980s. During Mike Warnke's *20/20* appearance, *Satanis* clips were accompanied by voice-overs claiming that "hearts were cut out, and . . . children were made to chew pieces of these children's hearts, pieces of their flesh." The rhetorical heft of the visuals made these fictions *feel* real. *Satanis* was also used in the previously mentioned Geraldo special, which rearranged the film's chronological order to fit the broadcast's narrative needs. "LaVey's playful attempts to re-signify highly connotative signifiers of darkness and evil as 'kitsch' backfired," Gunn writes, "as his church was later plagued by accusations of ritual murder, child abuse, and other occult crimes."[32]

Mike Warnke's *Satan-Seller* was but one of many hoaxes and cons that sparked the Satanic Panics. The highest profile survivor story was a 1980 memoir written by Michelle Smith and her psychiatrist, Lawrence Pazder, who diagnosed her with multiple personality disorder. Their book, *Michelle Remembers*, sold in the millions and was responsible for setting the "recovered memory" movement in motion. It was based on stories that Smith told Dr. Pazder, a devout Catholic whose strong religious convictions primed his dark imagination. He came to believe that Michelle's parents belonged to a secret order of Satanists that made her witness unspeakable acts in the mid-1950s. During one session, she recounted a horrifying scene orchestrated by a man named "Malachi," the head of a coven of witches (a.k.a. the "Bad Mommies"). "Malachi turned to a table and revealed another dead baby," Pazder wrote. "Before Michelle's eyes, he sliced the fetus in half, then turned to Michelle and rubbed half the body against her stomach." "No! No! Take it away!" she screamed. "They rubbed it all over me. Why did they do that?" Michelle allegedly developed symptoms during their sessions, called "body memories," such as a rash on her neck that Pazder believed was the mark of the devil's tail.[33]

Over the course of Michelle's two-year trauma, she witnessed spiders, snakes, rotting corpses, and people who ripped kittens apart with their teeth. She was vaginally penetrated with a crucifix (much like what happens in *The Exorcist*) and forced to urinate and defecate on the Bible. Demonic nurses pulled out her teeth, she was surgically implanted with horns, and Satan himself even dropped by for a visit. "Children shall disappear from the streets," she predicted, "never more to be seen, taken into covens and buried in their burial grounds." The book also included terrible poetry uttered by Satan. "When the year is seven and nine / Most of the world will be mine / They don't even know what I'm about / By 1980 they won't even shout." Just like what happened with Léo Taxil's Freemasonry hoax, the Catholic Church bought this story hook, line, and sinker. Michelle was invited to the Vatican, and the bishop of the diocese of Victoria, British Columbia wrote the book's foreword. Michelle and her doctor—who later married her—appeared throughout the 1980s on television as satanic-cult experts, further adding to the deluge of misinformation.[34]

Lauren Stratford's book *Satan's Underground* had a similar life cycle. Her experiences mirrored the stories in *Michelle Remembers*, as well as popular horror films (sticking to the script, Stratford says she was thrown into a small chamber with four dead babies until she took part in a ritual sacrifice). You could drive a Bible-filled Mack truck through all the holes in her holier-than-thou tales. For instance, Stratford said she escaped a satanic pornography ring after her father died in 1983—even though he actually passed away eighteen years earlier. *Cornerstone* magazine discovered that Stratford had a history of conning Christian organizations with stories that ranged from pretending to be blind to representing herself as a prostitute. Each time she was exposed, she garnered further sympathy by apologizing and claiming she was a lonely woman looking for attention. The book's publisher finally pulled it from distribution, but not before Stratford made several televised appearances—including that Geraldo special.[35]

Dozens more Satan-themed titles flew off the shelves throughout the 1980s. Jerry Johnston's *The Edge of Evil* made the dubious claim that forty to sixty thousand people were murdered annually in ritual sacrifices. Some of these books did make stabs at respectability, such as *Cult and Ritual Abuse: Its History, Anthropology, and Recent Discovery in Contemporary America*. Despite an attempt at balance, the book's authors recycled the same old secret-society-within-a-secret-society tales ("cultists operate within Freemasonry without the knowledge or consent of the majority of its membership"). They also rehash a Taxil-authored rumor about how Freemason Albert Pike was "associated with the cult of Lucifer." Several other Satanic Panic crusaders tried to cultivate an air of respectability by securing academic credentials. Former police officer Dale Griffis purchased a mail-order degree, added "PhD" to the end of his name, and showed up frequently on television, on the lecture circuit, and in courtrooms. His dissertation, "Mind Control Groups and Their Effects on the Objectives of Law Enforcement," argued that the brainwashing techniques employed by communist states were now being used by satanic cults.[36]

A Modern-Day Witch Hunt

It was Griffis's "expert" testimony that helped send three innocent teens to prison, despite a lack of any physical evidence. In 1993, three second-grade boys were murdered in West Memphis, Arkansas—a deeply conservative community in the heart of the Bible Belt. Suspicion was cast on a trio of outsiders: Damien Echols, Jason Baldwin, and Jessie Misskelley Jr. "Fears of satanic cults reached their peak last week when the teenagers were arrested," a local television station reported during the media firestorm. One resident told a news crew, "I heard things before about cults and I didn't really believe it, but some of the kids in the neighborhood said there is, and they found some animals back there that looked like they had been cut up." This was simply a rehashing of the old animals-mutilated-by-Satanists urban legend, so in the absence of concrete facts, people unleashed their darkest nightmares. A neighbor of one of the accused told reporters that she stopped letting her son play with Jason Baldwin after her husband saw some drawings he made. They featured snakes, weird sayings, and other sure signs of devil worship. "Some of them," she added, "they were *Latin* and stuff."[37]

These stories spread through word of mouth, got picked up by news media, and cycled back into the community's gossip mill. "At some time, all three suspects lived in the Lakeshore trailer park," another news program reported. "Residents here claim to have seen strange ritualistic meetings at the park prior to the murders." To call it a modern-day witch hunt wouldn't be too far off the mark. "I'm all for them burning 'em at the stake, just like they did in Salem," said Todd Moore, the father of a victim. West Memphis juvenile officer Jerry Driver recalled that the region had been bursting with rumors of devil worship in the years leading up to the murders. When the police department drew up a list of those who might be satanically inclined, Damien Echols was immediately singled out as the murderous ringleader. Many West Memphis residents also suspiciously noted that "Damien" was the name of the evil character from *The Omen* films (an insinuation that made little sense, given that he was born before the first movie was even released).[38]

"Damien's name was mentioned early on by a lot of people," said Gary Gitchell, chief investigator for the West Memphis Police. "He does act strange. He wears the black clothing which creates attention to him." When reporters asked Gitchell how sure he was of Echols's guilt, on a scale of one to ten, his *Spinal Tap*–esque reply was a confident "Eleven." Critics of the case argue that the West Memphis Three were targeted because they wore black, listened to heavy metal music, and seemed weird. That was pretty much all that was needed to sentence Echols to death and condemn the other two to life in prison. Their eighteen-year legal battle became a cause célèbre after the release of the 1996 documentary *Paradise Lost* and its two sequels. These films stirred the passions of thousands of people—including myself, a kid who grew up in the South at the height of the Satanic Panics. I wore black, didn't fit in, made weird art, and was prone to shouting "Satan!" in shopping malls, just to mess with people. Like many others who were moved to tears by *Paradise Lost,* I fear that my warped sense of humor and cynical attitude could have gotten me in serious trouble had I ever been in the wrong place at the wrong time. I was one of the lucky ones.[39]

During the trial's closing arguments, the prosecuting attorney told the jury, "Anything wrong with wearing black in and of itself? No. Anything wrong with the heavy metal stuff in and of itself? No. But when you look at it together and you begin to see inside Damien Echols, you see inside that person and there's *not a soul in there*." Earlier in the trial, expert witness Dale Griffis was asked what devil worshipers looked like and whether Echols fit the profile. Predictably, Griffis said Echols did show signs of being a homicidal Satanist—an opinion based on the old man's encounters with "people wearing black fingernails, having their hair painted black, wearing black t-shirts." The prosecution's case hinged on Griffis's testimony, despite his questionable training (he took no coursework to earn a PhD from Columbia Pacific University, an unaccredited distance-learning school later closed by court order). When the defense pointed this out, the gum-chewing judge grew irritated. "I'm not sure in Arkansas or any other state that you have to have any kind of degree to be an expert in a particular field," Judge Burnett snapped. After eighteen years in prison, the three walked free in 2011 when new DNA evidence proved their innocence. The prosecuting attorney told reporters, "Most likely these defendants, the state believes, could very easily have been acquitted."[40]

ΠATAS! Backmaskinɢ Πania Sweeps the Πation

Mountains of "satanic rock records" were thrown into bonfires in the 1980s, and rumors of subliminal messages raged. Tipper Gore's Parents' Music Resource Center sold fifteen-dollar "Satanism Research Packets" filled with all kinds of misinformation, and the Cult Awareness Network spread similar propaganda. Throughout the decade, parents sued several heavy metal artists and their record companies. Aside from the lawsuit brought against Ozzy Osbourne (infamous for his song "Mr. Crowley," among other things), the most prominent legal action involved Judas Priest. Two youths shot themselves after several hours of drinking, pot smoking, and listening to the metal group's albums, so their distraught parents filed suit. CBS Records and the band were accused of selling a "dangerous product"—the Judas Priest album titled *Stained Class*, which supposedly contained subliminal messages. The suit was dismissed after audio experts proved no such messages existed, but that didn't quell the backmasking rumors.[41]

"The cassette or CD player in too many teens' rooms is an altar to evil," radio evangelist Bob Larson warned, "dispensing the devil's devices to the accompaniment of a catchy beat." Jacob Aranza's *Backward Masking Unmasked* was one of many books that tried to expose these hidden messages. Aranza claimed that when the chorus of Queen's "Another One Bites the Dust" is played backward, one can hear, "Decide to smoke marijuana, marijuana, marijuana" (a message so hard to decipher, one probably needs to be under the influence of the devil's weed to perceive it). In Dan and Steve Peters's book *Rock's Hidden Persuader: The Truth about Backmasking,* they pick apart songs by Pink Floyd, the Rolling Stones, and the sinister Electric Light Orchestra. The sibling authors also note that Led Zeppelin guitarist Jimmy Page was fascinated by Aleister Crowley. Many rockers were also curious about him—including the Beatles, who included the occultist on the *Sgt. Pepper's* album cover. In the 1960s, the John Birch Society implicated *Sgt. Pepper's* in a communist mind-control plot, and as recently as 1994 a high-level Vatican official called the Beatles "the Devil's musicians."[42]

The Peters brothers begin *Rock's Hidden Persuader* with an analysis of *The White Album*'s "Revolution 9." That Beatles song had previously figured heavily in the "Paul Is Dead" rumor—which originated in Iowa, of all places. On September 17, 1969, Drake University's *Drake Times-Delphic* printed the first account of the musician's alleged death, titled "Is Beatle Paul McCartney Dead?" The hoax initially spread through word of mouth until someone in the gossip chain made a call to a Detroit radio station. Like many FM stations of that era, WKNR was "freeform"—a format that allowed radio DJs to play, and say, just about anything they wanted. An eighteen-minute album cut, which would never *ever* be played on Top 40 AM stations, was as common as hearing extended "raps" by a radio announcer or the musings of listeners who dialed in. Four weeks after the Drake newspaper article appeared, a caller told DJ Russ Gibb that clues to McCartney's death could be found in Beatles records. "What you've got to do," the man said, "is play 'Revolution 9' backwards."[43]

A University of Michigan sophomore named Fred LaBour happened to be listening, and two days later he published an article in the *Michigan Daily.* He was originally assigned to review the Beatles' newly released *Abbey Road* album, but LaBour took a different approach after hearing that WKNR broadcast. His piece, "McCartney Dead; New Evidence Brought to Light," struck a subtly satirical tone as it identified hidden messages in the group's lyrics and album covers. LaBour concluded the article with a wink: "The Beatles are building a mighty church, and when you emerge from it, you will be laughing." By midmorning, all copies of the paper had been snatched up, and at the end of the day the *Michigan Daily* had gone through two more press runs. The University of Michigan allowed the article to be reprinted in at least a dozen campus newspapers, and many more underground papers pirated it. The *Detroit Free Press* reported that after the story appeared in the *Harvard Crimson*, a letter to the editor said, "[It] has got us so turned on that none of the guys in the house got stoned last night." Within a month, "Paul Is Dead" became a national story, despite Iowa's distance far from the country's cultural and media centers. If not for the alternative communication network built by the 1960s counterculture, it is unlikely that the hoax would have made it out of Des Moines.[44]

These Beatles rumors injected the concept of backmasking into the public imagination at a time when musicians were experimenting with tape technologies to achieve psychedelic effects. The concept of backmasking also gained traction in part because it resonated with Cold War brainwashing discourses. Vance Packard first raised alarm bells about subliminal messages with his 1957 book *Hidden Persuaders*, which claimed marketers were placing covert commands in movies and television. Dan and Steve Peters drew on Packard's thesis in *Rock's Hidden Persuader*, and they also cited Wilson Bryan Key's 1977 bestseller *Media Sexploitation*. Looking at advertisements closely enough, Key saw everything from skulls and humping donkeys to the word *sex* spelled out in ice cubes. Key's book revived the subliminal-message meme just before the first major Satanic Panic outbreaks in the 1980s. This had the humorous effect of sending people on fool's errands such as decoding secret symbols in Proctor & Gamble products. "Whether these messages are Satan-created, or simply Satan-inspired," the Peters brothers write, "subliminal stimuli certainly must have the 'Satanic Seal of Approval.'" Their proof? "One never hears of secular rock albums promoting secretly the gospel of Christ—or even simply wholesome thoughts, such as 'Eat all your vegetables, Maynard,' or 'Would it hurt to visit your grandmother once in a while?'"[45]

The popular role-playing game Dungeons & Dragons was also lumped in with heavy metal and backmasking as a tool of the devil. A large anti-D&D cottage industry churned out propaganda such as the 1982 made-for-TV movie *Mazes & Monsters*. This craptastic film starred a young Tom Hanks, whose character was based on a Michigan State University student who went missing in 1979. His disappearance had nothing to do with D&D, but the narrative was set in motion when a private investigator floated a theory to the press that he might have wandered off into the school's steam tunnels while playing the game. Soon after, Rona Jaffe fictionalized the events in her best-selling novel *Mazes & Monsters*. Satanic Panic investigators often cited the book, and when it was adapted as a nationally distributed film, myth became fact. Radio evangelist Bob Larson's spin on the game was typical of the period. "The occult overtones of D&D are so explicit that virtually nothing in the world of Satanism is omitted," he says. "Players are told how to have their characters commune with nature spirits, consult crystal balls filled with human blood, and conjure the Egyptian deities that Moses opposed." Larson offered parents a checklist of telltale signs that their kids were worshiping Satan: a preoccupation with D&D, an interest in Ouija boards, listening to groups such as Slayer or Metallica, and sketching pentagrams or the number 666. His list describes, in part or in whole, most teenagers I knew during the 1980s.[46]

In the book *Teenage Wasteland*, sociologist Donna Gaines sought to understand the rise of teen suicide, especially among low-income kids who listened to metal. Gaines took Larson to task, arguing that "most kids view this stuff like carnival amusement, as art, as a means of expressing profound anxiety and frustrations of living. . . . Larson simply has no respect for kids' intellectual or aesthetic sensibilities." The teens who embraced H. P. Lovecraft's *Necronomicon*, Anton LaVey's *The Satanic Bible*, or Aleister Crowley's writings did so not because they were prone to murdering bunnies and babies. Those texts offered something exotic in a world of strip malls and monotonous minimum-wage jobs. Concerned adults such as Bob Larson may have had good intentions, but they had no clue about how music and popular culture works in the lives of teens. Nor did they have a very good BS detector. Larson's books uncritically quote absurd atrocity stories such as that of "Sean," whose testimony reads like the overactive imagination of a kid egged on by adults. "I became obsessively involved with Dungeons & Dragons," he said. "Through Ninjitsu, I delved into the violent aspects of the martial arts, learning how to conceal weapons and commit assassination. I once ate the leg off a live frog in biology class."[47]

jamming Mass Media

With a gullible audience ready to eat up all that devilish candy—and a cynical news media giving them what they wanted—Negativland leapt into action. Back in 1987, this satirically inclined San Francisco Bay Area sound-collage group released its fourth album, *Escape from Noise*. It contained a minor college-radio hit titled "Christianity Is Stupid," which sampled Rev. Estus W. Pirkle's sermon about state-sponsored mind-control programs. "He was talking about communism," Negativland member Don Joyce says, "and at one point he described Korean prisoner-of-war camps that had loudspeakers that kept repeating, 'Christianity is stupid, Communism is good.' So we used that sound bite as the basis of our song." *Escape from Noise* also incorporated contributions from the Church of the Subgenius's Ivan Stang, as well as several notable Bay Area artists. The Grateful Dead's Mickey Hart and Jerry Garcia played chimes, percussion, and "processed animals"; pop deconstructionists The Residents added hoots and clanging; and toilet-flushing sounds were credited to Dead Kennedy's Jello Biafra.[48]

Not long before Negativland's tour was to begin, the group realized that none of them could afford to take time off from their day jobs. They needed a reason to cancel but not just *any* reason. "One of the band members, Richard Lyons," Joyce recalls, "found this news article in the *New York Times* about a kid, David Brom, who had killed his family in Minnesota with an ax. The story mentioned his parents were very religious." Negativland drafted a press release that suggested the FBI asked them to stay home while it investigated what role "Christianity Is Stupid" might have had in the killings. "What really made the story work," says Negativland member Mark Hosler, "and what gave it legs was that it was tied into the fears about backmasking and hidden messages in rock music." Every media virus needs a host body to feed on, and the Satanic Panics carried Negativland's prank far and wide. The California music and culture magazine *BAM* reprinted the press release almost verbatim, and Channel 5, the local CBS affiliate, ran with the story. "Good evening," the news report began. "Topping Nightcast—a possible link between murder and music. . . . Four members of a midwestern family were murdered. The sixteen-year-old son is the prime suspect. Members of the experimental rock group Negativland have been drawn into the case."[49]

"We couldn't believe what was happening," Hosler tells me. Even though the band spent much of the interview talking about the news media's appetite for the sensational, predictably, none of that made it on air. Viewers were instead treated to the following conjecture: "A Negativland album may have sparked the last family dispute, and in particular, the song 'Christianity Is Stupid' may have been involved." Soon after, the *San Francisco Chronicle* gave Negativland a ring. Because the group was growing uneasy about the nature of this attention, they told reporters that the FBI asked them not to discuss the case. After the *Chronicle* went forward with an article that recycled Negativland's unsubstantiated claims, the group observed, "It's now abundantly clear that a major source for news stories is often other news." Validation from just one respectable outlet can help grease the wheels for the rapid dissemination of a prank or hoax. "We noticed right away when each new article appeared that the same errors would pop up," Joyce says. The only exception was the *Village Voice*, which reported on the band's press release with some skepticism. Music critic R. J. Smith and media critic Geoffrey Stokes even went so far as to track down a Negativland member at his job to confirm the story. "I do remember sitting there at the *Voice* processing this story," Smith tells me two decades later. "I was talking about it with Geoffrey, watching his response, and just thinking it didn't smell right, that it seemed outlandish on the face." Of all the reporters who covered this story, they were the only ones who didn't credulously rehash the original press release and subsequent news reports.[50]

Given that Negativland was already in the habit of taping television and radio broadcasts for its sound collages, the band documented the snowballing story. "When it had all blown over, we decided to make a record out of the whole thing," says Don Joyce, referring to Negativland's 1989 album *Helter Stupid*. "It was about fears of Satanism and music's influence over people and how it can make people kill. *Helter Stupid* was also about the media and how cannibalistic they are." Mark Hosler adds, "We explained in the liner notes our lie, saying very clearly how we manipulated people and what we'd done. You know, it's not enough to just hoax someone and laugh at how you fooled them, *ha ha*. There has to be a point to it all." Even though Negativland was fascinated by the results, they felt somewhat guilty because they were exploiting a real, horrible human tragedy. "To be honest, I don't think I'd do that type of thing now with the age I'm at," Hosler tells me. "We did it once and we learned a lot. I feel like now I view TV and news and information so utterly differently than when we started out as a band in 1980. It was a real eye-opener."

The Hip-Hop Illuminati

By the mid-1990s, the Satanic Panics had been debunked by sociologists, mainstream media, and evangelical publications such as *Cornerstone*. Attacks on popular music largely subsided until the 1999 Columbine school shootings stirred the pot again. Eric Harris and Dylan Klebold were said to be a part of a social circle called the "Trench Coat Mafia," but the truth is that the killers had virtually no affiliation with that clique—which by then had more or less disbanded. After news broadcasts claimed the Trench Coat Mafia might be responsible for the shootings, students trapped inside the school heard these reports and repeated this information back to reporters on their cell phones (this myth, it turns out, evolved through a very literal game of telephone). Blame was predictably cast on the pop culture that the killers consumed, such as Marilyn Manson, whose cartoonish "evil" iconography was designed to rile up fundamentalists—and, of course, to sell records. The provocative entertainer set off a few anti-Satan alarm bells, but for the most part the religious right was refocusing its attention elsewhere. In the 1990s and beyond, conservatives obsessed over another issue promoted by Christian con man Mike Warnke. "Whether Mike realized it or not," *Cornerstone* reported, "the Illuminati thread would become one of the most attractive and enduring themes of his entire improbable Satanist tale."[51]

Rock music served as a scapegoat for decades, but hip-hop added a new twist to the Illuminati myth. Jay-Z, for example, has received widespread scrutiny for imagery used in his music videos, clothing, lyrics, photo ops, and interviews. In the video for 2009's "Run This Town," the rapper wears a hoodie sweatshirt bearing the phrase "do what thou wilt" (a famous maxim of Aleister Crowley's). Jay-Z's clothing line, Roc-A-Wear, often bears symbols such as obelisks, pyramids, the all-seeing eye, and the occasional pentagram. Additionally, his record company name, Roc-A-Fella, is an allusion the Rockefeller family—the allegedly satanic dynasty that masterminded the New World Order. This is proof that he is in on the plot. Even though Jay-Z has explained that the name was chosen because it "was aspirational and confrontational," that hasn't stopped accusations that he is part of an elite secret society that runs the world. Other hip-hop artists have weathered similar charges, including Kanye West. During an interview on 96.3 NOW, a Minneapolis radio station, he was asked, "What is the craziest thing you've read about yourself and you were like, 'Well, where'd they get that from?'?" This line of questioning usually provokes an answer along the lines of "I can't believe people think I'm dating Jennifer Hudson!" Instead, Kanye stammered, in a rare loss for words, "Well, uh, the Illuminati thing. Because I, uh, I wanna know, at least I wanna know *what it is?*"[52]

The Illuminati has been a reoccurring theme in hip-hop since the early 1990s, when artists and fans embraced William Cooper's *Behold a Pale Horse*. The book's appeal stems from the fact that the author's economically deprived white followers had much in common with their black counterparts. During the go-go 1990s, a huge chunk of America was left out of the boom cycle, and a premillennial dread gripped the hip-hop generation. Journalist Jeff Chang recalls, "Youths trooped through the cities in camouflage jumpsuits and combat boots and called each other 'souljahs.'" Cooper's book could be found on urban street-vendor tables alongside such tracts as *The COINTELPRO Papers*, *Secrets of Freemasonry*, and *The Illuminati 666*. Mentions were also heard in such hip-hop songs as "Understandable Smooth," in which Ras-Kass raps that he is "still screaming *Behold a Pale Horse*." The Wu-Tang Clan exemplified this milieu, and the claustrophobic soundscapes conjured by ringleader/producer RZA complemented the group's cryptic rhymes. "Electric microbes, robotic probes / Taking telescope pictures of the globe / Exaggerated authorization, Food and Drug Administration / Testin' poison in prison population," RZA raps in "Impossible," from 1997's *Wu-Tang Forever*. Later in the song, U-God warns listeners to "get your shit together before the fuckin' Illuminati hit."[53]

Cee-Lo Green recalls an encounter in the mid-1990s with rapper Busta Rhymes, who approached his group Goodie Mob with a copy of *Behold a Pale Horse*. "I want to bless you all with some knowledge," he told them. "Read this." Cee-Lo adds, "I must say we were heavily influenced by it." These constant references to the Illuminati were a shorthand expression of the disquieting social changes African American communities confronted. With America becoming more of a separate and unequal caste system, prison was becoming a default reality for a large number of black men. "It's almost methodical / Education is false assimilation / Building prisons is economical," Ras-Kass raps in 1996's "Ordo Adchao (Order Out of Chaos)"—whose title is an oblique reference to Freemasonry. When I interviewed Ras-Kass in the mid-1990s, he said the lyric came from watching his friends getting sucked into what he called the "prison-industrial complex." Goodie Mob's breakout 1995 hit "Cell Therapy" makes a similar point during Cee-Lo's verse "Oh you know what else they trying to do? / Make a curfew, especially for me and you / The traces of the New World Order / Time is getting shorter / If we don't get prepared, people, it's gone be a slaughter." When Goodie Mob launches into the song's chorus—"Who's that peeking in my window? Pow! Nobody now"—they sound an awful lot like William Cooper at the end of his life. (Given the U.S. government's troubling history of using prisoners and people of color as medical test subjects, this paranoia was understandable.)[54]

The occultic, Egyptian-laden symbolism used by Jay-Z, Nas, the Wu-Tang Clan, and other popular hip-hop artists often gets interpreted as being purely Masonic. However, it can be more directly traced to the tradition of Afrocentrism and several quasi-mystical sects that African Americans have embraced since the mid-twentieth century. One such group is the Nation of Gods and Earths, founded in the early 1960s by a charismatic Nation of Islam student minister named Clarence 13X. He opened a street academy in Harlem and preached a condensed version of the Nation of Islam's "Lost-Found Lessons." These teachings rejected the idea of a supernatural "mystery god"; instead, the black man is his own god, the master of his destiny. Members of the Nation of Gods and Earths are commonly known as Five Percenters because they believe only 5 percent of the world's people are enlightened. The rest are the poor, ignorant, and uncivilized (the 85 percent) who are preyed on by bloodsuckers (the other 10 percent, who hold powerful positions in corporations and governments). Like many such sects, it takes a conspiratorial view of history. The plot can only be foiled by the few "poor righteous teachers" who were sent to emancipate the mentally deaf, dumb, and blind.[55]

The Nation of Gods and Earths was part of hip-hop culture from its beginnings. Afrika Bambaataa was affiliated, members sometimes provided security at 1970s hip-hop shows in the South Bronx, and it gained a large number of adherents by the late 1980s. Popular artists like Rakim, Big Daddy Kane, Busta Rhymes, and the aptly named Poor Righteous Teachers loaded their lyrics with references to this organization. They also popularized Five Percenter slang terms such as "dropping science," "break it down," and "word." (The Wu-Tang Clan's RZA explains, "That's what you say when someone expresses a deep truth: Word.") The Nation of Gods and Earths was one of many African American sects and secret societies that flourished in the 1950s and 1960s. Most can trace their roots back to the Moorish Science Temple of America, founded in 1913 by a man known as Noble Drew Ali. It heavily borrowed symbolism and ceremonies from Freemasonry's Ancient Arabic Order of the Nobles of the Mystic Shrine, better known as Shriners. This order was among the first to introduce Islamic imagery to America (along with fez-wearing old men who drive tiny cars). In the book *Occult America*, Mitch Horowitz writes, "a veritable who's who of early black-power figures joined or came in close contact with Moorish Science in the 1920s," including Nation of Islam architects Wallace D. Fard and Elijah Muhammad.[56]

Like these groups' nineteenth-century, white, European, occultic counterparts, they wove fantasy into their official histories. The Nation of Islam's science-fiction origin story involves a mad scientist named Dr. Yacub who created whites in order to place blacks in bondage. There was also a spacecraft, The Mother Ship, which would quite literally uplift the race. Far from being relegated to the obscure fringes of African American society, these stories resonated with many—including Muhammad Ali. "For Ali there was something in the notion of black superiority and the spaceship that was comforting and nourishing to him," said his friend Robert Lipsyte. "It gave him a sense of self, a connection to something larger and more important at the time." The Nation of Islam's teachings tapped into a strand of Afro-futurism that ran deep through twentieth-century black popular culture. Musicians such as avant-jazz legend Sun Ra, dub reggae pioneer Lee "Scratch" Perry, glam-funk trio LaBelle, Parliament-Funkadelic's George Clinton, Outkast's Andre 3000, and Janelle Monae have employed these tropes.

They mixed playful iconography, wild costumes, and out-there-but-funky music to express their alienation—all while joyfully voicing racial pride. Afro-futurism is a lively example of how fantasy can be empowering, because it allows people to imagine a newer, better world.[57] Sun Ra biographer John F. Szwed observes,

> This black cosmic vision is easily seen as part of the theme of travel, of journey, of exodus, of escape which dominates African-American narratives: of people who could fly back to Africa, travel in the spirit, visit or be visited by the dead; of chariots and trains to heaven, the Underground Railroad, Marcus Garvey's steamship line, Rosa Parks on the Mobile bus, freedom riders. It was also a vision which lurked distantly but stubbornly behind blues songs which praised the technology of motion and travel, where trains, cars, airplanes, buses—even transmission systems ("Dynaflow")—were celebrated as part of African-American postagricultural mobility within a Booker T. Washington / *Popular Science* optimism about the future.[58]

Born in Birmingham, Alabama at the height of segregation, Herman Poole Blount took on a new name and claimed Saturn as his homeland (which was a more hospitable environment than the Jim Crow South). Sun Ra began his musical career in the 1950s on the same Southside Chicago streets that embraced the Nation of Islam. The iconoclast never joined Elijah Muhammad's organization, but he was a member of a secret society named Thmei Research. Much like the Nation of Islam's bow-tied foot soldiers, Sun Ra could be seen on street corners lecturing and passing out his hand-typed tracts. Critic John Corbett called him "a supersonic cosmo-science sermonist," because pedagogy was part of the space-jazz package. While looking toward the future, Sun Ra kept his feet firmly planted in the past by studying Africa, Egyptology, numerology, mysticism, and biblical texts. He did not accept many of the Nation of Islam's teachings, including the belief that white people were devils ("black people can be devils, too," he countered). Nevertheless, their views did overlap at times. Sun Ra and Elijah Muhammad believed it was necessary to invert the Bible's symbolism because its text had been "poisoned," so they turned to secret and esoteric knowledge to free the minds of their people.[59]

Years later, these ideas were absorbed into hip-hop and fanned out into popular culture, via song. Rick Ross and Jay-Z's 2010 hit "Free Mason" contains similar imagery. "We the lost symbols, speak in cryptic codes," Ross raps, "ancient wisdom, valuable like gifts of Gold." The song is less a serious nod to occultism and more of a masculine boast about black power. In Jay-Z's verse, he dismisses conspiracy rumors with the couplet "I said I was amazin' / Not that I was a Mason." After an interviewer pressed him about being a member of a cult, Jay-Z more or less admitted that he was just messing with people's heads. "I'm an entertainer at the end of the day," he said. "Maybe I'll push your buttons." Black secret societies and sects emerged as a reaction to segregation, urban decay, and a desire for self-sufficiency. In the absence of that context, these coded lyrics have been used as evidence of a New World Order conspiracy. Moreover, a lack of familiarity with African American culture has led some whites to assume all kinds of outlandish things. For instance, Glenn Beck once aired footage of a Kansas City youth group practicing a step show (a foot-stomping style of synchronized dancing popular in traditionally black fraternities). Without this background knowledge, he informed viewers that "Obama's SS" was being trained in inner cities throughout America.[60]

The rising status of a few prominent African Americans has been unsettling for some of the United States' shrinking white majority. In 2012, the number of nonwhite babies surpassed Caucasian births for the first time, a demographic shift that coincided with an abysmal economy. Barack Obama (a Jay-Z-quoting Ivy Leaguer) has reinforced a variety of persecution complexes, including the idea that whites will soon become slaves. The rhetoric of slavery is quite common among contemporary Tea Partiers and old-school Illuminatiphobes. In the 1971 book *Richard Nixon*, the John Birch Society's Gary Allen wrote, "Americans are destined for slavery unless the CFR *Insiders* and those who are controlled by them can be purged from the government." Sarah Palin, Rush Limbaugh, and Glenn Beck use very similar metaphors. The latter asked his audience during a discussion of health-care reform, "Are we creating slaves?" Conservatives deploy that word to convey a loss of individual liberty or even the belief that they will *literally* be enslaved—though there are some contexts where its use is verboten. In 2009, the far-right Texas Board of Education voted to replace all mentions of "slavery" in public-school textbooks with the odd phrase "Atlantic Triangular Trade." At a time when the history of slavery is literally being erased, the right's appropriation of this word is troubling. Even more disturbing is how four centuries of trickery have produced a fantastical worldview that has reshaped the material world.[61]

💣 💣 💣

The Satanic Panics and the ongoing outbreaks of Illuminatiphobia demonstrate what can go wrong when fantasy takes on a life of its own. In the 1960s, the counterculture's dalliances with esoteric thought led Christian conservatives to believe that devilish forces were destroying civilization. One of the faces of this evil was Anton LaVey, who had a love of carnival entertainment and old-fashioned publicity stunts. His sense of humor wasn't shared by the religious right, which took his shock tactics at face value and promptly freaked out. They unleashed their sordid imaginations by mining pop-culture horror imagery and urban legends that were circulating in religious tracts, newsletters, and radio. This is yet another reminder of how alternative and mainstream media are locked in a dialogic relationship. Much of what surfaced in the "recovered" memories of alleged survivors of satanic ritual abuse came from a mixture of stories that appeared in Hollywood films (*Rosemary's Baby*, *The Omen*, and *Mazes & Monsters*), popular music (the Rolling Stones' "Sympathy for the Devil" and Ozzy Osborne's "Mr. Crowley"), religious books (by Christian con artists Mike Warnke, Michelle Smith, and Lauren Stratford), countercultural periodicals (the *Realist* and the *Los Angeles Free Press*), and sensationalistic news stories (from the 1960s coverage of the Manson murders to the 1980s Geraldo Rivera devil-worship television special). This head-spinning swirl of fact and fiction produced a paranoid feedback loop that sent three innocent teens to jail for eighteen years, and ruined countless other lives.

Showbiz Tricksters
and the Pop Underground

Popular culture is an inviting space for trickster figures. Entertainers generally have more leeway than your average person to push the boundaries of convention because they tend to be, well, *entertaining*. Bitter truths can be swallowed more easily with a dollop of sugar and spice. The eccentric Otherness exuded by early television star Korla Pandit, discussed in the next few pages, was made palatable by a spectacle that featured hypnotic music and striking costumes. One can get away with most anything by making people tap their toes, laugh, or shake their heads in disbelief. This was also true of Gorgeous George's gender-bending wrestling act, Muhammad Ali's in-and-out-of-ring dustups, and Andy Kaufman's dada displays on *The Dating Game, Late Night with David Letterman*, and other television staples. In spite of—or perhaps because of—their amusing idiosyncrasies, these men became household names. Conversely, Yoko Ono is often more despised than beloved because she never conformed to the showbiz rules that made her husband, John Lennon, a megastar. Yoko's prankish conceptual art and her uncompromising scream are two reasons why (along with sexism and racism) she provoked such visceral reactions among the public. Even noncelebrities have been able to break into the culture industry machine by using tricky tactics. Over the past half century, Jeanne and Alan Abel made headlines with pranks that ranged from a cryogenics-themed press conference involving billionaire recluse Howard Hughes to a long-running anticensorship satire that sought to clothe "naked" animals. As is true of the others discussed in this chapter, this couple's occasional night raids on mass media surely warped many a mind by suggesting that a world of weirdness was just over the horizon.

A Weird Musical Adventure

"Come with us through melody to the four corners of the earth," the KTLA station announcer said as an attractive and enigmatic man gazed into the camera. "Hear music exotic and familiar spring from the amaz-ing hands of Korla Pandit, *on a musical adventure!*" An androgynous figure massaged the organ with his slender fingers, looking a bit like *Purple Rain*–era Prince in a jeweled turban. *Korla Pandit's Adventures in Music* was the first all-music show on television, and it was an instant hit in 1948—airing five days a week for over nine hundred episodes. *TV Guide* named it the "Best Show" in Los Angeles, Pandit won the magazine's "Top Male Personality" honors, and he released more than two dozen records over the course of two decades. The mystic ascribed his success to the fact that music is a universal language, while also maintaining that television stations could transmit his brain waves. "I never spoke," he said, "yet I received letters from around the world that communicated as if people knew exactly what was on my mind." Even though Pandit was silent on camera, friends joked that he would never shut up in person. The organist loved to talk about his privileged child-hood in New Delhi, where his father was a government bureaucrat and a friend of Mohandas Gandhi. He also claimed his mother was a French opera singer, though the truth was more mundane: Pandit was a black man from the Midwest. "He was light-skinned, about the color of Gen-eral Colin Powell," said Stan Freberg, who worked with him at KTLA. "To tell you the truth, I think Korla Pandit invented himself."[1]

The St. Louis native was born in 1921 as John Roland Redd and began his radio career at a CBS affiliate in Iowa. In the late 1930s, he followed several of his sisters to California, where he worked as a staff musi-cian on network radio shows. Redd adopted the name Juan Rolondo and performed everything from country and western to big-band jazz. Then, in 1948, he dropped his Mexican identity and changed his name to Korla Pandit. That year he recorded "Stampede" with Roy Rogers and Sons of the Pioneers, who dubbed him "Cactus Pandit" (it was surely the first—and last?—time a black man passing as a turban-clad Indian ever played on a country record). Korla's beautiful blond wife, Beryl Pandit, a former Disney Studios airbrush artist, was instrumental in crafting his persona: a TV swami with hypnotic musical powers. She designed the sets, worked with lighting technicians, and costumed her husband. Outside the television studio, he remained a seasoned jazz musician who occasionally sat in with his idol, Art Tatum, who took a liking to the organist. But when posing as Pandit, he stripped any trace of African American musical styles from his repertoire to deflect unwanted scrutiny into his background. He died in 1998 having never told his two sons, Shari and Koram, the truth about his past.[2]

Korla Pandit remained silent on camera because his Indian accent didn't really pass muster, and, for that matter, neither did his outfit. Hindus typically didn't wear turbans—those were Sikhs, and they didn't put jewels in their headdress—but most Americans were not attuned to these cultural distinctions. He complemented his exotic headgear with a coat and tie, personifying the postwar stereotype of an Indian: a blend of mystical and modern. Pandit deeply believed in his music's potential to cross racial lines, but this utopian impulse was undermined by colonialist clichés. Musicologist Timothy Taylor notes that "Magnetic Theme," Pandit's signature song, "begins with a virtual catalogue of musical orientalisms, from near east to far east." The orientalist tropes did not end with the instrumentation. *Adventures in Music* presented Pandit as an unspeaking "Other" who was placed on display for the voyeuristic pleasure of Western eyes. He subverted these ideological constraints, to a certain extent, by staring back at the viewer for long periods without blinking. The effect was alternately seductive and unsettling.[3]

A program with no talking and only organ music surely would not fly today, but the rules of this new medium were still up for grabs. People didn't really know what TV was supposed to be. KTLA was also an independent broadcaster, which gave it a flexibility that its network competitors lacked. Shows were live, were rough around the edges, and offered a dizzying variety of musical entertainment: Harry Owens and His Royal Hawaiians, Ina Ray Hutton and Her All-Girl Orchestra, Liberace, and of course Pandit. There were also cooking programs, a variety show on ice, puppet theater, and a weird comedy named *Yer Ole Buddy* (in which a flustered man tried to explain the machinations of a television studio to viewers). Oddest of all was KTLA's decision to broadcast an atomic test explosion, live. "All this was done without any advance publicity," said Johnny Polich, who worked at the station. "Thirty seconds before the blast, we cut the food show off the air and just went on." That must have made for some jarring viewing! Early television created a semianarchic opening for pop-culture trickster figures to slip through the door and shape this new medium in their own image. With enough luck and pluck, border-crossing outsiders could become insiders. This gave a Jim Crow–era black man access to the nation's airwaves, enabling Korla Pandit to broadcast from an alternate universe located within his own imagination. "To have seen him on television," biographer R. J. Smith writes, "was to inhabit a perfumed realm."[4]

A Gorgeous Wrestler

Those who attended Gorgeous George wrestling matches quite literally entered a perfumed realm. A 1948 *Newsweek* article noted that "both in and out of the ring he affects a . . . swishy manner, and effeminate fragrance." As part of his prebout ritual, the wrestler dressed from head to toe in a frilly, beaded woman's nightgown. It was slowly and suggestively removed by his male valet, who then sprayed down the ring with an oversized canister of "Chanel No. 10" (which was, he said, twice as nice as Chanel No. 5). George then pompously bowed to the audience, mocking them. "Sissy!" they screamed back. "Who do you think you are?" The blue-collar crowd went berserk when he delayed the fight by *slooooooowly* folding his clothing with snobbish care. "The more they yelled," George recounted, "the more time I took." The preening wrestler's narcissistic persona and fluid sexual identity got him tagged as "a Liberace in tights" (George, like the gender-bending Liberace, regularly appeared on KTLA). Before matches, he held press conferences in women's beauty salons while getting his hair done, long golden locks and all. George stayed in character around sports reporters, whom he treated as inferiors—a shtick that was always good for a few column inches. Even though audiences retaliated with projectiles and verbal taunts, he was also widely beloved. A *Boxing Illustrated* profile noted that many people in the arena "jeered him with a smile and hated him with affection." Gorgeous George's outrageous performances gave audiences a license to respond with their own over-the-top behavior, joining in on the fun.[5]

In the late 1940s, televised wrestling matches aired every night on prime time, which made Gorgeous George as famous as just about any American celebrity. All the comedians of the day—from Jack Benny to Bob Hope—told Gorgeous George jokes, and his campy act helped move the shocking and outré into the televised mainstream. "He was bizarre, I'd never seen anything like it," John Waters said. "A man who wore women's clothes, who had bleached hair, who made people scared but also made them laugh." As Mr. and Mrs. Waters shouted at the television, offended by George's abominable behavior, their eleven-year-old son was awestruck. That night, he decided to go into show business. Waters started making underground films as a teenager and, eventually, directed gross-out classics such as *Pink Flamingos*, *Female Trouble*, and *Polyester*. "Gorgeous George inspired me to think up bizarre characters with humor," he said. "In my films, I'm beginning to realize, all of my characters have something to do with him, subliminally." Few entertainers—or anyone, for that matter—can claim such an eclectic and iconic list of devotees: John Waters, James Brown, Bob Dylan, Muhammad Ali, and Andy Kaufman. Each borrowed a different element from his transgressive persona, adding their own spin.[6]

Gorgeous George influenced James Brown's live shows by displaying, as the singer put it, "a special flamboyance." He also shaped Brown's wardrobe choices and other elements of his stagecraft, including the famous cape routine—which Brown claimed began as an improvised tribute to the wrestler. George's boastful nicknames ("The Toast of the Coast," "The Sensation of the Nation") also gave rise to Brown's memorable taglines ("The Godfather of Soul," "The Hardest Working Man in Show Business"). Another musical trickster figure he inspired was Bob Dylan, who first witnessed the wrestler's act in Hibbing, Minnesota during the late 1950s. "It was Gorgeous George, in all his magnificent glory," Dylan recalled. "He had valets and was surrounded by women carrying roses, wore a majestic fur-lined gold cape and his long blond curls were flowing." The aspiring musician was performing in the National Guard Amory, the same venue where a wrestling match was about to take place. As the beautiful showman walked by the stage with his entourage, the singer claims George winked at him and mouthed the following words: "You're making it come alive." He could have been saying anything, but Dylan insists that this chance encounter "was all the recognition and encouragement" he would need "for years to come." The times were a-changing, indeed.[7]

When Muhammad Ali (then known as Cassius Clay) first witnessed a Gorgeous George match, he saw the path to stardom. The wrestler walked down the aisle to the tune of "Pomp and Circumstance" while dressed in a formfitting red velvet gown and a lush white satin robe. With his nose held high, George surveyed his domain and addressed the crowd: "Peasants!" He relished the insults, screams, and foot stomping. "Oh, everybody just *booed* him," Clay recalled. "I looked around and I saw everybody was mad. *I was mad!* I saw 15,000 people coming to see this man get beat, and his talking did it. And I said, 'This is a *gooood* idea.'" After the match, George gave him some advice. "You just gotta have a gimmick, polish your act," he said. "Boxing, wrestling—it's all a show. You gotta get the crowd to react." He added, "You got your good looks, a great body, and you've got a good mouth on you. Talk about how pretty you are, tell 'em how great you are. And a lot of people will pay to see somebody shut your big mouth. So keep bragging, keep on sassing, and *always be outrageous.*" Though Gorgeous George didn't explicitly say it, he was surely aware that millions of white Americans wanted to see this "uppity" black man have his piehole wired shut. This tension helped make Ali one of the most controversial and beloved figures of the 1960s.[8]

A Beautiful Boxer

At the beginning of Cassius Clay's professional boxing career, he was primarily known for winning an Olympic gold medal and possessing a loud mouth. Most sportswriters hated him, especially the old guard, who felt he was not properly deferential. The racist treatment by boxing crowds and journalists certainly would have justified Clay's decision to throw his Olympic medal into the Ohio River in disgust. It is one of the most memorable stories in sports history, but the truth is that Clay simply lost it. This fiction first appeared in his autobiography, *The Greatest*, which was a mix of fact and folklore ghostwritten by the Nation of Islam. "The story about the Olympic medal wasn't true, but we had to take it on faith," said James Silberman, the editor and chief of Random House. "When he was young he took everything with a wink, even the facts of his life." This tale resonated during the civil rights era because it conveyed a deeper truth about the indignities that African Americans suffered in America, the supposed "land of the free." As cultural critic John Leland reminds us, "Tricksters tell small lies to reveal bigger ones."[9]

In early 1964, this fast-footed boxer shook up the world in spectacular fashion. Clay faced heavyweight champion Sonny Liston, a favorite of the white establishment because he didn't rock the racial boat. Most everyone believed the champ would destroy this inexperienced upstart, and bookies set the odds seven to one against Clay. A *New York Times* editor even instructed the young sports writer Robert Lipsyte to map out the quickest route from the arena to the hospital. Liston was an imposing man, but that didn't stop Clay from publicly mocking him: "Who would have thought / When they came to the fight / That they'd witness the launching / Of a human satellite? / Yes, the crowd did not dream / When they laid down their money / That they would see / A total eclipse of Sonny!" When Liston arrived at Miami International Airport, his opponent was waiting for him on the tarmac, shouting, "Chump! Big ugly bear! I'm gonna whup you right now!" Liston fled the airport for a rented beach house, but Clay chased him in a car, hurling more insults until a fuming Liston pulled over. "Listen, you little punk," Liston screamed. "I'll punch you in the mouth. This has gone too far!" They were separated, but the staged drama resumed in front of Liston's rental property, where Clay held court with reporters and fans in the front yard.[10]

At the weigh-in on the morning of the fight, Clay became even more erratic. "Float like a butterfly! Sting like a bee!" he famously shouted, warming up his act. "Round eight to prove I'm great!" No one had ever seen this kind of behavior in the world of boxing, where anything less than stoicism gave off a whiff of panic and fear. Liston stood on the scales as his bug-eyed opponent kept flinging abuse. "Hey, sucker! You're a chump! You been tricked, chump!" Clay ignored warning after warning until he was fined $2,500. "I suspected that there was a plan in his public clowning," Clay's friend Malcolm X later said. "I suspected, and he confirmed to me, that he was doing everything possible to con and to 'psyche' Sonny Liston into coming into the ring angry, poorly trained, and overconfident, expecting another of his vaunted one-round knockouts." The psychological warfare worked. Clay's corner man, Ferdie Pacheco, said, "It convinced Liston to the end of his life that Ali was crazy."[11]

The moment the first-round bell rang, Clay launched himself into the ring and began circling—bouncing from foot to foot, head twitching from side to side. Liston lunged with a left jab, missed by two feet, and things went downhill from there. After six rounds, an exhausted Liston refused to fight anymore and forfeited the match. Cassius Clay then jumped on the ropes, leaned into the sportswriters sitting nearby, and taunted them. "Eat your words! Eat your words! . . . I am the greatest!" he shouted. "I shook up the world. I'm the prettiest thing that ever lived." He also threw in a line that most people missed in the heat of the moment. "I talk to God every day," he said, "the *real* God!" Malcolm X, who laid low before the bout to avoid controversy, had now returned to his friend's side. The next day, Clay announced that he had joined the Nation of Islam, whose leader, Elijah Muhammad, soon gave him a new name: Muhammad Ali. The boxer respected Martin Luther King Jr. but was more compelled by Malcolm X's fiery rhetoric and messages of self-reliance. Not surprisingly, this lost the boxer a large chunk of his white fans. They could tolerate Clay's clownish behavior, but not Ali's association with an imposing and inscrutable black nationalist group.[12]

Like the other pop-culture trickster figures profiled in this chapter, Muhammad Ali straddled the center and margins—remaking America's social landscape in the process. He became even more politically outspoken after converting to Islam and was openly defiant when drafted into the military in 1966. If Ali had served, he almost certainly wouldn't have seen conflict and instead would have been allowed to continue boxing as a representative of the U.S. Army. But Ali stuck with his principles and was exiled from the ring at the height of his career, while in his physical prime. During this time, Ali uttered what became one of his most well-known lines: "I ain't got no quarrel with them Viet Cong." The antiwar and civil rights movements quickly turned it into the more dramatic "No Viet Cong ever called me Nigger." The phrase was later appropriated by the Viet Cong themselves, who dropped propaganda leaflets stating, "black soldiers: no vietnamese ever called you nigger." This game of telephone underscores how much of an influential global figure Muhammad Ali had become by the end of the 1960s. It also demonstrates how a single provocative or prankish statement can powerfully reframe a debate, especially when amplified through mass media.[13]

YES, SHE IS A WITCH

Yoko Ono also used media to shock, confuse, annoy, and amuse. Rather than praising her as a groundbreaking artist, angry Beatles fans spent years blaming her for their beloved group's breakup. She arrived in New York City in 1957 after studying composition at Sarah Lawrence College and philosophy in Japan, where she was the first woman admitted into a prestigious program at Gakushuin University. Both experiences constrained her too much, so Yoko set out on her own iconoclastic path. "I always liked her," says Roz Payne, a founder of the Women's International Terrorist Conspiracy from Hell, or WITCH. She tells me, "I liked the way she and John mixed art and politics and had a sense of humor about it—like their Bed-In for Peace." For this prank-cum-conceptual-art-piece, staged in 1969, the couple leveraged their celebrity status to spread antiwar messages. John and Yoko invited reporters to cover their weeklong stint in bed, but if media outlets wanted this entertaining spectacle, they had to broadcast the couple's critiques as well. "There were commercials for war," Lennon observed at the time, "so why don't we do a commercial for peace?" This "happening" was an extension of the work Yoko had done for a decade, but many people still think she's just a groupie. *New York Times* music critic Robert Palmer summed up the price she paid: "It is quite likely that having John Lennon fall in love with her was the worst thing that could have happened to Yoko Ono's career as an artist."[14]

Yoko was a key player in Fluxus, a 1960s art movement that was, according to its 1965 manifesto, "the fusion of Spike Jones, Vaudeville, gag, children's games and Duchamp." She organized downtown Manhattan's first loft events, the Chambers Street Series, which were ground zero for the city's experimental art scene. Yoko also collaborated with seminal avant-garde composers and musicians such as La Monte Young, John Cage, and Ornette Coleman—as well as visual artists, dancers, and poets. She moved on to more established venues such as Carnegie Recital Hall and London's Indica Gallery, but it wasn't always easy. "I feel that even in the avant-garde world, what I was doing was seen as a little bit out of line," she tells me. "They had their own set of rules, you know? 'You can't do that! You can't do certain things!'" For Yoko's *Cut Piece*, the audience was invited to cut off bits of her clothes until nothing remained. It was a radical statement, especially for 1964. She sat onstage with her legs folded in a traditional Japanese pose of feminine submissiveness, embodying the kind of vulnerability women experienced in Asian and American societies. "Although audience members' reactions at each venue varied in the reserve or abandon with which they cut off her clothing," art historian Jayne Wark writes, "the implications of the piece always invoked tensions between exhibitionism and voyeurism, victim and assailant, sadist and masochist, subject and object."[15]

Yoko spent most of her life stirring it up. "Yeah, 'stirring up' is the right word," she says. "Stirring up. Period." When I ask her to elaborate, she points to a song of hers titled "Yes, I'm a Witch." It begins in true punk-rock fashion: "Yes, I'm a witch / I'm a bitch / I don't care what you say / My voice is real / My voice speaks truth / I don't fit in your ways." Yoko reversed the meaning of the words "witch" and "bitch" much like how gay-rights activists later appropriated *queer*, turning an insult into a provocative badge of honor. "The line 'Yes, I am a witch,'" she says, laughing, "that one line stirs up a lot, doesn't it?" She then bemoans the fact that the public still doesn't get it. "Some people," Yoko sighs, "take it very seriously and get very angry." Despite caricatures to the contrary, her brand of 1970s feminism was definitely not strident. Take the song "What a Mess," in which she wryly tells the guys, "If you keep hammering antiabortion / We'll tell you no more masturbation for men / Every day you're killing living sperm in the billions / So how do you feel about that, brother?" Yoko's absurdist humor was on display in her conceptual piece *Questionnaire, 1966 spring*, which included such lines as "Happenings were first invented by Greek gods" and "The word 'manila envelope' comes from a deeply-rooted racial prejudice." There's plenty more where that came from. *Do It Yourself Fluxfest Presents Yoko Ono and Dance Co.* instructed its audience to "Face the wall and imagine throughout the year banging your head against it: A) Slowly until the wall collapses B) Violently until your head is gone."[16]

Her 1971 piece *Museum of Modern [F]art* embodies her irreverent attitude toward the art world's more staid conventions. It consists of a photo of Yoko walking underneath the Museum of Modern Art's entrance sign in New York City, capturing her midstride. While standing at the gap between the words "Modern" and "Art," she holds a shopping bag with an "F" that matches the size and font of the signage above. (As the old saying goes, art is merely the last three letters of the word *fart*.) "I could have been killed because of my sense of humor," she laughs, mischievously. "I have to be very careful." Yoko is referring, in part, to the sorts of "ugly bitch" verbal assaults she endured after meeting Beatle John. In the face of the racism, sexism, and pure unadulterated hatred—directed not just at women, generally, but at her, specifically—this trickster figure responded by laughing and screaming at the world. "When I said, 'Yes, I am a witch,' don't you think that is a kind of, you know, *ha ha* to them?" She sighs again. "But people take it seriously. That's the problem."[17]

Andy Kaufman Melts Minds

Growing up in Virginia Beach during the early 1980s, I often watched professional wrestling with my best friend, the television. I knew that those carefully choreographed body slams were pretty much a hoax, but I must admit that my twelve-year-old self was suckered by Andy Kaufman. When the *Taxi* star showed up in 1982 at the Mid-Atlantic Coliseum in Memphis, Tennessee, he mocked everyone. "I'm from Hollywood," he said, pointing at his cranium as he mouthed off about his higher intelligence and how southerners were *stupid*. Kaufman also claimed he was the world's greatest "Intergender Wrestling Champion," bragging that he could beat any woman in the ring. After he went too far with his antics, I cheered when wrestler Jerry Lawler stepped in and shoved him to the ground. "Lawler, you think you're really being smart," Kaufman ranted. "Look, I'm from Hollywood. That's where we make movies and TV shows. . . . I'm not from down here in men-fus ten-uh-see, okay?" *What a total jerk*, I thought. Kaufman kept needling the crowd about how his matches with women were real and that professional wrestlers were phonies. I was seething. *Andy Kaufman is such a jerk, and I really, really hate him.* I even stopped watching *Taxi* because of it.

Eventually, this ugly display overflowed into another favorite show of mine. "On April 5th, 1982, in Memphis, Tennessee," David Letterman said, introducing the *Late Night* segment, "Andy Kaufman—the actor-comedian and Intergender Wrestling Champion—had his first wrestling match with a member of his own sex." Cue footage: Lawler delivers a pile-driver move, and Kaufman crashes to the ground, head first, body crumpled. Off he goes in an ambulance! "Tonight, for the first time on network television," Letterman said, "they meet face to face. Here are Andy Kaufman and Jerry Lawler!" Cheers and boos erupted as they walked on. "Now, I don't know a great deal about wrestling," Letterman said to Lawler, "but it looks to me like you gave Andy that second pile-driver *after* the bell. Now, that didn't seem like a really sportsmanlike thing to do." Lawler was unfazed. "You say that wasn't a sportsmanlike thing to do," he drawled, "but everybody that sees Andy Kaufman, the way he is now, you know, Mr. Nice Guy—the very loveable little Latka character and everything—this is not the Andy Kaufman that I saw." *Damn right*, I thought. *That guy is a grade-A moron!* "It's the way I make my living," Lawler said, "and he comes in making a joke of it." On the show, Kaufman kept antagonizing Lawler until Lawler finally snapped, delivering a slap across Andy's face that knocked him to the ground.

Cut to commercial.

"Hi there, and welcome back to the show," Letterman said, right before Kaufman unleashed a torrent of obscenities at Lawler. "I am sick of this bleep! You are full of bleep, my friend! I will sue you for everything you have!" He walked backstage for a few seconds, then returned. "I am sorry," Kaufman said, turning to the audience, "I am sorry to use those words on television. I apologize to all my fans. I'm sorry, I'm sorry. But you! You're a bleep bleep!!!" Kaufman then pounded Letterman's desk, hurled a cup of coffee at Lawler, and ran away again. After an awkward pause, the host deadpanned, "I think, uh, I think you can use *some* of those words on TV. But what you *can't do* is throw coffee.

I've said it over and over." I had never seen anything like that on television, and my adolescent mind was blown wide open. In my defense, I only knew Kaufman as the affable Latka Gravas character on *Taxi* and had no clue about his previous history of trickery. I was too young to have seen his offbeat *Saturday Night Live* performances in the 1970s, nor did I witness his other surreal televised acts. It took me years to catch on, and only then did I realize Kaufman's hijinks had body-slammed my consciousness. It all came into focus long after his death, when his friend and collaborator Bob Zmuda finally confirmed that Lawler had conspired with them. "Jerry is quite the gentleman," Zmuda said, "and a helluva good sport." After all, it was just showbiz.[18]

"I wanted to recapture the old days of the carnivals," Kaufman said of his wrestling act, which tapped into a decades-old tradition. In the early twentieth century, carnies moved the sport away from its more respectable Greco-Roman-styled roots and into shadier territories. Collusion and fight fixing became the norm, and the 1930s saw the rise of bad-guy "heels." Early television made wrestling more popular than ever—accelerating the trend toward outrageous showmanship, stylized mock violence, and gaudy garb. "Whenever I play a role," Kaufman said, "whether it's good or bad, an evil person or a nice person, I believe in being a purist and going all the way with the role. If I'm going to be a villainous wrestler, I believe in going all the way with it." When he screamed that women were only good for "washing the dishes" and "peeling the potatoes," it was an homage to Gorgeous George. "I'll kill him," the cross-dressing wrestler would scream. "I'll tear his arm off. If the bum beats me, I'll crawl across the ring and cut off my hair, but it's not gonna happen because I'm the greatest wrestler in the world." One of the many things the comedian-cum-performance-artist borrowed from George's act was a promise to shave his head if he was defeated. Kaufman staged his act in an era when feminism was gaining acceptance, and he knew his male-chauvinist-pig routine would provoke audiences. Inversely, Gorgeous George's gender-bending performances took place when sex roles were much more rigidly defined. It didn't take much for a man dressed in a frilly nightgown—in a wrestling ring—to send postwar crowds through the roof.[19]

Early in Kaufman's career as a stage performer, he sometimes opened for musicians—including, implausibly, schlock-popper Barry Manilow and R&B greats the Temptations. His inept Foreign Man routine certainly did not win over the latter group's predominantly black fan base, who unleashed an avalanche of boos. Kaufman wept uncontrollably, pulled out a large cap gun, walked behind the curtains, fired the pistol into the microphone, and thudded to the ground. Deafening silence followed. The audience came to hear "My Girl" and "Just My Imagination," so this was not exactly what they paid for. The Temptations reportedly "sang extra hard that night to make up for it." Kaufman caused a similar stir when warming up for Barry Manilow's white-bread audience a couple of years later. He had such an effect on the crowd that the crooner said it was all he could do "to try to bring them back from the edge of revolution." A Barry Manilow audience on the edge of revolution must have been a sight to see![20]

When Kaufman appeared as the boorishly unfunny lounge lizard Tony Clifton, he was unrecognizable in a fat suit, sunglasses, wig, and prosthetic makeup. And in 1981, all hell broke loose when he opened for comedian Rodney Dangerfield. After arriving twenty-five minutes late, the crowd grew irritated when Clifton insisted he would not perform until all cigarettes were extinguished. When he finally swaggered onstage, Clifton lit up a cigar, blew smoke at the audience, and warbled "I Left My Heart in San Francisco." Tomatoes and eggs rained down as he plodded on with the next number, "Yankee Doodle," and then a banana cake splattered on his shoulder. On cue, Clifton shouted, "Drop the net!" A protective barrier came down as someone screamed, "*you suck!*" When he dedicated the next song "to the hostages," someone else shouted back, "*they should take you hostage!*" A coin flew through the net and barely missed Clifton's face, so he donned San Francisco Police Department riot gear—complete with a microphone mounted on the helmet. After an apple ripped through the net and exploded on his helmet, he spent the remainder of the show berating everyone from the wings. Promoter Bill Graham, who previously had booked the chaotic final Sex Pistols gig, had never seen anything like this.[21]

When Kaufman was offered a posh job on *Taxi*, he refused to sign on unless Clifton was given a guest-star turn. After the show's producers caved, they discovered Clifton could not act, was rude to other actors, and strutted around the set with a prostitute on each arm. Clifton was escorted off the studio lot, screaming, "I'll sue your fucking asses! You'll never work in Vegas again!" Kaufman showed up to work the next week as if nothing had happened, which further incensed the cast. "I don't know if I'd want to go through that again," Danny DeVito grumbled. "We all felt it was a big waste of time." Clifton was also ejected from *The Dinah Shore Show* after a cooking demonstration gone awry. The rogue performer nearly caused a fire when he threw a whole stick of butter into a hot frying pan, and then he crushed a dozen eggshells in Shore's hands. "Do you know who I am?!" Clifton yelled as security dragged him out. "I'm a big star!" Jean Stapleton, who played Edith Bunker on the 1970s sitcom *All in the Family*, locked herself in the greenroom with another guest, David Copperfield. The magician recalled, "She was weeping and sobbing when all the pandemonium broke loose in the studio. It was amazing."[22]

Tony Clifton could be mean-spirited, in an over-the-top cartoonish way, but this was an anomaly in the pantheon of Kaufman characters. Mostly, Andy exuded a sweet, naive charm. This distanced him from edgier comedians such as Lenny Bruce, who shocked audiences with obscene and sacrilegious quips. In *Andy Kaufman: Wrestling with the American Dream*, Florian Keller writes, "What ultimately sets him apart from Lenny Bruce is that he does not interfere with the symbolic order by bringing to light the 'sick' fantasies that are disavowed, and prohibited by, the letter of the law." Instead, Kaufman enacted "healthy" public fantasies—being famous, normal, and loved—and exaggerated them to the point of cognitive dissonance. His overly literal performance of the American Dream evokes Slavoj Žižek's concept of "overconformity," which emerged from the critic's reading of *The Good Soldier Švejk*, by Jaroslav Hašek. The novel's main character, Žižek notes, "wreaks total havoc by simply executing the orders of his superiors in an overzealous and all-too-literal way." Overconformity is a counterintuitive tactic. Instead of belligerently challenging authority, one excessively celebrates and embraces it to the point of absurdity. The labor-protest tactic known as "work-to-rule," or a "rulebook slowdown," uses a similar approach. Rather than an outright strike, employees slow productivity to a molasses pace by following an ultraliteral interpretation of workplace regulations.[23]

Kaufman's earnest Foreign Man character was an extension of this overconformist tradition. He confounded nightclub audiences by

transforming from a bumbling entertainer to a spot-on Elvis imper-
sonator. "I come down tonight from downtown Wisconsin," Foreign
Man would say in faintly Slavic-sounding accent. When the crowd tit-
tered nervously, he shot back, "No, no. Wait teel I give you thee punch."
Catch a Rising Star comedy club owner Rick Newman recalled, "I really
didn't know he was putting me on. He did Foreign Man until the audiences were booing and walking out. Then, suddenly, he broke into his
incredible Elvis imitation and caught us so completely by surprise that
we ended up crying, we were laughing so hard." Audiences returned
for the act—not so much to watch Kaufman as to see the crowd trying to process what was happening. Television producers began inviting Foreign Man on the air for similar reasons. His 1978 appearance
on *The Dating Game* pitted the hapless character against two quintessential seventies studs: a bearded man with a wide-open lapel exposing
his hairy chest, and another who was tanned, permed, and dressed to
the nines. "How ya doing, Patrice," Studs #1 and #2 said with smooth
confidence, while Foreign Man let out a meek, "Hee-lo Pat-reese." After
Patrice picked Stud #2, Kaufman burst into tears and protested that he
correctly answered the questions and followed all the rules. It was just
one of many moments in a long line of televised insanity.[24]

During Kaufman's 1981 appearance on a short-lived *Saturday Night
Live* rip-off named *Fridays*, he broke character and mumbled that he
couldn't play along anymore. Chaos ensued during the live broadcast
after Michael Richards—one of only two people who were in on the
prank—got up and threw a stack of cue cards at him. After Kaufman
got into a shoving match with the cast and crew, the show abruptly cut
to commercials. When invited back next season, he took a different
tack. Kaufman was now a clean-cut born-again Christian engaged to
Kathie Sullivan, a gospel singer from *The Lawrence Welk Show*. Sullivan
(an actual *Lawrence Welk* cast member who inexplicably played along)
spoke of his religious conversion and her love for him. She enthused,
"We'll probably end up with a bunch of little kids running around saying *tenk you veddy much!*" The only time Kaufman antagonized anyone
was when, right before a performance by The Pretenders, he criticized
a drug-related sketch that had just aired. It was Kaufman in overconformist mode, and the audience booed when his lecture on clean living
delayed the start of the song. After this health-food nut and nonsmoker

was diagnosed with a rare form of lung cancer at the age of thirty-five, many people were sure it was another one of his stunts. "Andy, come *on*, man," people said to the wheelchair-bound entertainer. "This dying thing is just too much!" He passed away on May 16, 1984—or maybe he didn't. Some people insist that he faked his death, and if that was the case, Kaufman surely got the idea from Alan Abel.[25]

THE ABELS RAISE CAIN

In 1955, "professional hoaxer" Alan Abel began a long career making mischief with media. Gleaning lessons from the PR world and P. T. Barnum, Abel staged a marriage of an Idi Amin impostor to a white American bride, launched a goofily lurid event named the International Sex Bowl, and founded Omar's School for Beggars, among many other things. It was a lively thirty-five-year career that was tragically cut short when he died of a heart attack in Sundance, Utah. "Alan Abel, Satirist Created Campaign to Clothe Animals," the *New York Times* obituary announced on January 2, 1980. It turned out that the report of his death was greatly exaggerated—or, to be more accurate, fabricated. Three days later, the *Miami Herald* ran a front-page story with a very different banner: "Report of Death . . . 'Fit to Print.'"[26]

> He who had tweaked America when he invented a nitwit organization called the Society for Indecency to Naked Animals and barnstormed the nation's talk-show circuit, earnestly urging citizens everywhere to clothe their pets. . . . He who had run a wholly fictitious Bronx house-wife named Yetta Bronstein for the U.S. Presidency ("Vote for Yetta And Things Will Get Betta!"). He who, at the height of the Watergate frenzy, had called a Washington press conference, gravely declared himself to be the Deep Throat of the Woodward-Bernstein reportage, announced that he was about to disclose very important things and then suddenly col-lapsed on the spot, leaving assembled newsgathers agape.[27]

It was the first time the *New York Times* had to retract an obituary. Abel tells me he got the idea to fake his death after overhearing a conver-sation between two Hollywood lawyers. He was negotiating the rights to his life story, and the attorneys—unaware that the prankster was standing next to them in an elevator—said that the studio should wait to purchase the rights until after he died, so that Universal could "get it for peanuts." An annoyed Abel then hired a tearful actress to pose as his widow, walk into the newspaper's offices, and deliver the news. Discussing a well-worn strategy, he says, "I decided to approach the *Times* because if they printed it, I knew others would pick it up." Alan gave his family and friends advance warning, though his longtime collaborator Jeanne Abel wanted nothing to do with this hoax. Alan had done a lot of crazy things over the years, but she worried that her husband was going too far. "I *definitely* wasn't for it," Jeanne tells me, laughing. The same year, in 1980, Alan Abel was introduced to Andy Kaufman. "We had a special kinship," he tells me, explaining how they bonded over their pranks. The comedian obsessed over the details of how he faked his death, and he pumped Abel for more information about how he pulled it off.[28]

Alan Abel said he never took money from the gullible, but he was still walking a fine line. Memories of charlatans were still fresh in the public's mind because scam artists had grown adept at using media to rip people off in the first half of the twentieth century. Shady figures such as John R. Brinkley sold the public fraudulent goods and services by using a massive radio station that broadcast at *one million watts* (today, the FCC limits FM stations to one hundred thousand watts). Just over the border in Mexico, XER saturated the Northern Hemisphere's airwaves with talk of Brinkley's world-famous "goat gland transplantation" breakthrough. Goat glands were sewn into a man's nether regions, a technique that often ended in infection, death, or, at the very least, a drained bank account. During this time, elaborate cons such as "the wire game" emptied people's pockets by using props and sets that looked like Western Union offices. Sharpers used these fake telegraph offices to convince marks they had access to horse-racing results moments before they were reported to the public. That way, suckers would place huge bets that didn't pay off. Media and fraud were so intertwined that Alan Abel needed to distance himself from these associations. He once returned a $40,000 donation check sent by a woman who fell for his most notorious prank: the Society for Indecency to Naked Animals.[29]

SINA advocated dressing naked animals—especially horses, cows, dogs, cats, and "other domestic animals that stand higher than 4 inches or are longer than 6 inches." Its motto? "Decency Today Means Morality Tomorrow." In 1958, Abel recruited Buck Henry to play SINA president G. Clifford Prout Jr. (the writer and actor went on to a successful career penning screenplays for *The Graduate* and *Catch-22* and hosting *Saturday Night Live* several times). The skinny, diminutive man with thinning hair and glasses was tailor-made for this role, especially because he could deliver surreal monologues without cracking a smile. "Well, during the days of the ancient Vikings," he soberly explained on one television broadcast, "in the great drinking halls where they held their feasts, they had huge dogs with long hair that were used as napkins." Henry/Prout made the rounds on programs such as NBC's *Tonight Show* and *Today Show*, where he delivered an impassioned ten-minute lecture. "There are naked animals everywhere! . . . And these animals are not grazing, they are hanging their heads in shame!" As the baffled *Today* host looked on, he concluded, "I am spending every single minute of every single day and every last dollar of my father's money to correct this evil."[30]

It was around this time that Jeanne met Alan. "I guess you could say I was attracted to funny men," she tells me. "That was part of the appeal. So it wasn't long before I was writing material for SINA, licking stamps and stuffing envelopes, picketing various events with signs, and so on." It was the beginning of a creative partnership that has lasted over half a century (they celebrated their fiftieth wedding anniversary in 2009). Of the dozens of schemes they hatched, SINA remains the high-water mark of the couple's conceptual genius. "It didn't take much back then to get on national television," Jeanne recalls. "All we needed was a drawing of a clothed animal and a graph of some sort, and producers were more than willing to put SINA on the air." It also helped to have fancy stationery, an impressive-sounding address on Manhattan's Fifth Avenue, charts and illustrations, and a memorable telephone number (Morality 1-1963). "It was a lot of work maintaining a nonexistent organization," Jeanne tells me. "There were numerous requests from media and people wanting SINA literature. It became a full-time occupation."[31]

The Internet greatly accelerated the speed that hoaxes can be revealed, but back then Jeanne and Alan Abel were able to keep their ruse going. And going—and *going*. In 1962, four years after the initial burst of press coverage, the *San Francisco Chronicle* ran a front-page article about SINA. In one-inch-high letters, the headline announced a "'war' against naked animals." The story was accompanied by an absurd photograph of SINA's president holding up a pair of pants in front of an elephant. While in San Francisco, the Abels dashed off a quick note with press clippings to CBS News anchor Walter Cronkite: "Just a quick note to say hello from San Francisco. This city is going crazy over these nuts who want to clothe animals. And they're serious! Might be something here for you. Expect to hit New York by Christmas. Will call if and when. Regards to you and your family, Bill." *CBS Evening News* took the bait and aired a seven-minute news story. Henry/Prout finished the interview by singing the SINA marching song while playing the ukulele. As a *now-I've-seen-everything* expression flashed across Cronkite's face, he signed off the air with a bemused "And that's the way it is."[32]

Abel tells me that the anchor remained furious about the incident for decades. "Of all the things he could hold a grudge about," he laughs, "*it was that?*" The *CBS Evening News* appearance generated lots of hate mail, which was piling up in the Abels' residence. "It certainly takes a filthy and maladjusted mind to think evil (or believe that others may be erotically aroused) by the sight of an Animal in his God given furred, featured, or finned state," one letter writer fumed. "It would certainly be a sad commentary on the state of the nation's mental health if advocates of such a monstrous scheme are permitted to roam at large." Another man told Mr. Prout, "You sure make me mad enough to write anybody for the first time. Thank God we don't have your kind around here." Not all the letters were hostile. One writer explained that he was "currently writing a paper on a Freudian approach to the self sex education of younger children." The researcher wanted more information about SINA's studies and requested outlines of the procedures used to prevent anxiety complexes in children who viewed naked animals.[33]

The couple stirred up more controversy in 1963 when the U.S. Postal Service declined to mail their literature. Their *Inside SINA* magazine— "The Official Organ of the Society for Indecency to Naked Animals"— contained press clippings, anti-nude-animal crossword puzzles, manifestos, images of clothed animals, and nuggets of advice.

WHAT TO DO IF YOU SEE A NAKED ANIMAL

   1. Provide temporary covering for the animal using an overcoat, shawl or blanket.

2. If no immediate covering is available, lead animal gently to nearest
   shed or area hidden from public view.

3. Report the location, complete description of animal and any iden-
   tifying marks by telephone to your nearest SINA headquarters.[34]

Soon after they mailed it, a post office inspector told them that the
materials had to be cleared through Washington. When they asked why,
he responded, "Well, we found them to be questionable." Jeanne Abel—
who did the layout and much of the writing for the magazine—points
out, "Keep in mind, the only thing in the SINA magazine was pictures
of *clothed animals*." Thumbing through *Inside SINA* today, it's difficult
to conceive what could possibly have raised an objection, aside from its
inherent weirdness. Government bureaucracies are not the best arbi-
ters of reason, and when you add nonsense to the equation, life can get
silly very quickly. The Abels sent out a press release voicing "a strong
protest to Attorney General Robert Kennedy over the United States
Post Office's seizure of SINA mail." They organized pickets in front of
the White House and orchestrated altercations with post office officials
until the magazine was finally deemed fit for public consumption. "We
later met Jackie Kennedy's half brother, who was visiting the day we
were picketing," Jeanne says. "He related that the president thought it
was really funny, though Jackie well, not so much." Inspired, Jeanne
ran for U.S. president in 1964 posing as a Bronx-based Jewish house-
wife. Yetta Bronstein's platform included dosing Congress's drinking
fountains with truth serum and installing a "mental" detector in the
entrance to the Senate.[35]

Fun and frivolity drive the couple's exploits, but they are also quite
serious about what they do. Alan's goal is to shake people up, "so they
are able to suddenly stop and look at themselves and laugh more and to
participate in life rather than just be passive bystanders." Jeanne adds,
"With SINA, it was a comment on censorship. The purpose of satire
is to get people to look at something again with a little more thought-
fulness." She then points out the most obvious clue that should have
tipped everyone off: SINA's name! The Society for Indecency to Naked
Animals explicitly made it clear that they were *for* indecency—but no
one seemed to notice. Jeanne and Alan Abel's career path never really
paid the bills, but it was still rewarding. "It's fun to get people thinking,

even if you're infuriating them in the process," Jeanne tells me. "And those endorphins that run through your body, it's better than any paycheck." Unlike many of the entertainers the Abels hung out with, they chose not to write for television. Alan says that TV satires are "viewed passively and then forgotten," which is why he wasn't interested in that line of work. "When I moved to New York, I wanted to be an actress," Jeanne recalls. "But when I met Alan, I realized that it was more fun to make people laugh *and* think. It hasn't always been very, shall we say, *remunerative*, but oh well." Rather than walking a straight and narrow path down the middle of the road, the Abels headed for the proverbial ditches. It was just more exciting down there.[36]

HACKING CULTURE

Dead Kennedys were punk provocateurs who also dwelled in the margins. Beginning in 1978, lead singer Jello Biafra made satire a central part of the group's concerts, song lyrics, and boomer-baiting name (which was meant as a metaphor for the death of the American dream). They were political pranksters in the tradition of the Fugs, whose song "Kill for Peace" shares its DNA with Dead Kennedys' "Kill the Poor"— and, for that matter, Jonathan Swift's *A Modest Proposal*. As with many satirists, the group walked a fine line between humor and bad taste. One time Biafra and his bandmates mounted the stage in Ku Klux Klan hoods, then pulled them off to reveal Ronald Reagan masks. Rightwingers weren't their only targets. The 1979 single "California Über Alles" skewered the New Agey worldview of the state's highest elected official. "I am Governor Jerry Brown," Biafra warbled. "My aura smiles and never frowns. Soon I will be president!" In this antihippy musical rant, the fictional Jerry Brown warned everyone to "mellow out," or else they would get dosed with "organic poison gas."[37]

Around this time, Jello Biafra ran for mayor of San Francisco (his campaign slogan appropriated the old ad tagline "There's Always Room for Jell-O"). The singer's platforms were both serious and irreverent, like banning cars within city limits and making businessmen wear clown costumes to work. Biafra finished third out of a field of nine candidates (Diane Feinstein, who later became a U.S. senator, won after a runoff election). Because he remained a thorn in the side of the political establishment, it came as no surprise that one day in the mid-1980s Biafra woke up to find nine police officers standing over him. "You are under suspicion of trafficking in harmful matter," they said. *Harmful matter?* Biafra thought. *What's that?* (As he later put it, "Can you imagine any matter more harmful than finding a *cop* in your *bedroom*?") The matter in question was a poster his band included inside its 1985 album *Frankenchrist*—a surrealistic H. R. Giger painting depicting a landscape of penises and vaginas. Soon after, a politically motivated district attorney prosecuted Dead Kennedys and its record company (charges were pressed just before Election Day). The trial ended in 1987 with an, um, hung jury, but not before the band broke up and its indie label, Alternative Tentacles, nearly went out of business.[38]

Jello Biafra was one of the leading lights of the 1980s "pop underground," a loose confederation of punks, pranksters, hackers, hippies, and other subcultural types. At first glance, the links between its various constituencies appear random. For instance, many computer nerds revered Robert Anton Wilson (the Discordian prankster and *Illuminatus!* author discussed throughout chapter 7). The connection between Wilson and hackers was first documented in a glossary of computer slang, *The Jargon File*, that has been maintained online since 1975. This glossary also includes an entry on Discordianism, which it defines as "the veneration of *Eris*, a.k.a. Discordia; widely popular among hackers." The appeal that this joke religion had within computer culture can best be understood through the lens of hacking, which is a close cousin of pranking. For instance, *The Jargon File* defines a *neat hack* as "a clever technique. Also, a brilliant practical joke, where neatness is correlated with cleverness, harmlessness, and surprise value. Example: the Caltech Rose Bowl card display switch circa 1961." Students from Caltech—which wasn't playing in this championship football game—broke into the Washington Huskies cheerleaders' hotel rooms and switched out 2,232 flip-card instruction sheets. During the game, the crowd thought team planners made a mistake when "HUSKIES" was spelled "SEIK-SUH." But when "CALTECH" appeared in the next card display, the stadium briefly went quiet before erupting into laughter.[39]

Another form of hacking was phone phreaking. Back in the early 1960s, MIT Lab engineers began building "blue boxes" that could manipulate telephone networks by playing specific tones. Phone phreaks used their technical know-how to hack the system, but they also relied on old-fashioned tricks. MIT engineers impersonated phone employees by reading manuals such as *Principles of Electricity and Electronics Applied to Telephone and Telegraph Work* or recent issues of the *Bell System Technical Journal*. With this authoritative knowledge, they could con operators into connecting them anywhere. Around the same time, similarly inclined students gravitated to Harvard University's student radio station, WHRB. Journalist and alum Sam Smith recalled that the station "functioned as a counter-fraternity, a *salon des refusés* for all those who because of ethnicity, class or inclination did not fit the mold of Harvard." (The word *fraternity* was accurate, because the phone-phreaking world was pretty much one big sausage party.) These Ivy League misfits started their telephonic explorations on the "tie lines" that connected Harvard and MIT. As the author Phil Lapsley characterizes it in *Exploding the Telephone*, "Okay, dial 83 to get to MIT. Now what? What if we dial 83 here? Oh, look, that connected us back to Harvard! Hey, if we dial 83 repeatedly we can tie up all the lines between the two schools. Whee!" Soon, they graduated to the harder stuff.[40]

A few years earlier, in 1955, someone had already figured out how to hack the phone network . . . with a plastic toy. David Condon's breakthrough came when he found a forty-nine-cent Davy Crockett Cat and Canary Bird Call Flute at Woolworth's department store. He adjusted it to play a specific pitch—about two octaves above middle C, or 1,000 Hz—which gave Condon access to the telephone system. After asking a local operator to connect him to another one in a distant city, he blew the flute and was automatically sent to an intermediate switchboard. Only employees had access to these internal lines, so Condon was able to get operators to forward his calls pretty much anywhere. Later on in the 1950s, a blind kid from Richmond, Virginia discovered he could do the same thing just by whistling. Joe Engressia had been obsessed with telephones since he was four, and throughout his childhood he stockpiled a library of technical manuals (which his very patient mother read to him). "I was seven or eight years old and I was sitting on a long-distance circuit, and I heard the background hum of the tone that controls it," he says. "I started whistling along with it and all of a sudden the circuit cut off!" By whistling in seventh-octave E—2,600 Hz—Engressia could disconnect long-distance calls. At first he didn't know what to do with this knowledge, save for a little pranking (such as whistling loudly to terminate people's pay phone calls, which was always good for a laugh).[41]

In one of those kooky cosmic coincidences, Engressia shared a birthday with another blind kid who had the same fixation. When Bill Acker was five or six, he first noticed the tones that came out of the telephone. And at the age of fourteen, he mapped the phone network in his head by dialing every area code, followed by 555-1212 (the universal number for information at the time). Acker recalled, "I'd just talk to the operator and say, 'Where are you? Where are you located?'" The operators were surprisingly game, perhaps because they were bored and/or bemused. Acker was fascinated by what he heard on his long-distance adventures—not just the operators' different accents but the sounds of circuits making connections. It was music to his ears, so he joined the concert with a Tonette toy flute that approximated that magical seventh-octave E note. The plastic flute was a bit unreliable, so Acker wired a Morse code practice oscillator to a rotary phone in order to send short 2,600 Hz bursts down the line. He then he got his hands on a tape machine, which led to one of the more unusual jam sessions in telephone-music history. On a Hammond organ, Acker and some phone-phreak friends recorded notes that could trigger certain numbers. "You know, KP, 1, 2, 3, 4, 5, 6, 7, 8, 9, ST, and a lot of 2,600 Hz," he says. It was "a bucket of fun!" Other hackers discovered that a cheap plastic whistle from a Cap'n Crunch cereal box could produce a 2,600 Hz signal. (A well-known phone phreak named John Draper dubbed himself Captain Crunch in its honor.)[42]

By the time Joe Engressia entered college, the whistling hacker mastered long-distance dialing. To get the area code 212, for instance, he blew two quick 2,600 Hz tones, then one, then two more—followed by the seven digits of a phone number. "I can whistle like a bird and get any number you want anywhere," Engressia told his fellow students. "I'll bet you a dollar I can." To everyone's amazement, it worked! "Joybubbles," as he dubbed himself, charged students one dollar per whistled call, but mainly this lonely kid liked how it made him a campus celebrity. Crowds of up to forty people gathered to watch—until the phone company busted him in 1968. Not long after news stories about Engressia circulated, his phone began ringing. Some teens in Los Angeles told him about strange things they were doing on their local phone network, as did a group of blind kids elsewhere in California. Most had no idea there were others like them out there until they heard about Engressia, who subsequently put them in touch with each other. Another hacker spread the word up and down the West Coast by putting small stickers on phone booths that instructed people to call a mysterious number. On the other end of the line was a recording that revealed the secrets of phone phreaking. Someone in Seattle saw one of those stickers and told a friend who attended a winter camp for the blind in Los Angeles. When the session ended, the secret migrated to towns all over the West and, eventually, to a summer camp for the blind in Vermont—where it fanned out further. These initiates developed sophisticated ways to hack the AT&T network, which, in turn, provided the medium they used to share this information.[43]

Because of social awkwardness, blindness, or both, many of these phone phreaks had few friends they could relate to. The telephone changed that, and by 1970 scattered clusters of phone phreaks around the country were talking to each other. The first step in making this connection was the discovery of "loop arounds," an internal phone-company circuit that could easily be hacked and used to talk to other phreaks. Sometimes they hit the jackpot and found hidden conference lines that could handle multiple callers at one time. A phone company in Vancouver, Canada unwittingly hosted an influential conference line that was populated by callers from all over the world. It facilitated a massive amount of information sharing and even the occasional musical phone-tone performance. "Day and night the conference line was never dead," journalist Ron Rosenbaum wrote in 1971. "Blind phone phreaks all over the country, lonely and isolated in homes filled with active sighted brothers and sisters . . . knew that no matter how late it got they could dial up the conference and find instant electronic communion with two or three other blind kids awake over on the other side of America." Four decades before Facebook debuted, hackers had already developed their own electronic social network.[44]

In the 1930s, when Bell Labs engineers set out to build an automated long-distance switching network, they overlooked the massive security flaw in its architecture. "The next thing you know," Phil Lapsley writes, "it's the 1960s and—*bleeeeep kerchink*—your network has blind kids and mobsters and college students making free calls with blue boxes." To AT&T's horror, its attorneys determined there was no federal law that definitively made phreaking illegal. The company became more paranoid when Yippie radicals spread the word in the underground about how to make free calls. "FUCK THE BELL SYSTEM" was the rallying cry of the Yippie newsletter *YIPL, the Youth International Party Line*. Then came Ron Rosenbaum's 1971 *Esquire* magazine article, "Secrets of the Little Blue Box," which blew the lid off this subculture. Rosenbaum still recalls what drew him to this story. "These people had managed to create a sort of network, a parallel communications network, of their own," he says. "I think I was also influenced in my vision of the phone phreaks by the Thomas Pynchon novel *The Crying of Lot 49*, which also describes this kind of underground communication network. They seemed to be living it out, in a way." This underworld—populated with shadowy figures who used blue boxes to contact AT&T's "Inward Operators"—was a bit Pynchon-esque (adding to the conspiratorial tone, Rosenbaum's article referred to these hackers as the "phone-phreak illuminati").[45]

That *Esquire* article turned future Apple cofounders Steve Jobs and Steve Wozniak into phreaking fanboys. "Halfway through the article," Woz said, "I had to call my best friend, Steve Jobs, and read parts of this long article to him." It mentioned that an issue of the *Bell System Technical Journal* had the key to rerouting AT&T calls. It was housed in a Stanford University library that was closed at the time, so the two broke in through a side door and dug through the stacks until Wozniak found the right issue. "It was like, holy shit," Jobs recalled, "and we opened it and there it was." Woz adds, "I was practically shaking, with goose bumps and everything. It was such a Eureka moment." Soon after, they were making and selling blue boxes on the black market, and Wozniak even used one to call the Vatican. "Ve are at de summit meeting in Moscow," he said, pretending to be Secretary of State Henry Kissinger, "and ve need to talk to de pope." They nearly got the pontiff on the line, but someone on the other end finally caught on. "They realized that Woz wasn't Henry Kissinger," Jobs said. "We were at a public phone booth." The dynamic duo adopted hacker handles—Woz and Jobs were known as Berkeley Blue and Oaf Tobark, respectively—and they sold about a hundred blue boxes before quitting the crime game. The two were scared straight after some more conventional crooks robbed them, and to top that off, they were nearly arrested by the police. (After convincing the officers their device was a synthesizer, one cop told them, "A guy named Moog beat you to it.")[46]

Wozniak, reflecting on his phone phreaking exploits, observes, "every hacker I've ever run into is always trying to explore the little tiny nuances of anything looking for a mistake, a crack they can get through." Irreverence and rule-breaking are embedded in computer culture's DNA, which helps explain the allure of *Principia Discordia* and the *Illuminatus!* trilogy. These texts appealed to those who resisted social, technological, and legal systems that constrained how people play with—or hack—computer code and everyday culture. Similarly, computer geeks of the late 1970s and 1980s were drawn to the role-playing game Dungeons & Dragons. (The 1978 *Advanced D&D Players Handbook* stresses that a "fantasy role playing game is an exercise in imagination and personal creativity.") The game placed an emphasis on fantasy and ingenuity, which are key ingredients for pranks, hacks, and other out-of-the-box ideas. Discussing campus hacks and pranks, MIT alum André DeHon explains that at his former school "intellect and its applications are valued," not athletic prowess. "It's not that we can run faster than you can," DeHon says. "It's that we can manipulate the physical world to do things you hadn't imagined were possible."[47]

SNAIL-MAIL SOCIAL NETWORKS

The New Hacker's Dictionary (which includes entries that date back to the mid-1970s) contains several mentions of Dungeons & Dragons, *Illuminatus!*, and the Discordians. The book also has an entry on a fake religion beloved by many a computer geek, the Church of the SubGenius. Its origin story begins in the 1950s with J. R. "Bob" Dobbs ("the world's greatest salesman"), though it was actually invented in 1979 by the Reverend Ivan Stang. Inspired by the weird religious tracts produced by Jack Chick and other conservative crackpots, Stang and his collaborators created *SubGenius Pamphlet #1*—also known as *The World Ends Tomorrow and You May Die!* This zine (a term for a cheap, independently produced publication) was laced with a heavy dose of dada humor. It drew its collage-heavy style from *Principia Discordia*, as well as the cut-and-paste aesthetics of punk-rock show flyers and indie album covers. Misfits of all stripes embraced the Church of the SubGenius, which quickly developed a cult following. Stang sent copies of *SubGenius Pamphlet #1* to leading figures in the music, zine, and underground comic scenes—including Devo's Mark Mothersbaugh and cartoonist Robert Crumb. "Finally," Crumb responded, "a religion even *I* can believe in." Robert Anton Wilson called it "the best of all the One True Religions," and Mothersbaugh declared, "'Bob' is an enema for a constipated society."[48]

"I found *The Book of the SubGenius* in college and I glommed onto it," says Pagan Kennedy, a writer who was involved in the zine scene beginning in the early 1980s. She tells me, "I first read it when I was nineteen or twenty, and it was just this transmission that I connected to. Its visual language and weirdness made a lot of sense back in the 1980s." Stang maintained that he and his followers were waging a war against a "Conspiracy" perpetrated by "The Normals," or those who preached conformity. The SubGenii's highest transcendent state, "slack"—the pursuit of perpetual leisure, independence, and original thinking— proved to be a powerful meme. It left traces on everything from the open-source operating system Slackware to *Slacker*, Richard Linklater's zeitgeist-defining 1991 film. The Church of the SubGenius even infiltrated the mainstream when a picture of J. R. "Bob" Dobbs appeared in the opening title sequence of the popular Saturday-morning children's show *Pee-wee's Playhouse*. This "religion" found an enthusiastic audience on university campuses during the 1980s, especially after college radio stations began airing Stang's syndicated weekly radio show, *Hour of Slack*. During this time, SubGenius enthusiasts connected with likeminded freaks through the Postal Service—which functioned as a kind of snail-mail social network.[49]

In 1992, the pop underground's varied constituencies converged in Atlanta, Georgia at "Phenomicon: America's Most Dangerous Convention." The World Wide Web didn't yet exist, so Phenomicon was publicized primarily through mailed flyers and ads placed in zines. Over the course of a weekend, punks, cyberpunks, collage artists, Discordian and SubGenius prophets, underground comic-book aficionados, role-playing gamers, and other esoteric nerds attended panels and speeches. Kerry Thornley spoke as an ambassador of the Discordians, and Rev. Ivan Stang represented the Church of the SubGenius.

Conspiracy-culture researcher and law professor Mark Fenster recalls how there was an eccentric cohesiveness to the Phenomicon attendees (though he notes that the mischievous "Sub-Genius 'followers' at times disrupted the proceedings of conspiracy theory panels"). One panel featured Ivan Stang, Robert Anton Wilson, and William Cooper, of *Behold a Pale Horse* infamy. Sparks flew when the conspiracy theorist grew irritated with Wilson and Stang's irreverent attitude. Cooper claimed they were trivializing "the most serious issues facing us today." Stang recalls that an audience member stood up and said, "The only reason most of us are here at all is because these two guys have written, in entertaining but sensible ways, how fringe extremists like you *might* be worth listening to."[50]

During the 1980s, Stang and his collaborators produced a number of SubGenius zines and spin-off books. Most notable was *High Weirdness by Mail: A Directory of the Fringe—Mad Prophets, Crackpots, Kooks and True Visionaries*. It was like a Postal Service search engine that offered one-paragraph descriptions of, and mailing addresses for, organizations that produced nutty reading materials. The zine world's most important resource was *Factsheet 5*. This publication organized the chaos by offering an exhaustive listing of short reviews, addresses, and purchasing information for zines, cassettes, videotapes, and other odd ephemera. The *Realist*'s Paul Krassner described it as a "central clearing house for the new underground." The cover illustration for *Factsheet 5* issue 35 highlighted the diverse constituencies that composed this paper-based social network: a spiked-haired white punk hands a comic to a young black man, a bearded hippie receives a poetry zine, a straight-laced businessman shares a film with a space alien, and so on.[51]

"My theory has always been that people were trying to create the web before there was a web," says Pagan Kennedy, who reviewed zines for the *Village Voice* in the 1980s. It is no coincidence that *BoingBoing*, among the most influential and heavily trafficked online blogs today, began in 1988 as a photocopied zine. Another key node in this subterranean network was the *Loompanics* catalog. Over the course of three decades, it reviewed and distributed books, audiotapes, and videocassettes aimed at—as the 1993 catalog states—"anarchists, survivalists, iconoclasts, self-liberators, mercenaries, investigators, dropouts, researchers, and just about anyone interested in the strange, the useful, the arcane, the oddball, the unusual, the unique and the diabolical." Owned and operated by Mike Hoy, an avowed "egoist" in the tradition of Ayn Rand, this mail-order catalog specialized in left-leaning libertarian manifestos, conspiracy rants, bomb-making manuals, utopian essays, and SubGenius odes to slack. In the late 1970s, Loompanics began reprinting *Principia Discordia*, which introduced this prank religion to a new generation of freaks. Anarchist-satirist-political-essayist Bob Black described *Loompanics* as "*The Whole Earth Catalog* ruthlessly re-edited by Friedrich Nietzsche."[52]

There has been a lot of celebratory talk in recent years about how the Internet made possible the existence of "participatory media" (e.g., materials made and shared by everyday people, as opposed to mass-mediated products consumed by passive audiences). However, these social practices existed long before the rise of online media. Aside from disseminating information, art, and culture, the zine network helped build communities of like-minded people across the globe. "Before the Internet, there was such an intense sense of 'us and them,' because it was so hard to find people who thought like you did," Pagan Kennedy tells me. "I remember being so alienated from the values of the country, so we reacted by making zines, doing pranks, and having fun." Kennedy's zine *Pagan's Head* offers a vibrant snapshot of this milieu. Mocking some of the predominant trends in 1980s indie culture, the first issue promised,

> In this issue you WON'T find:
> - An interview with John Wayne Gacy
> - Endless references to "Bob" and Slack . . .
> - Drawings of rotting corpses
> - Anarchist rants[53]

"I had just come back from a zine convention not far from where I lived," Kennedy says, explaining what inspired her sarcasm. "I found it so compelling that people were making their own media—the DIY thing—but it was incredibly disappointing to me what people were doing with it." By the mid-1980s, the counterculture had grown much darker and hardened, which was reflected in its preoccupation with serial killers, conspiracy theories, self-mutilation, and other sordid topics. "It was just *so* grim and joyless," Kennedy recalls. One key text that brought together these strands of underground culture was Adam Parfrey's *Apocalypse Culture*, a 1988 book that compiled rants, writings, and interviews with misanthropic envelope pushers. Parfrey's book fit snugly alongside a series of influential titles published by the San Francisco Bay Area imprint RE/Search (i.e., *Industrial Culture Handbook*, *Modern Primitives*, and *Pranks!*). These books were an integral part of a hardboiled milieu that included Survival Research Laboratories' DIY machine-versus-machine robot battles and the punk-rock shock tactics of the Butthole Surfers, whose multimedia stage shows included flaming drums, a naked dancer, and nauseating sex-change-operation film montages.[54]

Even though this subculture was male dominated—and, on occasion, a bit mean-spirited—Pagan Kennedy has fond memories. "When I moved to Boston, I fell into a whole nest of SubGenii," she says. "I remember Ivan Stang came up for a big convention. They all stayed at our house and on our floor, and I was made Pope of All New England for a while." They created zines, staged nonsensical street-theater actions, consumed drugs, and played freaky music on homemade instruments (such as a ski strung with piano wire). By waging psychological warfare against "The Normals" who populated Reagan's America, they carved out idiosyncratic spaces to express themselves. During this time, the pop underground's alternative communication network developed mutually constitutive links with mainstream media. Much of the fringe music, art, publications, and performances created during that decade used mass culture as a foil or as source material for sound and visual collages. By the 1990s, elements of this loopy shadow world infiltrated the pop world. Many critics cite the Nirvana-led "grunge explosion" as the quintessential example of this cultural shift, but symptoms of that viral infection manifested themselves a few years earlier—from a much more unlikely source.

The Justified Ancients of Mu Mu

What do the Illuminati, Discordians, pranks, country-music legend Tammy Wynette, and the incineration of £1 million have in common? Answer: the anarchic British pop duo Bill Drummond and Jimmy Cauty, who worked under several pseudonyms (The Timelords, The

Justified Ancients of Mu Mu, the JAMS, and the KLF). Between 1987 and 1992, they racked up seven UK top-ten hits and crossed over in America with the songs "3 A.M. Eternal" and "Justified and Ancient." The latter was a one-off collaboration with Wynette—a catchy, puzzling pop confection that featured the country diva uttering such lines as "They're Justified and Ancient, and they drive an ice cream van" and "All bound for Mu Mu Land!" This (od)ditty's lyrics alluded to the *Illuminatus!* trilogy, whose protagonists included the Justified Ancients of Mummu. Robert Shea and Robert Anton Wilson's books shaped the cryptic cosmology of the KLF, who sang about epic battles between the Illuminati and the revolutionary order of Mu Mu. "Both secret societies," Drummond notes, "have had a long history in fact and fiction and in the minds of conspiracy theorists everywhere." Drummond's links to Discordianism go back many years. In 1976, British theater iconoclast Ken Campbell enlisted him to design the set for his twelve-hour stage adaptation of *Illuminatus!*[55]

The KLF's brief but ubiquitous international stardom often overshadowed their biting lampoons of the culture industry. They were like a goofy Theodore Adorno whose praxis—or pranxis—involved a sampler and drum machine. One of Drummond and Cauty's sound collages, "All You Need Is Love," satirized the media coverage of the AIDS crisis by mixing together news broadcasts and unauthorized musical samples. Their guerrilla tactics also included the "illegal but effective use of graffiti on billboards and public buildings," as a KLF press release stated. "This was done in a way where the original meaning of the advert would be totally subverted." In one instance, they altered an outdoor advertisement that featured Greater Manchester police chief James Anderton, who blamed AIDS on gays. This approach to activism is sometimes called "culture jamming," a tactic used by those who want to speak back to the spectacle (replacing a corporate monologue with a dialogue). Negativland coined this expression in the mid-1980s on its cassette-tape release *Over the Edge, Vol. 1: JAMCON '84.* "The studio for the cultural jammer is the world at large," says Crosley Bendix, a fictional character who lectures over a collaged audio bed. "His tools are paid for by others, an art with *real* risk." Negativland's Mark Hosler later disassociated himself from the term, telling me, via Groucho Marx, "I don't care to belong to any club that would have me as a member."[56]

After becoming critics' darlings, Drummond and Cauty focused their crosshairs on an adoring British music press. Under the moniker The Timelords, they released "Doctorin' the Tardis," a *Doctor Who*–themed novelty hit. "We thought, this is going to be massive, let's go for it, and we went the whole hog," Bill Drummond recalled. "The lowest common denominator in every respect." *Melody Maker* dismissed it as "pure, unadulterated agony," and *Sounds* said it was "a record so noxious that a top ten place can be its only destiny." Sure enough, the song went to number one. The KLF's next release was a self-published a book titled *The Manual (How to Have a Number One Hit the Easy Way)*. It was packed with music-industry addresses, phone numbers, and sarcastic instructions.[57]

THE RECORDING STUDIO

DON'T BE TEMPTED TO SKIP THIS SECTION ON STUDIOS. IT MUST BE READ OVER LUNCH—BEFORE BOOKING YOUR STUDIO.

The recording studio is the place where you will record your Number One hit single. There are hundreds of recording studios scattered across the country, from the north of Scotland to deepest Cornwall. . . .

CHORUS AND TITLE

The next thing you have got to have is a chorus. The chorus is the bit in the song that you can't help but sing along with. . . . Do not attempt writing chorus lyrics that deal in regret, jealousy, hatred or any other negative emotions. These require a vocal performer of great depth to put it over well. . . .

THE GROOVE

In days gone by it was provided by the bass guitar player, now it is all played by the programmed keyboards. Even if you want it to sound like a real bass guitar, a sampled sound of a bass guitar will be used, then programmed. It's easier than getting some thumb-slapping dickhead in.[58]

At least one group scored a number-one single by following *The Manual*'s instructions. Two men from Vienna, who went by the name Edelweiss, stopped by in 1988 and chatted up Drummond and Cauty about an idea that involved hip-hop beats and lederhosen. "They wanted Jimmy and me to produce their concept for them," Drummond says. "We said, 'We don't need to, you can do it yourself,' handed them a copy of *The Manual* and sent them packing back to Austria." Within the year, "Bring Me Edelweiss" was a number-one hit in several countries, even cracking the U.S. pop charts. It featured turntable scratching, yodels, a chorus that ripped off ABBA's "S.O.S.," and a bizarre music video with awful Austrian rappers and a dwarf. "It was as bad a record as (or an even greater record) than our Timelords one," Drummond notes, "with the added bonus of a truly international appeal." After the KLF was voted "Best British Group" at the Brit Awards, the UK music industry's annual back-slapping ceremony, they bit the hand that fed them. Hard. During the 1992 awards show, they performed an ear-bleeding rendition of their dance-pop hit "3 A.M. Eternal" with the grindcore metal band Extreme Noise Terror. As they pummeled the audience with deafening decibels and distortion, Drummond fired on the audience with a real machine gun loaded with blanks.[59]

Echoing the famous exit line used after Elvis performances, the song concluded with the announcement, "The KLF have now left the music business." Later that night, they dumped the carcass of a sheep bought from a butcher—along with eight gallons of blood—on the red-carpeted entrance of the show's after party. Around the carcass's neck was a sign: "I DIED FOR YOU—BON APPETIT." Scott Piering, a record promoter who worked with the KLF, said, "They really wanted to cleanse themselves and be ostracized by the music industry." Drummond and Cauty both had a genuine love of pop music, which was equally matched by contempt for the music *industry*. To prove this wasn't a publicity stunt to boost sales, they deleted their entire music catalog, making it commercially unavailable. It was a feat made possible by the fact that, in the DIY spirit of punk, the duo owned their own independent record label. "We have been following a wild and wounded, glum and glorious, shit but shining path these past five years," they wrote in the final KLF Communications "Info Sheet." "The last two of which has led us up onto the commercial high ground— we are at a point where the path is about to take a sharp turn from these sunny uplands down into a netherworld of we know not what."[60]

Drummond and Cauty morphed into the K Foundation, whose first order of business was lampooning the Turner Prize—an honor given to establishment-approved artists such as Rachel Whiteread, who was 1993's winner. The K Foundation offered Whiteread a "Worst Artist of the Year" prize, along with a £40,000 stipend that doubled the Turner award amount. After she refused this "honor," Drummond and Cauty came within minutes of igniting the cash in a field near London's Tate Modern, where the Turner Prize ceremony was being held. Whiteread finally relented, claiming that she would distribute the money to ten needy artists. The duo followed through with their cash-burning idea when they torched the remaining money that the KLF had earned as pop stars. In 1994, Drummond and Cauty flew to a remote Scottish island accompanied by journalist Jim Reid and their roadie Gimpo, who filmed the blaze. In an article for the *Observer*, Reid soberly explained, "The £1 million was burnt without ceremony in an abandoned boat-house on the Isle of Jura, in the Inner Hebrides, between 12.45am and 2.45am on Tuesday, 23 August. It was a cold night, windy and rainy. The money, practically all the former chart-topping duo had left in their account, made a good fire." Describing what it felt like to watch £1 million vanish into ash, Reid wrote, "I could tell you that you watch it at first with great guilt and then, after perhaps 10 minutes, boredom. And when the fire has gone out, you just feel cold." The same might be said of consumer culture itself.[61]

💣 💣 💣

The pop-culture trickster figures who populate this chapter—from Korla Pandit and Gorgeous George to Muhammad Ali and Yoko Ono— reveal once again how the distinctions between mainstream and alternative media can be muddy. The KLF, for instance, kept their feet in both worlds. The group owned an independent record company but also used corporate channels to circulate their danceable critiques to millions. More than anyone featured in these pages, they bridged the two archetypes on display in this chapter's title. Celebrity gadflies and obscure cult artists regularly blur the lines between insider and outsider. The 1980s pop underground left an imprint on the next decade's mass culture by bringing together a disparate cast of characters connected by common artistic, cultural, and political inclinations. Discordian and SubGenius pranksters, street-theater provocateurs, and other like-minded weirdos injected creativity, fantasy, and play into everyday life. In those pre-Internet days, they often found each other through a snail-mail social network that was centered around zines.

The phone phreaks and computer hackers who penetrated AT&T's telecommunication system also reshaped the social landscape with their border-crossing transgressions. They used communication technologies to make their mischief, but their envelope pushing also *remade* these media. "It was the magic of the fact that two teenagers could build this box for $100 worth of parts," Jobs said, "and control hundreds of billions of dollars of infrastructure in the entire telephone network of the whole world." With enough imagination, even a toy whistle could rewire an international telephone system. The ripple effects created by phone phreaking altered the nation's telecommunication network and helped usher in a new information age. After discovering this menace in the 1960s, AT&T engineers began designing a new digital switching system that was not susceptible to blue-box hacking. This eventually made it possible to connect computers to the telephone network—and with a little help from ARPANET, the U.S. Department of Defense's communication system, the Internet was born. (Many major advances in media have involved making military technologies do things they weren't designed to do, something communication theorist Friedrich Kittler calls "the abuse of military equipment.") Several phone phreaks went on to successful careers as software engineers, and Jobs and Wozniak started a little company named Apple. Others, such as John "Captain Crunch" Draper, landed in jail a few times. After being sentenced to a work-furlough program in 1979, Draper split his time between jail and writing the code for EasyWriter (the first word processor for the Apple II and, later, the widely adopted IBM PC). Therefore, it is not a stretch to say that the Internet and the home-computer revolution grew out of amateur, underground, and criminal communication networks.[62]

When writing history, jesters and fringe figures are often ignored in favor of the usual suspects typically found in textbooks. But as *Pranksters* shows, mischief makers impacted modern life in profound ways. Whether they were socially conscious pranksters, villainous con artists, self-promoting hoaxers, or even conspiracy theorists suffering from self-deception—whatever their intentions, their blurring of fact and fiction transformed the world they lived in.

10

An Education
in Pranks

I have a confession. The subject matter covered in the previous chapter is very close to my heart, for I myself am a former computer hobbyist, Dungeons & Dragons nerd, zinester, Church of the SubGenius member, indie music fan, and mainliner of pop culture. It's in many ways a stealth autobiography, because all of those things fundamentally shaped who I am today. That is one reason why this book's closing pages take a personal turn—though not entirely, because several other people have shared the same kinds of experiences. I'm merely a minor actor in a comedic drama that played out in the 1990s and beyond. This final chapter begins with my first high dive into prankster pond, when I learned firsthand how easy it was to manipulate media with nothing more than my imagination and a little help from my friends. Around the same time, I witnessed firsthand the effects of someone else's satirical April Fools' prank after it was published in a national magazine. Both events altered the way I view the world and changed my relationship with media, but I certainly wasn't the only one. Over the past few decades, pranking developed into a legible style of political protest that has been popularized by new-model activists such as the Yes Men, Billionaires for Bush, and an army of other lesser-known troublemakers.

ATTACK OF THE THREE-EYED PIG WITH ANTLERS

Perhaps it was boredom, or maybe we just couldn't help ourselves. When I was twenty, in 1991, a few friends began staging spontaneous spectacles around James Madison University. My pal Phil Sweeney and a core group of self-described "freaks" started small but soon began aiming for a university-wide audience. *What better way to get people riled up*, we thought, *than to threaten the school mascot?* This idea culminated in a fictitious movement to replace the JMU Duke Dog—a steel-blue bulldog with a cape and crown—with a bright-pink, three-eyed pig with antlers, nicknamed Dukie. It was a class project (for which I got school credit!), but many others also played directorial and acting roles. At the time, I had no idea we were tapping into a venerable tradition, though I now realize our prank was akin to the sorts of campus hacks discussed in chapter 9. Hacking and pranking can help us figure out how stuff works, whether we are talking about the physical universe or the world of media. "A successful hack brings the satisfaction of having brightened the days of many people," an MIT alum notes. "An unsuccessful hack teaches valuable principles of engineering—plan ahead and check theory with experiment. What better pastime for aspiring scientists and engineers?" Or, for that matter, silly social engineers.[1]

After reserving the school Commons area for our pro-pig rally, I submitted letters to the campus newspaper about why our mascot should be replaced. Written at the height of the backlash against political correctness, they intentionally pushed buttons with lines such as "it is degrading to celebrate a dog that yearns to be free, but can't" and "it seems sexist to honor an aggressive, masculine dog wearing a crown— a symbol of historical patriarchal oppression." We hoped some people might get bent out of shape, but it seemed unrealistic to think it would become a scandal. Boy were we wrong. After I collected over four hundred signatures in favor of our alternative mascot, a countermovement sprang up to "Save the Duke Dog." Then, when a friend in the Student Government Association submitted a bill in favor of the mascot change, the poop hit the fan. During that year's homecoming football game, the marching band spelled out "We Love the Duke Dog" in its tubas and wore plastic dog bones around their necks in solidarity. When a student threw a makeshift three-eyed-pig-with-antlers effigy into the stands, loyal fans destroyed it. "Why are they ripping that stuffed animal to shreds?" someone was overheard asking. "Oh, some faggots are trying to change the mascot," came the nonchalant reply.[2]

That week our student newspaper, the *Breeze*, listed the top stories in order of importance: "Duke Dog Controversy," followed by "Traumatic Drama at Gunpoint: Find Out How a JMU Grad Dealt with Being Shot." This was the first time I went for a spin in the media machine, and it was illuminating. Our pro-pig rally was planned for Halloween, and it took the form of a fifty-person-strong mass wedding that I officiated. During the lead-up to the event, we offered several clues that our "movement" was a prank. The publicity flyers noted that we were marrying ourselves to bananas to demonstrate the "seriousness" of the cause, but our humor was lost on many people. As Phil Sweeney noted in his senior honors thesis—"Conscious and Unconscious Political Symbolism: A Study of a College 'Prank'"—these types of statements "served to reinforce the idea in most of the students' minds that we were very unreasonable people." I dressed for the occasion by rocking a priest's collar, strap-on pig nose, antlers, and a third eye glued to my forehead. It made for good television. Two stations showed up to cover the event, and all NBC affiliates in the state of Virginia aired the story on their local newscasts. A few weeks later, the footage was incorporated into a CNN piece about opposition to racially offensive team names and mascots, such as the Washington Redskins and the Atlanta Braves. Dukie the three-eyed pig with antlers sure was a strange fit.[3]

Newspapers also jumped on the bandwagon, and when the *Roanoke Times & World-News* called, I conducted a few experiments. To see what the reporter would print without fact checking, I fabricated over-the-top stories about the origins of the proposed mascot. I spoke of a nonexistent woman named Nancy X who dreamt up the mascot during an LSD-inspired vision quest at one of JMU's many "naked parties." I spun a ludicrous tale, casually telling the reporter, "I mean, of course everybody knows that the antlered pig was a pagan symbol of sexuality, right?" The published article stated, "Nancy X—who prefers to keep her identity hidden, although apparently nothing else—proposed a regular two-eyed pig with antlers, a pagan symbol of fertility and sexuality. But another faction wanted a three-eyed clown, so they compromised." Straight from my loose-cannon lips and onto the front page of a newspaper, with no qualifiers or quotation marks. The mascot-changing prank helped me better understand how trickery can shape mass media and, to a certain extent, how we perceive the world. Think about what I was able to do—a college student with little money and no formal media experience—and compare that to the resources available to PR firms, lobbyists, and the corporate interests they represent. In that regard, this prank can be understood as a performance-art-inflected form of media criticism.[4]

It was also something of an activist response to two recent political events. In 1989, the Supreme Court provoked a conservative backlash when it ruled that flag burning was a free-speech right, and the jingoistic tide surged a couple of years later when the United States went to war in Iraq. The first Gulf War politicized JMU's freaks, who engaged in traditional march 'n' chant protests *and* comical mind-bending tactics. Instead of burning an American flag to shake people up, we targeted another weighty icon: the holy sports mascot. Our violence was symbolic, not literal. "Sports is regarded by the majority of university students as a symbol of the positive aspects of competition, hard work, and team work," Phil Sweeney wrote not long after the three-eyed-pig-with-antlers prank concluded. "When the freaks tried to change the mascot from a vicious animal representing the seriousness of sports to a deranged, mutated pig, representing silliness, it was a metaphorical attack on the values and contradictions represented by the Duke Dog." The student body and administration could find no conventional way of countering our scheme, because we hadn't broken any official rules. This experience taught me that creativity, interactivity, and playfulness are key ingredients for a successful prank. Everyone had an opportunity to play an active role in a public spectacle that encouraged role-playing, experimentation, and humor. Because of our isolated location in rural Virginia, we had little idea that there were other people like us out there—that a cultural shift was happening. The first clue we were not alone arrived a year later, in the form of a mass-mediated prank.[5]

THE NEW MARKET AFFAIR

"The ironically named New Market, Virginia, might not seem the likeliest spot for America's most promising new music scene," *SPIN* magazine's Jim Greer observed at the height of the 1990s alternative-rock explosion, "but its very remoteness may provide an important creative spark." This was the first line of a 1993 April Fools' joke that took on a life of its own, jumping off the magazine's pages and into our lives. A few days later, the phone began ringing at WXJM, James Madison University's student-run radio station, where I was a DJ. At the other end of the line were record company A&R representatives, a term used in "the biz" that means, essentially, talent scouts. "What about this New Market scene? Any hot bands you can recommend?" The ensuing events played out like a morality play that dramatized the absurdities and economic excesses of that decade. Greer's prank also illustrates how new forms of media have transformed social relations, because it simply would not work today. A&R reps performed their jobs back then—in ye olden days—using phones and planes. Their current corporate kin are more likely to let their fingers do the clicking by trolling for artists online. Additionally, the simplest Internet keyword search would reveal that a club named Stinky's didn't exist in New Market, Virginia and that the bands Sweet Draino and Faghag were fictions. But back in 1993, prompted by little more than a ludicrous magazine article and some phone calls to our student radio station, the major labels rushed to our neck of the woods.[6]

Jim Greer, who went on to play bass for a while in the critically adored indie-rock band Guided By Voices, wrote the piece when he was making a living as a senior editor at *SPIN*. His "Smells Like Scene Spirit" article hit the newsstands of the Shenandoah Valley in mid-March, just as winter was receding from the area. "Eighteen miles north of Harrisonburg, Virginia, and a two-hour drive from Washington, D.C.," Greer breathlessly wrote, "New Market may one day supersede Seattle. The one thing that puzzles me about New Market is that there aren't *already* hordes of A&R weasels sniffing around here. I can't be the first person to hear about this scene." The article made repeated references to Seattle, which had been engulfed in an inferno of hype after the commercial rise of Pearl Jam, Soundgarden, and Kurt Cobain's little band that could. "Seattle," the same magazine declared a few months earlier, "is currently to the rock 'n' roll world what Bethlehem was to Christianity." The hunt was on for the next big thing, and *SPIN* had discovered the newest scene. Sort of.[7]

We lived next door to New Market, in Harrisonburg, a little college town near the border of West Virginia. It was one of the chicken-killing capitals of the country, and pretty much the biggest event to happen there was the annual "Poultry Parade" sponsored by the area's largest industry. Every summer, children and adults alike rode on tractor-pulled floats dressed like chickens and other fowl (presumably right before they were to be slaughtered by Tyson, one of the parade's sponsors). If there was gold to be had in the hills of the Shenandoah Valley, it was most definitely fool's gold. Greer's piece pretended to be "news," but there were many screamingly obvious clues that indicated it was not to be trusted. It was about a town named *New Market*, there was that "Smells Like Scene Spirit" headline, and the article—published in *SPIN*'s April issue—ended with the line, "For the briefest moment I wonder if she is putting me on." Amazingly, none of these fair warnings stopped the culture vultures from swooping down on us.[8]

Not long after WXJM received its first call, we were paid a visit from a living, breathing emissary from the recording industry: an A&R rep from Giant Records. The company's name, by the way, isn't an arch literary device like, say, "Big Culture, Inc." Giant Records was in fact a division of Time-Warner, and its employee was a walking, talking cliché. Jon Bohland, WXJM's programming director from 1992 to 1994, tells me, "I remember the guy had some seriously moussed hair and was really into Soundgarden and anything resembling the so-called Seattle Sound." Back then virtually no one had a mobile phone, except for this jet-setter, which we all thought was ridiculous. The Giant Records man was supplemented a few days later by an additional A&R rep, who was slick in spirit though not in dress. There was a third, probably a fourth, and each had his own particular style: one wore a white linen shirt and was described as "kind of *Miami Vice*-ish"; a different one wore Dockers and a dress shirt; and another tried to blend in with Doc Martins and skateboard shorts (though his silver metal briefcase made him quite conspicuous).

This feeding frenzy was a sign of the times, when major labels threw lucrative recording contracts at obscure artists. Why? "One word: Nirvana," Sonic Youth's Lee Ranaldo tells me. "The record companies were throwing money at 'quirky,' 'alternative' bands of all sorts, like blind men on a dark night." We weren't the first to have our own private bohemia served back to us on a blue-plate special, nor were we naive enough to think our situation was unique. But I'll be the first to admit there were moments when I let my critical guard down. There were a few good reasons for this optimism. "Something was happening in '90s music that isn't happening *anywhere* in pop culture these days, with women making noise in public ways that seem distant now," *Rolling Stone's* Rob Sheffield wrote in his 2007 memoir *Love Is a Mix Tape.* My old friend remembers it as a time pregnant with possibilities, when real change seemed around the corner—even if it was just at the level of significa-tion. Kurt Cobain was wearing dresses on MTV's macho-metal show *Headbanger's Ball* and alarming homophobes by French-kissing his bandmates on live TV. Women-led Riot Grrrl bands popped up every-where, even in the Shenandoah Valley. "It seemed inconceivable that things would ever go back to the way they were in the '80s," Sheffield writes, "when monsters were running the country and women were only allowed to play bass in indie-rock bands."[9]

The idea that mass culture would embrace the values of a few freaks was a dream, of course, one we woke up from the day those record-com-pany men arrived in Virginia. Of all the A&R reps who came to town, the Giant Records employee made the deepest impression. Jon Bohland and WXJM music director Mike McElligott agreed to drive him up to New Market, even though the two DJs were convinced the article was a joke. "I guess Mike and I led him on a bit," Bohland shrugs. "I recall that once in New Market we actually stopped at a gas station or two where he got out and asked about the club mentioned in the article." One of the faux-locals quoted in *SPIN* said Stinky's was "basically the only place to play now," adding, preposterously, "unless you count the Sheraton in Harrisonburg. They now have Alternative Night on Wednesday." Boh-land still remembers watching the man from Giant Records talking to a grubby attendant at one of the only gas stations in New Market, a tiny town known around those parts mostly for a Confederate battlefield and a big statue of Johnny Appleseed. "That was really amusing, as nobody knew what the hell he was going on about," Bohland said. "He fully expected to find these places when we got there."[10]

Upon returning to WXJM empty-handed, the A&R rep made a call back to his employer. "He was really agitated," Bohland says. "I think he was afraid of being fired." The guy had every right to be concerned, given that his boss was the notorious industry hit man Irv Azoff—a diminutive record exec nicknamed "the poison dwarf." Before founding Giant Records, Azoff managed the Eagles in the 1970s and ran MCA Records in the 1980s. He was exactly the sort of old-school shark that the alt-rock explosion promised to exterminate but didn't. Today he manages the career of pop diva Christina Aguilera, among many others, and in 2008 he became CEO of concert-industry behemoth Ticketmaster/Live Nation. Azoff's agitated A&R man was looking to invest in the New Market bands name-checked in Jim Greer's article—such as Frail, "whose feedback driven slacker anthem 'Whatever,' b/w 'I Don't Know,'" Greer wrote, "was easily one of the top two or three singles of last year." A generic, blurry action shot of three musicians rocking out was offered as evidence. "Frail: America's *best* new band," read the photo caption, with sarcasm dripping from the italics. McElligott took pity on the A&R rep and offered some advice. "If you really want to find the area's biggest unsigned band," he said, "you should drive an hour to Charlottesville and . . ." Already weary, wary, and annoyed, the rep cut Mike off with a curt, "No *fucking way.*" The recommendation? The Dave Matthews Band.[11]

The Giant Records man was suckered twice: once by Jim Greer's *SPIN* article and then by JMU's freak population. After flying from LA to DC and then driving two and a half hours in a rental car, he was conned into attending a supposed "Special Showcase Performance"—or, as the freaks wryly called it, "The Sellout Show." It was held in the basement of my next-door neighbor's house, which occasionally hosted punk acts such as Nation of Ulysses and Bikini Kill. It also housed members of a group called Cörn Röcket (spelled with umlauts, naturally). Setting up for the "showcase," my neighbors tricked out their skuzzy basement— an underground lair marinated in spilled beer, vomit, cigarette ash, and straw. The band placed a La-Z-Boy in front of a bank of amplifiers, for maximum effect. Next to the ratty leather recliner was an ashtray stand loaded with cigars because, as we all know, they are the accouterments of choice for major-label execs. No other prop works better when exclaiming, "You're gonna be huge!" Their guest barely lasted two songs. Cörn Röcket was an abrasive group that made ears and noses bleed; they were inspired by malt liquor, punk rock, and James Joyce. But before the man from Giant Records could leave, a freak blocked the door, stripped off all his clothes, and performed a full-frontal interpretive dance at close range. WXJM staffer Ben Davis remembers the rep's reaction: "Watching him grow increasingly bewildered and frustrated was amazing. It was really hard to keep a straight face."

Not only was Cörn Röcket ridiculing this cog in the culture-industry machine, but they also poked fun at their peers who were all too ready to sign at the dotted line. WXJM staffer Dave Cour remembers how the lead singer of a jammy alt-country group named Fried Moose stopped him with some urgency, asking how he could slip a demo tape to one of the visiting A&R reps. John Dinsmore, Fried Moose's former drummer, confesses, "I do remember being astounded but excited that New Market was the next Seattle." He tells me that it took some people in town up to a month to realize that Greer's article was a gag. "I guess if you really want something to be true, you will readily believe it," Dinsmore observes. Because this drummer's name is just one letter away from that of a more famous drummer—The Doors' John Densmore—a cautious reader might question the veracity of this story, but I swear it's true. I can assure you that my friend is no fiction and that I have known John Dinsmore since we attended Virginia Beach Junior High in the mid-1980s. However, even if you remain a little leery, that's great; a healthy skepticism is quite useful in everyday life.

THE GREAT GRUNGE PRANK OF '92

Jim Greer's 1993 *SPIN* article wasn't the first to satirize the alt-rock "revolution." Four months earlier, Megan Jasper masterminded a prank that was revealed in the pages of the *Baffler*, an independently produced publication founded by Thomas Frank. Jasper is now executive vice president of Sub Pop Records, but back then she was working as a twenty-five-year-old receptionist for the label. Because the company released the first records by "grunge" acts Mudhoney, Soundgarden, and Nirvana, it was a magnet for reporters working the youth-culture beat. Fatigued by clueless queries phoned in by journalists, Jasper provided the *New York Times* with slang terms supposedly used by Seattle scenesters—you know, familiar phrases such as "harsh realm," "lamestain," and the perennial favorite, "swingin' on the flippety-flop."

During the interview, the *Times* reporter would feed Jasper a phrase such as "hanging out," which she had to translate into "grunge speak." A couple, such as "score" and "rock on," were commonly used by hipsters at the time, but she made most of them up off the top of her head.

The resulting article resembled the *SPIN* piece, only this time it was a prank pulled *on* mass media. "I waited for the reporter to bust me," she tells me, "but it never happened. I then expected an editor to cut the section, but that didn't happen either. I was shocked when I saw it in print." The article's credibility was immediately torpedoed by a cringe-inducing, mathematically challenged error in its opening paragraph— which at the time of this writing *still* remains uncorrected on the paper's website. "When did grunge become *grunge*? How did a five-letter word meaning dirt, filth, trash become synonymous with a musical genre, a fashion statement, a pop phenomenon?" It was accompanied by the following condescending sidebar:

Lexicon of Grunge: Breaking the Code

All subcultures speak in code; grunge is no exception. Megan Jasper . . . provided this lexicon of grunge speak, coming soon to a high school or mall near you:

WACK SLACKS: Old ripped jeans

FUZZ: Heavy wool sweaters

PLATS: Platform shoes

KICKERS: Heavy boots

SWINGIN' ON THE FLIPPETY-FLOP: Hanging out

BOUND-AND-HAGGED: Staying home on Friday or Saturday night

SCORE: Great

HARSH REALM: Bummer

COB NOBBLER: Loser

DISH: Desirable guy

BLOATED, BIG BAG OF BLOATATION: Drunk

LAMESTAIN: Uncool person

TOM-TOM CLUB: Uncool outsiders

ROCK ON: A happy goodbye[12]

The *New York Times* article offered its readers a secret decoder ring that could crack the code of the latest subculture. But it was a faulty device that enveloped anyone who used it in an impenetrable force field of squareness. Jasper's friends in Mudhoney helped perpetrate the gag in magazines and newspapers when the band was playing in England. Lead singer Mark Arm confirms this, telling me, "Yes, we did pepper our interviews with those terms, mostly to amuse ourselves while on tour." Smartass T-shirts emblazoned with "Lamestain" began popping up around Seattle, and the *Baffler* revealed Jasper's prank soon after. When the *New York Times* demanded a retraction, Thomas Frank replied in a statement, "when The Newspaper of Record goes searching for the Next Big Thing and the Next Big Thing piddles on its leg, we think that's funny." But in an irony of meta-tastic proportions, Frank's own publication fell for Jim Greer's New Market prank. The *Baffler's* fifth issue included a piece titled "Brain Dead in Seattle," which used Greer's *SPIN* article as a sober example of how entertainment magazines didn't fact check and were, as they say, without clue. After describing how *Entertainment Weekly*, *Rolling Stone*, *Details*, and *Esquire* had slashed and burned their way through Seattle, Chapel Hill, and other fertile music towns, the author smugly stated that "*SPIN* had settled on New Market, Virginia"—adding, "I kid you not." The joke, it turned out, was also on the *Baffler*.[13]

BETTER LIVInG THROUGH PRAnKS

The New Market Affair subtly, but profoundly, changed the way I view the world. As I have suggested throughout this book, a clever deception can help generate an honest discussion—in this case, by revealing how the "music biz" works. Here are four lessons I gleaned from the New Market Affair:

> *Industry Rule #4,080: Record people are shady.* "A&R folks had huge travel budgets and other such expense accounts," says Jenny Toomey, who played in the Washington, DC–based group Tsunami throughout the 1990s and cofounded the indie label Simple Machines. "These expenses are absorbed not by record companies but by other artists signed to major labels, which is one reason why so many musicians never see a

penny of royalties." Creative accounting might not have originated in the music industry, but the two go together like peanut butter and jelly. Using the New Market Affair as an example, Toomey says that recording contracts are stacked against artists "because the major labels have to pay for the tremendous amount of waste that goes on when you have people flying off to Virginia with checkbooks in hand." She also notes that the post-Nirvana indie boom was much like the irrational exuberance of the dot-com period, in the late 1990s. "It was just too good to be true," Toomey says. "In both cases, there was a moment of sustained energy supporting a myth."

Industry Rule #5,218: Exploit the freshest music scene. Back when Greer's *SPIN* article was published, Glenn Boothe was employed as an A&R rep. Though he was amused when I recounted the New Market story, Boothe admits he fell for the hype surrounding another far-fetched scene/scheme: Halifax, Nova Scotia. In 1993, he almost flew up to the "Seattle of the North" but ultimately decided not to go. "The idea that you'll find good music solely based a geographic location is pretty absurd," he says. Though this desire to discover or invent music scenes happened in the early 1990s, the record biz had already descended into self-parody many years earlier. For instance, the "British Invasion" (The Beatles, The Rolling Stones) gave way to the "San Francisco Sound" (Jefferson Airplane, The Grateful Dead), which led to the next Next Big Thing in Boston (um, The Ultimate Spinach, Eden's Children). "The Bosstown Sound" was a marketing slogan concocted in 1968 to promote the nascent Boston psych-rock scene. "The Sound Heard 'Round the World: Boston! Where the new thing is making everything else seem like yesterday," the zippy ad copy read. While not as ludicrous as CBS Records' 1969 marketing slogan "The Man Can't Bust Our Music," listeners still didn't buy the hype.

Industry Rule #7,203: Nothing is guaranteed. There is no wizard behind the culture-industry curtain pulling levers that deliver surefire results. Music-industry history is littered with failed million-dollar publicity campaigns, such as what happened with Point Blank at Irv Azoff's MCA Records. This generic late-1970s/early-1980s corporate boogie band remains deservedly forgotten, despite the label's best promotional efforts pushing 1979's ironically titled *Airplay*. A counterexample is the Dave Matthews Band, whose regional rise occurred during the grunge craze, heavy guitars and all. Matthews's sweeter, more upbeat sound was at odds with the prevailing trends of the day, and major labels initially ignored his group. This is a reminder that corporations don't have all-knowing, powerful computer brains. *People* run them, and sometimes they aren't smart enough to mount a conspiracy against consumers. Jay Zehr—who owned the only record store in downtown Harrisonburg—recalls that an A&R rep "straight out of central casting" came in looking for bands mentioned in the *SPIN* article. After humoring his delusions, Zehr inadvertently sent the A&R rep on a fool's errand after jokingly suggesting that he sign Washington, DC's Fugazi (an uncompromising postpunk band that ran its own indie label, Dischord). "He hadn't heard of them before," Zehr says, "took me seriously, and got real excited. That's where he said he was going when he left."

Industry Rule #9,416: The revolution won't be televised. "Nirvana's *Nevermind*, it helped create a pop-culture version of this underground thing that had been bubbling up since the 1980s," Jim Greer says. "The reason you loved it was because it was your own. And then, you know, it was just bizarre: around '92, '93, everything took off." The Flaming Lips were a relatively obscure indie band from the 1980s that landed a major-label contract during this time. They scored one Top 40 radio and MTV hit, "She Don't Use Jelly," which briefly allowed them entry into the entertainment-industrial complex. Lead singer Wayne Coyne tells me, "Our level of fame was such that we got to revel in the silliness of it all," referring to the time they made a lip-synced appearance on the prime-time teen soap *Beverly Hills 90210*. (Sample dialogue: "You know, I've never been a big fan of alternative music, but these guys rocked the house!") Similarly, Sonic Youth's journey through the 1990s offered the group, as guitarist Lee Ranaldo calls it, "a wild, privileged vantage point for four punk flies on the wall." Not many noise bands guest star as themselves on *The Simpsons*, as his group did in 1996.

Despite our cautious optimism, we knew in our guts there would be no revolution—televised, recorded, or otherwise. And pretty soon, it was all over; the countercultural bubble burst. "After Kurt died, stuff started to collapse," Greer says. "Bands with one hit ended up tanking on their second major-label album, and what was left was a bunch of corporate-grunge bands and, later, Britney Spears and the Backstreet Boys—you know, just *total product*." The investments in alt-rock didn't pay off, so the major labels went back to pushing boy bands, teen teases, cock rock, and other safe bets. But before that happened, we watched as the biz's funhouse mirrors distorted a musical culture we loved. Our response? Irreverence, irony, and pranks—that three-in-one toolkit for better living. Away from the cosmopolitan centers, living in the geographic and cultural margins, the JMU freaks were left alone to build our own community. I'm reminded of something zinester Pagan Kennedy said about her network of friends around this time. It's a lonely world, she writes, "a place of Personal ads, identical Burger Kings, strip malls, TV laugh tracks, lite rock. But luckily we don't need mass culture, because we can stay home and make our own fun." We were a bunch of goofballs, misfits, slackers, and nerds who liked spending time together *making* and *doing* stuff. The New Market Affair offered us an amusing playground for our experiments, and when Big Culture, Inc., came calling—in person—we had fun, a whole lotta fun. It was a life-affirming lesson I never forgot.[14]

Well, actually, I almost did. The New Market Affair is a memory that should have been erased by the sandblaster of time because, in order to reconstruct this narrative, I had to sift through artifacts pried from damaged and conflicting memories. This was made even more difficult because the story's very foundation was built on a sinkhole of deception. When I started my research in 2007, the *SPIN* article wasn't included in a single electronic database index, and there was absolutely no mention of it on the Interweb. It's like it never happened, and I began to question whether it did. But when I called the Center for Popular Music at Middle Tennessee State University—a place with such an unlikely name couldn't possibly exist, right?—a faxed copy finally fell into my hands. My next big challenge was tracking down one or more of the A&R guys who visited Virginia, but I repeatedly hit dead ends. I guess nobody wants to volunteer himself as the butt of an elaborate joke. At least I acquired some colorful *Spinal Tap*–esque gossip about various "suits" from that era: "Yeah, he was fired after being 'serviced' in his office by a female staffer with his window shades up, and he was later murdered"; "Man, that dude nearly got kicked in the head, and so he quit, but he was also on a lot of drugs"; and so on.

I said earlier that Jim Greer's prank wouldn't have worked in the age of the Internet, but I also could not have told my tale without this medium. Email and social-networking sites allowed me to tap into personal memories and archives that would have been inaccessible to me in another moment in history. In digging up this story, sorting fiction from reality was hard, especially when some factoids seemed too good to be true. The biggest head-scratcher was discovering that Greer modeled the *SPIN* article not on the area where I lived in the early 1990s but on where I have now resided for years. "I originally set it in Iowa City," he tells me, explaining that he grew fond of this college town when passing through on a road trip. "I really liked the fact that Iowa City was in the middle of nowhere, and if the joke worked, then people would have to make a very, very long trek." *SPIN* editor Craig Marks changed the location after he saw New Market, Virginia in an atlas and figured it would be a dead giveaway that the article was a satire. Could this be true? Was I somehow propelled on a Cörn Röcket from rural Virginia to Iowa City? Is it possible that Greer's story caused a small tear in the space-time continuum, folding together the middle-of-nowhere places where I was an undergrad, then a professor? For the briefest moment, I wondered if he was putting me on.

An Army of Pranksters

Of all the things that sent me packing on my long, strange trip, a 1987 book named *Pranks!* blazed the path. This edited collection of interviews served as an operator's manual not only for me but also for a generation of pranksters such as the Yes Men—a duo that uses humorous deceptions to get their political points across. Mike Bonanno recalls that he and his future partner in crime, Andy Bichlbaum, read the *Pranks!* book when they "were just spring chickens." He says it "was out on the floor for people to read": "We had a big group, and we were doing all kinds of strange things in Portland, Oregon. And that was the *reference* book, the source that you cite. It was very important in our development." Bonanno's first attempt at "cultural sabotage" was the Barbie Liberation Front (BLO), launched in 1993 during the Christmas season. The BLO purchased multiple Barbie and G.I. Joe dolls, switched their voice boxes, and "reverse shoplifted" them back into stores. Holiday shoppers brought home Barbies that grunted, "Dead men tell no lies," while gender-bending G.I. Joes gushed, "I like to go shopping with you!" After the BLO sent out press kits to news organizations, the story broke nationally.[15]

By the late 1990s, Mike and Andy joined forces. One of the Yes Men's first pranks was a George W. Bush parody site, gwbush.com, developed in collaboration with computer consultant Zack Exley. "In the beginning, I wanted to do a copy of the Bush site," said Exley. "I thought it would be funny if the Bush people finally stumbled upon the site and found an exact copy—maybe with a few minor and unsettling changes." They duplicated the layout of the Bush campaign site and filled it with slogans such as "Hypocrisy with Bravado." The parallel-universe political page invited people to engage in acts of symbolic subterfuge, such as inserting "slaughtered cow" plastic toys into Happy Meals or jumping the fence into Disneyland and demanding political asylum. Candidate Bush was frighteningly candid when commenting on his doppelganger site: "There ought to be limits to freedom." This reaction demonstrates the pedagogical possibilities of pranks, because the Yes Men's little lie exposed George W. Bush's true feelings not long before he began dramatically chipping away at civil liberties as president.[16]

The Yes Men grew more ambitious after registering the web domain name GATT.org. The General Agreement on Tariffs and Trade, or GATT, was a treaty governing international trade that was replaced in 1995 by the World Trade Organization (WTO). Mike and Andy set up a website that copied the graphic design and repeated the rhetoric used by GATT and the WTO—with a few glaring differences, of course. Some credulous visitors read straight through the satire and sent emails with speaking invitations. The organizers of the Textiles of the Future Conference in Tampere, Finland, needed a WTO representative to deliver a keynote address, so in August 2001 the merry pranksters flew to Scandinavia. Posing as "Dr. Hank Hardy Unruh of the WTO," Andy Bichlbaum delivered a speech that used such terms as "market liberalization" to favorably compare sweatshops to slavery. In a subsection of his speech, titled "British Empire: Its Lessons for Managers," Dr. Unruh dismissed Mohandas Gandhi as "a likeable, well-meaning fellow who wanted to help his fellow workers along but did not understand the benefits of open markets and free trade." The Yes Men's subsequent pranks followed the same template: outrageously caricature an opponent's position, document the performance, reveal their trickery in a press release, and spark a public discussion.[17]

The Yes Men's web pages and public speeches employ corporate-speak to reveal how bland jargon can mask troubling ideas. "We use this language because it is so effective," says "Frank Guerrero," another pseudonym used by the duo. "We think that by adopting the language, mannerisms, legal rights and cultural customs of corporations we are able to engage them in their own terms, and also perhaps to reveal something about how downright absurd it can get." The Yes Men owe a great debt to the Situationists and other radical artists who sought to transform everyday life. "It is impossible to get rid of a world," wrote Situationist Mustapha Khayati in 1966, "without getting rid of the language that conceals and protects it." These tactics include the détournement of corporate slogans and pop-culture detritus, in which words and images are recontextualized to reveal hidden truths. This approach can be used to subvert what social theorist Guy Debord called "the spectacle" (a hypercommercialized media space where virtually everything is turned into a detached representation of reality).[18]

The Yes Men's most controversial prank involved Dow Chemical and its subsidiary Union Carbide India Limited. In 1984, the Union Carbide pesticide plant negligently leaked poisonous chemicals in Bhopal, India. Hundreds of thousands of people were exposed, thousands died immediately, and the long-term effects on the population were disastrous. It remains the world's worst industrial accident, but the corporation's relief efforts were minimal. Three years after Dow purchased the company in 2001, the Yes Men leveraged the twentieth anniversary of the catastrophe to bring attention to this issue. They started by creating a fake Dow Chemical web page that many journalists mistook for the real deal. The site claimed Dow was going to sell off Union Carbide and use the billions of dollars to pay for medical care and the cleanup of the Bhopal site. BBC World, the British Broadcasting Company's global news network, invited a Dow spokesperson to discuss the announcement on air. Instead, it got a Yes Man. Andy appeared as "Jude Finisterra," and within two hours this news fanned out internationally, prompting celebrations in Bhopal. Before Dow had a chance to deny the story, the corporation's stock plummeted in value by $2 billion.

When asked about the crushing disappointment many Indian revelers must have felt when they discovered the news was not true, Andy replied that it was nothing compared to the distress Union Carbide caused them. It's a question the Yes Men have been asked a lot, but unfortunately—perhaps because the repeated queries can get annoying—their responses can sometimes sound a bit curt. Pranks are very much a rhetorical high-wire balancing act, one that can backfire if the proper care and sensitivity are not taken (and even then, there are no guarantees). From an activist perspective, another problem is that the pleasure of pranking can sometimes override its underlying purpose. "A lot of people approach what we're doing as something totally new and unique and that we are changing the face of social protest," Bonanno says, "but no, it's not actually new and it's not necessarily better." Echoing the Yes Men's insistence that pranks are no substitute for grassroots organizing and direct actions, media scholar and activist Stephen Duncombe warns, "This politics is also not without its dangers." When the means are valued as much as the end goal, it can create a slippery slope into apolitical apathy.[19]

The Yes Men's most successful merging of grassroots political action and pranks occurred on the one-year anniversary of Hurricane Katrina. On August 28, 2006, Andy Bichlbaum stood onstage alongside the mayor of New Orleans and the governor of Louisiana. Posing as "Rene Oswin"—an assistant undersecretary of the Department of Housing and Urban Development (HUD)—he announced a New Deal–like plan for the Gulf Coast. It included requiring oil companies to set aside some of their profits for wetland renewal (the lack of which exacerbated flooding during the storm). In his speech, Bichlbaum/Oswin emphasized that HUD's mission was to provide affordable housing but added, "I am ashamed to say we have failed." To correct this problem, the agency was going to halt plans to demolish five thousand units that former occupants desperately wanted to move back into. These apartment complexes received only minor damage from the storm, but because of their close proximity to valuable downtown-area real estate, they were condemned. The audience burst into applause when he declared, "With your help, the prospects of New Orleanians will no longer depend on their birthplace, and the cycle of poverty will come to an end." Soon after leaving the podium, reporters discovered his imposture, and a HUD spokesperson denounced it as a "sick" hoax. This opinion wasn't shared by Survivors Village, a tent-city protest group that collaborated with the Yes Men. Their media coordinator, Annie Chen, insisted, "Right now, a lie is better than the truth."[20]

Not all of these contemporary pranksters are explicitly political. Groups such as the New York City–based Improv Everywhere are mostly interested in catching unsuspecting audiences off guard. During a 2006 event, dozens of people descended on a Best Buy consumer electronics store wearing blue polo shirts and tan slacks that matched the store's employee uniform. They went in, fanned out, and nonchalantly stood at either end of an aisle. As you can imagine, Best Buy shoppers and workers were baffled. Improv Everywhere's most famous prank is the annual "No Pants Subway Ride." Since 2002, strangers have congregated at a set time in designated subway stations to wait for trains, read newspapers, and casually converse. Without pants. This idea may have been partially inspired by a series of New York City subway parties staged at the beginning of the decade. Large crowds would enter a train, cover the advertisements with streamers, place colored gels over the lights, and blast music. In doing so, they transformed city subway cars into a celebration of public space. "There was a brass band on one side, and a boy with a boom box pumping techno on the other," said Sheena Bizarre, a participant. "We immediately started to dance around." Not only did their action politicize the divide between public and private space; it allowed participants and observers to feel this critique viscerally.[21]

Subversive messages can be made palatable with the aid of satire, camp, and pure fun—a lesson that the Billionaires for Bush took to heart. The activist group's multiple street-theater events generated a ton of news coverage throughout the 2004 presidential election season. At a "protest" against Democratic Party presidential candidate Howard Dean, a Fox News crew interviewed an impeccably dressed young man wearing a double-breasted suit, bowler hat, and monocle. "Yes, I'm a Billionaire," he said. "And, yes, I'm for Bush." He looked like a cartoon Monopoly-board-game version of a rich man or, as Stephen Duncombe put it, "someone trying to look like someone trying to look like a billionaire." In the months leading up to voting day, dozens of men and women showed up at campaign rallies uncorking champagne bottles and unloading quotable irony for reporters. The prank spread quickly because the presidential campaign served as a host body for this media virus. Billionaires for Bush mastermind Andrew Boyd designed these events to attract journalists who wanted to spice up their tediously predictable election coverage with novelty and humor. By way of illustration, he describes a memorable prank they staged at a fund-raiser attended by Bush adviser Karl Rove.[22]

> When we reached the club where the fund-raiser was being held some protestors from the Sierra Club were already there. You could tell they were protesters because, unlike us, they didn't have matching outfits, and their signs were hand-scrawled, unlike our perfectly lettered placards. You could also tell they were protesters because the NYPD had stuck them in a protest pen on the other side of the street. Where did they put us? Right in front of the club, right next to all these buttoned-down Wall Street execs lined up waiting to get inside. We turned to them and chanted, "Write big checks!" Then we turned to face the Sierra Club protesters and chanted, "Buy your own president!"[23]

The Billionaires for Bush strategically distinguished themselves from ragtag activists that can easily be placed in a box (literally and metaphorically). They did so by taking cues from Madison Avenue advertising agencies and corporate media. Using high production values, the Billionaires branded themselves with a flashy logo—a red, white, and blue piggy bank—and a carefully conceived public-relations campaign. Their ten-thousand-strong email list facilitated the organization of six nationwide days of action and several local events that garnered widespread mainstream coverage. "Content and humor were tightly meshed," Boyd noted. "Not only did the humor help carry the content (in the way that laughter makes it easier to bear the truth), but if the media wanted the humor (and they did), they had to take the content too." The Billionaires' prank was designed to be participatory, which also aided in its success. They set up a website with customizable materials that could be used in local actions—including templates for posters, flyer designs, and press releases. The role-playing aspect of this prank encouraged people to have fun while at the same time spreading a focused message about economic inequality and political alienation.[24]

💣 💣 💣

Like all good pranksters, the Billionaires for Bush encouraged viewers to stop and think about what they were witnessing. Their top hats, monocles, and other faux displays of wealth allowed them to wink and let the audience in on the joke. Some spectators surely did not agree with the group's message, but at least their critiques were not passively absorbed or ignored altogether. This is one of the many ways pranking can shake people out of their daily routines and rewire taken-for-granted realities. By turning the world upside down—even for a brief moment—it can be seen from a new vantage point. This can spur people to imagine a better society and, occasionally, turn fantasy into reality through the hard work of community building and activism. Commentators often bemoan the apathetic state of our citizenry, but media scholar and activist Stephen Duncombe believes the problem is not that people are uninterested or lazy. They just don't want to take part in a professionalized political process that offers them little freedom to explore new ideas and express themselves. For citizens to feel part of the process, whether we are talking about cultural politics or electoral politics, they should feel like active contributors. Pranking is certainly not the only way to make this happen, but it can spark public conversations (which is a first step in working toward change). The more spaces we can open up to cultivate creativity and criticism—both in politics and everyday life—the better.[25]

Conclusion:
Reflections of a Prankster

Tapping into a rich, centuries-old tradition, pranksters infuse their performances with humor, irony, and satire. They reject the dominant protest model—march, chant, and listen—in favor of one that is more dynamic, engaging, and social. Before this new form of activism made its presence known in the 1990s, most political rallies were quite predictable. They required passive spectatorship: leaders organized and made speeches while followers listened and sometimes got arrested. The mass anti–Vietnam War demonstrations of the 1960s embodied this approach, which was at odds with the counterculture's radical pretentions. Ken Kesey noted this contradiction when he took the stage at a 1965 demonstration dressed in an orange military coat and Day-Glo World War One helmet. "You know, you're not gonna stop this war with this rally, by marching," he told the assembled crowd in Berkeley, California. Talking at a leisurely pace in a folksy tone, the Merry Prankster punctuated his speech with plenty of pauses. "That's what *they* do. . . . They hold rallies and they march. . . . They've been having wars for ten thousand years and you're not gonna stop it this way. . . . You're playing . . . their game." Kesey believed any revolution was meaningless without a new vision for humanity. The shape our society takes is rooted in our rituals, and we are doomed to repeat past mistakes unless we break bad habits.[1]

"Lockdowns and marches aren't the world we want to create," argues William Etundi, the New York organizer of Reclaim the Streets, a protest project that began in the early 1990s. "It's through our parties and our performances that we imagine liberation." The Youth International Party was founded on similar participatory ideals. The Yippies publicized their 1968 protests in Chicago by word of mouth, through the underground press, and, eventually, with the help of mainstream news outlets. "A *Yippie!* button produces a question. The wearer must answer," Abbie Hoffman explained. "He tells a little story. He mentions Chicago, a festival of music, violence (Americans love to go to accidents and fires), guerrilla theater, Democrats. Each story is told in a different way. There is mass participation in the Yippie! myth." Yippies were among the first contemporary activists to stage playful critiques with mass media in mind. Stephen Duncombe observes that this approach was later adopted by the sea-turtle-costumed environmentalists at the 1999 antiglobalization protests in Seattle, the Clandestine Insurgent Rebel Clown Army that flooded London's streets with revolutionary jesters in 2003, and other such street-theater dramas. These large, coordinated actions show there is strength in numbers, though sometimes all it takes is a single individual to stir it up.[2]

i, RoboProfessor

While slipping into my metallic costume, not far from where Bill Clinton was speaking, I didn't know if I would be fired upon, fired from my job, or sent to Guantanamo Bay. So I wasn't taking any chances. Well, I was taking a *few* risks, but for someone who was about to confront a former U.S. president dressed like a robot, I was being as cautious as humanly possible. It was the beginning of another presidential primary season, a month before the 2008 Iowa caucuses, and I was surrounded by news media. You couldn't throw a rock in Iowa City without hitting out-of-state reporters, and they all seemed to have descended on this rally. Hillary Clinton was the Democratic Party's heir apparent and was leading Barack Obama in the polls, so there was a lot of energy and attention focused on her husband's visit. I smooth-talked my way into the raised press area, which gave me a visible stage from which to execute the prank. My outfit: silver gym shorts, a reversible black-and-silver ski vest, a chrome bicycle helmet, metallic sneakers, wraparound "Electronic Rap Shades," and a *High School Musical* microphone/speaker combo. I stuffed it all in a gym bag, which no one thought to search (hey, it's Iowa!).

When Bill Clinton took the stage, the photographers and other reporters stood up, some on their toes, vying to get a good view of the man. The wall of bodies provided the cover I needed to hunch down on the floor, don the costume, and climb atop a wobbly chair. The toy microphone amplified and distorted my voice, making me sound like an agitated Hal 9000 from *2001: A Space Odyssey*. "Bill Clinton, apologize to Sister Souljah," I abruptly announced, stopping him midspeech. "Robots of the world want you to apologize to Sister Souljah!" I tossed into the air hundreds of tiny flyers that offered journalists clues about my motives, along with my contact information in case they wanted more commentary. Immediately, several power-suited Hillary staffers and Secret Service agents surrounded me. The Clintonite crowd turned to me and then turned *on* me, letting out a massive roar: "boooooooooo!" "He has nothing to apologize for," someone shouted. Then a grandmotherly woman snapped, "Screw *you*, pal." Security yanked the plastic mic from my hands before I could get in another word. "You need to get down, right now!" Not wanting to be Tased, shot, or sent to Gitmo, I complied as they whisked me away to be debriefed.

The incident I wanted Bill Clinton to apologize for took place many years before. Sister Souljah was a young black activist who joined the provocative hip-hop group Public Enemy as their "Sister of Instruction / Director of Attitude" in 1990. A couple of years later, in the summer of 1992, she made headlines when Slick Willie intentionally took her words out of context. In an interview with *Washington Post* reporter David Mills, she paraphrased the mind-set of a gang member involved in the racially charged Los Angeles riots. "I mean, if Black people kill Black people every day," she said, "why not have a week and kill white people?" That was the money quote Clinton latched on to. However, Souljah unequivocally stated she did not advocate violence against whites, nor was she airing her own personal views. She was simply answering the reporter's question about why Reginald Denny (a white

277

truck driver caught in the riots) was dragged from his vehicle and bru-
tally attacked. Souljah also criticized the institutions that looked the
other way as blacks were being murdered in the streets of LA on a daily
basis. "In other words," she said, "white people, this government, and
that mayor were well aware of the fact that Black people were dying
every day in Los Angeles under gang violence. So if you're a gang member and you would normally be killing somebody, why not kill a white
person?"[3]

Clinton's campaign was flagging at the time, so he pulled a surprise political stunt by blasting Souljah at a meeting of Jesse Jackson's
Rainbow Coalition. "If you took the words 'white' and 'black' and you
reversed them, you might think David Duke was giving that speech,"
Clinton said, referring to the Louisiana Klansman-turned-politician
who was running for state office at the time. After his speech, Jackson was hopping mad, but it was political gold for the candidate. "At
the time," rapper Jay-Z recalls, "everyone knew he was trying to prove
to white America that he could stand up to black people, particularly
young black people involved in hip-hop, and especially in the aftermath
of the L.A. riots." In 2008, *New York Times* columnist Michael Cohen
called it the most influential campaign speech of the past twenty years,
one that "fundamentally changed the popular perception of the Democratic Party" (and, to be more precise, moved it further to the right).
The candidate's actions resembled a prank, though with an intellectually
dishonest dark side. "Clinton really *did* take her comment out of context," said David Mills, who wrote the *Post* article. "Souljah was describing the attitude of the L.A. rioters, not prescribing future action." This
incident revealed Bill Clinton to be just another opportunistic politician, rather than a genuine advocate for social justice. Years later, I had
a chance to hold him accountable—in my own peculiar way.[4]

After RoboProfessor's debut, I sat in my Iowa City living room slack-
jawed as the story looped on television over the next few days. "Well,
Hillary Clinton may have lost the robot vote," CNN anchor Kiran
Chetry soberly reported, as though she were covering Israeli-Palestin-
ian peace talks. Another newscast: "Bill Clinton has seen a lot in his
decades in politics, but probably it's safe to say that he has never ever
ever ever *ever* been heckled by a man dressed as a robot. Let's take a
look now at how it went down." The cable-news echo chamber distorted

my intended message, morphing the story in an elaborate game of telephone. I recall that one blog facetiously claimed I said, "Don't Tase me, human!" (a reference to a protestor who had recently pleaded "Don't Tase me, bro!" when confronted by an officer at a speech by then-senator John Kerry). I never said that or anything of the sort—RoboProfessor is not quick enough on his feet—but some journalists misread the joke and reported that I did. "Did they Taser him, à la John Kerry?," talk-show host Tucker Carlson asked. "As a matter of fact, they did not," the commentator replied. "He said, 'We are polite in Iowa. They were polite to me, I was polite to them, and they escorted me out,' and that was the end of it."[5]

My favorite moment occurred on MSNBC's *Countdown with Keith Olbermann*, which inexplicably ranked my confrontation as the number-one story of the night. During the broadcast, the show's host asked a *Washington Post* columnist about the security implications of my stunt, which got me within close range of Clinton. Dana Milbank replied, "Well, robots are not yet on any terrorist watch list, so there wasn't necessarily anything nefarious about him." Why a robot costume? I chose this ridiculous persona because I had no desire to play the role of an aggressive, chest-thumping activist screeching away at a politician. One can catch more flies with honey—or in my case, tasty robot motor oil. I also knew my android outfit was the sort of look, and hook, reporters would go for. Spectacle-over-substance is the stock and trade of news media, which churned out wacky headlines such as "Roboprofessor Heckles Clinton." I figured one reaction would be, "Why is a robot complaining about this obscure sixteen-year-old issue?" or "Why in the world is a white professor from *Iowa* demanding that Clinton apologize to *Sister Souljah*?" I hoped to shock, befuddle, and/or amuse, as well as annoy the former president. The incident didn't leave a lasting mental scar on him, but it sure was cathartic for me.[6]

As I have noted, the most important stage of a prank is "the reveal"—the teaching moment that comes in its wake. Before my robotic intervention, no paper would have printed an op-ed that criticized Bill Clinton for his Sister Souljah Moment. The subject was deemed old and irrelevant, but after I strapped on that silver outfit, the *Washington Post* published my column about it. Nevertheless, my message was lost in a sea of disinformation. Clinton's 1992 comments about Souljah shaped our collective memories of that incident, leading to lazy coverage then and in 2008. Two days after my debut as RoboProfessor, a CNN anchor informed viewers that Souljah was a rapper who "asked for a Kill White People Week, which Clinton called racist." She asked for a *Kill White People Week?* Which *Clinton called racist?!?* Flatly untrue. It would have taken an intern with access to an Internet search engine less than a minute to discover the falsity of that statement. I assume the good folks in the CNN newsroom figured that because Souljah was an Angry Black Rapper, she surely wanted to Kill Whitey. Therefore, no need to fact-check. In trying to correct the record about Clinton's demonization of Souljah and his sometimes-problematic relationship with African Americans, my prank utterly failed. Journalists repeated a more simplistic and inaccurate version of this story than they did back in 1992. For those who forgot or never knew, all they learned was that Sister Souljah was a scary black woman who called for a "Kill White People Week." I'm sorry to say that I probably did more harm than good.[7]

When executing a prank, it is important to clearly communicate, something that didn't happen during my face-off with Bill Clinton. Picking an obscure issue made this difficult, for it required too much explanation and backstory to successfully make my point. I was quite conscious of this problem four years later when my prankster alter ego encountered antigay Republican presidential candidate Michele Bachmann. This time I made sure my message was sharp (though still silly). "Not only are you a homophobe," RoboProfessor said as she got off her campaign bus, "you are a robophobe!" I trailed close behind her and spoke through a small silver megaphone so I could be heard over the background noise. By calling out Bachmann on an issue that was a central part of her public persona, I knew my actions would be understood—even by those who did not agree. And, boy, some folks *really* disliked what I did. The Bachmann supporters packed inside the Hamburg Inn restaurant booed and shoved me, and after I came out as a gay robot, some started a "Stay in the closet!" chant. "I cannot help myself. I was programmed to do this. I am gay," pleaded RoboProfessor, further infuriating them. When a harried restaurant manager asked me to leave, I immediately agreed. After all, we are polite in Iowa.

Reporters soon came calling, and I got the chance to explain myself. But even without any follow-up commentary, the prank's point was fairly legible because I customized it with Bachmann in mind. "I am a gay robot," RoboProfessor said. "I oppose bachmann's position on gays, whether human or robot." I also knew the phrase "gay robot" would be an irresistible hook that could get reporters to spread the story far and wide. England's *Daily Mail* trumpeted, "Republican Candidate Michelle Bachmann Harangued by 'Gay Robot' on the Campaign Trail in Iowa," and the *International Business Times* ran the headline "Gay Robot 'RoboProf' Crashes Michele Bachmann Rally in Iowa City." Another tactical choice I made, in order to publicize the story, was to document the encounter. A friend followed me with an inexpensive handheld HD camera, and an hour after leaving the campaign stop I edited the material and uploaded it to the video-sharing platform YouTube. That encouraged online news sites to embed the eye-popping visuals in their articles, and because the video quality was fairly good, MSNBC used a full minute of the footage in its coverage. This playful source material also allowed news outlets to have fun with their reporting. "Many of her views seem to come from outer space," the MSNBC segment began, "so it would be of little surprise that at a campaign stop in Iowa Michele Bachmann got a visit from a *robot*. Take a look."[8]

Making Mischief in the Modern World

The coverage of the RoboProfessor-versus-Bachmann incident shows how pranking can blur the boundaries between corporate and DIY media. My footage was seen by millions of people, despite being shot by an amateur in Iowa City—about as far away from the country's cultural and media epicenters as one can get. As I have emphasized throughout *Pranksters*, this back-and-forth movement between center and margin is nothing new. The phone phreaks of the 1960s and 1970s, for instance, manipulated a multibillion-dollar telecommunication system using toy whistles, tape recorders, and blue boxes. With a little ingenuity, a bunch of blind and socially awkward outsiders were able to break into AT&T's network and use it as a playground. That sort of border crossing is one of the defining features of trickery in the modern era, which is one reason why I started with Benjamin Franklin. Among other things, he created the template for slippery nineteenth-century celebrities like P. T. Barnum and Mark Twain. Those two famous white men certainly did not exist in the periphery of society, as opposed to Henry "Box" Brown—the slave-turned-entertainer who lived during the same period. Nevertheless, each of them creatively used media to engage the public, such as how Brown reenacted his escape from bondage in an elaborate edutainment spectacle. This showbiz trickster attracted audiences with state-of-the-art panoramic images and dazzling stage magic, but it was his compelling narrative about freedom and rebirth that fully captured the public's imagination. (A good story or hook is an essential ingredient for a successful prank, PR stunt, hoax, or swindle.)

Pranksters, hoaxers, and con artists use media to make their mischief, but their actions can also remake the media landscape in profound ways. P. T. Barnum thrived in an era when deceptions were common occurrences, and the showman's exhibitions cultivated habits of mind that could help his audiences guard against the schemes of confidence men. This normalization of deceit produced ripple effects that transformed media, such as how the nineteenth-century culture of cons and humbugs helped instigate the "Truth-in-Advertising" movement early in the next century. Consumers got fed up with being lied to, so marketers toned down their more outrageous claims after public pressure mounted. In the world of journalism, new ethical codes emerged in reaction to the hoaxes pulled by the likes of Mark Twain, Edgar Allan Poe, and others. The irreverent impulses that marked journalism throughout the 1800s began to wane by the end of century. By this time, the newspaper industry was transforming itself into a truly big business, and the production of news became standardized. This left less room for dissonance on the printed page, though these changes did allow for a more respectable form of hoaxing to emerge: public relations. Since the early days of the PR industry, publicists and pranksters have shared similar tactics (a reality that further muddies the distinctions between professional and amateur media production).

Nineteenth-century life was also impacted by another major social force: Spiritualism. Inspired by the emergence of the telegraph, Spiritualists used this new technology as a model for speaking to the Other Side. They believed the fairer sex's intrinsic sensitivity and passivity primed them to receive messages from the dead. This enabled female mediums to gain more control over their lives by moving the site of religion from the patriarchal public sphere to the private sphere of the home. In doing so, Spiritualism ignited the feminist movement, along with a firestorm of fear among religious conservatives. The late-nineteenth-century occult revival exacerbated their anxieties, as did the simultaneous resurgence of Rosicrucian thought. This myth, which originated as a satirical prank hatched in the early modern period, laid the foundation for the post–French Revolution Illuminati conspiracy theories that proliferated throughout the 1800s. Later in that century, Léo Taxil provoked more prank blowback by spreading wild lies about Masonic devil worship during an elaborate joke that targeted right-wing Catholics. Unfortunately, his hoax publications indirectly inspired those who fabricated *The Protocols of the Elders of Zion*, which was drafted around the time of Taxil's prank. That anti-Semitic literary forgery left its own black mark on modern history, and it serves as a cautionary reminder of trickery's unintended consequences.

Early-twentieth-century author Nesta Webster was instrumental in keeping the Judeo-Masonic conspiracy-theory flame alive. Her anti-Semitic books continue to be cited today, even though they were based in part on Taxil's hoaxes and the creations of other unreliable narrators. In the 1950s and 1960s, the John Birch Society gave Webster's grand unified conspiracy theory a new audience by promoting it within the American far right. This inspired a group of left-leaning weirdos to satirize those beliefs by planting fake news reports in mainstream and underground media outlets. The Discordians claimed that the Bavarian Illuminati was responsible for the turmoil of the sixties, and soon others joined in on the fun. This "guerrilla ontology" experiment spiraled out of control when credulous conservatives projected their darkest fantasies on the silly/sinister stories that circulated at the time. Activist pranks by the Women's International Terrorist Conspiracy from Hell (WITCH) and the self-serving publicity stunts of Church of Satan founder Anton LaVey also freaked out true believers. These events lit a fuse that fed into a powder keg of paranoia. History repeated like a skipping record, and fictions morphed into widely believed truths.

Beginning in the 1960s, Tim LaHaye and Pat Robertson shouted those "truths" from the rooftops. To counterbalance the influence of secular media, the religious right built an alternative communication network that reached huge numbers of people through books, newsletters, radio, and television. Of particular importance was Mike Warnke's

1973 memoir *The Satan-Seller*, which unleashed fantastical urban legends that fueled the Satanic Panics of the 1980s. The Christian con man's long-term legacy, however, was publicizing the Illuminati myth among the millions of evangelicals who read his book. In the 1990s, *Behold a Pale Horse* author William Cooper greatly expanded this conspiracy theory's audience. His book appealed to an odd mixture of right-wing militiamen, left-wing radicals, white religious conservatives, and hip-hop-generation African Americans. Each used Cooper's explanatory narrative to make sense of the social upheavals they experienced, but many were unaware that lots of his sources started out as satires or outright frauds. In the early 2000s, Tea Partiers carried the torch by sounding alarms about Rothschild bankers, Bilderberg schemers, and New World Order shadow governments. In doing so, they echoed anxieties about string-pulling elites that date back to the anti-Masonism movement of the early nineteenth century. In both eras, economic recessions and demographic changes instilled the belief that a privileged minority was blocking the common man's way to wealth. It's the same old story— one told again and again throughout this book.

Despite some amusing moments sprinkled throughout *Pranksters*, I can't shake the feeling of dread that runs through it. Rather than celebrating trickery in all its forms, this book reveals the ways that deception has shaped the modern world in some very disturbing ways. The early-seventeenth-century Protestant pranksters who invented the Rosicrucian Brotherhood wanted to stir up a public debate about ideas the Catholic Church opposed. Their humorous shock tactics backfired when they were taken at face value by those who were predisposed to believe that evil puppet masters walked among them. The Rosicrucian myth also inspired some liberals to found their own esoteric secret societies. This feedback loop cultivated an influential worldview that was stitched together from a jumble of verifiable facts and far-out fictions. Satanic ritual abuse! Devilish Freemasons! Sinister social engineers! Death panels! World Government! The aftershocks from a four-hundred-year-old prank ensured that the Ages of Reason and Enlightenment would not necessarily be reasonable or all that enlightened—nor would our own era, for that matter. Imagination is a powerful tool that can point us to more ethical and just ways of living, but we should approach unchecked fantasy with caution. We tend to fall for pranks, hoaxes, cons, and conspiracy theories when they validate our belief systems, which is why we should be vigilant in challenging those assumptions. One useful model is Jonathan Swift, the self-described "rational surgeon" who dissected popular delusions with his rapier wit. His legacy reminds us that we need to develop more critical habits of mind, so that next time—hopefully—we won't get fooled again.

NOTES

NOTES TO THE INTRODUCTION

1. Lutz, *Doing Nothing*, 59; Green and Stallybrass, *Benjamin Franklin*; "Just published for" quote from Isaacson, *Benjamin Franklin*, 95; "at the very instant" quote from Franklin, *Fart Proudly*, 37; "But at length" quote from Franklin, "Poor Richard vs. Mr. Leeds," in *Benjamin Franklin Reader*, 94.

2. Highet, *Anatomy of Satire*, 97–98; "false predictor" quote from Franklin, *Fart Proudly*, 38–40; "Having received much" quote from Franklin, *Fart Proudly*, 40; "plain to everyone" quote from Isaacson, *Benjamin Franklin*, 96.

3. D. Anderson, *Radical Enlightenments*, 100; "Mr. Leeds was" quote from Franklin, *Fart Proudly*, 39; "I did actually" quote from Isaacson, *Benjamin Franklin*, 97.

4. Juno and Vale, *Pranks!*, 4.

5. "Rats. Rats. Rats." quote from Marks, "Dot-Dash-Diss."

6. Thanks to Ben Peters for the neologism "trickstory."

7. "Freedom of Expression" quote from Ives, "When Marketers Trip over Trademarks."

8. H. Sullivan, "New Survey Delivers"; "self-reinforcing news wave" coined by Vasterman, "Media Hype"; "I can turn" quote from Holiday, *Trust Me I'm Lying*, 18.

9. "Imagination is the" quote from Dewey, *Art as Experience*, 362; "Much like artists" quote from Jasper, *Art of Moral Protest*, 13, 369; "Jokes are active" quote from Duncombe, *Dream*, 130–32.

10. All quotes from McMillian, *Smoking Typewriters*, 66–67, 70–71.

11. McMillian, *Smoking Typewriters*, 66–67, 71; "From bananas, it" quote from B. Wolfe, *Hippies*, 175.

12. Lachman, *Turn Off Your Mind*, 292; "These circumstances come" quote from McMillian, *Smoking Typewriters*, 79.

13. "The second half" quote from Lapsley, *Exploding the Phone*, 224–25; remaining quotes from Isaacson, *Steve Jobs*, 12, 27

14. Jordan, *Hacking*, 9–10; Friedman, *Electric Dreams*, 172–73; Levy, *Hackers*, 10; all quotes from Peterson, *Nightwork*, 3, 5, 198.

15. "If it hadn't" quote from Isaacson, *Steve Jobs*, 30; remaining quotes from Wozniak, foreword to *Exploding the Phone*, xi–xii.

16. Lapsley, *Exploding the Phone*, 174, 296–97; Thornton, *Club Cultures*, 96–97, 116.
17. Hebdige, *Hiding in the Light*, 243; Hyde, *Trickster Makes This World*, 188; all quotes from Bakhtin, "From *Rabelais and His World*," 84, 88; Baxter, *Voicing Relationships*.
18. "When the Church" quote from Nissenbaum, *Battle for Christmas*, 7.
19. Codrescu, *Posthuman Dada Guide*, 23–24; "Every so often" and "The ritual container" quotes from Hyde, *Trickster Makes This World*, 188; "The dust and" quote from Hebdige, *Hiding in the Light*, 243.
20. Hynes, "Mapping the Characteristics," 37; Brooks, *Bodies in Dissent*, 66–69, 85–86, 91.
21. "Some stockies booed" quote from Sanders, *Fug You*, 268.
22. Reed, *Art of Protest*, 182, 188–89, 196–97; Crimp and Rolston, *AIDS Demo Graphics*, 112–13.
23. Schwartz, "CIA Website Hacked."
24. Zehme, *Lost in the Funhouse*, 205; "I like to" quote from Abel, *Confessions of a Hoaxer*.
25. "Antics did indeed" quote from Aufderheide and Jaszi, *Reclaiming Fair Use*, 63.
26. De Hoyos and Morris, *Is It True What They Say about Freemasonry?*, 200.
27. Halttunen, *Confidence Men and Painted Women*.
28. Cook, introduction, 4, 28–29; N. Harris, *Humbug*, 77.
29. Horowitz, *Occult America*, 230; John, *Network Nation*; "The Edgar Cayce" and "People were calling" quotes from Robertson, *Shout It from the Housetops!*, 249–50.
30. Lachman, *Turn Off Your Mind*, 255; Lyons, *Satan Wants You*.
31. Horowitz, *Occult America*, 164–65; Lachman, *Turn Off Your Mind*, 256.
32. Hendershot, *Shaking the World for Jesus*, 4; "People that are" quote from Horowitz, *Occult America*, 164.

NOTES TO CHAPTER 1

1. Milner, *Perfecting Sound Forever*, 108; E. Morris, *Believing Is Seeing*, 92.
2. Love, *Attributing Authorship*, 187–99 (quote from 186–87); Chalmers, *General Biographical Dictionary*, 140; Goldwag, *New Hate*, 28.
3. Horowitz, *Occult America*, 26; Carr-Gomm and Heygate, *Book of English Magic*, 386; Didier Kahn, "Rosicrucian Hoax in France," 238; Yeats, *Rosicrucian Enlightenment*, 235–36, 295; Churton, *Golden Builders*, 81–82; Churton, *Invisible History*, 27, 103; McIntosh, *Rosicrucians*, ix, 25; McIntosh, *Astrologers and Their Creed*, 119.
4. Williamson, *Rosicrucian Manuscripts*, 10; Churton, *Invisible History*, 184, 267.
5. Churton, *Golden Builders*, 91–92, 130–31; Churton, *Invisible History*, 27–28; McIntosh, *Rosicrucians*, 9, 13–14, 27; McIntosh, *Astrologers and Their Creed*, 70.
6. Baigent and Leigh, *Temple and the Lodge*, 144–45; Yeats, *Rosicrucian Enlightenment*, 104, 113–14; Carr-Gomm and Heygate, *Book of English Magic*, 232; Horowitz, *Occult America*, 7; Churton, *Golden Builders*, 154, 168; Churton, *Invisible History*, 17, 31, 75, 86, 101, 109, 271; Eisenstein, *Printing Revolution*, 87.

7. "In theology as" and "Olof Rudbeck is" quotes from King, *Finding Atlantis*, 210.

8. McIntosh, *Rosicrucians*, 24; Horowitz, *Occult America*, 26; "The invisibility of" quote from Yeats, *Rosicrucian Enlightenment*, 49; "adherents of the" quote from Churton, *Invisible History*, 165.

9. Yeats, *Rosicrucian Enlightenment*, 237–38, 49–51; Churton, *Golden Builders*, 107, 130, 141, 152–53; Horowitz, *Occult America*, 26; Williamson, *Rosicrucian Manuscripts*, 17, 137–38; "When . . . some on" quote from Churton, *Invisible History*, 311; "Listen ye mortals" quote from McIntosh, *Rosicrucians*, 20.

10. "We, being deputies" quote from Yeats, *Rosicrucian Enlightenment*, 103–4; "The Rose Cross" quote from Churton, *Invisible History*, 29–30.

11. "There are no" quote from Didier Kahn, "Rosicrucian Hoax in France," 246.

12. Somerset, *Affair of Poisons*; Lyons, *Satan Wants You*, 53; Didier Kahn, "Rosicrucian Hoax in France," 307–8; Churton, *Golden Builders*, 130; Carr-Gomm and Heygate, *Book of English Magic*, 387.

13. Brands, *First American*, 125; D. Anderson, *Radical Enlightenments*, 93; Bullitt, *Jonathan Swift*, 2; Suarez, "Swift's Satire and Parody," 122; Mayhew, "Swift's Bickerstaff Hoax," 272; McIntosh, *Astrologers and Their Creed*, 85; "a yearly stock" quote from Swift, *Bickerstaff-Partridge Papers*, 1.

14. Mayhew, "Swift's Bickerstaff Hoax," 272–77; "My first Prediction" quote from D. Anderson, *Radical Enlightenments*, 100.

15. Mayhew, "Swift's Bickerstaff Hoax," 275; "Now can any" quote from Swift, *Bickerstaff-Partridge Papers*, 19.

16. Swift, *Bickerstaff-Partridge Papers*, 11.

17. Swift, *Bickerstaff-Partridge Papers*, 14; Fedler, *Media Hoaxes*, 4; D. Anderson, *Radical Enlightenments*, 100; Bullitt, *Jonathan Swift*, 105–6; Yapp, *Great Hoaxes*, 174; McIntosh, *Astrologers and Their Creed*, 84–85; Weed, *Wisdom of the Mystic Masters*; "Here, five Foot" quote from Swift, *Bickerstaff-Partridge Papers*, 11.

18. Mayhew, "Swift's Bickerstaff Hoax," 279; Highet, *Anatomy of Satire*, 99; Bullitt, *Jonathan Swift*, 105–6; Swift, *Bickerstaff-Partridge Papers*, 20, 23.

19. Suarez, "Swift's Satire and Parody," 112–16; Mayhew, "Swift's Bickerstaff Hoax," 271; Bullitt, *Jonathan Swift*, 6–7; Fedler, *Media Hoaxes*, 3; E. Sullivan, *Concise Book of Lying*, 59; H. Davis, *Jonathan Swift*, 117.

20. Hyde, *Common as Air*, 148; Isaacson, *Benjamin Franklin*, 28; McPharlin, "Ridicule," 87; Bullitt, *Jonathan Swift*, 24.

21. Highet, *Anatomy of Satire*, 58; Swift, *Modest Proposal*, 53–54.

22. E. Rosenheim, *Swift and the Satirist's Art*, 49, 51; Swift, *Modest Proposal*, 55; Reilly, *Jonathan Swift*, 150, 234; Bullitt, *Jonathan Swift*, 6.

23. "When any young" quote from Swift, *Modest Proposal*, 55; "at my arrival" quote from Psalmanazar, *Memoirs of* ****, 164.

24. Psalmanazar, *Memoirs of* ****, 164; Keevak, *Pretended Asian*, 4–5, 11–13.

25. Collins, *Banvard's Folly*, 140; Rosenblum, *Practice to Deceive*, 6; Keevak, *Pretended Asian*, 5–6; Day, "Psalmanazar's 'Formosa,'" 200; "My complexion, indeed" quote from Psalmanazar, *Memoirs of* ****, 165.

26. Rosenblum, *Practice to Deceive*, 11; Psalmanazar, *Memoirs of* ****, 166; "The Memoirs, in short" quote from Keevak, *Pretended Asian*, 61.

27. Spence, *Question of Hu*, 3–5, 42, 62, 82–85.

28. Collins, *Banvard's Folly*, 142–43; Rosenblum, *Practice to Deceive*, 13.

29. Rosenblum, *Practice to Deceive*, 8; Psalmanazar, *Historical and Geographical Description*, 177–78, 200.

30. Keevak, *Pretended Asian*, 34; Collins, *Banvard's Folly*, 143, 146–47; "On the first" quote from Rosenblum, *Practice to Deceive*, 13.

31. Keevak, *Pretended Asian*, 9–10; Psalmanazar, *Memoirs of* ****.

32. Rosenblum, *Practice to Deceive*, 15; "The last will" quote from Psalmanazar, *Memoirs of* ****, 1; "I never sought" quote from Keevak, *Pretended Asian*, 103.

33. Isaacson, *Benjamin Franklin*, 14; Hyde, *Common as Air*, 42; "the first in" quote from Burns, *Infamous Scribblers*, 33.

34. McPharlin, introduction to *Spectator Papers*, 3–4; Bullitt, *Jonathan Swift*, 29; Green and Stallybrass, *Benjamin Franklin*, 7–8; "it is no" quote from Hyde, *Common as Air*, 147; "Scarce one part" quote from Isaacson, *Benjamin Franklin*, 228.

35. Franklin, *Fart Proudly*, 57; Franklin, "Silence Dogood Introduces Herself," in *Benjamin Franklin Reader*, 11; Waldstreicher, *Runaway America*, 44; Burns, *Infamous Scribblers*, 63; "I made bold" quote from Isaacson, *Benjamin Franklin*, 31.

36. Keyes, *Ben Franklin*, 25; Isaacson, *Benjamin Franklin*, 32; Green and Stallybrass, *Benjamin Franklin*, 7; "I began to" quote from Waldstreicher, *Runaway America*, 45.

37. Keyes, *Ben Franklin*, 52; Isaacson, *Benjamin Franklin*, 60–61; Waldstreicher, *Runaway America*, 75; Brands, *First American*, 103; Green and Stallybrass, *Benjamin Franklin*, 7, 33.

38. Green and Stallybrass, *Benjamin Franklin*, 7; Hyde, *Common as Air*, 42; "In order to" quote from Lindberg, *Confidence Man in American Literature*, 80; "Printers were, without" quote from Waldstreicher, *Runaway America*, 55.

39. Farquhar, *Treasury of Deception*, 31; "Burlington, Oct. 12" quote from Franklin, "A Witch Trial at Mount Holly," in *Benjamin Franklin Reader*, 58–59.

40. All quotes from Franklin, *Fart Proudly*, 18–21.

41. M. Hall, *Benjamin Franklin and Polly Baker*, 3–4, 14–15, 21, 24–25.

42. Block, *Benjamin Franklin*, 233; M. Hall, *Benjamin Franklin and Polly Baker*, 21, 34–35, 42, 46; Tucker, *Bolt of Fate*, 74.

43. E. Morgan, *Benjamin Franklin*, 17; M. Hall, *Benjamin Franklin and Polly Baker*, 51–56.

44. All quotes from M. Hall, *Benjamin Franklin and Polly Baker*, 51–62.

45. All quotes from M. Hall, *Benjamin Franklin and Polly Baker*, 62, 80–81, 87–88.

46. Fedler, *Media Hoaxes*, 7; Rigal, "Imperial Attractions," 31.

47. Isaacson, *Benjamin Franklin*, 151; Waldstreicher, *Runaway America*, 23, 80–81.

48. Rush, "Biographical Anecdotes," 297; Rigal, "Imperial Attractions," 28; all quotes from Waldstreicher, *Runaway America*, 81–82.

49. Waldstreicher, *Runaway America*, 231; Isaacson, *Benjamin Franklin*, 465; Fedler, *Media Hoaxes*, 11; all quotes from Franklin, "The Final Parody, on Slavery," in *Benjamin Franklin Reader*, 373.

50. Fedler, *Media Hoaxes*, 12–13; all quotes from Franklin, "The Final Parody, on Slavery," in *Benjamin Franklin Reader*, 373.

51. "I read from" quote from Lopate, *Getting Personal*, 200; "great tradition of" quote from Marr, *History of Modern England*, 223.

NOTES TO CHAPTER 2

1. Lindberg, *Confidence Man in American Literature*, 62; Adams, *E Pluribus Barnum*, 4; N. Harris, *Humbug*, 71–72; Cook, *Arts of Deception*, 78; Sante, *Low Life*, 214; Goodman, *Sun and the Moon*, 263; Shields, *Reality Hunger*, 34; "Perhaps the first" quote from Poe, "The Man That Was Used Up," in *Complete Works*, 213; "Now and then" quote from Barnum, *Struggles and Triumphs*, 120.

2. "If there is" quote from Hyde, *Trickster Makes This World*, 296.

3. Lindberg, *Confidence Man in American Literature*, 62; "childish and almost" quote from Goodman, *Sun and the Moon*, 245; "It seems impossible" quote from Standage, *Turk*, 23, 27–28, 32.

4. Standage, *Turk*, 36–38, 40–45, 47–48; "Napoleon was delighted" quote from Wallace, *Fabulous Showman*, 13.

5. Goodman, *Sun and the Moon*, 248; Standage, *Turk*, 150; Reiss, *Showman and the Slave*, 28–29.

6. S. Rosenheim, *Cryptographic Imagination*, 101; "Perhaps no exhibition" quote from Standage, *Turk*, 177; "the most successful" quote from Goodman, *Sun and the Moon*, 249.

7. Standage, *Turk*, 200.

8. All quotes from Wallace, *Fabulous Showman*, 26, 28.

9. Wallace, *Fabulous Showman*, 30–31; all quotes from Barnum, *Struggles and Triumphs*, 53, 55.

10. Reiss, *Showman and the Slave*; Wallace, *Fabulous Showman*, 6–9, 12; Goodman, *Sun and the Moon*, 121–22; "I see that" quote from Standage, *Turk*, 173.

11. Goodman, *Sun and the Moon*, 123–25; Barnum, "Chapter X," 35; Reiss, *Showman and the Slave*, 2; Wallace, *Fabulous Showman*, 10.

12. Goodman, *Sun and the Moon*, 251; all quotes from Cook, *Arts of Deception*, 8–9.

13. Cook, *Arts of Deception*, 9.

14. Goodman, *Sun and the Moon*, 251; Adams, *E Pluribus Barnum*, 3; "the deadpan denials" quote from Cook, *Arts of Deception*, 8–12; "the funniest part" quote from Reiss, *Showman and the Slave*, 1, 3.

15. N. Harris, *Humbug*, 57; Adams, *E Pluribus Barnum*, 83; "Bowery museums were" quote from Sante, *Low Life*, 99; "Powerful Drummond lights" quote from Barnum, *Struggles and Triumphs*, 112.

16. Reiss, *Showman and the Slave*, 3–4; Sante, *Low Life*, 59–60; all quotes from Barnum, *Struggles and Triumphs*, 112.

17. Bode, "Introduction," 16; Cook, *Arts of Deception*, 81; Reiss, *Showman and the Slave*, 182; all quotes from Wallace, *Fabulous Showman*, 67, 79.

18. Farquhar, *Treasury of Deception*, 9; Reiss, *Showman and the Slave*, 35, 181; all quotes from Barnum, *Life of P. T. Barnum*, 231.
19. Cook, *Arts of Deception*, 84.
20. Cook, *Arts of Deception*, 16, 77–78, 84; Cook, introduction to *The Colossal P. T. Barnum Reader*, 4, 6–7, 85; Papanikolas, *Trickster in the Land of Dreams*, 96; "In other words" quote from N. Harris, *Humbug*, 68, 71–72, 77.
21. L. Cohen, *Fabrication of American Literature*, 170–71; Lindberg, *Confidence Man in American Literature*, 6; Sante, *Low Life*, 168–69; Halttunen, *Confidence Men and Painted Women*, 7–8; "the stranger, at" quote from Bergmann, *God in the Street*, 195.
22. Halttunen, *Confidence Men and Painted Women*, 6–7, 17; Ewen, *All Consuming Images*, 62–63.
23. Hyde, *Common as Air*, 112–13; Halttunen, *Confidence Men and Painted Women*, 32, 193; Melville, *Confidence-Man*; all quotes from Lindberg, *Confidence Man in American Literature*, 89, 233.
24. Adams, *E Pluribus Barnum*, 1; L. Cohen, *Fabrication of American Literature*, 162, 173; Hyde, *Trickster Makes This World*, 297; N. Harris, *Humbug*, 79; Cook, *Arts of Deception*, 27–28.
25. Lindberg, *Confidence Man in American Literature*, 8; Radin, *Trickster*, xxiii; Hyde, *Trickster Makes This World*; Pelton, "West African Tricksters," 134, 139; "use impersonation, disguise" quote from Landay, *Madcaps, Screwballs, and Con Women*, 2.
26. Leland, *Hip*, 169; Gates, *Signifying Monkey*, 55–56; Roberts, *From Trickster to Badman*, 34–39.
27. Brooks, *Bodies in Dissent*, 66–69, 85–86, 91; all quotes from Brown, *Narrative of the Life*, 58–59, 62.
28. All quotes from Brooks, *Bodies in Dissent*, 85–86, 118–19.
29. All quotes from Hyde, *Trickster Makes This World*, 189, 228, 241, 243.
30. All quotes from Hyde, *Trickster Makes This World*, 189, 244–45, 250.
31. Rahn, *Wizard of Oz*, 5; all quotes from Baum, *Annotated Wizard of Oz*, 18.
32. Baum, *Annotated Wizard of Oz*, xxviii; Culver, "What Manikins Want," 106; all quotes from Papanikolas, *Trickster in the Land of Dreams*, 102.
33. Rahn, *Wizard of Oz*, 6; Culver, "What Manikins Want," 102; Papanikolas, *Trickster in the Land of Dreams*, 104; "If you did" quote from Baum, *Annotated Wizard of Oz*, 171.
34. Culver, "What Manikins Want," 100, 102; Baum, *Annotated Wizard of Oz*, xxiii.
35. Culver, "What Manikins Want," 102–4; Bronfen, "There's No Place Like Home," 50; "Many shops stood" quote from Baum, *Annotated Wizard of Oz*, 177; "Are scarecrows and" quote from Papanikolas, *Trickster in the Land of Dreams*, 105.
36. Bogart, *Artists, Advertising, and the Borders of Art*, 48.

NOTES TO CHAPTER 3

1. Rue, *By the Grace of Guile*, 55; Cook, *Arts of Deception*, 22, 167, 179; Lamont, "Spiritualism and a Mid-Victorian Crisis of Evidence," 903; Schmidt, "From Demon

Possession to Magic Show," 275, 293; Carr-Gomm and Heygate, *Book of English Magic*, 281.

2. Schmidt, "From Demon Possession to Magic Show," 274, 294, 299; Weisberg, *Talking to the Dead*, 91–92; McGarry, *Ghosts of Futures Past*, 6–8; "From the late" quote from Connor, *Dumbstruck*, 209.

3. Schmidt, "From Demon Possession to Magic Show," 293; Barnouw, *Magician and the Cinema*, 19; Robinson, Herbert and Crangle, *Encyclopaedia of the Magic Lantern*, 227–28; "Enlightenment fought constantly" quote from Cook, *Arts of Deception*, 170; "Through this art" quote from Kittler, *Optical Media*, 101.

4. Tebra, "Robertson and His Phantasmagoria," 21; Weisberg, *Talking to the Dead*, 27; Kalush and Sloman, *Secret Life of Houdini*, 21; Lamont, "Spiritualism and a Mid-Victorian Crisis of Evidence," 904–5; all quotes from Cook, *Arts of Deception*, 172–74, 205.

5. Owen, *Darkened Room*, 18; McGarry, *Ghosts of Futures Past*, 123; Sconce, *Haunted Media*, 22–23; Randi, *Encyclopedia of Claims, Frauds, and Hoaxes*, 101; Parfrey and Heimbichner, *Ritual America*, 308.

6. Owen, *Darkened Room*, 18; McGarry, "The Quick, the Dead, and the Yet Unborn," 252–53; Weisberg, *Talking to the Dead*, 6, 55–56; "What would I" quote from Carroll, *Spiritualism in Antebellum America*, 1.

7. Weisberg, *Talking to the Dead*, 65; Bednarowski, "Outside the Mainstream," 213; Carroll, "Religious Construction of Masculinity," 28; McGarry, *Ghosts of Futures Past*, 123; Owen, *Darkened Room*, 11; Sconce, *Haunted Media*, 29, 49; "The only religious" quote from Braude, *Radical Spirits*, 2; "Victorian mediums were" quote from Tromp, "Spirited Sexuality," 78.

8. McGarry, *Ghosts of Futures Past*, 41; Brooks, *Bodies in Dissent*, 14–15; "characters that had" quote from Mattison, *Spirit Rapping Unveiled!*, 81.

9. All quotes from Carroll, "Religious Construction of Masculinity," 27, 34, 47.

10. McGarry, *Ghosts of Futures Past*, 158–61; Buescher, *Other Side of Salvation*, 152; "unmanly and effeminating" quote from Emerson, "Worship," in *Complete Prose Works*, 543; remaining quotes from Carroll, "Religious Construction of Masculinity," 38, 43–47.

11. McGarry, *Ghosts of Futures Past*, 46; Sconce, *Haunted Media*, 27, 45–46, 29.

12. Stuart, *Reluctant Spiritualist*, 44; Sconce, *Haunted Media*, 33; J. Peters, *Speaking into the Air*, 90; Horowitz, *Occult America*, 33; Reynolds, *Waking Giant*, 232; Buescher, *Other Side of Salvation*, 86.

13. Spence and Hazard quotes from McGarry, *Ghosts of Futures Past*, 46, 51.

14. S. Rosenheim, *Cryptographic Imagination*, 92, 120–21; Carroll, *Spiritualism in Antebellum America*, 69; "The whole mystery" quote from Sconce, *Haunted Media*, 30; "heavenly news along" quote from Buescher, *Other Side of Salvation*, 121.

15. Weisberg, *Talking to the Dead*, 102; Sconce, *Haunted Media*, 25, 30, 38–39, 48; "Mysteries are going" quote from Stuart, *Reluctant Spiritualist*, 59.

16. J. Peters, *Speaking into the Air*, 94, 96, 100; Sconce, *Haunted Media*, 21; Thurschwell, *Literature, Technology and Magical Thinking, 1880–13*; Kittler, *Discourse Networks*.

17. Sconce, *Haunted Media*, 34; Horowitz, *Occult America*, 33, 37–38; Fedler, *Media Hoaxes*, 33; all quotes from S. Rosenheim, *Cryptographic Imagination*, 89, 103.

18. Cowan, *Social History of American Technology*, 126; David Kahn, *Code Breakers*, 416; S. Rosenheim, *Cryptographic Imagination*, 88–89, 120–21; Weisberg, *Talking to the Dead*, 146–47.

19. Houdini, *Magician among the Spirits*, 229; Stuart, *Reluctant Spiritualist*, 57; Hammond, *Light from the Spirit World*, vii, ix; all quotes from Collins, *Trouble with Tom*, 90, 138–39.

20. Hammond, *Light from the Spirit World*, 28–29.

21. Brooks, *Bodies in Dissent*, 14; Stuart, *Reluctant Spiritualist*, 173; "I will write" quote from Hammond, *Light from the Spirit World*, 259.

22. Braude, *Radical Spirits*, 181; "Well, you've caught" quote from Houdini, "How I Unmask the Spirit Fakers."

23. A. Anderson, *Snake Oil, Hustlers, and Hambones*, 88–90; "I was chagrined" quote from Kalush and Sloman, *Secret Life of Houdini*, 63.

24. Polidoro, *Final Séance*; Kalush and Sloman, *Secret Life of Houdini*, 379, 383; all quotes from Randi, *Encyclopedia of Claims, Frauds, and Hoaxes*, 42.

25. Owen, "Borderland Forms," 50–51, 50, 54, 67–68; Carpenter, *J. R. R. Tolkien*, 55; Kalush and Sloman, *Secret Life of Houdini*, 384.

26. Houdini, *Magician among the Spirits*, 151; Miller, *Adventures of Arthur Conan Doyle*; Randi, *Encyclopedia of Claims, Frauds, and Hoaxes*, 123; all quotes from Kalush and Sloman, *Secret Life of Houdini*, 388, 395.

27. Polidoro, *Final Séance*, 102, 242; Houdini, *Magician among the Spirits*, xix; all quotes from Kalush and Sloman, *Secret Life of Houdini*, 396, 411.

28. Randi, *Encyclopedia of Claims, Frauds, and Hoaxes*, 58; Silverman, *Houdini!*, 339; Lycett, *Man Who Created Sherlock Holmes*, 441; all quotes from Kalush and Sloman, *Secret Life of Houdini*, 433–35, and Doyle, *Pheneas Speaks*, 55.

29. Kalush and Sloman, *Secret Life of Houdini*, 393, 437, 440, 466; Silverman, *Houdini!*, 393.

30. Kalush and Sloman, *Secret Life of Houdini*, 439–40, 499–500; Silverman, *Houdini!*, 391, 411; all quotes from Bell, *Man Who Killed Houdini*, 48.

31. Kalush and Sloman, *Secret Life of Houdini*, 512–13; all quotes from Segal, "Why Not Just Hold a Seance?"

32. Stuart, *Reluctant Spiritualist*, 297; Weisberg, *Talking to the Dead*, 239–44.

33. Braude, *Radical Spirits*, 162; McGarry, *Ghosts of Futures Past*, 65; Cowan, *Social History of American Technology*, 162–65; Thurschwell, *Literature, Technology and Magical Thinking*, 23; "if it is possible" quote from Horowitz, *Occult America*, 45.

34. Kirkpatrick, *Edgar Cayce*, 124; Weisberg, *Talking to the Dead*, 261–62; Horowitz, *Occult America*, 254; "The roots of" quote from Thurston, introduction to *Essential Edgar Cayce*, 112.

35. Sugrue, *There Is a River*, 151; Thurston, introduction to *Essential Edgar Cayce*, 12; Horowitz, *Occult America*, 231, 235; McIntosh, *Astrologers and Their Creed*, 99–101; Kirkpatrick, *Edgar Cayce*, 10–11, 24, 29.

36. Stearn, *Edgar Cayce*, 14, 37; Lachman, *Turn Off Your Mind*, 361–63; "Expect it in" quote from Edgar Cayce, *Edgar Cayce*, 522; "When we see" quote from Kirkpatrick, *Edgar Cayce*, 125.

37. Horowitz, *Occult America*, 229; Kirkpatrick, *Edgar Cayce*, 234–35, 423; *Tourist Guide Book of Virginia*, 148; Goldblatt, "Once There Was a University," 4; Cayce, "Report of Edgar Cayce Reading."

NOTES TO CHAPTER 4

1. Aaronovitch, *Voodoo Histories*, 84; "In 1959, the" quote from Robertson, *Shout It from the Housetops!*, 137; "The New Age" quote from Robertson, *New World Order*, 273.

2. Barkun, *Culture of Conspiracy*, 46; Wilgus, *Illuminoids*, 18–19; Pipes, *Conspiracy*, 31–32, 59; McLeod, "Evolution of Masonic History," xv; Baigent and Leigh, *Temple and the Lodge*, 54–55, 123.

3. Wilgus, *Illuminoids*, 18–19; B. Ellis, *Raising the Devil*, 127; Goldwag, *New Hate*, 159; "depraved and perverted" quote from de Hoyos and Morris, *Is It True What They Say about Freemasonry?*, 16.

4. Jay, "Darkness Over All"; Webster, *Secret Societies and Subversive Movements*, 228; Aaronovitch, *Voodoo Histories*, 217; "method for filling" quote from Hofstadter, *Paranoid Style in American Politics*, 11.

5. Jay, "Darkness Over All"; Cohn, *Warrant for Genocide*, 25–27; Pipes, *Conspiracy*, 64.

6. Pipes, *Conspiracy*, xi, 67; Segel, *Lie and a Libel*, 52; Streeter, *Behind Closed Doors*, 108; Welch, "Cross Section of the Truth," 5–6; "We shall demonstrate" quote from Goldwag, *New Hate*, 149.

7. Hofstadter, *Paranoid Style in American Politics*, 10; J. Morse, *Sermon Exhibiting the Present Dangers*, 15–16; Wilgus, *Illuminoids*, 26; Pipes, *Conspiracy*, 65; "I have, my" quote from Stauffer, *New England and the Bavarian Illuminati*, 292.

8. Pace, *Benjamin Franklin and Italy*; Goldwag, *New Hate*, 166; Fine and Ellis, *Global Grapevine*, 91; Wilgus, *Illuminoids*, 26; "Shall our sons" quote from Hofstadter, *Paranoid Style in American Politics*, 13; "It is not" quote from Hatonn, *Through Darkness into Light*, 45.

9. Pipes, *Conspiracy*, 47; Goldwag, *New Hate*, 24; Horowitz, *Occult America*, 27; Reynolds, *Waking Giant*, 69; Hofstadter, *Paranoid Style in American Politics*, 14–17.

10. Katsoulis, *Literary Hoaxes*, 41–43; Goldwag, *New Hate*, 216; all quotes from Hofstadter, *Paranoid Style in American Politics*, 8, 21.

11. Katsoulis, *Literary Hoaxes*, 45–47; all quotes from Hofstadter, *Paranoid Style in American Politics*, 21.

12. Goldwag, *New Hate*, 24; Hofstadter, *Paranoid Style in American Politics*, 19; Dunkerley, *Americana*, 116; John, *Network Nation*, 27; "A conspiracy exists" quote from S. Morse, *Foreign Conspiracy against the Liberties of the United States*, 33.

13. Cohn, *Warrant for Genocide*, 41–44; E. Peters, *Inquisition*, 77–78; Laqueur, *Changing Face of Anti-Semitism*, 3, 55–56; Codrescu, *Posthuman Dada Guide*, 24.

14. Cohn, *Warrant for Genocide*, 41–44; "intimate alliance with" quote from Michael and Rosen, "Gougenot de Mousseax, Henri Roger," in *Dictionary of Antisemitism*, 187.

15. Pipes, *Conspiracy*, 74; Goldwag, *New Hate*, 57; "unmasked the hellish" quote from Cohn, *Warrant for Genocide*, 27.

16. Barruel quote from Cohn, *Warrant for Genocide*, 31.

17. Laqueur, *Changing Face of Anti-Semitism*, 73; E. Peters, *Inquisition*, 83–86; Segel, *Lie and a Libel*, 53; Cohn, *Warrant for Genocide*, 29.

18. Pipes, *Conspiracy*, 40, 74; Laqueur, *Changing Face of Anti-Semitism*, 79; all quotes from Cohn, *Warrant for Genocide*, 24, 30, 48.

19. Katsoulis, *Literary Hoaxes*, 48–50; Segel, *Lie and a Libel*, 56, 58, 99; Aaronovitch, *Voodoo Histories*, 22–24; Silverstein and Arnold, *Hoaxes That Made Headlines*, 38–39; all quotes from Cohn, *Warrant for Genocide*, 23.

20. Katsoulis, *Literary Hoaxes*, 51; Laqueur, *Changing Face of Anti-Semitism*, 96; all quotes from Cohn, *Warrant for Genocide*, 36.

21. Cohn, *Warrant for Genocide*, 34–37; Katsoulis, *Literary Hoaxes*, 51.

22. Segel, *Lie and a Libel*, 108–9; Pipes, *Conspiracy*, 85; "We must disarm" quote from LaHaye and Jenkins, *Left Behind*, 274.

23. Sachar, *History of the Jews in the Modern World*, 383, 471; Goldwag, *New Hate*, 92; Stein and MacNee, *Hoaxes!*, 47; Katsoulis, *Literary Hoaxes*, 48; "According to the" quote from Cohn, *Warrant for Genocide*, 181; "I hope that" quote from McConnachie and Tudge, *Rough Guide to Conspiracy Theories*, 111.

24. Laqueur, *Changing Face of Anti-Semitism*, 99; Cohn, *Warrant for Genocide*, 41–44; Baker, *Human Smoke*, 6; Webster, *Socialist Network*, 9; Kovalio, *Russian Protocols of Zion in Japan*, 4; "tells us against" quote from Aaronovitch, *Voodoo Histories*, 26; "world-wide conspiracy" quote from Michael and Rosen, "Winston Churchill," in *Dictionary of Antisemitism*, 96.

25. Fine and Ellis, *Global Grapevine*, 62; "Beneath all these" quote from Webster, *Secret Societies and Subversive Movements*, 166; "In those days" quote from Robertson, *Shout It from the Housetops!*, 77.

26. Lyons, *Satan Wants You*, 80; Horowitz, *Occult America*, 51–53; "the real directors" quote from Gumaer, "Satanism," 63; remaining quotes from Webster, *Secret Societies and Subversive Movements*, 119, 178.

27. Goldwag, *Cults, Conspiracies, and Secret Societies*, 112–13; Thurschwell, *Literature, Technology and Magical Thinking*, 6–7; Webster, *World Revolution*, 35; Robertson, *New World Order*, 17, 177–78; B. Ellis, *Raising the Devil*, 127.

28. Segel, *Lie and a Libel*, 117–18; "Leo Taxil and His 'Greatest Joke of All Times,'" 176; Byrnes, *Antisemitism in Modern France*, 306–9; Marsh, *Word Crimes*, 140–42.

29. Gilgoff, "Devil in a Red Fez"; Medway, *Lure of the Sinister*, 10–11; Byrnes, *Antisemitism in Modern France*, 307–11; "The Masonic Religion" quote from Robinson,

Pilgrim's Path, 56; remaining quotes from de Hoyos and Morris, *Is It True What They Say about Freemasonry?*, 209, 212.

30. Byrnes, *Antisemitism in Modern France*, 313; Waite, *New Encyclopedia of Freemasonry*, 252–53; Medway, *Lure of the Sinister*, 11–14.

31. Medway, *Lure of the Sinister*, 10–16; Waite, *New Encyclopedia of Freemasonry*, 252, 254; Byrnes, *Antisemitism in Modern France*, 313–14; "Leo Taxil and His 'Greatest Joke of All Times,'" 176.

32. Gilgoff, "Devil in a Red Fez"; Medway, *Lure of the Sinister*, 14–16; Byrnes, *Antisemitism in Modern France*, 315.

33. Waite, *New Encyclopedia of Freemasonry*, 257; Byrnes, *Antisemitism in Modern France*, 317–18; Medway, *Lure of the Sinister*, 17; "My Reverend Fathers" quote from de Hoyos and Morris, *Is It True What They Say about Freemasonry?*, 197.

34. Taxil quote form Medway, *Lure of the Sinister*, 16–17.

35. Gilgoff, "Devil in a Red Fez"; Waite, *New Encyclopedia of Freemasonry*, 263; Robinson, *Pilgrim's Path*, 59; "Palladism, my most" quote from Medway, *Lure of the Sinister*, 17; "For all our" quote from "Leo Taxil and His 'Greatest Joke of All Times,'" 176.

36. Segel, *Lie and a Libel*, 118; Gilgoff, "Devil in a Red Fez"; de Hoyos and Morris, *Is It True What They Say about Freemasonry?*, 27; Parfrey and Heimbichner, *Ritual America*, 71; "it was not" quote from Medway, *Lure of the Sinister*, 97.

37. "It is self-evident" quote from Robertson, *New World Order*, 273.

NOTES TO CHAPTER 5

1. Weisberg, *Talking to the Dead*, 107; Goodman, *Sun and the Moon*, 20–21, 262; Maliszewski, *Fakers*, 104.

2. Silverstein and Arnold, *Hoaxes That Made Headlines*, 76; Fedler, *Media Hoaxes*, 57; Maliszewski, *Fakers*, 104, 109; "There appeared as" quote from Goodman, *Sun and the Moon*, 137.

3. Reiss, *Showman and the Slave*, 147; Farquhar, *Treasury of Deception*, 35; all quotes from Goodman, *Sun and the Moon*, 167, 173.

4. *War of the Worlds*, 83; Fedler, *Media Hoaxes*, 63; Goodman, *Sun and the Moon*, 12, 178.

5. Silverstein and Arnold, *Hoaxes That Made Headlines*, 79; Fedler, *Media Hoaxes*, 65; all quotes from Goodman, *Sun and the Moon*, 218, 224–25, 227.

6. L. Cohen, *Fabrication of American Literature*, 60; Fedler, *Media Hoaxes*, 18, 66; Maliszewski, *Fakers*, 117–18; Reiss, *Showman and the Slave*, 147; Goodman, *Sun and the Moon*, 235.

7. C. MacDougall, *Hoaxes*, 231; S. Rosenheim, *Cryptographic Imagination*, 183; Goodman, *Sun and the Moon*, 240–41.

8. Fedler, *Media Hoaxes*, 25.

9. All quotes from Goodman, *Sun and the Moon*, 243–44.

10. L. Harris, "From Abolitionist Amalgamators to 'Rulers of the Five Points,'" 208; Kaplan, "Miscegenation Issue in the Election of 1864," 279, 284; Lemire, *"Miscegenation,"* 129; all quotes from *Miscegenation*, 50.

11. Lemire, *"Miscegenation,"* 116, 118, 137; all quotes from Kaplan, "Miscegenation Issue in the Election of 1864," 280, 284.

12. Lemire, *"Miscegenation,"* 138; all quotes from Kaplan, "Miscegenation Issue in the Election of 1864," 289, 294, 296, 328.

13. Collins, *Trouble with Tom*, 164; all quotes from Kaplan, "Miscegenation Issue in the Election of 1864," 275–76, 309–10, 319, 325.

14. All quotes from Kaplan, "Miscegenation Issue in the Election of 1864," 142, 277–78, 299, 331–32, 326–27.

15. Fedler, *Media Hoaxes*, 85.

16. All quotes from Fedler, *Media Hoaxes*, 37, 89–91.

17. Fedler, *Media Hoaxes*, 40, 96; C. MacDougall, *Hoaxes*, 232; Silverstein and Arnold, *Hoaxes That Made Headlines*, 74; Collins, *Sixpence House*, 157; all quotes from Farquhar, *Treasury of Deception*, 39.

18. Sims, "Chicago Style of Journalism," 29–32, 34, 44; R. Morris, *Lighting Out for the Territory*, 107–8; Silverstein and Arnold, *Hoaxes That Made Headlines*, 80; all quotes from Fedler, *Media Hoaxes*, xvi–xvii.

19. Katsoulis, *Literary Hoaxes*, 65; Sims, "Chicago Style of Journalism," 37; Silverstein and Arnold, *Hoaxes That Made Headlines*, 82; "with his throat" quote from C. MacDougall, *Hoaxes*, 234; "Well, in all" quote from Fedler, *Media Hoaxes*, 34.

20. R. Morris, *Lighting Out for the Territory*, 122; Silverstein and Arnold, *Hoaxes That Made Headlines*, 82; all quotes from Fedler, *Media Hoaxes*, 46.

21. Simonson, *Refiguring Mass Communication*, 119; Ewen, *PR!*, 108–11; "the first organized" quote from Bernays, *Biography of an Idea*, 155.

22. Ewen, *PR!*, 116–17; Goldberg, *Liberal Fascism*, 109–10.

23. Bernays, *Biography of an Idea*, 205; Ewen, *All Consuming Images*, 267; Lippmann, *Public Opinion*, 19, 158; all quotes from Ewen, *PR!*, 9, 10, 12, 380, 379.

24. Milbank, *Tears of a Clown*, 127; Welch, "Truth about Vietnam," 3; Welch, "Republics and Democracies," 18; Welch, "Truth in Time," 2–3, 9; "It was under" quote from Welch, *New Americanism*, 128.

25. Kirkpatrick, *Edgar Cayce*, 10, 198, 231; "Since Dewey began" quote from Robertson, *New World Order*, 164.

26. Ewen, *PR!*, 176; Bernays, "Manipulating Public Opinion"; "We are dominated" quote from Jackson, *Conspiranoia!*, 94.

27. Ewen, *Captains of Consciousness*, 160; "the engineer of" quote from Ewen, *PR!*, 379; "If the publicity" quote from Lippmann, *Public Opinion*, 218; "Our parade of" quote from Bernays, *Biography of an Idea*, 386.

28. Cowan, *Social History of American Technology*, 75, 94; Sims, "Chicago Style of Journalism," 20–28, 38.

29. Lin, *Kid A*, 41; Sconce, *Haunted Media*, 21; "It seems impossible" quote from R. MacDougall, "Wire Devils," 737; "When it was" quote from Cowan, *Social History of American Technology*, 155–56.

30. Carey, *Communication as Culture*, 210–11.

NOTES TO CHAPTER 6

1. Turner, *From Counterculture to Cyberculture*; all quotes from T. Wolfe, *Electric Kool-Aid Acid Test*, 67–69, 71, 250–51.

2. Sanders, *Fug You*, 2; McMillian, *Smoking Typewriters*, 30, 37–38, 77, 99.

3. Duncombe, *Notes from the Underground*, 138; Krassner, *Confessions of a Raving, Unconfined Nut*, 46; McMillian, *Smoking Typewriters*, 33–36, 99.

4. "Write a letter" quote from Krassner, *Confessions of a Raving, Unconfined Nut*, 48.

5. "If the post" quote from Krassner, *Confessions of a Raving, Unconfined Nut*, 93–94.

6. "It only worked" quote from Juno and Vale, *Pranks!*, 81; "During that tense" quote from Krassner, *Winner of the Bicycle Race*, 287.

7. Krassner, *Winner of the Bicycle Race*, 288.

8. All quotes from Krassner, *Confessions of a Raving, Unconfined Nut*, 139.

9. All quotes from Juno and Vale, *Pranks!*, 38–39.

10. All quotes from Juno and Vale, *Pranks!*, 38–40.

11. Hultkrans, "Joey Skaggs," 41; all quotes from Juno and Vale, *Pranks!*, 40–41.

12. Krassner, *Who's to Say What's Obscene?*, 112; Hoffman, *Steal This Book*, 67; "As a co-founder" quote from Krassner, *Confessions of a Raving, Unconfined Nut*, 152; "We had $200" quote from Juno and Vale, *Pranks!*, 66.

13. Roszak, *Making of a Counterculture*, 124; "an event in" quote from Krassner, *Confessions of a Raving, Unconfined Nut*, 152; "There were 50,000" quote from Juno and Vale, *Pranks!*, 65–66.

14. Juno and Vale, *Pranks!*, 65–66.

15. B. Ellis, *Raising the Devil*, 175–76; I. Ellis, *Rebels Wit Attitude*, 102–6; Lachman, *Turn Off Your Mind*, 301; Sanders, *Fug You*, 281; all quotes from Roszak, *Making of a Counterculture*, 124.

16. Hoffman, "Revolution for the Hell of It," 329; Juno and Vale, *Pranks!*, 40; "The Yippies themselves" quote from Krassner, *Confessions of a Raving, Unconfined Nut*, 157; "We are faced" quote from Duncombe, *Dream*, 22.

17. All quotes from McLeese, *Kick Out the Jams*, 1–2, 11.

18. Reed, *Art of Protest*, 61–62; all quotes from Cuddihy, *Ordeal of Civility*, 191, 194.

19. Cuddihy, *Ordeal of Civility*, 190, 192, 194; "This image of" quote from Reed, *Art of Protest*, 61–62.

20. All quotes from Reed, *Art of Protest*, 41, 50.

21. Churchill and Vander Wall, *COINTELPRO Papers*, 123; Reed, *Art of Protest*, 53.

22. Duncombe, *Dream*, 21, 57, 155; Reed, *Art of Protest*, 59–61; "The purpose of" quote from Churchill and Wall, *COINTELPRO Papers*, 92.

23. McMillian, *Smoking Typewriters*, 115–16, 124; "The Bureau is" quote from Churchill and Wall, *COINTELPRO Papers*, 212; "I've hated fraternities" quote from Juno and Vale, *Pranks!*, 66.

24. "The only solution" quote from Krassner, *Winner of the Bicycle Race*, 24.

25. "Some leaders of" quote from Churchill and Wall, *COINTELPRO Papers*, 184, 205–6; "Gentlemen, you must" quote from Krassner, *Winner of the Bicycle Race*, 23–24.

26. All quotes from Echols, *Daring to Be Bad*, 120.

27. All quotes from Echols, *Daring to Be Bad*, 93–94.

28. R. Morgan, *Word of a Woman*, 21, 27; Echols, *Daring to Be Bad*, 94; "Picket Lines; Guerrilla" quote from "No More Miss America," in R. Morgan, *Sisterhood Is Powerful*, 521.

29. "No More Miss America," 521; Echols, *Daring to Be Bad*, 94; "We estimated correctly" quote from R. Morgan, *Word of a Woman*, 21, 27.

30. "Bras, girdles, and" quote from Zeisler, *Feminism and Pop Culture*, 53; "was translated by" quote from R. Morgan, *Word of a Woman*, 26; "Those feminists who" quote from Echols, *Daring to Be Bad*, 94.

31. "No More Miss America," 522–23; all quotes from Echols, *Daring to Be Bad*, 96.

32. Echols, *Daring to Be Bad*, 97; "A certain common" quote from "WITCH Documents," in R. Morgan, *Sisterhood Is Powerful*, 538–39.

33. "WITCH Documents," 544.

34. "We promise to" quote from "WITCH Documents," 544; "Incredibly, they had" quote from Echols, *Daring to Be Bad*, 97–98.

35. Greeley, "There's a New-Time Religion on Campus," 14.

36. Gumaer, "Satanism," 72; Carr-Gomm and Heygate, *Book of English Magic*, 182–83; Larson, *Satanism*, 166.

NOTES TO CHAPTER 7

1. Melley, "Brainwashed!," 147; Melley, *Empire of Conspiracy*; Root, *Brainwashing in the High Schools*, 3–5; all quotes from Seed, *Brainwashing*, 29, 106.

2. Seed, *Brainwashing*, 27, 67; Biderman, "Image of 'Brainwashing'"; "like witchcraft, with" quote from Melley, "Brainwashed!," 146, 148.

3. Melley, "Brainwashed!," 154; "not recommend testing" quote from Lee and Shlain, *Acid Dreams*, 29, 40.

4. "What is the" quote from Lee and Shlain, *Acid Dreams*, 31, 37.

5. Gorightly, *Prankster and the Conspiracy*, 27, 57, 62.

6. Gorightly, *Prankster and the Conspiracy*, 61–62.

7. *Principia Discordia*, 22, 28.

8. "Many people consider" quote from Gorightly, *Prankster and the Conspiracy*, 11; "The Believer had" quote from Krassner, *Who's to Say What's Obscene?*, 140; "We were both" quote from Wilson, *Cosmic Trigger I*, 56.

9. Thornley, *Idle Warriors*; Gorightly, *Prankster and the Conspiracy*, 32–33; "You might say" quote from President's Commission on the Assassination of President Kennedy, *Report*, 686.

10. McConnachie and Tudge, *Rough Guide to Conspiracy Theories*, 26; Gorightly, *Prankster and the Conspiracy*, 92; "Thornley and Garrison" quote from Wilson, *Cosmic Trigger I*, 61.

11. Gorightly, *Prankster and the Conspiracy*, 97.

12. "In the underground" quote from Wilson, *Cosmic Trigger I*, 62; remaining quotes from Gorightly, *Prankster and the Conspiracy*, 97, 100.

13. "Synchronicity, by Goddess" quote from Wilson, *Cosmic Trigger I*, 64; "had laid out" quote from Gorightly, *Prankster and the Conspiracy*, 154.

14. "For only five" quote from Gorightly, *Prankster and the Conspiracy*, 142–43; "There simply were" quote from Wilson, *Cosmic Trigger I*, 63.

15. Pipes, *Conspiracy*, 65; Blumenthal, *Republican Gomorrah*, 18; Wilentz, "Confounding Fathers"; Welch, *Politician*, 133.

16. Welch, "More Stately Mansions," 12; Webster, *World Revolution*, 109; "They will sometimes" quote from Fourier, *Utopian Vision of Charles Fourier*, 251–52.

17. Welch, "Truth in Time," 2–3; C. Mills, *Power Elite*; Welch, "Cross Section of the Truth," 11; "This incredibly ambitious" quote from Welch, *New Americanism*, 130–31.

18. All quotes from W. Carr, *Pawns in the Game*, x, xix, 129.

19. B. Ellis, *Raising the Devil*, 132; Welch, "What Is the John Birch Society?," 1; "both sides of" quoted Welch, *Neutralizers*, 15.

20. "We're amused you've" quote from Gorightly, *Prankster and the Conspiracy*, 143; "We accused everybody" quote from Wilson, *Cosmic Trigger I*, 63.

21. Gorightly, *Prankster and the Conspiracy*, 141–42; "some less gullible" quote from Wilson, *Cosmic Trigger I*, 63; "I recently heard" quote from Shea and Wilson, *Illuminatus Trilogy!*, 20.

22. Wilson, *Cosmic Trigger I*, 63.

23. Wilson, *Cosmic Trigger I*, 64; Fenster, *Conspiracy Theory*, 164; Wilgus, *Illuminoids*, 21, 31.

24. Shea and Wilson, *Illuminatus Trilogy!*, 104.

25. "[Weishaupt's] conspiracy was" quote from Robertson, *New World Order*, 98; "This lodge, in" quote from Shea and Wilson, *Illuminatus Trilogy!*, 146; "a rare example" quote from Gorightly, *Prankster and the Conspiracy*, 151; "experiences with the" quote from Wilson, *Illuminati Papers*, 19.

26. Pipes, *Conspiracy*, 15; Kellner, "X-Files and Conspiracy," 206–7; "Sometimes it seemed" quote from Hine, *Great Funk*, 51; "Conspiracy mythology is" quote from Wilgus, *Illuminoids*, 21.

27. Gorightly, *Prankster and the Conspiracy*, 152, 193; all quotes from Wilson, *Cosmic Trigger I*, 59, 150, 154.

28. "The logic of" quote from Wilson, *Cosmic Trigger I*, 154; remaining quotes from Gorightly, *Prankster and the Conspiracy*, 193, 206, 258.

29. Lewin, *Report from Iron Mountain*, 119; "The book is" quote from Navasky, introduction to *Report from Iron Mountain*, v.

30. "Its acceptance by" quote from Navasky, introduction to *Report from Iron Mountain*, v.

31. All quotes from Navasky, introduction to *Report from Iron Mountain*, ix–x; and Lewin, *Report from Iron Mountain*, 11–12, 69.

32. Lewin, *Report from Iron Mountain*, 94–95.

33. Lewin, *Report from Iron Mountain*, 134; all quotes from Navasky, introduction to *Report from Iron Mountain*, xiii.

34. "All leaders of" quote from Prouty, *JFK*, 31.

35. Pipes, *Conspiracy*, 16; Navasky, introduction to *Report from Iron Mountain*, xiv; all quotes from Prouty, *JFK*, xi.

36. Barkun, *Culture of Conspiracy*, 7; Fenster, *Conspiracy Theory*, 116; Lewin, *Report from Iron Mountain*, 120; "are the victims" quote from Kelly, *Conspiracy against God and Man*, 223; "Authors who expose" quote from Robertson, *New World Order*, 72.

37. Juno and Vale, *Pranks!*, 82; all quotes from Krassner, *Winner of the Bicycle Race*, 21–22.

38. Chang, *Can't Stop Won't Stop*, 438; Pipes, *Conspiracy*, 8.

39. Pipes, *Conspiracy*, 8; Pierce, *Turner Diaries*; Fenster, *Conspiracy Theory*, 279; Lampley, *Universal Church of God Newsletter*, Summer 1994, 1, 3.

40. Lampley, *Universal Church of God Newsletter*, Summer 1994, 2; "The American people" quote from Lampley, *Universal Church of God Newsletter*, August 12, 1994, 1; "We are getting" quote from Lampley, *Universal Church of God Newsletter*, August 30, 1994, 1; "35,000 Communist Chinese" quote from Hofstadter, *Paranoid Style in American Politics*, 29.

41. Festinger, Riecken, and Schachter, *When Prophecy Fails*, 17–23, 216–29; Liddy, Barrett, and Selanikio, *Fighting Back*, 85; "I made a" quote from Lampley, *Universal Church of God Newsletter*, September 23, 1994, 1–2.

42. Pipes, *Conspiracy*, 88; "It is reported" quote from Robertson, *New World Order*, 126.

43. Cooper, *Behold a Pale Horse*, 78; Barkun, *Culture of Conspiracy*, 60; "Fox Mulder's Cooper-esque" quote from Chang, *Can't Stop Won't Stop*, 439.

44. Pipes, *Conspiracy*, 7.

45. "The numbers 3" quote from Cooper, *Behold a Pale Horse*, 92.

46. Barkun, *Culture of Conspiracy*, 95; Chang, *Can't Stop Won't Stop*, 438.

47. Blumenthal, "James O'Keefe's Race Problem"; "As you can" quote from Shane, "Political Gadfly Lampoons the Left."

48. Goldberg, *Liberal Fascism*, 270–73; Blumenthal, "James O'Keefe's Race Problem."

49. Shane, "Political Gadfly Lampoons the Left."

50. Newman, "Advice to Fake Pimp Was No Crime"; "heavily edited to" quote from California Department of Justice, Office of the Attorney General, *Report of the Attorney General*, 23–24; "That 20-minute video" quote from Urbina, "ACORN on Brink of Bankruptcy."

51. All quotes from Wilentz, "Confounding Fathers."

52. Bunch, *Backlash*, 171; "When I was" quote from Wilentz, "Confounding Fathers"; "It is not" quote from Allen, *Kissinger*, 139.

53. Milbank, *Tears of a Clown*, 56–58; Skousen, *Communist Attack on U.S. Police*, 21–23; Bunch, *Backlash*, 44–45; Wilentz, "Confounding Fathers."

54. Christenson, "Quigley"; Allen, *Man behind the Mask*, 59, 60–61; "a bold and" quote from Skousen, *Naked Capitalist*, 6.

55. Allen and Abraham, *None Dare Call It a Conspiracy*, 17; "Skousen's book is" quote from Wilentz, "Confounding Fathers"; "I know it's" quote from Milbank, *Tears of a Clown*, 55–56.

56. Skousen, *Five Thousand Year Leap*, 1; Milbank, *Tears of a Clown*, 56–60; Skousen, *Communist Attack on U.S. Police*, 21–23; Bunch, *Backlash*, 44–45; Wilentz, "Confounding Fathers."

57. Wilentz, "Confounding Fathers"; Fine and Ellis, *Global Grapevine*, 60; Goldberg, *Liberal Fascism*, 81–82; "As I study" quote from Milbank, *Tears of a Clown*, 128; "By 1920 the" quote from Welch, "Looking Ahead," 17.

58. Harp, "Church of Humanity"; "Who will be" quote from Goldberg, *Liberal Fascism*, 100.

59. Brock, *Charlatan*, 82; Wilentz, "Confounding Fathers."

60. "So in some ways" quote from Bunch, *Backlash*, 263, 270.

61. TNR Staff, "TNR Exclusive"; Amato and Neiwert, *Over the Cliff*, 19; all quotes from Elliott, "Rand Paul in '08."

62. "A superb analysis" quote from Griffin, *Creature from Jekyll Island*, back-cover blurb.

NOTES TO CHAPTER 8

1. B. Ellis, *Raising the Devil*, 177; "What *is* new" quote from Roszak, *Making of a Counterculture*, 167.

2. B. Ellis, *Raising the Devil*, 128; Roberts and Olson, *John Wayne*, 523; Wilentz, "Confounding Fathers"; Arellano, *Orange County*, 12.

3. Medway, *Lure of the Sinister*, 21; Gunn, *Modern Occult Rhetoric*, 183; Lyons, *Satan Wants You*, 107; "The true magus" quote from LaVey, *Satanic Bible*, 21; "My mother was" quote from Lamothe-Ramos, "Beelzebub's Daughter," 91.

4. Hertenstein and Trott, *Selling Satan*, 92; all quotes from Gumaer, "Satanism," 45–47, 67.

5. Medway, *Lure of the Sinister*, 26, 127; B. Ellis, *Lucifer Ascending*, 87–89; Horowitz, *Occult America*, 164–65; Lachman, *Turn Off Your Mind*, 77, 256.

6. Austen, "Sammy Devil Jr."; Medway, *Lure of the Sinister*, 26, 127; B. Ellis, *Lucifer Ascending*, 87–89; Horowitz, *Occult America*, 164–65; Lachman, *Turn Off Your Mind*, 77, 256.

7. Carr-Gomm and Heygate, *Book of English Magic*, 431; Parfrey and Heimbichner, *Ritual America*, 272; Larson, *Satanism*, 151; Lyons, *Satan Wants You*, 77; M. Davis, *City of Quartz*, 59–60; Baddeley, *Lucifer Rising*, 23; all quotes from Gunn, *Modern Occult Rhetoric*, 156–57, 175.

8. LaVey, *Satanic Bible*, 10; Lachman, *Turn Off Your Mind*, 250–52; "Beware, you psychedelic" quote from Baddeley, *Lucifer Rising*, 67.

9. S. Gaines, *Heroes and Villains*, 213; Quantick, *Revolution*, 188; B. Ellis, *Raising the Devil*, 177–78.

10. All quotes from B. Ellis, *Raising the Devil*, 179–80.

11. Gunn, *Modern Occult Rhetoric*, 185.

12. Lachman, *Turn Off Your Mind*, 270; Lyons, *Satan Wants You*, 88–90; Versluis, *New Inquisitions*, 112–13; "Black is the" quote from Bainbridge, *Satan's Power*, 3; "There was a" quote from Blumenthal, *Republican Gomorrah*, 219.

13. Ammerman, "North American Protestant Fundamentalism," 56, 67–68, 87; Erickson, *Religious Radio and Television*, 82–83; Hendershot, *Shaking the World for Jesus*, 167; Arellano, *Orange County*, 130–31.

14. Robertson, *Shout It from the Housetops!*, 75, 249–50; Cayce, *Edgar Cayce*, 17; Kirkpatrick, *Edgar Cayce*, 345–46; Sugrue, *There Is a River*, 230.

15. Berlet, "Who Is Mediating the Storm?," 249; Erickson, *Religious Radio and Television*, 53–54; all quotes from Robertson, *Shout It from the Housetops!*, 137, 151.

16. Berlet, "Who Is Mediating the Storm?," 249; Erickson, *Religious Radio and Television*, 53–54; "When I visited" quote from Armstrong, *Electric Church*, 101; "(1) wisdom to know" quote from Robertson, *Shout It from the Housetops!*, 145.

17. Ammerman, "North American Protestant Fundamentalism," 88; Barkun, *Culture of Conspiracy*, 48–49; "My circumstances necessitate" quote from Sutton, *Illuminati 666*, 176–77.

18. Erickson, *Religious Radio and Television*, 61–64; Irr, *Suburb of Dissent*, 100; Cohn, *Warrant for Genocide*, 233–36; Pipes, *Conspiracy*, 65.

19. Ammerman, "North American Protestant Fundamentalism," 87; Frankl, *Televangelism*, 70; Horsfield, *Religious Television*, 8–10; Lesage, "Christian Media," 21–22.

20. B. Ellis, *Raising the Devil*, 192–94; Hertenstein and Trott, *Selling Satan*, 165; Versluis, *New Inquisitions*, 117.

21. Martin and Segrave, *Anti-Rock*, 283; "lit the way" quote from LaHaye, *Rapture*, 217; "The Christmas holiday" quote from Welch, "Our Only Weapon," 12.

22. Victor, *Satanic Panic*, 15; B. Ellis, *Raising the Devil*, 117; Hicks, *In Pursuit of Satan*, 182–83, 188.

23. B. Ellis, *Aliens, Ghosts, and Cults*, 199–200; "Papa Smurf, a" quote from Hicks, *In Pursuit of Satan*, 25.

24. Hicks, *In Pursuit of Satan*, 167; Johnston, *Edge of Evil*, xi, 167; Medway, *Lure of the Sinister*, 208–9; Victor, *Satanic Panic*, 60–64.

25. Victor, *Satanic Panic*, 7; Baddeley, *Lucifer Rising*, 135–36; Hicks, *In Pursuit of Satan*, 332; Lyons, *Satan Wants You*, 138.

26. Victor, *Satanic Panic*, 13–14; Hicks. *In Pursuit of Satan*, 335; Bromley, Shupe, and Ventimiglia, "Role of Anecdotal Atrocities," 141–43.

27. Medway, *Lure of the Sinister*, 165–67; B. Ellis, *Raising the Devil*, 189; Warnke, *Satan-Seller*, 63, 87, 93.

28. B. Ellis, *Raising the Devil*, 189; "A worldwide, super-secret" quote from Warnke, *Satan-Seller*, 93; "I brought up" quote from Hertenstein and Trott, *Selling Satan*, 101; "the satanically inspired" quote from LaHaye, *Rapture*, 208.

29. Hicks, *In Pursuit of Satan*, 21; Hertenstein and Trott, *Selling Satan*, 256; "I've been waiting" quote from Medway, *Lure of the Sinister*, 168.
30. Hertenstein and Trott, *Selling Satan*, 290; Lyons, *Satan Wants You*, 2; B. Ellis, *Raising the Devil*, xv; "A generation of" quote from Versluis, *New Inquisitions*, 113; remaining quotes from Gunn, *Modern Occult Rhetoric*, 196–200.
31. Lyons, *Satan Wants You*, 153; Bettelheim, *Uses of Enchantment*, 122.
32. Hicks, *In Pursuit of Satan*, 176; all quotes from Gunn, *Modern Occult Rhetoric*, 174, 193, 196–200.
33. Hertenstein and Trott, *Selling Satan*, 281; Hicks, *In Pursuit of Satan*, 142; Loftus and Ketcham, *Myth of Repressed Memory*, 55; B. Ellis, *Raising the Devil*, 105–6; Smith and Pazder, *Michelle Remembers*, 162.
34. Victor, *Satanic Panic*, 81–82, 99–100; B. Ellis, *Raising the Devil*, 111; all quotes from Smith and Pazder, *Michelle Remembers*, ix, 189.
35. Gunn, *Modern Occult Rhetoric*, 172; Victor, *Satanic Panic*, 99–100; Hicks, *In Pursuit of Satan*, 179.
36. Versluis, *New Inquisitions*, 114–15; Noblitt and Perskin, *Cult and Ritual Abuse*, 100–101; Hicks, *In Pursuit of Satan*, 85–87.
37. *Paradise Lost: Purgatory.*
38. *Paradise Lost: The Child Murders at Robin Hood Hills.*
39. *Paradise Lost: Purgatory.*
40. *Paradise Lost: Purgatory.*
41. Victor, *Satanic Panic*, 165, 168–69; Weinstein, *Heavy Metal*, 248.
42. Aranza, *Backward Masking Unmasked*, 7; Peters and Peters, *Rock's Hidden Persuader*, 34–57; Jackson, *Conspiranoia!*, 182; Baddeley, *Lucifer Rising*, 144; "The cassette or" quote from Larson, *Satanism*, 81.
43. Reeve, *Turn Me On, Dead Man*, 11–13.
44. LaBour, "McCartney Dead"; Harper, "Is Beatle Paul McCartney Dead?," 1; Reeve, *Turn Me On, Dead Man*; Patterson, *Walrus Was Paul*, 31–35.
45. McLaren, "Subliminal Seduction," 223–25; "Whether these messages" quote from Peters and Peters, *Rock's Hidden Persuader*, 59.
46. Victor, *Satanic Panic*, 172–74; Dear, *Dungeon Master*; Hicks, *In Pursuit of Satan*, 45, 288; "The occult overtones" quote from Larson, *Satanism*, 52.
47. Weinstein, *Heavy Metal*, 262; Larson, *Satanism*, 106; "most kids view" quote from D. Gaines, *Teenage Wasteland*, 188.
48. Negativland, *Helter Stupid.*
49. Negativland, *Helter Stupid.*
50. Negativland, *Helter Stupid.*
51. D. Carr, *Pretty Hate Machine*, 2–3; "Whether Mike realized" quote from Hertenstein and Trott, *Selling Satan*, 101.
52. "Jay-Z"; Jay-Z, *Decoded*, 247; "Kanye West Listening Party."
53. Chang, *Can't Stop Won't Stop*, 437–39.
54. Bazell, "U.S. Apologizes to Guatemala"; Chang, *Can't Stop Won't Stop*, 437; "I want to" quote from "Cee Lo," 61.

55. Parfrey and Heimbichner, *Ritual America*, 64.
56. RZA, *Wu-Tang Manual*, 43–44; "A veritable who's" quote from Horowitz, *Occult America*, 138–42.
57. Corbett, *Extended Play*, 150; "For Ali there" quote from Remnick, *King of the World*, 134.
58. Szwed, *Space Is the Place*, 142–43.
59. Szwed, *Space Is the Place*, 105–6; Corbett, Elms, and Kapsalis, *Pathways to Unknown Worlds*, 7–8; Corbett, *Extended Play*, 169.
60. RZA, *Wu-Tang Manual*, 169; Goldwag, *New Hate*, 187; Blumenthal, *Republican Gomorrah*, 328.
61. Allen, *Man behind the Mask*, 424; Goldwag, *New Hate*, 19; C. Hall, "Glenn Beck Blames Evils of Slavery"; Paulson, "Texas Textbook War."

1. Williams, "Entertaining 'Difference,'" 22–23; "Come with us" quote from Taylor, "Korla Pandit," 23; "He was light-skinned" quote from R. Smith, *Great Black Way*, 223, 230.
2. Williams, "Entertaining 'Difference,'" 21; R. Smith, *Great Black Way*, 223–26, 231–32.
3. R. Smith, *Great Black Way*, 227; Taylor, "Korla Pandit," 26, 32; Williams, "Entertaining 'Difference,'" 22–23, 25–26; Juno and Vale, *Incredibly Strange Music*, 18.
4. R. Smith, *Great Black Way*, 222; "All this was" quote from Kisseloff, *Box*, 171, 181.
5. Lemert, *Muhammad Ali*, 45; Beekman, *Ringside*, 87; all quotes from Capouya, *Gorgeous George*, 3–5, 8, 85, 105, 226.
6. R. Smith, *Great Black Way*, 229; all quotes from Capouya, *Gorgeous George*, 270–71.
7. R. Smith, *One*, 143–44; all quotes from Capouya, *Gorgeous George*, 89–91, 210–11.
8. All quotes from Capouya, *Gorgeous George*, 245–47.
9. Leland, *Hip*, 163; "The story about" quote from Remnick, *King of the World*, 90.
10. All quotes from Remnick, *King of the World*, 148, 173, 175.
11. All quotes from Remnick, *King of the World*, 169, 178–80.
12. Lemert, *Muhammad Ali*, 73, 77–78; all quotes from Remnick, *King of the World*, xiv, 137.
13. Lemert, *Muhammad Ali*, 106, 113.
14. Palmer, *Blues and Chaos*, 263; "There were commercials" quote from *Classic Albums: John Lennon Plastic Ono Band*.
15. Danto, *Unnatural Wonders*, 70; Palmer, *Blues and Chaos*; Banes, *Greenwich Village 1963*, 52, 60; Gruen, *New Bohemia*, 125–29; "Although audience members'" quote from Wark, *Radical Gestures*, 46.
16. Hendricks, "Yoko Ono and Fluxus," 47; "Face the wall" quote from Ono, *Grapefruit*.
17. Concannon, "Works," 195.
18. Zmuda, *Andy Kaufman Revealed!*, 237.

19. Margulies, *Dear Andy Kaufman*, 5; Beekman, *Ringside*, 35–40, 81–82; *I'm from Hollywood*; Lemert, *Muhammad Ali*, 46.

20. Keller, *Andy Kaufman*, 139–40, 23.

21. Hirshey, "Andy Kaufman beyond Laughter," 16–19; Hecht, *Was This Man Insane?*; Zmuda, *Andy Kaufman Revealed!*, 198–99.

22. Hirshey, "Andy Kaufman beyond Laughter," 16–19; Zehme, *Lost in the Funhouse*, 269–70.

23. Keller, *Andy Kaufman*, 44–45; "wreaks total havoc" quote from Žižek, *Plague of Fantasies*, 22.

24. Zehme, *Lost in the Funhouse*.

25. Zehme, *Lost in the Funhouse*, 301–2; *I'm from Hollywood*.

26. Abel, *How to Thrive on Rejection*, 16, 20.

27. Abel, *How to Thrive on Rejection*, 22.

28. *Abel Raises Cain*.

29. Maurer, *Big Con*, 16–17; Brock, *Charlatan*, 83, 176.

30. *Abel Raises Cain*; Abel, *Great American Hoax*, 25.

31. Abel, *Great American Hoax*, xi.

32. Abel, *Great American Hoax*, xi, 106, 112, 116.

33. Abel, *Confessions of a Hoaxer*, 1–2; all quotes from Abel, *Great American Hoax*, 36, 43.

34. Abel, *Inside SINA*, 3.

35. Abel, *Great American Hoax*, 211.

36. Juno and Vale, *Pranks!*, 107; Abel, *Great American Hoax*, xi; Abel, *Confessions of a Hoaxer*, 242.

37. Belsito, ed., *Notes from the Pop Underground*; I. Ellis, *Rebels Wit Attitude*, 176–79.

38. Biafra, *High Priest of Harmful Matter*.

39. Raymond, *New Hacker's Dictionary*, 154; Boese, *Museum of Hoaxes*, "a clever technique" quote from Spurgeon, "Computer Slang.".

40. Levy, *Hackers*, 86–87; all quotes from Lapsley, *Exploding the Phone*, 68–70.

41. "I was seven" quote from Lapsley, *Exploding the Phone*, 122.

42. Levy, *Hackers*, 86–87; all quotes from Lapsley, *Exploding the Phone*, 135–43, 151.

43. Lapsley, *Exploding the Phone*, 123–24; Rosenbaum, "Secrets of the Little Blue Box," 22–23, 30–31.

44. All quotes from Rosenbaum, "Secrets of the Little Blue Box," 22–23, 28–29, 31.

45. Rosenbaum, "Secrets of the Little Blue Box," 22; all quotes from Lapsley, *Exploding the Phone*, 86, 167, 170–71, 185–86.

46. Lapsley, *Exploding the Phone*, 218–19, 222–25; Levy, *Hackers*, 251–54; Hine, *Great Funk*, 208; all quotes from Isaacson, *Steve Jobs*, 25–27, 28–29.

47. Wozniak, foreword to *Exploding the Phone*, xii; Peterson, *Nightwork*, 3; Gygax, *Advanced Dungeons & Dragons Players Handbook*, 7.

48. Raymond, *New Hacker's Dictionary*; W. Smith, *Act Like Nothing's Wrong*; Belsito, Davis, and Kester, *Street Art*; SubGenius Foundation, *Book of the SubGenius*, back cover.

49. Duncombe, *Notes from the Underground*, 86.

50. Fenster, *Conspiracy Theory*, 155–56; "The only reason" quote from Stang, "Pope Bob Remembrance."

51. Stang, *High Weirdness by Mail*; SubGenius Foundation, *Revelation X*; Duncombe, *Notes from the Underground*, 51, 157, 159.

52. *Loompanics Unlimited Main Catalog*, iv ; Black, *Beneath the Underground*, 145.

53. "In this issue" quote from Kennedy, *Zine*, 11.

54. Parfrey, *Apocalypse Culture*; Parfrey, *Apocalypse Culture II*.

55. Webb, "Pop," 14; "Both secret societies" quote from Drummond, *.45*, 231.

56. KLF Communications, "KLF Biography as of 20th July 1990."

57. Sharkey, "Trash Art & Kreation"; Wilkinson, "Ford Every Scheme"; "Doctorin' the Tardis."

58. KLF Communications, *Manual*, 25, 59, 65.

59. Drummond, *.45*, 191–92.

60. Shaw, "Who Killed the KLF?"; "We have been" quote from "Timelords, Gentlemen Please!," 3.

61. Reid, "Money to Burn," 28.

62. Dayal, "Phreaks and Geeks"; Wozniak, foreword to *Exploding the Phone*, xii; Lapsley, *Exploding the Phone*, 269–67, 319, 329, 334; Kittler, *Gramophone, Film, Typewriter*, 97.

NOTES TO CHAPTER 10

1. Sweeney, "Conscious and Unconscious Political Symbolism," 94; Peterson, *Nightwork*, 42.

2. Sweeney, "Conscious and Unconscious Political Symbolism," 94; Peterson, *Nightwork*, 104.

3. Sweeney, "Conscious and Unconscious Political Symbolism," 94; Peterson, *Nightwork*, 103.

4. "Nancy X—who" quote from Yancey, "JMU Fans Fight to Replace Bark with Oink," A19.

5. Peterson, *Nightwork*, 113–14; "Sports is regarded" quote from Sweeney, "Conscious and Unconscious Political Symbolism," 94.

6. Greer, "Smells Like Scene Spirit," 112.

7. Greer, "Smells Like Scene Spirit," 112.

8. Greer, "Smells Like Scene Spirit," 112.

9. Greer, "Smells Like Scene Spirit" 112; Sheffield, *Love Is a Mix Tape*, 214.

10. Greer, "Smells Like Scene Spirit," 112.

11. Greer, "Smells Like Scene Spirit," 112.

12. Marin, "Grunge."

13. "When The Newspaper" quote from Frank, "Harsh Realm, Mr. Sulzberger!," 206; "*SPIN* had settled" quote from Iversen, "Brain Dead in Seattle," 24.

14. "A place of" quote from Kennedy, *Zine*, 184.

15. All quotes from Vale, *Pranks 2*, 33.

16. All quotes from Meikle, *Future Active*, 113–14.
17. All quotes from *Yes Men*.
18. Yes Men and Khayati quotes from Meikle, *Future Active*, 126–27; Debord, *Society of the Spectacle*.
19. "This politics is" quote from Duncombe, *Dream*, 69; all remaining quotes from Vale, *Pranks 2*, 32.
20. Koppelman, "HUD Hoax"; all quotes from "Oops."
21. All quotes from Duncombe, *Dream*, 97–98.
22. Boyd, "Truth Is a Virus," 373; all quotes from Duncombe, *Dream*, 43.
23. Duncombe, *Dream*, 45.
24. "Content and humor" quote from Boyd, "Truth Is a Virus," 371, 373.
25. Harold, *Ourspace*; Duncombe, *Dream*, 72, 76–77.

NOTES TO THE CONCLUSION

1. Duncombe, *Dream*, 22–23; Kent, *From Slogans to Mantras*, 18; Plummer, *Holy Goof*, 137; "You know, you're" quote from T. Wolfe, *Electric Kool-Aid Acid Test*, 222.
2. "Lockdowns and marches" quote from Duncombe, *Dream*, 70; "A *Yippie!* button" quote from Hoffman, "Revolution for the Hell of It," 81.
3. Chang, *Can't Stop Won't Stop*, 394; D. Mills, "Sister Souljah's Call to Arms," B1.
4. Jay-Z, *Decoded*, 166; M. Cohen, "Souljah Legacy"; Garofalo, *Rockin' Out*, 263.
5. *CNN Newsroom*, CNN, December 13, 2007; *Tucker*, MSNBC, December 13, 2007.
6. *Countdown with Keith Olbermann*, MSNBC, December 14, 2007; Clayworth, "Roboprofessor Heckles Clinton," B1.
7. McLeod, "I, Roboprofessor."
8. Jones, "Gay Robot 'RoboProf' Crashes Michele Bachmann Rally"; Gayle, "Republican Candidate Michele Bachmann Harangued"; *The Ed Show*, MSNBC, December 23, 2011.

BIBLIOGRAPHY

Aaronovitch, David. *Voodoo Histories: The Role of the Conspiracy Theory in Shaping Modern History*. New York: Riverhead Books, 2010.

Abel, Alan. *Confessions of a Hoaxer*. Toronto: Macmillan, 1970.

———. *The Great American Hoax*. New York: Trident, 1966.

———. *How to Thrive on Rejection: A Manual for Survival*. New York: Dembner Books, 1984.

———. *Inside SINA*. New York: SINA, 1963.

Abel Raises Cain. Dir. Jenny Abel and Jeff Hockett. Crashcourse Documentaries, 2005. Film.

Adams, Bluford. *E Pluribus Barnum: The Great Showman and the Making of U.S. Popular Culture*. Minneapolis: University of Minnesota Press, 1997.

Allen, Gary. *Kissinger: The Secret Side of the Secretary of State*. Boston: Western Islands, 1976.

———. *The Man behind the Mask*. Boston: Western Islands, 1971.

Allen, Gary, and Larry Abraham. *None Dare Call It a Conspiracy*. Seal Beach, CA: Concord, 1972.

Amato, John, and David Neiwert. *Over the Cliff: How Obama's Election Drove the American Right Insane*. Sausalito, CA: Polipoint, 2010.

Ammerman, Nancy T. "North American Protestant Fundamentalism." In *Media, Culture, and the Religious Right*, edited by Linda Kintz and Julia Lesage, 55–105. Minneapolis: University of Minnesota Press, 1998.

Anderson, Ann. *Snake Oil, Hustlers, and Hambones: The American Medicine Show*. New York: McFarland, 2005.

Anderson, Douglas. *The Radical Enlightenments of Benjamin Franklin*. Baltimore: Johns Hopkins University Press, 1997.

Aranza, Jacob. *Backward Masking Unmasked: Backward Satanic Messages of Rock and Roll Exposed*. Shreveport, LA: Huntington House, 1983.

Arellano, Gustavo. *Orange County: A Personal History*. New York: Simon and Schuster, 2008.

Armstrong, Ben. *The Electric Church*. Nashville, TN: Thomas Nelson, 1979.

Aufderheide, Patricia, and Peter Jaszi. *Reclaiming Fair Use: How to Put Balance Back in Copyright*. Chicago: University of Chicago Press, 2011.

Austen, Jake. "Sammy Devil Jr." *Vice.com*, May 2, 2008. http://www.vice.com/read/sammy-devil-jr-v15n5.

Baddeley, Gavin. *Lucifer Rising: Sin, Devil Worship and Rock 'n' Roll*. London: Plexus, 1999.

Baigent, Michael, and Richard Leigh, *The Temple and the Lodge*. New York: Arcade, 2011.

Bainbridge, William Sims. *Satan's Power: A Deviant Psychotherapy Cult*. Berkeley: University of California Press, 1978.

Baker, Nicolson. *Human Smoke: The Beginning of World War II, the End of Civilization*. New York: Simon and Schuster, 2009.

Bakhtin, Mikhail. "From *Rabelais and His World*." In *Cultural Resistance Reader*, edited by Stephen Duncombe, 82–88. New York: Verso, 2002.

Banes, Sally. *Greenwich Village 1963: Avant-Garde Performance and the Effervescent Body*. Durham: Duke University Press, 1993.

Barkun, Michael. *A Culture of Conspiracy: Apocalyptic Visions in Contemporary America*. Berkeley: University of California Press, 2003.

Barnouw, Erik. *The Magician and the Cinema*. New York: Oxford University Press, 1981.

Barnum, P. T. "Chapter X." In *The Colossal P. T. Barnum Reader: Nothing Else Like It in the Universe*, edited by James W. Cook, 233–41. Urbana: University of Illinois Press, 1995.

———. *The Life of P. T. Barnum*. New York: Cosino, 2006.

———. *Struggles and Triumphs*. Edited by Carl Bode. New York: Penguin, 1981.

Baum, L. Frank. *The Annotated Wizard of Oz: Centennial Edition*. Edited by Michael Patrick Hearn. New York: Norton, 2000.

Baxter, Leslie. *Voicing Relationships: A Dialogic Perspective*. Los Angeles: Sage, 2011.

Bazell, Robert. "U.S. Apologizes to Guatemala for STD Experiments." *MSNBC.com*, October 1, 2010. http://www.msnbc.msn.com/id/39456324/ns/health-sexual_health/.

Bednarowski, Mary Farrell. "Outside the Mainstream: Women's Religion and Women Religious Leaders in Nineteenth-Century America." *Journal of the American Academy of Religion* 48.2 (1980): 208–30.

Beekman, Scott M. *Ringside: A History of Professional Wrestling in America*. Westport, CT: Praeger, 2006.

Bell, Don. *The Man Who Killed Houdini*. Montreal: Véhicule, 2005.

Belsito, Peter, ed. *Notes from the Pop Underground*. San Francisco: Last Gasp, 1985.

Belsito, Peter, Bob Davis, and Marian Kester. *Street Art: The Punk Poster in San Francisco, 1977–1982*. San Francisco: Last Gasp, 1981.

Bergmann, Hans. *God in the Street: New York Writing from the Penny Press to Melville*. Philadelphia: Temple University Press, 1995.

Berlet, Chip. "Who Is Mediating the Storm? Right-Wing Alternative Information Networks." In *Media, Culture, and the Religious Right*, edited by Linda Kintz and Julia Lesage, 249–74. Minneapolis: University of Minnesota Press, 1998.

Bernays, Edward L. *Biography of an Idea: Memoirs of Public Relations Counsel Edward L. Bernays*. New York: Simon and Schuster, 1965.

———. "Manipulating Public Opinion: The Why and the How." In *Mass Communication and American Social Thought: Key Texts, 1919–1968*, edited by John Durham Peters and Peter Simonson, 51–57. Lanham, MD: Rowman and Littlefield, 2004.

Bettelheim, Bruno. *The Uses of Enchantment: The Meaning and Importance of Fairy Tales*. New York: Vintage, 1977.

Biafra, Jello. *High Priest of Harmful Matter: Tales from the Trial*. Alternative Tentacles, 1989. CD.

Biderman, Albert D. "The Image of 'Brainwashing.'" *Public Opinion References Quarterly* 26 (1962): 547–63.

Black, Bob. *Beneath the Underground*. Portland, OR: Feral House, 1994.

Block, Seymour Stanton. *Benjamin Franklin, Genius of Kites, Flights and Voting Rights*. Jefferson, NC: McFarland, 2004.

Blumenthal, Max. "James O'Keefe's Race Problem." *Salon.com*, February 3, 2010. http://www.salon.com/news/feature/2010/02/03/james_okeefe_white_nationalists.

———. *Republican Gomorrah: Inside the Movement That Shattered the Party*. New York: Nation Books, 2009.

Bode, Carl. "Introduction: Barnum Uncloaked." In *Struggles and Triumphs*, by P. T. Barnum, edited by Carl Bode, 5–38. New York: Penguin, 1981.

Boese, Alex. *The Museum of Hoaxes: A Collection of Pranks, Stunts, Deceptions, and Other Wonderful Stories Contrived for the Public from the Middle Ages to the New Millennium*. New York: Dutton, 2002.

Bogart, Michele H. *Artists, Advertising, and the Borders of Art*. Chicago: University of Chicago Press, 1997.

Boyd, Andrew. "Truth Is a Virus: Meme Warfare and the Billionaires for Bush (or Gore)." In *Cultural Resistance Reader*, edited by Stephen Duncombe, 369–78. New York: Verso, 2002.

Brands, H. W. *The First American: The Life and Times of Benjamin Franklin*. New York: Anchor Books, 2000.

Braude, Ann. *Radical Spirits: Spiritualism and Women's Rights in Nineteenth-Century America*. Bloomington: Indiana University Press, 2001.

Brock, Pope. *Charlatan: America's Most Dangerous Huckster, the Man Who Pursued Him, and the Age of Flimflam*. New York: Three Rivers, 2008.

Bromley, David G., Anson D. Shupe, Jr., and J. C. Ventimiglia. "The Role of Anecdotal Atrocities in the Social Construction of Evil." In *The Brainwashing/Deprogramming Controversy: Sociological, Psychological, Legal and Historical Perspectives*, edited by David G. Bromley and James T. Richardson, 139–60. New York: Edwin Mellen, 1983.

Bronfen, Elisabeth. "'There's No Place Like Home': The Aporia of Homecoming *The Wizard of Oz* (Victor Fleming)." *Parallax* 6.3 (2000): 49–62.

Brooks, Daphne A. *Bodies in Dissent: Spectacular Performances of Race and Freedom, 1850–1910*. Durham: Duke University Press, 2006.

Brown, Henry Box. *Narrative of the Life of Henry Box Brown*. New York: Oxford University Press, 2002.

Buescher, John B. *The Other Side of Salvation: Spiritualism and the Nineteenth-Century Religious Experience*. Boston: Skinner House Books, 2004.

Bullitt, John M. *Jonathan Swift and the Anatomy of Satire: A Study of Satiric Technique*. Cambridge: Harvard University Press, 1953.

Bunch, Will. *The Backlash: Right-wing Radicals, High-Def Hucksters, and Paranoid Politics in the Age of Obama*. New York: Harper, 2010.

Burns, Eric. *Infamous Scribblers: The Founding Fathers and the Rowdy Beginnings of American Journalism*. New York: PublicAffairs, 2006.

Byrnes, Robert F. *Antisemitism in Modern France*. Vol. 1, *The Prologue to the Dreyfus Affair*. New Brunswick: Rutgers University Press, 1950.

California Department of Justice, Office of the Attorney General. *Report of the Attorney General on the Activities of ACORN in California*. April 1, 2010. http://ag.ca.gov/cms_attachments/press/pdfs/n1888_acorn_report.pdf.

Capouya, John. *Gorgeous George: The Outrageous Bad-Boy Wrestler Who Created American Pop Culture*. New York: HarperCollins, 2008.

Carey, James. *Communication as Culture: Essays on Media and Society*. New York: Routledge, 1988.

Carpenter, Humphrey. *J. R. R. Tolkien: A Biography*. Boston: Houghton Mifflin, 1987.

Carr, Daphne. *Pretty Hate Machine*. New York: Continuum, 2011.

Carr, William Guy. *Pawns in the Game*. Glendale, CA: St. George.

Carr-Gomm, Philip, and Richard Heygate. *The Book of English Magic*. New York: Overlook, 2012.

Carroll, Bret E. "The Religious Construction of Masculinity in Victorian America: The Male Mediumship of John Shoebridge." *Religion and American Culture: A Journal of Interpretation* 7.1 (1997): 27–60.

———. *Spiritualism in Antebellum America*. Bloomington: Indiana University Press, 1997.

Cayce, Edgar. *Edgar Cayce: Modern Prophet—Four Complete Books*. New York: Gramercy Books, 1990.

———. "Report of Edgar Cayce Reading 254-48." March 7, 1929.

"Cee Lo: Southern Hip-Hop." *Rolling Stone*, October 27, 2011, 61.

Chalmers, Alexander. *The General Biographical Dictionary Containing an Historical and Critical Account of the Most Eminent Persons*. London: J. Nichols, 1814.

Chang, Jeff. *Can't Stop Won't Stop: A History of the Hip-Hop Generation*. New York: St. Martin's, 2005.

Christenson, Wes. "Quigley . . . Making Birchers Bark." *Georgetown Today* 4.4 (March 1972): 12–13.

Churchill, Ward, and Jim Vander Wall. *The COINTELPRO Papers: Documents form the FBI's Secret Wars against Dissent in the United States*. Cambridge, MA: South End, 2002.

Churton, Tobias. *The Golden Builders. Alchemists, Rosicrucians, and the First Freemasons*. Boston: WeiserBooks, 2002.

———. *The Invisible History of the Rosicrucians*. Rochester, VT: Inner Traditions, 2009.

Classic Albums: John Lennon Plastic Ono Band. Dir. Matthew Longfellow. BBC, 2008. Film.

Clayworth, Jason. "Roboprofessor Heckles Clinton." *Des Moines Register*, December 12, 2007, B1.

Codrescu, Andrei. *The Posthuman Dada Guide: Tzara and Lenin Play Chess*. Princeton: Princeton University Press, 2009.

Cohen, Lara Langer. *The Fabrication of American Literature: Fraudulence and Antebellum Print Culture*. Philadelphia: University of Pennsylvania Press, 2012.

Cohen, Michael A. "The Souljah Legacy," *Campaign Stops* (blog), *New York Times*, June 15, 2008. http://campaignstops.blogs.nytimes.com/2008/06/15/the-souljah-legacy/.

Cohn, Norman. *Warrant for Genocide: The Myth of the Jewish World-Conspiracy and the Protocols of the Elders of Zion*. Chico, CA: Scholars, 1981.

Collins, Paul. *Banvard's Folly: Thirteen Tales of People Who Didn't Change the World*. New York: Picador, 2002.

———. *Sixpence House: Lost in a Town of Books*. New York: Bloomsbury, 2003.

———. *The Trouble with Tom: The Strange Afterlife and Times of Thomas Paine*. New York: Bloomsbury, 2005.

Concannon, Kevin. "Works." In *Yes Yoko Ono*, edited by Alexandra Munroe with Jon Hendricks, 208–27. New York: Harry N. Abrams, 2000.

Connor, Steven. *Dumbstruck: A Cultural History of Ventriloquism*. New York: Oxford University Press, 2000.

Cook, James W. *The Arts of Deception: Playing with Fraud in the Age of Barnum*. Cambridge: Harvard University Press, 2001.

———. Introduction to *The Colossal P. T. Barnum Reader: Nothing Else Like It in the Universe*, edited by James W. Cook, 1–8. Urbana: University of Illinois Press, 1995.

Cooper, William Milton. *Behold a Pale Horse*. Flagstaff, AZ: Light Technology.

Corbett, John. *Extended Play: Sounding Off from John Cage to Dr. Funkenstein*. Durham: Duke University Press, 1994.

Corbett, John, Anthony Elms, and Terri Kapsalis. *Pathways to Unknown Worlds: Sun-Ra, El Saturn, and Chicago's Afro-Futurist Underground, 1954–68*. Chicago: WhiteWalls, 2006.

Cowan, Ruth Schwartz. *A Social History of American Technology*. New York: Oxford University Press, 1997.

Crimp, Douglas, and Adam Rolston. *AIDS Demo Graphics*. Seattle: Bay, 1990.

Cuddihy, John Murray. *The Ordeal of Civility: Freud, Marx, Lévi-Strauss, and the Jewish Struggle with Modernity*. New York: Basic Books, 1974.

Culver, Stuart. "What Manikins Want: *The Wonderful Wizard of Oz* and *The Art of Decorating Dry Goods Windows*." *Representations* 21 (1988): 97–116.

Danto, Arthur Coleman. *Unnatural Wonders: Essays from the Gap between Art and Life*. New York: Columbia University Press, 2007.

Davis, Herbert. *Jonathan Swift: Essays on His Satire and Other Studies*. New York: Oxford University Press, 1964.

Davis, Mike. *City of Quartz: Excavating the Future in Los Angeles*. New York: Verso, 2006.

Day, Robert Adams. "Psalmanazar's 'Formosa' and the British Reader (Including Samuel Johnson)." In *Exoticism in the Enlightenment*, edited by George Sebastian Rousseau and Roy Porter, 197–233. Manchester: Manchester University Press, 1990.

Dayal, Geeta. "Phreaks and Geeks." *Slate*, February 11, 2013. http://www.slate.com/articles/technology/books/2013/02/steve_jobs_and_phone_hacking_exploding_the_phone_by_phil_lapsley_reviewed.single.html.

Dear, William. *The Dungeon Master: The Disappearance of James Dallas Egbert III*. New York: Ballantine Books, 1985.

Debord, Guy. *Society of the Spectacle*. Detroit: Black and Red.

de Hoyos, Arturo, and S. Brent Morris. *Is It True What They Say about Freemasonry?* Lanham, MD: M. Evans, 2010.

Dewey, John. *Art as Experience*. New York: Penguin, 2005.

"Doctorin' the Tardis." *Melody Maker*, May 28, 1988. http://www.libraryofmu.org/display-resource.php?id=78.

Doyle, Sir Arthur Conan. *Pheneas Speaks: Direct Spirit Communication in the Family Circle*. London: Psychic Press and Bookshop, 1927.

Drummond, Bill *.45*. London: Abacus, 2001.

Duncombe, Stephen. *Dream: Re-imagining Progressive Politics in an Age of Fantasy*. New York: New Press, 2007.

———. *Notes from the Underground: Zines and the Politics of Alternative Culture*. New York: Verso, 1997.

Dunkerley, James. *Americana: The Americas in the World, around 1850*. New York: Verso, 2000.

Echols, Alice. *Daring to Be Bad: Radical Feminism in America, 1967–1975*. Minneapolis: University of Minnesota Press, 1989.

Eisenstein, Elizabeth L. *The Printing Revolution in Early Modern Europe*. Cambridge: Cambridge University Press, 1983.

Elliott, Justin. "Rand Paul in '08: Beware the NAFTA Superhighway!" *Talking Points Memo*, May 21, 2010. http://tpmmuckraker.talkingpointsmemo.com/2010/05/rand_paul_beware_the_nafta_superhighway_video.php.

Ellis, Bill. *Aliens, Ghosts, and Cults*. Jackson: University Press of Mississippi, 2001.

———. *Lucifer Ascending: The Occult in Folklore and Popular Culture*. Lexington: University of Kentucky Press, 2004.

———. *Raising the Devil: Satanism, New Religions, and the Media*. Lexington: University of Kentucky Press, 2000.

Ellis, Iain. *Rebels Wit Attitude: Subversive Rock Humorists*. New York: Soft Skull, 2008.

Emerson, Ralph Waldo. *The Complete Prose Works of Ralph Waldo Emerson*. New York: Ward, Lock, 1891.

Erickson, Hal. *Religious Radio and Television in the United States, 1921–1991*. Jefferson, NC: McFarland, 1992.

Ewen, Stuart. *All Consuming Images: The Politics of Style in Contemporary Culture.* New York: Basic Books, 1984.

———. *Captains of Consciousness: Advertising and the Social Roots of the Consumer Culture.* New York: McGraw-Hill, 1976.

———. *PR! A Social History of Spin.* New York: Basic Books, 1996.

Farquhar, Michael. *A Treasury of Deception.* New York: Penguin, 2005.

Fedler, Fred. *Media Hoaxes.* Ames: Iowa State University Press, 1989.

Fenster, Mike. *Conspiracy Theory: Secrecy and Power in American Culture.* Minneapolis: University of Minnesota Press, 2008.

Festinger, Leon, Henry W. Riecken, and Stanley Schachter. *When Prophecy Fails: A Social and Psychological Study of a Modern Group That Predicted the Destruction of the World.* Mansfield Centre, CT: Martino, 2011.

Fine, Gary Alan, and Bill Ellis. *The Global Grapevine: Why Rumors of Terrorism, Immigration, and Trade Matter.* New York: Oxford University Press, 2010.

Fourier, Charles. *The Utopian Vision of Charles Fourier.* Edited by Jonathan Beecher and Richard Bienvenu. Boston: Beacon, 1971.

Frank, Thomas. "Harsh Realm, Mr. Sulzberger!" In *Commodify Your Dissent: The Business of Culture in the New Gilded Age,* edited by Thomas Frank and Matt Weiland, 203–06. New York: Norton, 1997.

Frankl, Razelle. *Televangelism: The Marketing of Popular Religion.* Carbondale: Southern Illinois University Press, 1987.

Franklin, Benjamin. *A Benjamin Franklin Reader.* Edited by Walter Isaacson. New York: Simon and Schuster, 2003.

———. *Fart Proudly: Writings of Benjamin Franklin You Never Read in School.* Edited by Carl Japikse. Berkeley, CA: Frog, 2003.

Friedman, Ted. *Electric Dreams: Computers in American Culture.* New York: NYU Press, 2005.

Gaines, Donna. *Teenage Wasteland: Suburbia's Dead End Kids.* New York: Pantheon Books, 1991.

Gaines, Steven. *Heroes and Villains: The True Story of the Beach Boys.* New York: Signet, 1986.

Garofalo, Reebee. *Rockin' Out: Popular Music in the USA.* New York: Prentice Hall, 2011.

Gates, Henry Lewis, Jr. *The Signifying Monkey: A Theory of African-American Literary Criticism.* New York: Oxford University Press, 1988.

Gayle, Damien. "Republican Candidate Michele Bachmann Harangued by 'Gay Robot' on the Campaign Trail in Iowa." *Daily Mail,* December 23, 2011. http://www.dailymail.co.uk/news/article-2078011/Republican-candidate-Michelle-Bachmann-harangued-gay-robot-campaign-trail-Iowa.html.

Gilgoff, Dan. "Devil in a Red Fez." *U.S. News and World Report,* August 26–September 2, 2002, 46.

Goldberg, Jonah. *Liberal Fascism: The Secret History of the American Left from Mussolini to the Politics of Meaning.* New York: Doubleday, 2007.

Goldblatt, Abe. "Once There Was a University in Virginia Beach with a Football Team." *Virginian-Pilot*, March 21, 1971.

Goldwag, Arthur. *Cults, Conspiracies, and Secret Societies: The Straight Scoop on the Freemasons, Illuminati, Skull and Bones, Black Helicopters, the New World Order, and Many, Many More.* New York: Random House, 2009.

———. *The New Hate: A History of Fear and Loathing on the Populist Right.* New York: Pantheon, 2012.

Goodman, Matthew. *The Sun and the Moon: The Remarkable True Account of Hoaxers, Showmen, Dueling Journalists, and Lunar Man-Bats in Nineteenth-Century New York.* New York: Basic Books, 2008.

Gorightly, Adam. *The Prankster and the Conspiracy: The Story of Kerry Thornley and How He Met Oswald and Inspired the Counterculture.* New York: Paraview, 2003.

Greeley, Andrew M. "There's a New-Time Religion on Campus." *New York Times Magazine*, June 1, 1969.

Green, James N., and Peter Stallybrass. *Benjamin Franklin: Writer and Printer.* Philadelphia: Oak Knoll, 2006.

Greer, Jim. "Smells Like Scene Spirit." *SPIN*, April 1993, 112.

Griffin, Edward G. *The Creature from Jekyll Island: A Second Look at the Federal Reserve.* Thousand Oaks, CA: American Media, 1998.

Gruen, John. *The New Bohemia.* Pennington, NJ: A Capella Books, 1990.

Gumaer, David Emerson. "Satanism: A Practical Guide to Witch Hunting." *American Opinion*, September 1970, 42–72.

Gunn, Joshua. *Modern Occult Rhetoric: Mass Media and the Drama of Secrecy in the Twentieth Century.* Tuscaloosa: University of Alabama Press, 2005.

Gygax, Gary. *Advanced Dungeons & Dragons Players Handbook.* New York: Random House / TSR Games, 1978.

Hall, Colby. "Glenn Beck Blames Evils of Slavery on Government Regulation." *Mediaite.com*, October 4, 2010. http://www.mediaite.com/online/glenn-beck-blames-evils-of-slavery-on-government-regulation/.

Hall, Max. *Benjamin Franklin and Polly Baker: The History of a Literary Deception.* Pittsburgh: University of Pittsburgh Press, 1990.

Halttunen, Karen. *Confidence Men and Painted Women: A Study of Middle-Class Culture in America, 1830–1870.* New Haven: Yale University Press, 1982.

Hammond, Charles. *Light from the Spirit World: The Pilgrimage of Thomas Paine and Others to the Seventh Circle in the Spirit World.* New York: Partridge and Brittan, 1852.

Harold, Christine. *Ourspace: Resisting Corporate Control of Culture.* Minneapolis: University of Minnesota Press, 2007.

Harp, Gillis J. "The Church of Humanity: New York's Worshipping Positivists." *Church History* 60.4 (1991): 508–23.

Harper, Tim. "Is Beatle Paul McCartney Dead?" *Drake Times-Delphic*, September 17, 1969, 1.

Harris, Leslie M. "From Abolitionist Amalgamators to 'Rulers of the Five Points': The Discourse of Interracial Sex and Reform in Antebellum New York City." In

Sex, Love, Race: Crossing Boundaries in North American History, edited by Martha Hodes, 191–212. New York: NYU Press, 1999.

Harris, Neil. *Humbug: The Art of P. T. Barnum*. Chicago: University of Chicago Press, 1981.

Hatonn, Gyeorgos C. *Through Darkness into Light: Endless Cycles of the Divine Plan*. Carson City, NV: America West, 1992.

Hebdige. Dick. *Hiding in the Light*. New York: Routledge, 1988.

Hecht, Julie. *Was This Man Insane? Talks with Andy Kaufman*. New York: Random House, 2001.

Hendershot, Heather. *Shaking the World for Jesus: Media and Conservative Evangelical Culture*. Chicago: University of Chicago Press, 2004.

Hendricks, Jon. "Yoko Ono and Fluxus." In *Yes Yoko Ono*, edited by Alexandra Munroe with Jon Hendricks, 38–50. New York: Harry N. Abrams, 2000.

Hertenstein, Mike, and Jon Trott. *Selling Satan: The Tragic History of Mike Warnke*. Chicago: Cornerstone, 1993.

Hicks, Robert D. *In Pursuit of Satan: The Police and the Occult*. Buffalo, NY: Prometheus Books, 1991.

Highet, Gilbert. *The Anatomy of Satire*. Princeton: Princeton University Press, 1962.

Hine, Thomas. *The Great Funk: Styles of the Shaggy, Sexy, Shameless 1970s*. New York: Sarah Crichton Books, 2007.

Hirshey, David. "Andy Kaufman beyond Laughter." *Rolling Stone*, April 30, 1981, 15–21.

Hoffman, Abbie. "Revolution for the Hell of It." In *Cultural Resistance Reader*, edited by Stephen Duncombe, 327–29. New York: Verso, 2002.

———. *Steal This Book*. New York: Pirate Editions, 1971.

Hofstadter, Richard. *The Paranoid Style in American Politics*. New York: Vintage Books, 2008.

Holiday, Ryan. *Trust Me I'm Lying: Confessions of a Media Manipulator*. New York: Portfolio/Penguin, 2012.

Horowitz, Mitch. *Occult America: White House Séances, Ouija Circles, Masons, and the Secret Mystic History of Our Nation*. New York: Bantam Books, 2009.

Horsfield, Peter G. *Religious Television: The American Experience*. New York: Longman, 1984.

Houdini, Harry. "How I Unmask the Spirit Fakers." *Popular Science Monthly*, November 1925, 12–14, 152-56.

———. *A Magician among the Spirits*. Amsterdam: Fredonia Books, 1924.

Hultkrans, Andrew. "Joey Skaggs." In *The Happy Mutant Handbook*, edited by Mark Frauenfelder, Carla Sinclair, and Gareth Branwyn, 40–43. New York: Riverhead Books, 1994.

Hyde, Lewis. *Common as Air: Revolution, Art, and Ownership*. New York: Farrar, Straus and Giroux, 2010.

———. *Trickster Makes This World*. New York: North Point, 1998.

Hynes, William J. "Mapping the Characteristics of Mythic Tricksters: A Heuristic Guide." In *Mythical Trickster Figures: Contours, Contexts, and Criticisms*, edited by

William J. Hynes and William G. Doty, 33–45. Tuscaloosa: University of Alabama Press, 1993.

I'm from Hollywood. Dir. Lynne Margulies and Joe Orr. Joe Lynne Productions, 1989. Film.

Irr, Caren. *The Suburb of Dissent: Cultural Politics in the United States and Canada during the 1930s*. Durham: Duke University Press, 1998.

Isaacson, Walter. *Benjamin Franklin: An American Life*. New York: Simon and Schuster, 2003.

———. *Steve Jobs*. New York: Simon and Schuster, 2011.

Iversen, Eric. "Brain Dead in Seattle." *Baffler* 5 (1993): 21–24.

Ives, Nat. "When Marketers Trip over Trademarks, the Fun Begins." *New York Times*, January 23, 2003. http://www.nytimes.com/2003/01/23/business/media-business-advertising-when-marketers-trip-over-trademarks-fun-begins.html.

Jackson, Devon. *Conspiranoia! The Mother of All Conspiracy Theories*. New York: Penguin, 1999.

Jasper, James M. *The Art of Moral Protest: Culture, Biography, and Creativity in Social Movements*. Chicago: University of Chicago Press, 1997.

Jay, Mike. "Darkness Over All: John Robison and the Birth of the Illuminati Conspiracy." *The Daily Grail*, July 20, 2010. http://www.dailygrail.com/Guest-Articles/2010/7/The-Birth-the-Illuminati.

Jay-Z. *Decoded*. New York: Spiegel and Grau, 2011.

"Jay-Z: A Master of Occult Wisdom?" *NPR.org*, September 20, 2009. http://www.npr.org/templates/story/story.php?storyId=112998783.

John, Richard R. *Network Nation: Inventing American Telecommunications*. Cambridge: Harvard University Press, 2010.

Johnston, Jerry. *The Edge of Evil: The Rise of Satanism in North America*. Dallas: Word, 1989.

Jones, Melanie. "Gay Robot 'RoboProf' Crashes Michele Bachmann Rally in Iowa City." *International Business Times*, December 23, 2011. http://www.ibtimes.com/gay-robot-roboprof-crashes-michele-bachmann-rally-iowa-city-video-387070#.

Jordan, Tim. *Hacking: Digital Media and Technological Determinism*. Cambridge, UK: Polity, 2008.

Juno, Andrea, and V. Vale. *Incredibly Strange Music*. Vol. 1. San Francisco: RE/Search, 1993.

———. *Pranks!* San Francisco: RE/Search, 1987.

Kahn, David. *The Code Breakers*. New York: Signet, 1973.

Kahn, Didier. "The Rosicrucian Hoax in France (1623–4)." In *Secrets of Nature: Astrology and Alchemy in Early Modern Europe*, edited by Anthony Grafton, 235–344. Cambridge: MIT Press, 2001.

Kalush, William, and Larry Sloman. *The Secret Life of Houdini: The Making of America's First Superhero*. New York: Atria Books, 2006.

"Kanye West Listening Party with 963 NOW Minneapolis Part One." *YouTube.com*, November 23, 2010. http://www.youtube.com/watch?v=EnWQeiCrcMM&feature=player_embedded#!.

Kaplan, Sidney. "The Miscegenation Issue in the Election of 1864." *Journal of Negro History* 34.3 (1949): 274–343.

Katsoulis, Melissa. *Literary Hoaxes: An Eye-Opening History of Famous Frauds*. New York: Skyhorse, 2009.

Keevak, Michael. *The Pretended Asian: George Psalmanazar's Eighteenth-Century Formosan Hoax*. Detroit: Wayne State University Press, 2004.

Keller, Florian. *Andy Kaufman: Wrestling with the American Dream*. Minneapolis: University of Minnesota Press, 2005.

Kellner, Douglas. "The X-Files and Conspiracy: A Diagnostic Critique." In *Conspiracy Nation: The Politics of Paranoia in Postwar America*, edited by Peter Knight, 205–32. New York: NYU Press, 2002.

Kelly, Clarence. *Conspiracy against God and Man: A Study of the Beginnings and Early History of the Great Conspiracy*. Boston: Western Islands, 1974.

Kennedy, Pagan. *Zine: How I Spent Six Years of My Life in the Underground and Finally . . . Found Myself . . . I Think*. New York: St. Martin's Griffin, 1995.

Kent, Stephen. *From Slogans to Mantras: Social Protest and Religious Conversion in the Late Vietnam Era*. Syracuse: Syracuse University Press, 2001.

Keyes, Nelson Beecher. *Ben Franklin: An Affectionate Portrait*. Garden City, NY: Hanover House, 1956.

King, David. *Finding Atlantis: A True Story of Genius, Madness, and an Extraordinary Quest for a Lost World*. New York: Harmony Books, 2005.

Kirkpatrick, Sidney D. *Edgar Cayce: An American Prophet*. New York: Riverhead Books, 2000.

Kisseloff, Jeff. *The Box: An Oral History of Television*. New York: Penguin, 1995.

Kittler, Friedrich. *Discourse Networks, 1800/1900*. Stanford: Stanford University Press, 1990.

———. *Gramophone, Film, Typewriter*. Stanford: Stanford University Press, 1999.

———. *Optical Media: Berlin Lectures 1999*. Malden, MA: Polity, 2010.

KLF Communications. "The KLF Biography as of 20th July 1990 (KLF BIOG 012)." *Library of Mu*, 1990. http://libraryofmu.org/display-resource.php?id=512.

———. *The Manual (How to Have a Number One the Easy Way)*. London: Ellipsis, 1998.

Koppelman, Alex. "The HUD Hoax." *Salon.com*, August 29, 2006. http://www.salon.com/news/feature/2006/08/29/yes_men.

Kovalio, Jacob. *The Russian Protocols of Zion in Japan: Yudayaka/Jewish Peril Propaganda Debates in the 1920s*. New York: Peter Lang, 2009.

Krassner, Paul. *Confessions of a Raving, Unconfined Nut: Misadventures in the Counterculture*. New York: Simon and Schuster, 1993.

———. *One Hand Jerking: Reports from an Investigative Satirist*. New York: Seven Stories, 2005.

———. *Who's to Say What's Obscene? Politics, Culture and Comedy in America Today*. San Francisco: City Lights Books, 2009.

———. *The Winner of the Bicycle Race: The Satirical Writings of Paul Krassner*. New York: Seven Stories, 1996.

LaBour, Fred. "McCartney Dead: New Evidence Brought to Light." *Michigan Daily*, October 14, 1969, 2.

Lachman, Gary. *Turn Off Your Mind: The Mystic Sixties and the Dark Side of the Age of Aquarius*. New York: Disinformation, 2001.

LaHaye, Tim. *The Rapture: Who Will Face the Tribulation?* Eugene, OR: Harvest House, 2002.

LaHaye, Tim, and Jerry B. Jenkins. *Left Behind: A Novel of the Earth's Last Days*. Wheaton, IL: Tyndale House, 1995.

Lamont, Peter. "Spiritualism and a Mid-Victorian Crisis of Evidence." *Historical Journal* 47.4 (2004): 897–920.

Lamothe-Ramos, Annette. "Beelzebub's Daughter." *Vice*, January 2012, 90–92.

Lampley, Ray. *Universal Church of God Newsletter*, Summer 1994.

———. *Universal Church of God Newsletter*, August 12, 1994.

———. *Universal Church of God Newsletter*, August 30, 1994.

———. *Universal Church of God Newsletter*, September 23, 1994.

Landay, Lori. *Madcaps, Screwballs, and Con Women: The Female Trickster in American Culture*. Philadelphia: University of Pennsylvania Press, 1998.

Lapsley, Phil. *Exploding the Phone: The Untold Story of the Teenagers and Outlaws Who Hacked Ma Bell*. New York: Grove, 2013.

Laqueur, Walter. *The Changing Face of Anti-Semitism*. New York: Oxford University Press, 2006.

Larson, Bob. *Satanism: The Seduction of America's Youth*. Nashville, TN: Thomas Nelson, 1989.

LaVey, Anton Szandor. *The Satanic Bible*. New York: Avon Books, 1969.

Lee, Martin A., and Bruce Shlain. *Acid Dreams: The Complete Social History of LSD— The CIA, the Sixties, and Beyond*. New York: Grove Weidenfeld, 1992.

Leland, John. *Hip: The History*. New York: HarperCollins, 2004.

Lemert, Charles. *Muhammad Ali: Trickster in the Culture of Irony*. Cambridge, UK: Polity, 2003.

Lemire, Elise. *"Miscegenation": Making Race in America*. Philadelphia: University of Pennsylvania Press, 2002.

"Leo Taxil and His 'Greatest Joke of All Times.'" *Literary Digest*, June 5, 1897.

Lesage, Julia. "Christian Media." In *Media, Culture, and the Religious Right*, edited by Linda Kintz and Julia Lesage, 21–50. Minneapolis: University of Minnesota Press, 1998.

Levy, Steven. *Hackers*. Cambridge, MA: O'Reilly, 2010.

Lewin, Leonard C. *Report from Iron Mountain: On the Possibility and Desirability of Peace*. New York: Free Press, 1996.

Liddy, G. Gordon, J. Michael Barrett, and Joel Selanikio. *Fighting Back: Tackling Terrorism, Liddy Style*. New York: Macmillan, 2007.

Lin, Marvin. *Kid A*. New York: Continuum, 2011.

Lindberg, Gary. *The Confidence Man in American Literature*. New York: Oxford University Press, 1982.

Lippmann, Walter. *Public Opinion*. New York: Simon and Schuster, 1922.

Loftus, Elizabeth, and Katherine Ketcham. *The Myth of Repressed Memory: False Memories and Allegations of Sexual Abuse*. New York: St. Martin's Griffin, 1994.

Loompanics Unlimited Main Catalog. Port Townsend, WA: Loompanics Enterprises, 1993.

Lopate, Phillip. *Getting Personal: Selected Writings*. New York: Basic Books, 2003.

Love, Harold. *Attributing Authorship: An Introduction*. New York: Cambridge University Press, 2002.

Lutz, Tom. *Doing Nothing: A History of Loafers, Loungers, Slackers, and Bums in America*. New York: Farrar, Straus and Giroux, 2006.

Lycett, Andrew. *The Man Who Created Sherlock Holmes: The Life and Times of Sir Arthur Conan Doyle*. New York: Simon and Schuster, 2008.

Lyons, Arthur. *Satan Wants You: The Cult of Devil Worship in America*. New York: Mysterious, 1988.

MacDougall, Curtis D. *Hoaxes*. New York: Dover, 1958.

MacDougall, Robert. "The Wire Devils: Pulp Thrillers, the Telephone, and Action at a Distance in the Wiring of a Nation." *American Quarterly* 58.3 (2006): 715–41.

Maliszewski, Paul. *Fakers: Hoaxers, Con Artists, Counterfeiters, and Other Great Pretenders*. New York: New Press, 2008.

Margulies, Lynne. *Dear Andy Kaufman, I Hate Your Guts!* Los Angeles: Process, 2009.

Marin, Rick. "Grunge: A Success Story." *New York Times*, November 15, 1992. http://www.nytimes.com/1992/11/15/style/grunge-a-success-story.html.

Marks, Paul. "Dot-Dash-Diss: The Gentleman Hacker's 1903 Lulz." *New Scientist*, September 18, 2009. http://www.newscientist.com/article/mg21228440.700-dotdash-diss-the-gentleman-hackers-1903-lulz.html#.UcbFBlNvX_o.

Marr, Andrew. *A History of Modern Britain*. New York: Macmillan, 2009.

Marsh, Joss. *Word Crimes: Blasphemy, Culture, and Literature in Nineteenth-Century England*. Chicago: University of Chicago Press, 1998.

Martin, Linda, and Kerry Segrave. *Anti-Rock: The Opposition to Rock 'n' Roll*. New York: Da Capo, 1993.

Mattison, Hiram. *Spirit Rapping Unveiled! An Exposé of the Origin, History, Theology and Philosophy of Certain Alleged Communications from the Spirit World, by Means of "Spirit Rapping," "Medium Writing," "Physical Demonstrations," Etc*. New York: Mason Brothers, 1853.

Maurer, David W. *The Big Con: The Story of the Confidence Man*. New York: Anchor Books, 1940.

Mayhew, George P. "Swift's Bickerstaff Hoax as an April Fools' Joke." *Modern Philology* 61.4 (1964): 270–80.

McConnachie, James, and Robin Tudge. *The Rough Guide to Conspiracy Theories*. New York: Rough Guides, 2005.

McGarry, Molly. *Ghosts of Futures Past: Spiritualism and the Cultural Politics of Nineteenth-Century America*. Berkeley: University of California Press, 2008.

———. "'The Quick, the Dead, and the Yet Unborn': Untimely Sexualities and Secular Hauntings." In *Secularisms*, edited by Janet R. Jakobsen and Ann Pellegrini. 247–82. Durham: Duke University Press, 2008.

McIntosh, Christopher. *The Astrologers and Their Creed: An Historical Approach*. New York: Praeger, 1969.

———. *The Rosicrucians: The History, Mythology, and Rituals of an Esoteric Order*. San Francisco: Weiser Books, 1997.

McLaren, Carrie. "Subliminal Seduction: How Did the Uproar over Subliminal Manipulation Affect the Ad Industry?" In *Ad Nauseam: A Survivor's Guide to American Consumer Culture*, edited by Carrie McLaren and Jason Torchinsky, 223–46. New York: Faber and Faber, 2009.

McLeese, Don. *Kick Out the Jams*. New York: Continuum, 2005.

McLeod, Kembrew. "I, Roboprofessor." *Washingtonpost.com*, December 19, 2007. http://www.washingtonpost.com/wp-dyn/content/article/2007/12/19/AR2007121901000.html.

McLeod, Wallace. "Evolution of Masonic History." In *Freemasonry on Both Sides of the Atlantic*, edited by R. William Weisberger, Wallace McLeod, and S. Brent Morris, xv–xvii. Boulder, CO: East European Monographs, 2002.

McMillian, John. *Smoking Typewriters: The Sixties Underground Press and the Rise of Alternative Media in America*. New York: Oxford University Press, 2011.

McPharlin, Paul. Introduction to *Spectator Papers: Satirical and Philosophical Extracts from the Journal of That Name Written 1711–5 by Addison and Steele, Etc.*, edited by Paul McPharlin. Mount Vernon, NY: Peter Pauper, 1950.

———. "Ridicule." In *Spectator Papers: Satirical and Philosophical Extracts from the Journal of That Name Written 1711–5 by Addison and Steele, Etc.*, edited by Paul McPharlin. Mount Vernon, NY: Peter Pauper, 1950.

Medway, Gareth J. *Lure of the Sinister: The Unnatural History of Satanism*. New York: NYU Press, 2001.

Meikle, Graham. *Future Active: Media Activism and the Internet*. New York: Routledge, 2002.

Melley, Timothy. "Brainwashed! Conspiracy Theory and Ideology in the Postwar United States." *New German Critique* 35.1 (2008): 146–65.

———. *Empire of Conspiracy: The Culture of Paranoia in Postwar America*. Ithaca: Cornell University Press, 2000.

Melville, Herman. *The Confidence-Man: His Masquerade*. 1857. Reprint, New York: Norton, 1971.

Michael, Robert, and Philip Rosen. *Dictionary of Antisemitism from the Earliest Times to the Present*. Lanham, MD: Scarecrow, 2007.

Milbank, Dana. *Tears of a Clown: Glenn Beck and the Tea Bagging of America*. New York: Doubleday, 2010.

Miller, Russell. *The Adventures of Arthur Conan Doyle: A Biography*. New York: Macmillan, 2008.

Mills, C. Wright. *The Power Elite*. New York: Oxford University Press, 1956.

Mills, David. "Sister Souljah's Call to Arms." *Washington Post*, May 13, 1992, B1.

Milner, Greg. *Perfecting Sound Forever: An Aural History of Recorded Music*. New York: Faber and Faber, 2009.

Miscegenation: The Theory of the Blending of the Races Applied to the American White Man and Negro. New York: H. Dexter, Hamilton, 1864.

Morgan, Edmund S. *Benjamin Franklin*. New Haven: Yale University Press, 2002.

Morgan, Robin, ed. *Sisterhood Is Powerful: An Anthology of Writings from the Women's Liberation Movement*. New York: Vintage Books, 1970.

————. *The Word of a Woman: Feminist Dispatches, 1968–1992*. New York: Norton, 1992.

Morris, Errol. *Believing Is Seeing: Observations on the Mysteries of Photography*. New York: Penguin, 2011.

Morris, Roy, Jr. *Lighting Out for the Territory: How Samuel Clemens Headed West and Became Mark Twain*. New York: Simon and Schuster, 2010.

Morse, Jedediah. *A Sermon Exhibiting the Present Dangers and Consequent Duties of the Citizens of the United States*. Charlestown, MA: Samuel Etheridge, 1799.

Morse, Samuel F. B. *Foreign Conspiracy against the Liberties of the United States*. 7th ed. New York: American and Foreign Christian Union, 1855.

Munroe, Alexandra, with Jon Hendricks. *Yes Yoko Ono*. New York: Japan Society, 2000.

Navasky, Victor. Introduction to *Report from Iron Mountain: On the Possibility and Desirability of Peace*, by Leonard C. Lewin, 19–20. New York: Free Press, 1996.

Negativland. *Helter Stupid*. SST Records, 1989. CD.

Newman, Andy. "Advice to Fake Pimp Was No Crime, Prosecutor Says." *New York Times*, March 1, 2010. http://www.nytimes.com/2010/03/02/nyregion/02acorn.html.

Nissenbaum, Stephen. *The Battle for Christmas*. New York: Vintage Books.

Noblitt, James Randall, and Pamela Sue Perskin. *Cult and Ritual Abuse: Its History, Anthropology, and Recent Discovery in Contemporary America*. Westport, CT: Praeger, 1995.

Ono, Yoko. *Grapefruit: A Book of Instruction and Drawings by Yoko Ono*. New York: Simon and Schuster, 2000.

"On the Feejee Mermaid." In *The Colossal P. T. Barnum Reader: Nothing Else Like It in the Universe*, edited by James W. Cook, 185–90. Urbana: University of Illinois Press, 1995.

"Oops: Impostor Scams Louisiana Officials." *CNN.com*, August 28, 2006. http://www.cnn.com/2006/POLITICS/08/28/.

Owen, Alex. "'Borderland Forms': Arthur Conan Doyle, Albion's Daughters, and the Politics of the Cottingley Fairies." *History Workshop* 38 (1994): 48–85.

————. *The Darkened Room: Women, Power, and Spiritualism in Late Victorian England*. Chicago: University of Chicago Press, 1989.

Pace, Antonia. *Benjamin Franklin and Italy*. Philadelphia: American Philosophical Society, 1958.

Palmer, Robert. *Blues and Chaos: The Music and Writing of Robert Palmer*. New York: Simon and Schuster, 2011.

Papanikolas, Zeese. *Trickster in the Land of Dreams*. Lincoln: University of Nebraska Press, 1995.

Paradise Lost: The Child Murders at Robin Hood Hills. Dir. Joe Berlinger and Bruce Sinofsky, 1996.

Paradise Lost: Purgatory. Dir. Joe Berlinger and Bruce Sinofsky, 2011.

Parfrey, Adam, ed. *Apocalypse Culture*. Venice, CA: Feral House, 1990.

——, ed. *Apocalypse Culture II*. Venice, CA: Feral House, 2000.

Parfrey, Adam, and Craig Heimbichner. *Ritual America: Secret Brotherhoods and Their Influence on American Society*. Port Townsend, WA: Feral House, 2012.

Patterson, R. Gary. *The Walrus Was Paul: The Great Beatle Death Clues*. New York: Simon and Schuster, 1998.

Paulson, Amanda. "Texas Textbook War: 'Slavery' or 'Atlantic Triangular Trade'?" *Christian Science Monitor*, May 19, 2010. http://www.csmonitor.com/USA/Education/2010/0519/Texas-textbook-war-Slavery-or-Atlantic-triangular-trade.

Pelton, Robert D. "West African Tricksters: Web of Purpose, Dance of Delight." In *Mythical Trickster Figures: Contours, Contexts, and Criticisms*, edited by William J. Hynes and William G. Doty, 122–40. Tuscaloosa: University of Alabama Press, 1993.

Peters, Dan, and Steve Peters. *Rock's Hidden Persuader: The Truth about Backmasking*. Minneapolis: Bethany House, 1985.

Peters, Edward. *Inquisition*. Berkeley: University of California Press, 1988.

Peters, John Durham. *Speaking into the Air: A History of the Idea of Communication*. Chicago: University of Chicago Press, 1999.

Peterson, T. F. *Nightwork: A History of Hacks and Pranks at MIT*. Rev. ed. Cambridge: MIT Press, 2011.

Pierce, William. *The Turner Diaries*. Hillsboro, WV: National Vanguard Books, 1999.

Pipes, Daniel. *Conspiracy: How the Paranoid Style Flourishes and Where It Comes From*. New York: Free Press, 1997.

Plummer, William. *The Holy Goof: A Biography of Neil Cassady*. New York: Da Capo, 2004.

Poe, Edgar Allan. *The Complete Works of Edgar Allan Poe*. Vol. 4, *Tales*. New York: Thomas Y. Crowell, 1902.

Polidoro, Massimo. *Final Séance: The Strange Friendship between Houdini and Conan Doyle*. Amherst, NY: Prometheus Books, 2001.

President's Commission on the Assassination of President Kennedy. *Report of the President's Commission on the Assassination of President Kennedy*. Washington, DC: Government Printing Office, 1964. http://www.archives.gov/research/jfk/warren-commission-report/appendix-13.html.

Principia Discordia. 5th ed. Port Townsend, WA: Loompanics Unlimited, 1979.

Prouty, Fletcher L. *JFK: The CIA, Vietnam, and the Plot to Assassinate John F. Kennedy*. New York: Skyhorse, 1996.

Psalmanazar, George. *An Historical and Geographical Description of Formosa*. London, 1704.

———. *Memoirs of ****: Commonly Known by the Name of George Psalmanazar, a Reputed Native of Formosa*. Dublin: Printed for P. Wilson, J. Exshaw, E. Watts, S. Cotter, J. Potts, and J. Williams, 1765.

Quantick, David. *Revolution: The Making of the Beatles White Album*. Chicago: A Capella, 2002.

Radin, Paul. *The Trickster: A Study in American Indian Mythology*. New York: Schocken Books, 1972.

Rahn, Suzanne. *The Wizard of Oz: Shaping an Imaginary World*. New York: Twayne, 1998.

Randi, James. *An Encyclopedia of Claims, Frauds, and Hoaxes of the Occult and Supernatural: James Randi's Decidedly Skeptical Definitions of Alternate Realities*. New York: St. Martin's, 1995.

Raymond, Eric S. *The New Hacker's Dictionary*. Cambridge: MIT Press, 1996.

Reed, T. V. *The Art of Protest: Culture and Activism from the Civil Rights Movement to the Streets of Seattle*. Minneapolis: University of Minnesota Press, 2005.

Reeve, Andru J. *Turn Me On, Dead Man: The Beatles and the "Paul Is Dead" Hoax*. Bloomington, IN: AuthorHouse, 2004.

Reid, Jim. "Money to Burn." *Observer*, September 25, 1994, 28.

Reilly, Patrick. *Jonathan Swift: The Brave Desponder*. Manchester: Manchester University Press, 1982.

Reiss, Benjamin. *The Showman and the Slave: Race, Death, and Memory in Barnum's America*. Cambridge: Harvard University Press, 2001.

Remnick, David. *King of the World: Muhammad Ali and the Rise of an American Hero*. New York: Vintage Books, 1998.

Reynolds, David S. *Waking Giant: America in the Age of Jackson*. New York: Harper, 2008.

Rigal, Laura. "Imperial Attractions: Benjamin Franklin's *New Experiments* of 1751." In *Memory Bytes: History, Technology, and Digital Culture*, edited by Lauren Rabinovitz and Abraham Geil, 23–46. Durham: Duke University Press, 2004.

Roberts, John W. *From Trickster to Badman: The Black Folk Hero in Slavery and Freedom*. Philadelphia: University of Pennsylvania Press, 1989.

Roberts, Randy, and James Stuart Olson. *John Wayne: American*. Lincoln: University of Nebraska Press, 1997.

Robertson, Pat. *The New World Order*. Dallas: Word, 1991.

———. *Shout It from the Housetops! The Autobiography of Pat Robertson*. Alachua, FL: Bridge-Logos, 1995.

Robinson, David, Stephen Herbert, and Richard Crangle, eds., *Encyclopaedia of the Magic Lantern*. London: Magic Lantern Society, 2001.

Robinson, John. *A Pilgrim's Path: Freemasonry and the Religious Right*. New York: M. Evans, 1993.

Root, E. Merrill. *Brainwashing in the High Schools*. New York: Devin-Adair, 1958.

Rosenbaum, Ron. "Secrets of the Little Blue Box." In *The Secret Parts of Fortune: Three Decades of Intense Investigations and Edgy Enthusiasms*, 13–41. New York: Perennial, 2001.

Rosenblum, Joseph. *Practice to Deceive: The Amazing Stories of Literary Forgery's Most Notorious Practitioners.* New Castle, DE: Oak Knoll, 2000.

Rosenheim, Edward W., Jr. *Swift and the Satirist's Art.* Chicago: University of Chicago Press, 1963.

Rosenheim, Shawn James. *The Cryptographic Imagination: Secret Writing from Edgar Poe to the Internet.* Baltimore: Johns Hopkins University Press, 1997.

Roszak, Theodore. *The Making of a Counterculture.* New York: Anchor, 1969.

Rue, Loyal. *By the Grace of Guile: The Role of Deception in Natural History and Human Affairs.* New York: Oxford University Press, 1994.

Rush, Benjamin. "Biographical Anecdotes of Benjamin Lay." In *Essays: Literary, Moral and Philosophical,* 296–301. Charleston, SC: BiblioLife, 2009.

RZA. *The Wu-Tang Manual.* New York: Riverhead Freestyle, 2005.

Sachar, Howard M. *A History of the Jews in the Modern World.* New York: Knopf, 2005.

Sanders, Ed. *Fug You: An Informal History of Peace Eye Bookstore, the Fuck You Press, the Fugs, and Counterculture in the Lower East Side.* New York: Da Capo, 2011.

Sante, Luc. *Low Life: Lures and Snares of Old New York.* New York: Farrar, Straus and Giroux, 1991.

Schmidt, Leigh Eric. "From Demon Possession to Magic Show: Ventriloquism, Religion, and the Enlightenment." *Church History* 67.2 (1998): 274–304.

Schwartz, Mathew J. "CIA Website Hacked, Struggles to Recover." *InformationWeek,* February 13, 2012. http://www.informationweek.com/security/attacks/cia-website-hacked-struggles-to-recover/232600729.

Sconce, Jeffrey. *Haunted Media: Electronic Presence from Telegraphy to Television.* Durham: Duke University Press, 2000.

Seed, David. *Brainwashing: The Fictions of Mind Control.* Kent, OH: Kent State University Press, 2004.

Segal, David. "Why Not Just Hold a Seance?" *Washington Post,* March 24, 2007. http://www.washingtonpost.com/wp-dyn/content/article/2007/03/23/AR2007032301850.html.

Segel, Binjamin W. *A Lie and a Libel: The History of the Protocols of the Elders of Zion.* Translated by Richard S. Levy. Lincoln: University of Nebraska Press, 1995.

Shane, Scott. "A Political Gadfly Lampoons the Left via YouTube." *New York Times,* September 18, 2009. http://www.nytimes.com/2009/09/19/us/19sting.html?_r=1.

Sharkey, Alix. "Trash Art & Kreation." *Guardian,* May 21, 1994. Available at http://www.libraryofmu.org/display-resource.php?id=384.

Shaw, William. "Who Killed the KLF?" *Select,* July 1992.

Shea, Robert, and Robert Anton Wilson. *The Illuminatus Trilogy! The Eye of the Pyramid, the Golden Apple, Leviathan.* New York: Dell, 1983.

Sheffield, Rob. *Love Is a Mix Tape: Life and Loss, One Song at a Time.* New York: Three Rivers, 2007.

Shields, David. *Reality Hunger: A Manifesto.* New York: Knopf, 2010.

Silverman, Kenneth. *Houdini! The Career of Ehrich Weiss: American Self-Liberator, Europe's Eclipsing Sensation, World's Handcuff King and Prison Breaker*. New York: HarperCollins, 1996.

Silverstein, Herma, and Caroline Arnold. *Hoaxes That Made Headlines*. New York: Julian Messner, 1986.

Simonson, Peter. *Refiguring Mass Communication*. Urbana: University of Illinois Press, 2010.

Sims, N. H. "The Chicago Style of Journalism." PhD diss., University of Illinois–Urbana, 1979.

Skousen, Cleon W. *The Communist Attack on U.S. Police*. Salt Lake City, UT: Ensign, 1966.

———. *The Five Thousand Year Leap*. Franklin, TN: American Documents, 2009.

———. *The Naked Capitalist*. Catchoque, NY: Buccaneer Books, 1970.

Smith, Michelle, and Lawrence Pazder. *Michelle Remembers*. New York: Pocket Books, 1980.

Smith, R. J. *The Great Black Way: L.A. in the 1940s and the Lost African American Renaissance*. New York: PublicAffairs, 2006.

———. *The One: The Life and Music of James Brown*. New York: Gotham Books, 2012.

Smith, Winston. *Act Like Nothing's Wrong: The Montage Art of Winston Smith*. San Francisco: Last Gasp, 1994.

Somerset, Anne. *The Affair of Poisons: Murder, Infanticide and Satanism at the Court of Louis XIV*. London: Weidenfeld and Nicolson, 2003.

Spence, Jonathan D. *The Question of Hu*. New York: Vintage Books, 1989.

Spurgeon, Charles. "Computer Slang." *CoEvolution Quarterly*, Spring 1981, 31.

Standage, Tom. *The Turk: The Life and Times of the Famous Eighteenth-Century Chess-Playing Machine*. New York: Walker, 2001.

Stang, Ivan. *High Weirdness by Mail: A Directory of the Fringe—Mad Prophets, Crackpots, Kooks and True Visionaries*. New York: Fireside, 1988.

———. "Pope Bob Remembrance." *BoingBoing* (blog), January 15, 2012. http://boingboing.net/2012/01/15/raw-week-pope-bob-remembrance.html.

Stauffer, Vernon. *New England and the Bavarian Illuminati*. New York: Columbia University Press, 1918.

Stearn, Jess. *Edgar Cayce: The Sleeping Prophet*. New York: Doubleday, 1967.

Stein, Gordon, and Marie J. MacNee. *Hoaxes! Dupes, Dodges and Other Dastardly Deceptions*. Detroit: Visible Ink, 1995.

Streeter, Michael. *Behind Closed Doors: The Power and Influence of Secret Societies*. London: New Holland, 2008.

Stuart, Nancy Rubin. *The Reluctant Spiritualist: The Life of Maggie Fox*. New York: Harcourt, 2005.

Suarez, Michael F. "Swift's Satire and Parody." In *The Cambridge Companion to Jonathan Swift*, edited by Christopher Fox, 112–27. New York: Cambridge University Press, 2003.

SubGenius Foundation. *The Book of the SubGenius*. New York: Fireside, 1987.

———. *Revelation X: The "Bob" Apocryphon—Hidden Teachings and Deuterocanonical Texts of J. R. "Bob" Dobbs*. New York: Fireside, 1994.

Sugrue, Thomas. *There Is a River: The Story of Edgar Cayce*. Virginia Beach, VA: ARE, 1997.

Sullivan, Evelin. *The Concise Book of Lying*. New York: Farrar, Straus and Giroux, 2001.

Sullivan, Heidi. "New Survey Delivers Vital Message for PR." *Bulldog Reporter's Daily Dog*, February 23, 2010. http://www.bulldogreporter.com/dailydog/article/new-survey-delivers-vital-message-pr-transparency-social-media-crucial-building-cre.

Sutton, William Josiah. *The Illuminati 666*. Brushton, NY: TEACH Services, 1983.

Sweeney, Phil. "Conscious and Unconscious Political Symbolism: A Study of a College 'Prank.'" BA thesis, James Madison University, 1994.

Swift, Jonathan. *Bickerstaff-Partridge Papers, and a Modest Proposal*. Gloucester, UK: Dodo, 2007.

———. *A Modest Proposal and Other Satirical Works*. New York: Dover, 1996.

Szwed, John F. *Space Is the Place: The Lives and Times of Sun Ra*. New York: Pantheon Books, 1997.

Taylor, Timothy D. "Korla Pandit: Music, Exoticism and Mysticism." In *Widening the Horizon: Exoticism in Post-war Popular Music*, edited by Philip Hayward, 19–44. Sydney: John Libbey, 1999.

Tebra, William. "Robertson and His Phantasmagoria." *Magic Lantern Gazette* 21.3 (2009): 21–24.

Thornley, Kerry W. *The Idle Warriors*. Lilburn, GA: Illuminet, 1991.

Thornton, Sarah. *Club Cultures: Music, Media and Subcultural Capital*. Hanover, NH: Wesleyan University Press, 1996.

Thurschwell, Pamela. *Literature, Technology and Magical Thinking, 1880–1920*. Cambridge: Cambridge University Press, 2001.

Thurston, Mark. Introduction to *The Essential Edgar Cayce*, edited by Mark Thurston, 1–46. New York: Penguin, 2004.

"Timelords, Gentlemen Please!" *New Musical Express,* May 16, 1992.

TNR Staff. "TNR Exclusive: A Collection of Ron Paul's Most Incendiary Newsletters." *New Republic*, December 23, 2011. http://www.newrepublic.com/article/politics/98883/ron-paul-incendiary-newsletters-exclusive.

Tourist Guide Book of Virginia, The. Spring 1931.

Tromp, Marlene. "Spirited Sexuality: Sex, Marriage, and Victorian Spiritualism." *Victorian Literature and Culture* 31.1 (2003): 67–81.

Tucker, Tom. *Bolt of Fate: Benjamin Franklin and His Electric Kite Hoax*. New York: PublicAffairs, 2003.

Turner, Fred. *From Counterculture to Cyberculture: Stewart Brand, the Whole Earth Network, and the Rise of Digital Utopianism*. Chicago: University of Chicago Press, 2006.

Urbina, Ian. "ACORN on Brink of Bankruptcy, Officials Say." *New York Times*, March 19, 2010. http://www.nytimes.com/2010/03/20/us/politics/20acorn.html.

Vale, V. *Pranks 2*. San Francisco: RE/Search, 2006.

Vasterman, Peter L. M. "Media Hype: Self-Reinforcing News Waves, Journalistic Standards and the Construction of Social Problems." *European Journal of Communication* 20.4 (2005): 508–30.

Versluis, Arthur. *The New Inquisitions: Heretic-Hunting and the Intellectual Origins of Modern Totalitarianism*. New York: Oxford University Press, 2006.

Victor, Jeffrey S. *Satanic Panic: The Creation of a Contemporary Legend*. Chicago: Open Court, 1993.

Waite, Arthur Edward. *A New Encyclopedia of Freemasonry*. Vol. 2. London: William Rider and Son, 1921.

Waldstreicher, David. *Runaway America: Benjamin Franklin, Slavery, and the American Revolution*. New York: Hill and Wang, 2004.

Wallace, Irving. *The Fabulous Showman: The Life and Times of P. T. Barnum*. New York: Knopf, 1959.

Wark, Jayne. *Radical Gestures: Feminism and Performance Art in North America*. Montreal: McGill-Queen's University Press, 2006.

Warnke, Mike, with Dave Balsiger and Les Jones. *The Satan-Seller*. South Plainfield, NJ: Bridge, 1972.

War of the Worlds, The: Mars' Invasion of Earth, Inciting Panic and Inspiring Terror from H. G. Wells to Orson Welles and Beyond. Naperville, IL: Sourcebooks MediaFusion, 2005.

Webb, Robert. "Pop: It's in the Mix—Tammy Wynette and the KLF Justified and Ancient (Stand by the Jams); the Independent's Guide to Pop's Unlikeliest Collaborations." *Independent* (London), November 3, 2000, 14.

Webster, Nesta. *Secret Societies and Subversive Movements*. London: Britons, 1964.

———. *The Socialist Network*. London: Boswell, 1926.

———. *World Revolution: The Plot against Civilization*. Boston: Small, Maynard, 1921.

Weed, Joseph J. *Wisdom of the Mystic Masters*. New York: Prentice Hall, 1968.

Weinstein, Deena. *Heavy Metal: The Music and Its Culture*. New York: Da Capo, 2000.

Weisberg, Barbara. *Talking to the Dead: Kate and Maggie Fox and the Rise of Spiritualism*. San Francisco: HarperSanFrancisco, 2004.

Welch, Robert. "A Cross Section of the Truth." *Review of the News*, 1968.

———. "Looking Ahead." *American Opinion Reprint Series*, 1972.

———. "More Stately Mansions." *American Opinion Reprint Series*, 1964.

———. *The Neutralizers*. Belmont, MA: John Birch Society, 1963.

———. *The New Americanism: And Other Speeches and Essays*. Boston: Western Islands, 1966.

———. "Our Only Weapon." *American Opinion Reprint Series*, 1973.

———. *The Politician*. Belmont, MA: Belmont, 1963.

———. "Republics and Democracies." *American Opinion Reprint Series*, 1961.

———. "The Truth about Vietnam." *American Opinion Reprint Series*, 1967.

———. "The Truth in Time." *American Opinion Reprint Series*, 1966.

———. "What Is the John Birch Society?" *American Opinion Reprint Series*, 1965.

Wilentz, Sean. "Confounding Fathers: The Tea Party's Cold War Roots." *NewYorker.com*, October 18, 2010. http://www.newyorker.com/reporting/2010/10/18/101018fa_fact_wilentz.

Wilgus, Neal. *The Illuminoids: Secret Societies and Political Paranoia*. Santa Fe, NM: Sun Books, 1978.

Wilkinson, Roy. "Ford Every Scheme." *Sounds*, May 28, 1988. http://www.libraryofmu.org/display-resource.php?id=81.

Williams, Mark. "Entertaining 'Difference': Strains of Orientalism in Early Los Angeles Television." In *Living Color: Race and Television in the United States*, edited by Sasha Torres, 12–34. Durham: Duke University Press, 1998.

Williamson, Benedict J. *The Rosicrucian Manuscripts*. Arlington, VA: Invisible College Press, 2002.

Wilson, Robert Anton. *Cosmic Trigger I: Final Secret of the Illuminati*. Tempe, AZ: New Falcon, 1986.

———. *The Illuminati Papers*. Oakland, CA: Ronin, 1997.

Wolfe, Burton H. *The Hippies*. New York: New American Library, 1968.

Wolfe, Tom. *The Electric Kool-Aid Acid Test*. New York: Picador, 1968.

Wozniak, Steve. Foreword to *Exploding the Phone: The Untold Story of the Teenagers and Outlaws Who Hacked Ma Bell*, by Phil Lapsley, xi–xii. New York: Grove, 2013.

Yancey, Dwayne. "JMU Fans Fight to Replace Bark with Oink." *Roanoke Times and World-News*, November 19, 1991, A1, A19.

Yapp, Nick. *Great Hoaxes of the World and the Hoaxers behind Them*. London: Robson Books, 1992.

Yeats, Frances. *The Rosicrucian Enlightenment*. Boston: Routledge and Kegan Paul, 1972.

Yes Men, The. Dir. Sarah Price and Chris Smith. Yes Men Films, 2003. Film.

Zehme, Bill. *Lost in the Funhouse: The Life of Andy Kaufman*. New York: Delacorte, 1999.

Zeisler, Andi. *Feminism and Pop Culture*. Berkeley, CA: Seal, 2008.

Žižek, Slavoj. *Plague of Fantasies*. New York: Verso, 1997.

Zmuda, Bob. *Andy Kaufman Revealed!* Boston: Little, Brown, 1999.

ABOUT THE AUTHOR

Kembrew McLeod is a writer, a filmmaker, and Professor of Communication Studies at the University of Iowa. He has written and produced several books and documentaries about popular music, independent media, and copyright law. McLeod's 2007 book, *Freedom of Expression®*, received the American Library Association's Oboler book award, and his documentary *Copyright Criminals* aired in 2010 on PBS's Emmy Award–winning series *Independent Lens*. McLeod's writing has appeared in the *New York Times*, the *Los Angeles Times*, the *Village Voice*, *Slate*, *SPIN*, and *Rolling Stone*.